THE COOKIE
AND BISCUIT BIBLE

THE COOKIE
AND BISCUIT BIBLE

Over 400 delicious, easy-to-make recipes for brownies, bars, muffins
and crackers, shown step-by-step in over 1300 glorious photographs

By Catherine Atkinson with recipes by Joanna Farrow and Valerie Barrett

southwater

This edition is published by Southwater

Southwater is an imprint of Anness Publishing Ltd
Hermes House, 88–89 Blackfriars Road, London SE1 8HA
tel. 020 7401 2077; fax 020 7633 9499; info@anness.com

© Anness Publishing Ltd 2003, 2006

UK agent: The Manning Partnership Ltd, 6 The Old Dairy,
Melcombe Road, Bath BA2 3LR;
tel. 01225 478444; fax 01225 478440; sales@manning-partnership.co.uk

UK distributor: Grantham Book Services Ltd, Isaac Newton Way,
Alma Park Industrial Estate, Grantham, Lincs NG31 9SD;
tel. 01476 541080; fax 01476 541061; orders@gbs.tbs-ltd.co.uk

North American agent/distributor: National Book Network,
4501 Forbes Boulevard, Suite 200, Lanham, MD 20706;
tel. 301 459 3366; fax 301 429 5746; www.nbnbooks.com

Australian agent/distributor: Pan Macmillan Australia, Level 18,
St Martins Tower, 31 Market St, Sydney, NSW 2000;
tel. 1300 135 113; fax 1300 135 103;
customer.service@macmillan.com.au

New Zealand agent/distributor: David Bateman Ltd, 30 Tarndale Grove,
Off Bush Road, Albany, Auckland;
tel. (09) 415 7664; fax (09) 415 8892

A CIP catalogue record for this book is available from the British Library.

Publisher: Joanna Lorenz
Managing Editor: Linda Fraser
Editors: Susannah Blake and Jennifer Schofield
Production Controller: Ben Worley
Photographers: Frank Adam, Karl Adamson, Edward Allwright,
Martin Brigdale, Steve Baxter, James Duncan, John Freeman,
Michelle Garrett, Nelson Hargreaves, Amanda Heywood, David Jordan,
William Lingwood, Patrick McLeavey, Michael Michaels, Craig Robertson
and Polly Wreford
Additional recipes: Liz Trigg, Patricia Lousada, Carla Capalbo,
Laura Washburn, Frances Cleary, Norma MacMillan, Christine France,
Pamela Westland, Hilaire Walden, Elizabeth Wolf-Cohen, Janice Murfitt,
Carole Handslip, Steven Wheeler, Katherine Richmond, Joanna Farrow,
Judy Williams, Sue Maggs, Carole Clements, Jacqueline Clarke,
Sarah Maxwell, Sallie Morris, Lesley Mackley, Roz Denny, Sarah Gates,
Norma Miller, Maxine Clark, Shirley Gill, Judy Jackson, Gilly Love,
Janet Brinkworth, Elisabeth Lambert Ortiz and Sohelia Kimberley.
Designer: Paul Oakley

Previously published as The Cookie Book

10 9 8 7 6 5 4 3 2 1

NOTES

Bracketed terms are intended for American readers.

For all recipes, quantities are given in both metric and
imperial measures and, where appropriate, measures are
also given in standard cups and spoons. Follow one set,
but not a mixture, because they are not interchangeable.

Standard spoon and cup measures are level.
1 tsp = 5ml, 1 tbsp = 15ml, 1 cup = 250ml/8fl oz

Australian standard tablespoons are 20ml. Australian
readers should use 3 tsp in place of 1 tbsp for measuring
small quantities of gelatine, flour, salt, etc.

Medium (US large) eggs are used unless otherwise stated.

Main front cover image shows Greek honey crunch
creams – for recipe, see pages 114–5.

Contents

The Cookie-making Tradition

Left: *There is little so wonderful as sitting down to a cup of tea and a plate of freshly baked cookies.*

EARLY COOKIES

There are differences in opinion about the origins of the word biscuit, but whether it is derived from the French *cuit* or from the Latin *biscoctus*, all agree that it means twice-cooked.

Originally, cookies were double-baked. They were browned for a few minutes when the oven was at its hottest, then removed and returned to finish baking when the oven was cooling down. This time-consuming process dried out the cookies so that they kept well – essential in the days before airtight containers were available. At this time, not all cookie batters were baked; some were fried into wafers.

Rusks and ship's biscuits, which needed to keep for several months, were also baked in this way. The dough was first baked, then cooled, sliced, and dried in a gentle heat until crisp; Italian *biscotti* are still made in this way.

During the Middle Ages, improvements were made. Sugar and spices were added to biscuits, to make them more palatable and, in the late Middle Ages, it was discovered that adding beaten egg to biscuit dough made the finished cookie lighter and that ground nuts could be used instead of flour. This led to the creation of meringue, sponge and macaroon cookies.

Cookie mixtures changed significantly in the 18th and 19th centuries. The tradition of baking rusks and frying cookies virtually

No matter what age you are, there's little so enjoyable as a freshly baked cookie. They always feel like the ultimate treat, despite the fact that they're so simple to make. Cookies, in one form or another, have been around for centuries and some of the most popular cookies today derive from these original treats.

AN AMERICAN INVENTION

The term cookie was first used in the United States when early Dutch settlers brought their *koekje* (little cakes) to New York. At about the same time, wood-burning and coal-fired ovens were introduced, which made baking more reliable and the popularity of cookies and cookie-making soon spread.

Eastern European, Scandinavian and British immigrants who settled in the United States all made great contributions to the cookie-making tradition. For example, refrigerator cookies originated from German Heidesand cookies, which are made by shaping the dough into long, sausage-shaped rolls, cutting them into thin, round slices and then baking them.

In other parts of the world, the word for (and meaning of) cookie varies. In Scotland, a cookie is a sweetened bread bun that is either filled with whipped cream or thickly iced. In Britain and France, cookies are known as biscuits, while in the United States, the term biscuit is used to describe a large, soft scone.

disappeared – although in parts of Europe, India and the Middle East some cookies are still fried today – and enriched short cakes became very popular. These rich, buttery doughs still form the basis of many modern cookies.

Although savoury cheese biscuits (crackers) have their origins in medieval times, plain, savoury biscuits were not created until the 18th century. These later developed into salted crackers and cocktail savouries for nibbling with drinks.

During the 19th century, with the availability of cheap sugar and flour and chemical raising agents such as bicarbonate of soda (baking soda), cookie factories were able to open up. As the quality of factory-made cookies improved, more and more people began to buy rather than make their own cookies.

COOKIE-MAKING TODAY

In more recent years, consumers have started to turn away from foods containing artificial additives. Commercial cookies have become less popular and there has been a resurgence in home-baking.

Time-saving kitchen devices such as food mixers have helped to speed up cookie-making, and the widely available range of more unusual ingredients has opened up the possibilities for the modern cook who can make just about any cookie they want.

With the help of this book, you can learn everything you will ever need to know about cookie-making – from the basic techniques to the perfect cookie to serve with coffee, put in a lunchbox or offer as a gift.

CLASSIC COOKIES

Anzac A crunchy cookie from New Zealand, named after the Australia and New Zealand Army Corps (ANZAC). It is made with butter, golden (light corn) syrup, rolled oats and coconut.

Bath Oliver A hard, crisp savoury cracker created as a health product by Dr W. Oliver of Bath, England, in 1730.

Digestive/Graham Cracker Also known as sweetmeal or wheatmeal, this moderately sweet cookie is made with brown flour. Despite its name, it has no special digestive properties.

Maria Popular in Spain, this thin, plain crisp cookie was created in England to celebrate the wedding of the Grand Duchess Maria of Austria to the Duke of Edinburgh.

Fortune Cookie During the Ming Dynasty, political resisters baked cookies containing messages detailing secret meetings and plans. The idea was revived in San Francisco in the 19th century.

Below: Modern fortune cookies contain predictions of the future.

Above: Maryland cookies are one of the most popular and well-known types of chocolate chip cookie.

Jumble Well-known as early as the 17th century, this cookie was originally flavoured with rose water, aniseed or caraway seeds and tied into knots. The mixture is now made into S-shapes.

Petit Beurre This plain, crisp French cookie has been made in Nantes since the 1880s. It was created by Louis Lefevre-Utile and is also known as LU or *P'tit lu*.

Shortbread Scottish shortbread evolved from 16th-century short cakes. The main ingredients are usually flour, sugar and butter. Petticoat tails are shortbread baked in a round, named after the shape of an outspread petticoat.

Snickerdoodle A Pennsylvanian Dutch speciality, this spicy cookie contains nutmeg, nuts and raisins.

Chocolate Chip Cookies These are absolute classics; two of the best known being Toll House cookies and chocolate chip Maryland cookies.

The Art of Making and Baking Cookies

Cookies are simple to make but there is some basic know-how that will make cookie-making even easier. This chapter explains everything you will ever need to know – from basic equipment and ingredients to making, shaping and baking different types of cookie dough; decorating and storing cookies; and making pretty cookie gifts for friends and family.

Cookie Ingredients

Most cookies are made from a few basic ingredients – butter, sugar, flour and sometimes eggs and other ingredients and flavourings. To make the best cookies, always use really fresh, good quality ingredients.

BUTTER

Unsalted (sweet) butter is best for making cookies; it has a sweet, slightly nutty taste and a firm texture, which is particularly well-suited to cookies made using the the rubbed-in method.

The temperature of butter is important. For rubbed-in cookies butter should be cold and firm but not too hard; take it out of the refrigerator 5 minutes before using. To cream butter, it should be at room temperature. This is very important if you are beating by hand. If you forget to take butter out of the refrigerator in advance, soften it in the microwave on low power for 10–15 seconds.

If you need to melt butter, dice it so that it melts more quickly and evenly. Melt the butter over a very low heat to prevent it burning

and remove it from the heat when it has almost melted; the residual heat will complete the job. If you need to brush baking tins (pans) or sheets with melted butter, use unsalted butter rather than salted, which tends to burn and stick.

STORING BUTTER

Butter should be stored in the refrigerator or freezer. It can absorb other flavours easily so protect it from strong-smelling ingredients by wrapping tightly in greaseproof (waxed) paper or foil. If possible, store in a separate compartment.

Salted butter can be stored in the refrigerator for about a month but unsalted butter should be used within 2 weeks. Alternatively, you can store unsalted butter in the freezer and transfer it to the refrigerator 1–2 days before you need it. All butter can be frozen for up to 6 months.

Left: Unsalted butter produces cookies with a wonderfully rich flavour and warm golden colour.

Above: White vegetable fat (left) and block margarine (right) work well in some cookie recipes.

OTHER FATS

Margarine This won't produce the same flavour as butter but it is usually less expensive and can be used in the same way. Block margarines are better for cookie-making, although soft margarine may be used for creaming.

White cooking fats Made from blended vegetable oils or a mixture of vegetable and animal or fish oils, white fats are flavourless and create light, short-textured cookies. They work well in highly flavoured cookies, in which you wouldn't taste the butter. Lard is an opaque white fat made from rendered pork fat and features in some traditional cookie recipes.

Oil This may sometimes be used instead of solid fat. Sunflower and safflower oils are preferable as they are light in colour with a mild taste. Olive oil has a distinctive flavour but may be added to savoury crackers.

SUGAR

There are many different types of sugar, all of which add their own distinctive character to cookies.

REFINED SUGARS

Produced from sugar cane and sugar beet, refined white sugar is 99.9 per cent pure sucrose.

Granulated sugar This has large granules and can be used in rubbed-in mixtures or to make a crunchy cookie topping.

Caster/superfine sugar This is the most frequently used sugar for cookie-making. It has a fine grain so is ideal for creaming with butter. It is also used for melted mixtures, meringue toppings and sprinkling over freshly baked cookies.

Icing/confectioners' sugar This fine, powdery sugar is used to make smooth icings and fillings and for dusting cookies. It may also be added to some piped mixtures.

Soft brown sugar This is refined white sugar that has been tossed in molasses or syrup to colour and flavour it; the darker the colour, the more intense the flavour. It makes moister cookies than white sugar, so never substitute one for the other.

UNREFINED SUGARS

Derived from raw sugar cane, these retain some molasses. They often have a more intense flavour but tend to be less sweet than refined sugars.

Golden caster/superfine sugar and granulated sugar These are pale gold and are used in the same way as their white counterparts.

Demerara/raw sugar This rich golden sugar has a slight toffee flavour. The grains are large so it is only used in cookie doughs if a crunchy texture is required. It is good for sprinkling over cookies before they are baked.

Above: (Left to right) Soft brown sugar and demerara (raw) sugar give cookies a slightly caramel taste.

Muscovado/molasses sugar This fine-textured, moist soft brown sugar may has a treacly flavour.

STORING SUGAR

Sugar should always be stored in an airtight container. If white sugar forms clumps, break it up with your fingers. If brown sugar dries out and hardens, warm it in the microwave for about 1 minute.

OTHER SWEETENERS

There are many other ingredients that can be used as sweeteners.

Golden/light corn syrup Slightly less sweet than sugar, this produces moist, sticky cookies and is often used in no-bake recipes.

Maple syrup Thinner than golden syrup, this has a distinctive flavour.

Honey Use blended honey in cookie doughs as the flavour of milder honeys will be lost.

Malt extract This concentrated extract made from barley has a distinctive flavour, thick consistency and dark, almost black colour.

Molasses A by-product of sugar refining, molasses looks like malt extract but has a slightly bitter taste.

Above:
Coarse-grained granular sugar is good for sprinkling.

Left: Fine-grained caster sugar is widely used in cookie doughs.

FLOUR

Most cookie recipes use plain (all-purpose) flour as it has a low gluten content, resulting in a crumbly texture. The grains are processed then treated with chlorine to make the flour whiter. You can also buy unbleached flour, which has a greyish colour. Some flour is pre-sifted but you should sift it anyway as the contents tend to settle during storage. Flour, even the same type and brand, may vary slightly, so always hold a few drops of liquid back in case they aren't needed.

SELF-RAISING FLOUR

Known as self-rising flour in the United States, this flour contains raising agents that make cookies spread and rise, giving them a lighter texture. If you run out of self-raising flour, you can substitute plain flour, adding 5ml/1 tsp baking powder to each 115g/4oz/1 cup. Self-raising flour should not be kept for longer than 3 months because raising agents gradually deteriorate.

WHOLEMEAL FLOUR

Also known as whole-wheat flour, this is milled from the entire wheat kernel and contains all the nutrients and flavour of wheat. It is coarser than white flour, giving a heavier result. It absorbs more liquid than white flour so recipes should be adjusted if wholemeal flour is used.

Brown (wheatmeal) flour, contains only 80–90 per cent of the bran and wheat germ and has a finer texture and milder taste.

Left: Wholemeal (whole-wheat) flour gives cookies a lovely taste.

NON-WHEAT FLOURS

These can be great for cookie making, although some should be combined with wheat flour.

Potato flour This fine powder is made from potato starch and can be mixed with wheat flour to give a lighter texture to cookies.

Chestnut flour This light brown, nutty flavoured flour is made from ground chestnuts and is often sold in Italian delicatessens.

Cornmeal Also known as polenta or maizemeal, this is bright yellow and coarse or medium ground.

Cornflour/cornstarch This fine white powder is made from the middle of the maize kernel. It is often used in piped cookie mixtures to give a smooth texture.

Soya flour Made from soya beans, this has a distinctive nutty flavour. It has a high protein content. Medium- and low-fat varieties are available.

Rice flour This is made by finely grinding polished white rice and is used in many cookie recipes, to give a short, slightly crumbly texture.

Above: Rice flour is often added to shortbread to give a crumbly texture.

Left: Cornmeal produces cookies with a golden colour, delicious flavour and distinctive texture.

GLUTEN-FREE BAKING

Some people are allergic or intolerant to the protein gluten, which is found in both wheat and rye. Specially produced gluten-free and wheat-free flour mixtures can be used for baking, as can any of the naturally gluten-free flours such as cornmeal, potato flour, rice flour and soya flour.

Above:
Bicarbonate of soda (baking soda) and baking powder give cookies a lighter texture.

RAISING AGENTS

Although cookies are usually made with plain (all-purpose) flour, raising agents may be added to give them a lighter texture. Raising agents make cookies spread more, so space them well apart for baking.

Raising agents react when they come in contact with water and produce carbon dioxide bubbles that make the cookie rise during baking. Cookie doughs containing raising agents must therefore be shaped and baked as soon as liquid is added. Store raising agents in a dry place and use within their use-by date because they deteriorate with age, becoming less effective.

Baking powder This is a mixture of alkaline bicarbonate of soda (baking soda) and an acid such as cream of tartar.

Bicarbonate of soda/ baking soda This can be added to a cookie mixture that contains an acidic ingredient.

Right: Eggs are widely used in cookie-making and can help to produce rich, golden cookies with a great flavour.

EGGS

These are used to enrich cookie doughs and bind dry ingredients. They are often included in rolled doughs because they prevent the mixture from spreading too much during baking. If a recipe does not specify the size of an egg, use a medium (US large) one.

For baking, eggs should be at room temperature; cold egg yolks may curdle and cold egg whites will produce less volume when whisked. Add eggs to a creamed mixture a little at a time, beating after each addition and adding 15ml/1 tbsp sifted flour if the mixture starts to curdle. Whisk egg whites in a very clean bowl and use straight away.

BUYING AND STORING EGGS

Always check the use-by date on eggs and never buy cracked, damaged or dirty eggs. A fresh egg will have a round, plump yolk and a thick white that clings closely to the yolk. Store eggs in the refrigerator, pointed-end down. Do not store near strong-smelling foods or possible contaminants such as raw meat; their shells are porous and can absorb odours and bacteria.

SEPARATING EGGS

Some recipes require only an egg yolk or an egg white. Egg separating devices are available from kitchenware stores but it is easy to separate eggs by hand.

1 Tap the middle of the egg sharply against the rim of a bowl, then, holding the egg over the bowl, prise the shell apart with the tips of your thumbs.

2 Gently tip the white into the bowl, retaining the yolk in the shell. Tip the yolk into the other half-shell, letting any remaining white fall into the bowl.

Cook's Tip

You can also separate the yolk from the white by tipping the whole egg into the palm of your hand and letting the white drain into a bowl through your fingers.

FRUIT, NUTS AND SEEDS

Dried, candied and crystallized fruit, nuts and seeds can be added to cookie doughs to add flavour, colour and texture, or to decorate.

DRIED FRUIT

The drying process intensifies the flavour and sweetness of the fruit. Adding dried fruit does not affect the moisture of the dough so you can usually subsitute one type of dried fruit for another in a recipe.

Vine fruit These include sultanas (golden raisins), raisins and currants. Buy seedless fruit, choosing a reliable brand or go for fruit in clear bags so that you can check its softness and colour. As dried fruit ages, a white coating may develop; it is still usable, but you should never buy it in this condition. It can be kept in an airtight container for up to a year, but is best used within 6 months. Some brands are lightly tossed in oil before packing to keep the fruits separate; uncoated vine fruits may stick together and should be pulled apart before adding to cookies.

Apricots These are produced in California and other parts of the American Pacific coast, Australia, South Africa, Turkey and Iran. Some are very dry and need to be soaked in a little liquid before using; others, usually labelled ready-to-eat, have a softer texture and sweeter flavour and are generally better for cookie-making. After picking and stoning (pitting), the fruits may be treated with sulphur dioxide to retain their colour and prevent mould growing.

Unsulphured apricots, which are darker in colour and very sticky, are also available; they should be stored in the refrigerator.

Apples and pears Dried in rings or as halved fruit, these have a chewy texture. They are best used finely chopped and added to drop cookie mixtures.

Tropical fruits Exotic fruits such as papaya and mango are available dried and have an intense flavour and vibrant colour. They are often sold in strips, which can be easily chopped with a sharp knife or snipped into small pieces with a pair of scissors. Dried pineapple and dried banana are also available and make a tasty addition to cookies.

Left: Dried fruit such as apricots and pears make a delicious, healthy addition to cookies.

Above: Crystallized ingredients such as glacé cherries and angelica can be used both to flavour cookies and as decorations.

Cranberries and sour cherries These are brightly coloured and add a wonderful sweet-and-sour flavour to cookies. They make a very good addition to festive cookies.

Candied and crystallized fruit Fresh fruits such as whole pitted cherries and apricots or pieces of kiwi and pineapple are steeped in sugar. The process retains the original bright colour of the fruit. Angelica, the bright green stem of the herb, is candied in this way. Because of their pretty colour, candied and crystallized fruit are usually used to decorate cookies rather than in the dough.

Crystallizing fruit takes a long time, making the fruit expensive. Candied citrus peel is cheaper and can be bought ready-chopped. However, make sure that chopped candied peel is still soft and moist as it can dry out quickly; it is better to buy whole pieces of candied peel and chop or slice it as required.

NUTS

These can be added to cookie mixtures or chopped and sprinkled over unbaked cookies. Always buy really fresh nuts in small quantities, then chop as necessary. Store in an airtight container, ideally in the refrigerator or freezer.

Almonds Sweet almonds are available ready-blanched, chopped, split, flaked (sliced) and ground.

Brazil nuts These wedge-shaped nuts are actually a seed. Their creamy white flesh has a sweet milky taste and a high fat content. Store carefully and use within a few months. They can be grated.

Cashew nuts These kidney-shaped nuts are always sold shelled and dried. They have a sweet flavour and almost crumbly texture.

Coconut White, dense coconut flesh is made into desiccated (dried unsweetened shredded) coconut and flakes. It is also possible to find sweetened shredded coconut, which is good for decorating cookies.

Below: Hazelnuts have a lovely nutty taste and can be used whole or chopped into small pieces.

Hazelnuts These are particularly good chopped and toasted, as this brings out their flavour.

Macadamia nuts Also known as Queensland nuts, these round, white, buttery nuts are native to Australia but are now also grown in California and South America.

Peanuts Strictly speaking, these are a legume not a nut, as they grow underground. Peanuts may be used raw or roasted, but do not use salted nuts unless specified.

Pecan nuts These are rather like elongated walnuts in appearance, but with a milder, sweeter flavour.

Pine nuts These are the fruits of the stone pine, which grows in the Mediterranean. Small and creamy coloured, they have an almost oily texture and aromatic flavour.

Pistachio nuts Bright green in colour, these are often used for decorating cookies.

Walnuts These are well flavoured with a crunchy texture. In the United States there are several types: white walnuts or butternuts, the large pale-shelled variety called English or Californian, and strong-flavoured, black-shelled walnuts.

SKINNING NUTS

To make skinning easier, either roast or blanch the nuts first.

To roast nuts, spread them out in a single layer on a baking sheet and roast at 180°C/350°F/Gas 4 for 10–12 minutes, until the skins split and the nuts are golden. Tip the nuts on to a clean dishtowel and rub gently to loosen and remove the skins.

To blanch nuts, place in a bowl, pour over boiling water and leave for 5 minutes. Drain, then slip them out of their skins.

SEEDS

These are a popular ingredient in wholesome cookies and savoury crackers. They can be added to cookie doughs to give a crunchy texture or sprinkled over the tops of cookies before they are baked to give an attractive finish. Sesame and poppy seeds work particularly well because of their small size. However, larger seeds such as sunflower seeds work just as well.

Left: Sunflower and pumpkin seeds can be added to cookie doughs or sprinkled over unbaked cookies.

COOKIE FLAVOURINGS

There are many flavourings that can be added to cookies. They may add a subtle or strong taste, and some can also add texture.

CHOCOLATE

From cocoa-flavoured drop cookies to chocolate chip and chocolate-coated varieties, chocolate is the most popular cookie flavouring.

Dark/bittersweet chocolate
This has a bitter flavour and is the most popular chocolate for cookie-making. The degree of bitterness depends on the percentage of cocoa solids. Continental dark chocolate contains a minimum of 70 per cent cocoa solids so it is ideal for very sweet, sugar-laden cookies. Plain (semisweet) chocolate contains at least 50 per cent cocoa solids; the eating variety may contain as little as 25 per cent. It can be chopped and added to cookie doughs, but does not melt well.

Milk chocolate This contains milk powder and a higher percentage of sugar than plain chocolate. It is more difficult to melt.

White chocolate This contains no cocoa solids, only cocoa butter, milk solids and sugar. Some cheaper brands use flavourings and vegetable oil in place of cocoa butter. Brands that contain more cocoa butter are best for baking and melting. White chocolate may caramelize during baking due to its high sugar content.

Couverture This fine-quality plain, milk or white chocolate is used by professional cooks, and can be bought from specialist stores and by mail order. It melts beautifully and makes glossy cookie coatings.

Chocolate chips or dots These tiny chocolate pieces melt well and are easy to work with. The milk and white versions are more stable than bars of milk and white chocolate.

Chocolate cake covering This usually contains little real chocolate and is flavoured with cocoa powder. It melts well and is good for coating cookies, but has a poor flavour.

Unsweetened cocoa powder This bitter, dark powder can be added to cookie mixtures or dusted over the tops. (Drinking chocolate contains about 25 per cent cocoa powder and 75 per cent sugar. It is not suitable for baking.)

Complementary flavours Chocolate can be combined with many other flavourings. The most subtle is vanilla, which often goes unnoticed, yet greatly enhances the taste and aroma of chocolate. The bitterness of coffee can offset

Above: Chocolate – in its many forms – is a popular cookie ingredient.

the sweetness of chocolate, and caramel works well, especially if the sugar is cooked until it is dark, as this helps to reduce some of its sweetness. Both mint and orange add a subtle tang to chocolate cookies, and are especially good for fillings, frostings and icings; nuts are a classic addition.

STORING CHOCOLATE

Chocolate should always be wrapped in foil and kept in a dry, cool place. In hot weather, chocolate can be kept in the refrigerator but it may develop a whitish bloom; this is the cocoa butter rising to the surface. The chocolate will still be safe to use and won't alter the flavour of cookies but it can affect the final texture of the cookies.

SPICES AND HERBS

Adding spices to cookies is a great way to add flavour. Warm spices such as cinnamon, ginger and nutmeg are mainly used in sweet cookies, while whole spice seeds such as cumin and fennel and ground ones such as coriander and chilli are great in crackers.

Vanilla is perhaps the spice most frequently added to sweet cookies, providing a fragrant, delicate flavour. Vanilla sugar is one of the easiest ways to add the flavouring. Pure vanilla essence (extract), which is distilled from vanilla pods (beans), is also a good way to add the flavour. Vanilla flavouring is a synthetic product and may not actually contain any real vanilla.

Fresh or dried herbs can be added to savoury cookie doughs or sprinkled on top before baking.

Above: *Grated citrus rind can be added to cookie doughs to give them a lovely zesty citrus taste.*

Some, such as rosemary, are highly pungent and should be used sparingly. Milder herbs such as mint are good in fillings, and mint essence (extract) can be added to doughs.

Above: *Fresh mint can be added to delicately flavoured cookies and fillings to give them a fresh, aromatic flavour.*

OTHER FLAVOURINGS

There are also a great many cookie flavourings that do not fit into a particular category. These include grated lemon, lime or orange rind, the juice of citrus fruits, rose water, orange flower water and almond essence (extract),

ALCOHOL

Spirits, sherry and liqueurs can be added to cookie mixtures instead of liquid such as milk. They can also be used to soak dried fruit. During baking the alcohol will evaporate, leaving a subtle flavour. They can also be used in glacé icings.

SALT

This helps to bring out the flavour in both sweet cookies and crackers, but add only the tiniest pinch, especially if using salted butter. Coarse crystals of sea salt can be used to sprinkle over savoury cookies to decorate.

Equipment

Most cookies can be made with nothing more sophisticated than weighing scales or calibrated measuring cups, a mixing bowl, fine sieve, rolling pin, wooden spoon, baking sheet and a wire rack. However, there are a few pieces of equipment that can make cookie-making even easier.

Electric gadgets can really speed up the whole cookie-making process and more specialist equipment such as cookie presses, shortbread moulds and piping bags can produce really professional-looking cookies.

BOWLS

Large bowls are good for mixing doughs, while medium and small heatproof bowls are good for melting butter or chocolate and beating eggs. Small and medium bowls are also useful if you need to measure out ingredients beforehand. Some people may argue that a copper or steel bowl is desirable for whisking egg whites to their maximum volume but, for cookie-making, this really is not necessary.

Left: An electric food mixer takes the hard work out of cookie-making and can be a real time saver.

Above: A set of different sized, heatproof bowls for mixing, beating and melting ingredients is invaluable when making cookies.

ELECTRICAL APPLIANCES

Food mixers and processors are great for creaming together butter and sugar and for beating in eggs. However, if these machines are used, dry ingredients should always be folded in by hand as it is very easy to over-mix cookie dough, which will spoil the final texture.

A food processor is particularly useful for chopping and grinding large quantities of nuts and some come with a mini bowl specifically made for such tasks.

A hand-held electric whisk can be used for beating eggs, whisking egg whites and beating together butter and sugar and it has the advantage that it can be used in a pan over heat. Choose one with three speeds and beaters that can be removed for easy cleaning.

Above: Flexible palette knives and spatulas make cookie-making easier.

SPATULAS

A flexible rubber or plastic spatula can be used to scrape every last morsel of cookie dough from the mixing bowl. They are also very useful for folding dry ingredients such as flour into a creamed or whisked mixture.

PALETTE KNIVES AND METAL SPATULAS

Wide and round-bladed palette knives and metal spatulas are essential for lifting cookies from baking sheets and can also be used for mixing liquid into cookie doughs and mixtures. Small ones are very useful for spreading cookie fillings and icing on to cookies.

WHISKS

A wire balloon whisk or hand-held rotary whisk are useful for whisking egg whites for cookies such as macaroons and for whipping cream to use in fillings. They are also good for removing lumps in icing.

Below: The flexible wires of a balloon whisk will incorporate air into everything from eggs to cream.

MEASURING SPOONS, JUGS AND CUPS

A set of accurate measuring spoons is essential. Ordinary spoons vary in size so invest in a commercially produced set. For measuring larger volumes of dry ingredients and liquids, you will need a clearly calibrated measuring jug (cup). They are available in glass, plastic and stainless steel. Use a glass measuring jug for hot liquids; plastic may soften and stainless steel conducts heat.

Below: A set of special measuring spoons and jugs or measuring cups are essential for successful baking.

SIEVES

You should invest in a set of strong, fine sieves in at least two sizes; a large one for sifting dry ingredients such as flour, and a smaller one for dusting icing (confectioners') sugar or (unsweetened) cocoa powder over baked cookies. You can also buy dredgers with a very fine mesh or tiny holes in the top for dusting with icing sugar or cocoa powder but a sieve works just as well.

Below: A set of strong, fine-wire sieves will prove invaluable for cookie-making and last a lifetime.

ROLLING PINS

These come in all shapes and sizes, some with handles and some without. Rolling pins are usually made of wood but they are also available in marble. Mini rolling pins are sometimes available, which are perfect for small children who want to help out in the kitchen. Hollow plastic rolling pins, designed to be filled with iced water, are also available. These have no special advantage over ordinary rolling pins, providing the cookie dough is sufficiently chilled before rolling out.

PASTRY BOARDS

These flat, smooth boards are good for rolling cookie dough out to an even thickness. They are made from many different materials including wood, toughened glass and marble, which remains cool to the touch however warm the weather.

Smooth, laminated plastic kitchen surfaces provide a good alternative to a separate pastry board but take care not to scratch the surface when using cookie cutters and sharp knives.

Below: Wooden rolling pins are efficient, inexpensive and very easy to clean.

BAKING SHEETS

These are either entirely flat or have a lip along the length of one side; baking trays have a lip all around the edges. Baking sheets are preferable as they allow better air movement around the cookies, but be careful when removing cookies from the oven because they can slip off easily.

Always measure your oven before buying baking sheets to make sure they will fit. Large sheets will allow you to bake more cookies in each batch but there needs to be a small gap at either side and at the back of the baking sheet so that heat can circulate. Although non-stick varieties may save greasing or lining with greaseproof (waxed) paper; crisp cookies may not crisp quite so well on them and soft ones may spread out too much.

When buying baking sheets, always choose good-quality, heavy ones; they won't buckle in high temperatures, distort the shape of your cookies or develop hot-spots, which might cause burning. A good baking sheet can last you a lifetime. Avoid baking sheets that are very dark as they absorb more heat, which means cookies burn more easily. Dark baking sheets are intended for other kinds of baking such as bread-baking.

Left: Baking sheets can vary greatly in size, colour and quality.

TINS/PANS

These are available in many shapes and sizes from round, square and rectangular to petal-shaped. They are used for baking cookie doughs such as shortbread and bar and brownie mixtures. The cookies should be marked into squares, bars or wedges while warm, then cut and removed from the tin when cool. If possible, use tins with a dull finish rather than shiny aluminium ones, as they will give your cookies a crispier texture.

To bake bar cookies, use a rectangular tin measuring 28 x 18cm/ 11 x 7in or a square tin measuring 20 x 20cm/8 x 8in. (If you do not have a tin, you can use an ovenproof glass dish. However, this will not produce such good results and the oven temperature will need to be reduced slightly because glass takes longer than metal to heat up, but retains more heat when removed from the oven.

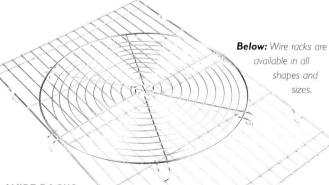

Below: Wire racks are available in all shapes and sizes.

WIRE RACKS

After baking, most cookies should be transferred to a wire rack to cool. The rack allows air to circulate, preventing trapped warmth turning into moisture and making the cookies soggy. Some cookies should be left on the baking sheet for a few minutes to firm up before transferring to a wire rack.

TIMERS

These are absolutely essential for baking. Even an extra 1 or 2 minutes in the oven can result in overbaked or burnt cookies. Many modern ovens are already fitted with a timer, but if you do not have an oven with a timer, it is well worth investing in one. The simplest timers have a rotating dial that registers any time up to 60 minutes. They are fairly accurate and are perfectly suitable for baking cookies. Modern, digital timers are very useful and accurate and will help ensure that your cookies are removed from the oven at exactly the right time. These small timers also have the advantage that you can take them with you if you need to go into another room while your cookies bake.

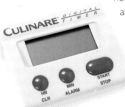

Above: Cookie dough can be pressed into tins to make squares and bars.

Above: Digital timers are inexpensive and help to ensure perfect baking.

COOKIE CUTTERS

These come in many different shapes and sizes from the simplest plain or fluted round cutters to people-, animal-, heart- and flower-shaped ones. You will also find tiny cutters that can be used for *petits fours* and savoury cocktail snacks, and multi-sided cutters that have six different shapes arranged around a cube.

For the best results, cutters should be sharp enough to give a clear, precise outline. The top side of the cutter will usually have a smooth, rounded finish for pressing down on.
More intricate cutters will retain their shape better if they have a handle on them as this helps to keep the cutter rigid.

Below: Metal cutters are better for cookie-making than plastic ones, which can compress the cut edges.

Below:
Pretty shortbread moulds are usually carved from sycamore wood, which gives a sharp outline.

SHORTBREAD MOULDS

You can buy shortbread moulds that are decorated with intricate patterns. These are perfect if you are making shortbread for a special occasion or if you are making shortbread to offer as a gift. The moulds are usually made of wood. The classic shortbread mould is traditionally engraved with a Scottish thistle motif and is usually about 18cm/7in in diameter.

They are simple to use; all you need to do is press the dough into the mould with the tips of your fingers, level off the surface with a palette knife and then turn out on to a baking sheet for baking.

Above: An aluminium cookie press comes with a choice of patterned discs to create different shapes.

COOKIE PRESSES

Soft cookie dough can be shaped using a cookie press. The presses look like an icing syringe and work in a similar way. The dough is forced through a disc, which shapes the dough into a pretty cookie.

Right: Piping (pastry) bags can be filled with dough and used to make cookie shapes, or filled with icing and used to decorate baked cookies.

PIPING/PASTRY BAGS AND NOZZLES

A medium to large piping bag and a selection of both plain and fluted nozzles is useful for piping uncooked cookie dough. Smaller piping bags are extremely good for decorating baked cookies with icing or buttercream.

Originally, piping bags were made of water-proofed canvas but these tended to weep and were difficult to wash; now piping bags are made of nylon. Look for bags that are double stitched along the seams as well as glued to avoid leakage or splitting. You can also buy disposable piping bags, which are ideal for piping fine lines of melted chocolate or icing as decoration. (A small plastic bag with the corner snipped off makes a good substitute if you don't have a piping bag.)

PASTRY BRUSHES

These brushes are used for glazing unbaked cookies with milk or beaten egg, or baked cookies with a thin sugar glaze. They can also be used for brushing surplus flour from rolled cookie dough and for greasing baking sheets with oil.

The best pastry brushes have natural bristles fixed in a wooden handle, although nylon bristles are sometimes considered more hygienic. Brushes that have been used for egg glazing should be rinsed in cold water before washing in hot soapy water. Flick them dry and leave to air before using again.

Below: A pastry brush is very useful for brushing unbaked cookies with a milk or beaten egg glaze.

PASTRY WHEELS

These make quick work of cutting rolled dough into squares, rectangles or diamonds, although some skill is needed to create even-sized cookies. They are particularly good for young children who want to help with cutting out cookie shapes. They are easy to use and do not have a sharp blade. They are available from kitchenware stores and are either made from wood or stainless steel, and have a plain or fluted blade. (A pizza cutter can be used in the same way.)

Below: A fluted pastry wheel gives a pretty zigzag edge to rectangular, square and diamond shaped cookies.

Methods of Making Cookies

There are many different ways of making cookie dough. Depending on the type of cookie you are baking, the method will vary, so it is useful to know all the techniques.

THE CREAMING METHOD

A wide variety of cookies are made using the creaming method. These include plain Shrewsbury cookies, French sablés, fork cookies, melting moments, snickerdoodles and Swiss butter cookies. The fat and sugar are creamed – or beaten – together either until just blended or, more usually, until they are well-aerated and have a light and fluffy texture. Eggs and dry ingredients are then added a little bit at a time.

The fat should be soft enough to beat easily, so remember to remove it from the refrigerator at least 30 minutes before you start mixing. Unsalted (sweet) butter is the best choice, but if you are going to use margarine, use the firm block type rather than softer margarine that is sold in tubs.

The eggs should also be at room temperature or they may curdle the creamed mixture when they are added. It is not essential to use an electric mixer or food processor for the creaming method – a wooden spoon does a perfectly good job – but it definitely makes the process easier and quicker.

Cook's Tip
Creamed mixtures have a tendency to curdle when the eggs are added. To avoid this, add the eggs a little at a time and beat well after each addition. If the mixture does curdle, beat in 15ml/1 tbsp of the flour before adding more egg.

SWISS BUTTER COOKIES

These crisp cookies are very easy to make and delicious to eat.

Makes 24
115g/4oz/½ cup unsalted (sweet)
   butter, softened
50g/2oz/¼ cup caster (superfine) sugar
1 egg
200g/7oz/1¾ cups plain (all-purpose) flour
30ml/2 tbsp cornflour (cornstarch)
15ml/1 tbsp ground almonds

1 Put the butter in a large mixing bowl and beat with an electric mixer or a wooden spoon until it is softened and creamy. Add the sugar and beat in until it is completely incorporated. Continue beating until the mixture is light, fluffy and much paler in colour.

2 Beat the egg lightly with a fork. Add the egg to the butter mixture, a little at a time, beating well after each addition.

3 Sift the flour and cornflour over the creamed ingredients. This will remove any lumps and incorporate air, making your cookies lighter. Add the ground almonds and stir together to make a soft dough.

4 Shape the dough into a ball, then flatten it slightly into a round – this makes it easier to roll out. Wrap the dough tightly in clear film (plastic wrap) and chill for about 30 minutes, or until the dough is fairly firm. Meanwhile, preheat the oven to 180°C/350°F/Gas 4. Lightly grease two baking sheets or line them with baking parchment.

5 Roll out the dough on a lightly floured surface to 3mm/⅛in thick. Cut the dough into rounds with a 7.5cm/3in plain cutter and place on the baking sheets. Bake for about 15 minutes until golden. Leave on the baking sheets for 5 minutes, then transfer to a wire rack to cool.

THE RUBBING-IN METHOD

Many traditional cookies, such as shortbread and digestives (Graham crackers) are made by rubbing the fat, which can be butter, margarine, white vegetable fat or lard, into the flour. The fat should be firm and cool but not straight from the refrigerator, so leave the fat at room temperature before using. Beaten eggs, milk or water may be added to bind the mixture.

CLASSIC SHORTBREAD

These buttery cookies are cooked in a round, then cut into wedges.

Makes 8 wedges

175g/6oz/1½ cups plain (all-purpose) flour
115g/4oz/½ cup butter, diced and chilled
50g/2oz/¼ cup caster (superfine) sugar, plus extra for sprinkling

1 Preheat the oven to 160°C/325°F/ Gas 3. Grease a baking sheet or line it with baking parchment. Sift the flour and salt into a large bowl. Use a palette knife (metal spatula) to stir in the diced butter until the pieces are coated with flour. Rub them between your fingertips, lifting the mixture and then letting it drop until it looks like fine breadcrumbs. Stir in the sugar.

2 Holding the bowl firmly, gather the dough into a ball – the warmth of your hand will help bring the dough together.

3 Gently knead the dough on a lightly floured surface for about 30 seconds until it is smooth.

4 Roll out the dough into a round about 15cm/6in in diameter and 1cm/½in thick. Transfer to the prepared baking sheet. Score the top deeply into eight sections, then prick a pattern with a fork. This will allow steam to escape during cooking and prevent the shortbread from rising in the middle. Chill the shortbread for 1 hour.

5 Sprinkle the top lightly and evenly with a little extra caster sugar. Bake the shortbread for 35 minutes, or until it is a pale, golden straw colour. Leave to cool on the baking sheet for 5 minutes, then transfer to a wire rack to cool.

MAKING RUBBED-IN COOKIES IN A FOOD PROCESSOR

This method of making cookies is especially useful where the cookie mixture contains a high proportion of fat.

1 Put the sifted flour and other dry ingredients, such as salt, into the food processor. Process for 4–5 seconds.

2 Sprinkle in the diced, chilled fat. Process for 10 seconds, or until the mixture resembles fine breadcrumbs.

3 Sprinkle any liquid, such as beaten egg, milk or water, over the mixture and, using the pulse button, process for just a few seconds until the mixture starts to hold together. Do not allow the cookie dough to form a ball in the food processor.

4 Remove the mixture from the food processor and form into a ball with your hands. Gently knead the dough on a lightly floured surface for a few seconds until smooth. Wrap the dough in clear film (plastic wrap) and then chill until fairly firm.

THE MELTED METHOD

Cookies, such as flapjacks and gingernuts (gingersnaps) are made by first melting the fat and sugar or syrup together. The dry ingredients are then stirred in to make a soft dough that firms as it cools. The baked cookies become crisp as they cool, so should be quickly shaped, or left on the baking sheets for a few minutes to firm up before transferring to a wire rack.

GINGERNUTS

When baked, these spiced cookies are slightly cracked on the top.

Makes 24
50g/2oz/¼ cup butter, diced
50g/2oz/¼ cup golden (light corn) syrup
40g/1½oz/3 tbsp granulated sugar
115g/4oz/1 cup self-raising
* (self-rising) flour*
5ml/1 tsp ground ginger
5ml/1 tsp bicarbonate of soda
* (baking soda)*

1 Preheat the oven to 180°C/350°F/ Gas 4. Lightly grease two large baking sheets. Put the butter, syrup and sugar in a heavy pan and heat gently until just melted, stirring occasionally until the ingredients are blended. Do not let the mixture boil or some of the liquid will evaporate, altering the proportions.

2 Remove the pan from the heat and leave the mixture to cool for a few minutes. (This is particularly important if you are adding eggs, as they will cook and curdle if the mixture is too hot.) Sift the flour, ginger and bicarbonate of soda over the mixture. Stir until the mixture has blended and is smooth. The raising agents will start to work straight away, so shape the cookie dough and bake as soon as possible.

3 Place small spoonfuls of the mixture on to the prepared baking sheets, spacing the mounds of cookie dough well apart to allow room for the cookies to spread.

4 Bake the gingernuts for about 10 minutes, or until they are golden brown and the top surfaces are crazed. Leave the cookies on the baking sheets for 2 minutes to firm up, then transfer them to a wire rack to cool and crisp.

THE WHISKED METHOD

Airy cookies or crisp, delicate cookies, such as tuiles, macaroons and *langues de chat* are made by folding the dry ingredients into a whisked mixture of eggs and sugar, or into a meringue (whisked egg whites and sugar) mixture.

TUILES

These delicate cookies are named after the French curved roof tiles, which they closely resemble if they are shaped into curls while still hot.

Makes 12
1 egg white
50g/2oz/¼ cup caster (superfine) sugar
25g/1oz/2 tbsp butter, melted
* and cooled*
25g/1oz/¼ cup plain
* (all-purpose) flour, sifted*
flaked (sliced) almonds, for sprinkling
* (optional)*

1 Preheat the oven to 190°C/375°F/ Gas 5. Lightly grease two or three baking sheets or line them with sheets of baking parchment.

2 Put the egg whites in a large, clean, grease-free mixing bowl and whisk until stiff peaks form. Gently fold in the caster sugar to make a stiff and glossy mixture. (It should resemble a meringue mixture.)

3 Trickle about a third of the melted butter down the side of the bowl and fold in with the same quantity of flour. Repeat until all the butter and flour are incorporated.

4 Place small spoonfuls of the mixture, at least 13cm/5in apart, on the prepared baking sheets, then spread out into thin rounds using the back of a spoon. Sprinkle flaked almonds over each round, if using.

5 Bake the tuiles for 6–7 minutes, or until the biscuits are pale beige in the middle and brown at the edges. Leave to cool on the baking sheets for a few seconds, then lift off carefully with a palette knife or metal spatula and cool on a wire rack. (If you want to curl the tuiles, do this while they are still hot.)

THE ALL-IN-ONE METHOD

Some cookies are made by simply placing all the ingredients in a bowl and beating them together. Drop cookies are usually made this way. This easy method can be made even faster by using a food processor, although chunky ingredients such as dried fruit and nuts may have to be stirred in after mixing the cookie dough. It is essential that the fat is soft enough to blend easily.

RAISIN COOKIES

The natural sweetness of raisins gives these cookies extra flavour and a chewy bite.

Makes 24
150g/5oz/1¼ cups plain (all-purpose) flour
2.5ml/½ tsp baking powder
pinch of salt
115g/4oz/generous ½ cup caster
  (superfine) sugar
115g/4oz/½ cup soft margarine
1 egg, lightly beaten
2.5ml/½ tsp vanilla essence (extract)
150g/5oz/1 cup seedless raisins

1 Preheat the oven to 190°C/375°F/ Gas 5. Lightly grease three baking sheets or line them with baking parchment. Sift together the flour, baking powder and salt into a mixing bowl or the bowl of a food processor. Add the sugar, margarine, egg and vanilla essence.

2 Beat with a wooden spoon or blend in a food processor until combined. Stir in the raisins.

3 Drop heaped dessertspoonfuls of the mixture about 5cm/2in apart on to the baking sheets. Bake the cookies for 15 minutes or until golden brown. Leave on the baking sheets for a few minutes then transfer to wire racks to cool.

MEASURING INGREDIENTS

Dry ingredients by weight

Whether you measure in imperial or metric, electronic and balance scales generally give more accurate readings than spring scales. Spoon or pour the dry ingredients into the bowl or tray on the scales and check the reading or dial carefully.

Dry ingredients in measuring cups or spoons

To measure a dry ingredient in a spoon, scoop it up in the spoon, then level the surface using the straight edge of a knife. If you are using measuring cups, make sure you have ¼, ⅓, ½, ⅔, ¾ and 1 cup sizes. Where a recipe calls for a scant cup, fill the cup with the dry ingredient, level with the back of a knife, then scoop out about 15ml/1 tbsp. Where a generous cup is called for, level with a knife then add about 15ml/1 tbsp.

Liquids in litres, pints or cups

Use a clear glass or plastic jug (cup) with calibrations in litres, pints or cups. Put it on a flat surface, pour in the liquid and check the markings by bending down and looking at eye level.

Liquids in spoons

Use proper measuring spoons and carefully pour in the liquid, filling it to the brim then pouring it into the mixing bowl. Do not hold the spoon over the bowl.

Drop Cookies

These are probably the simplest cookies to make. They are called drop cookies because the dough is soft enough to drop off the spoon and on to the baking sheet. The basic mixture is often made by the creaming method where butter and sugar are beaten together until light and fluffy. Eggs are then beaten in, followed by flour, raising agents and any flavourings.

CHOCOLATE CHIP COOKIES

Created in the 1930s, these were originally called Toll House cookies.

Makes 12
115g/4oz/½ cup butter, softened
115g/4oz/generous ½ cup caster (superfine) sugar
1 egg, lightly beaten
5ml/1 tsp vanilla essence (extract)
175g/6oz/1½ cups plain (all-purpose) flour
175g/6oz/1 cup plain (semisweet) chocolate chips

1 Preheat the oven to 180°C/350°F/Gas 4. Lightly grease two or three large baking sheets or line them with baking parchment. Cream the butter and sugar together in a bowl with a wooden spoon or an electric mixer until pale and fluffy. Beat in the egg and vanilla essence. Sift the flour over the butter mixture and fold in with the chocolate chips.

2 Drop tablespoonfuls of the mixture on to the prepared baking sheets. (It should fall off the spoon quite easily with a sharp jerk; if not, use another spoon to scoop it off.) Leave plenty of space between the cookies to allow for spreading.

3 Flatten each cookie slightly with the back of a fork, keeping the shape as even as possible. For dropped cookies that have a soft or cakey texture when cooked, the mixture should be left well mounded on the baking sheet and not flattened; very stiff mixtures should be more widely spread. The recipe instructions should indicate this – if you are unsure, test how much the mixture spreads by baking a single cookie.

4 Bake the cookies for about 10 minutes, or until golden. Using a palette knife or metal spatula, transfer to a wire rack to cool.

FLAVOURING DROP COOKIES

As long as you follow the basic recipe and techniques, you can make a huge variety of drop cookies. Remember, though, that some added ingredients may alter the consistency of the dough – chopped fresh fruit, for example, may make the mixture too wet, whereas rolled oats will soak up moisture, making the cookies dry and crumbly.

Chocolate Substitute 15ml/1 tbsp (unsweetened) cocoa powder for the same quantity of flour. For a chunkier texture, use coarsely chopped chocolate instead of chocolate chips. You can use milk chocolate or chocolate chips instead of the plain (semisweet) chocolate chips in the recipe on this page.

Mocha Use coffee essence (extract) instead of vanilla essence (extract).

Macadamia nut or hazelnut Add whole or coarsely chopped nuts instead of the chocolate chips. Alternatively, as nuts and chocolate are a classic combination, use 75g/3oz/½ cup of each.

Dried fruit In place of the chocolate chips, add chopped dried fruit, such as raisins, sultanas (golden raisins), apricots, glacé (candied) cherries, or a mixture of candied tropical fruit, such as pineapple, mango and papaya. Add fruit juice or milk instead of vanilla essence.

MELTED DROP COOKIES

Thin, crisp cookies, such as tuiles, florentines and brandy snaps, require the butter and sugar or syrup to be melted together first to start the caramelization process prior to baking. Such cookies usually contain little flour, which helps them spread on the baking sheet – so make sure they have plenty of room.

BRANDY SNAPS

These classic melted drop cookies have a wonderful brittle texture. They melt in the mouth to release a sweet, almost caramelized flavour.

Makes 12–14

75g/3oz/6 tbsp butter, diced
75g/3oz/scant ½ cup caster
  (superfine) sugar
45ml/3 tbsp golden (light corn) syrup
75g/3oz/⅓ cup plain
  (all-purpose) flour
5ml/1 tsp ground ginger
30ml/2 tbsp brandy
15ml/1 tbsp lemon juice

1 Preheat the oven to 190°C/375°F/ Gas 5. Lightly grease several baking sheets or line them with baking parchment. Put the butter, sugar and syrup in a heavy pan. Heat gently over a low heat, stirring occasionally until the mixture has melted and becomes smooth.

2 Remove the pan from the heat. Leave the mixture to cool for a few minutes or the flour will start to cook when it is added.

3 Sift together the flour and ginger and stir into the butter mixture with the brandy and lemon juice. Leave for a further 1–2 minutes to allow the flour to absorb some of the moisture.

4 Drop teaspoonfuls of the mixture at 4cm/1½in intervals on to the baking sheets. Do not attempt to cook any more than three or four on each sheet as they will need plenty of room to spread.

5 Bake, one sheet at a time, for about 8–10 minutes, or until the cookies turn bubbly, lacy in texture and golden brown. Remove the brandy snaps from the oven and leave for about 15 seconds to firm up slightly before attempting to move them.

6 Loosen the brandy snaps from the baking sheet one at a time using a palette knife or metal spatula, and shape before cooling on a wire rack.

SHAPING UP

Some melted drop cookies need to be reshaped or neatened before, part-way through or after cooking.

Tuiles Named after the curved roof tiles in France, these may be round but are usually slightly elongated. Drop heaped teaspoonfuls of the mixture on greased or lined baking sheets then spread each into an oval, measuring 10 x 5cm/4 x 2in.

Florentines The mixture often spreads out further than the fruit and nuts. Remove from the oven 2 minutes before the end of cooking time and press back the edges into a neat shape with a palette knife to create perfect rounds, then return to the oven.

Glass cookies After baking, trim these thin, delicate cookies into shape by pressing a round metal biscuit cutter, slightly smaller than the baked cookie, into each, then pull away or break off the excess.

SHAPING MELTED DROP COOKIES

Melted drop cookies are pliable enough to be shaped into curls, rolls or baskets when they are warm. As they cool, the cookies become crisp and hard, retaining their shape.

MAKING CURLS

Tuiles are usually curled after baking. They make a pretty accompaniment to serve with desserts. Remove the cookies from the oven, lift off the baking sheet and drape over a lightly oiled rolling pin, gently curling them around. Leave them to cool and crisp before removing.

MAKING ROLLS

These tightly rolled, wand-shaped cookies are great for serving as an accompaniment to any dessert. Cigarette Russes are a classic example of a rolled cookie.

1 Shape small spoonfuls of tuile mixture into 7.5 x 5cm/3 x 2in rectangles on greased or lined baking sheets, spacing them well apart, and bake at 190°C/375°F/ Gas 5 for 6–7 minutes.

2 Carefully lift off the cookies and place upside down on a flat surface. Wind each cookie tightly around a greased wooden spoon handle.

3 Cool slightly until firm, then ease the cookies off the handles and place them on a wire rack to cool completely. Brandy snaps can be shaped in the same way, but do not turn upside-down before rolling them up.

MAKING BASKETS

You can use either large brandy snaps or tuiles to make little bowl-shaped containers for desserts such as ice cream, sorbet, fresh fruit or mousse.

1 Bake heaped tablespoonfuls of brandy snap mixture or spread heaped teaspoonfuls of tuile mixture into 12cm/4½in rounds on a large baking sheet.

2 Once cooked, leave the cookies to cool for a few seconds, then lift from the baking sheet. Mould over lightly greased, upturned ramekin dishes, pressing the edges into soft folds with your fingers.

3 If you do not have suitable ramekins, then small bowls, cups or even small oranges can be used to produce a similar effect. If you use oranges to create the basic basket shape, then remember to pat the base flat before the cookie sets so that the baskets will be stable and stand upright. Lift off once set.

Variation
To make chocolate brandy snaps, use 65g/2½oz/9 tbsp plain (all-purpose) flour and 30ml/2 tbsp (unsweetened) cocoa powder. You can always omit the ground ginger, if you prefer.

FORTUNE COOKIES

Originally forming part of an ancient Chinese tradition, these are little folded cookies made from tuile mixture. They contain short messages that predict the future and they provide lots of fun for children and adults alike.

1 Spread out teaspoonfuls of tuile mixture to 7.5cm/3in rounds on greased or lined baking sheets and bake until the edges are just turning brown.

2 Working quickly so that the cookies do not cool before they are folded, lift the cookies off the sheets with a palette knife or metal spatula. Lay a folded paper fortune message in the centre and fold the cookie in half. Bend in half again over the edge of a bowl.

3 Leave the cookies to cool and harden, then lift them off the bowl and store in an airtight container.

Rolled Cookies

A cookie dough that is rolled and cut may be a creamed, melted or rubbed-in mixture, but it must have the right consistency. If the dough is too dry it will crack and crumble; too wet and it may stick when rolling and spread during baking.

SIMPLE ALMOND COOKIES
The addition of almonds gives these cookies a delicious crunch.

Makes 24

115g/4oz/½ cup butter, softened
50g/2oz/¼ cup caster (superfine) sugar
1 egg, lightly beaten
15ml/1 tbsp ground almonds
200g/7oz/1¾ cups plain (all-purpose) flour
30ml/2 tbsp cornflour (cornstarch)

1 Preheat the oven to 180°C/350°F/ Gas 4. Lightly grease two baking sheets or line them with baking parchment. Beat the butter and sugar together until creamy. Gradually add the egg, beating well after each addition, then beat in the almonds. Sift over the flour and cornflour and mix to a soft dough.

2 Lightly knead the dough on a floured surface for a few seconds, until smooth. Do not overwork the dough or the butter will start to melt and the gluten will "develop", giving the cookies a tough texture.

3 Shape the dough into a ball then flatten slightly into a round – this makes it easier when you begin to roll it out. Wrap in clear film (plastic wrap) to prevent the dough from drying out and chill for about 30 minutes, or until firm but make sure it is not too stiff to roll. If you are making a large amount of cookie dough, divide it into pieces so that you will be able to handle it more easily when rolling.

4 On a floured surface, roll out the dough lightly and evenly in one direction only to a thickness of about 3mm/⅛in. Roll from the centre to the far edge but not actually over the edge. Always roll away from you and rotate the cookie dough occasionally to prevent it from sticking and also to make sure it is evenly rolled. Avoid pulling the dough as you roll or rotate it, otherwise it may become misshapen when baked.

5 Stamp out 6.5cm/2½in rounds using a fluted cookie cutter, or use another similar-sized shape. Gather up the scraps and re-roll to make more cookies.

6 Transfer the cookies to the prepared baking sheets using a palette knife or metal spatula. Rolled out cookies shouldn't spread as much as drop cookies during baking, but you should still leave a space of at least 2.5cm/1in between each on the baking sheet. Chill the cookies for at least 30 minutes before baking them, as this helps to retain their shape.

7 Bake for 10 minutes until the cookies are a pale golden brown, making sure you rotate the baking sheets halfway through the cooking time. Remove the cookies from the oven and leave on the baking sheets for 2–3 minutes. This allows the biscuits to firm up so that they are less fragile when you handle them. Transfer the cookies to a wire rack using a metal spatula.

Cook's Tip
Cooling cookies on a wire rack allows air to circulate around them, preventing them from gathering moisture and becoming soggy as they cool.

ALL SHAPES AND SIZES

One of the greatest assets of rolled cookies is that they may be cut into any shape or size. There is a huge range of cutters available, but other ways of cutting and shaping cookies include using a pastry wheel or a knife, or even making your own template out of paper or card.

USING A KNIFE OR A PASTRY WHEEL TO SHAPE COOKIES

If you want to make squares, rectangles, triangles or bars, a sharp knife and a ruler are the perfect tools for the job. Instead of a knife, you could use a fluted pastry wheel to give an attractive edging.

1 Roll out the cookie dough to a square or rectangular shape, turning it frequently by 90 degrees. During the early stages of rolling out, push in the edges of the dough with your cupped palms to keep the shape.

2 To make square or rectangular cookies such as shortbread fingers or bourbons, use a ruler to measure the dough so that it is rolled to the appropriate shape and size, then cut with a sharp knife or pastry cutter. (For example, for custard creams, cut the dough into 4cm/1½in strips, then cut each strip at intervals of 5cm/2in to make rectangles.)

3 To make triangular cookies, cut the dough into strips then into squares, then cut each square in half diagonally to make triangles.

4 To make neat diamond-shaped cookies, cut the dough into strips and then cut diagonally across the strips to make diamonds.

MAKING A TEMPLATE

For special occasions you may want to create a more complex cookie shape for which you do not have a cutter. In this case you will need to make a template. It's probably best to avoid very intricate designs, especially those with small protrusions as these may distort or burn during baking, and will break off easily once cooked.

1 Select the design, then either draw the design straight on to a piece of thin cardboard or trace it on to tracing or greaseproof (waxed) paper first, then glue it on to cardboard. Wait for the glue to dry thoroughly before carefully cutting out the template.

2 Place the template on the rolled out cookie dough and hold it firmly in place. Using the point of a sharp knife, cut around the template to create the cookie shape.

MAKING RING COOKIES

It's hard to transfer ring cookies to baking sheets without pulling them out of shape. One solution is to place rounds of cookie dough on the baking sheet, then cut out the centres with a smaller cutter. To make perfect rings, bake round cookies, then stamp out the centres while the cookies are still warm.

1 Roll out the dough then stamp into rounds and transfer to a baking sheet. Bake the cookies according to the recipe instructions.

2 Remove the cookies from the oven and leave on the baking sheet. Using a small cookie cutter, stamp out the centres of the cookies before they have time to cool.

3 Leave the cookies on the baking sheet for 3–4 minutes, then transfer to a wire rack to cool completely.

Cook's Tips
• *To make pretty jammy sandwiches, only remove the centres from half the rounds, then sandwich the rounds and rings together with a little jam.*
• *Young children love the mini cookies that are left over after punching out holes in larger cookies. Drizzle with a little icing made from sugar and water for an extra special treat.*

MAKING MULTI-COLOURED ROLLED COOKIES

By using two or more different coloured doughs you can make a range of attractive cookies. The coloured doughs can be rolled, stamped out, then pieced together before baking, or the rolled doughs can be layered together then cut into cookie shapes.

TWO-TONE COOKIES

To make cookies with different coloured middles, leave half the dough plain and knead in a little cooled melted chocolate into the other half, or use a few drops of food colouring.

1 Roll out each piece of dough to about 3mm/⅛in thick. Stamp out an equal number of cookies (rounds or hearts) and place them on separate baking sheets. Chill for 30 minutes.

2 Using a smaller cutter, stamp out the centres from all of the cookies, then swap the plain centres for the flavoured or coloured centres and vice versa.

3 If you like, you can use a third, even smaller, cutter as well and swap the tiny centres once more to make triple-tone cookies.

PINWHEELS

These cookies are made by rolling together layers of coloured dough.

1 Divide the cookie dough into two. Leave half plain and flavour the other half by kneading in 15ml/1 tbsp sifted (unsweetened) cocoa powder and 5ml/1 tsp milk. Wrap and chill for about 30 minutes.

2 Roll out each piece of dough to a rectangle measuring 20 x 25cm/8 x 10in. Lightly brush the plain dough with lightly beaten egg white and place the coloured dough on top. Roll up tightly from a long side, then cut into 5mm/¼in thick slices.

NEAPOLITAN SLICES

These cookies resemble mini slices of Neapolitan ice cream.

1 Divide the dough into three. Leave one third plain, flavour one third with cocoa (as for pinwheels) and colour the remaining third pink. Wrap and chill for 30 minutes.

2 Roll out each piece of dough into a rectangle measuring 10 x 7.5cm/4 x 3in. Place the rectangles on top of each other, brushing between the layers with lightly beaten egg white. Cut the dough into 5mm/¼in thick slices, then cut each slice in half.

SEVEN STEPS TO SUCCESS

• Always chill the dough to firm it for at least 20 minutes and up to 1 hour before rolling. If you chill it for longer, leave it at room temperature for about 10 minutes before rolling out.
• Cookies should be rolled to a thickness of 3–5mm/⅛–¼in. Thicker cookies will have soggy centres when the outside has browned; thinner cookies will be very crisp and fragile.
• Use the minimum amount of flour when rolling out the dough. Lightly dust the work surface and the rolling pin using a flour dredger or fine sieve, sprinkling with a little more flour when needed. After cutting the cookies, brush off any excess flour with a dry pastry brush.
• If the dough is sticky, even after chilling, roll it out between two sheets of baking parchment or clear film (plastic wrap). After rolling, leave the parchment or clear film in place, slide the dough on to a baking sheet and chill before stamping out the cookies with a cookie cutter.
• When stamping out the cookies, dip the cutter into flour, then press down firmly to cut right through the dough.
• Cut cookies closely together to minimize re-rolling scraps. The first rolling is always better.
• If you haven't got a cutter, use a sharp knife or pastry wheel to cut the dough into squares or rectangles, or stamp out rounds using a thin-rimmed glass.

Piped Cookies

For this type of cookie the mixture needs to be soft enough to pipe but firm enough to keep its shape during baking. Piped cookies are usually made by the creaming method, which gives them a crumbly, airy texture and makes blending in flavourings easy. Make sure that the butter is very soft before you start as this will make mixing and piping quick and easy.

VIENNESE PIPED COOKIES

With a little practice, these cookies can be piped into any shape you like.

Makes 12

175g/6oz/¾ cup unsalted (sweet) butter, softened
40g/1½oz/3 tbsp icing (confectioners') sugar, sifted
2.5ml/½ tsp vanilla essence (extract)
175g/6oz/1½ cups plain (all-purpose) flour
40g/1½oz/3 tbsp cornflour (cornstarch)

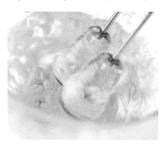

1 Preheat the oven to 180°C/350°F/ Gas 4. Grease or line two baking sheets. Cream the butter and icing sugar together until very pale and fluffy. Add the vanilla essence and beat for a few more seconds.

2 Sift the flour and cornflour together over the butter mixture and mix together until smooth.

3 Spoon the mixture into a piping (pastry) bag fitted with a large, star-shaped nozzle and pipe into the required shapes on the prepared baking sheets. Make sure the shapes are spaced well apart.

4 Bake the cookies for about 12 minutes, or until they are a pale golden colour. Leave for a few minutes on the baking sheets to firm up slightly before carefully transferring them to a wire rack with a palette knife or metal spatula to finish cooling.

Variations
Once you have mastered making and piping the basic recipe, try adding flavourings to vary the cookie mixture.
Chocolate *Substitute 30ml/2 tbsp (unsweetened) cocoa powder for the same quantity of flour.*
Coffee *Omit the vanilla essence and blend 5ml/1 tsp instant coffee powder with 5ml/1 tsp just boiled water. Leave to cool, then add to the mixture with the flour and cornflour.*
Strawberry *Use 40g/1½oz/3 tbsp strawberry flavour blancmange powder instead of the cornflour.*
Orange or lemon *Beat the finely grated rind of half an orange or lemon into the creamed mixture.*
Caramel *To give the cookies a mild caramel flavour, use unrefined icing sugar.*

PERFECT PIPING
To perfect your piping technique, follow these three simple steps.

1 Drop the nozzle into the bag, pushing it down to fit firmly. Twist the nozzle end round so that there is a twist in the bag just above it, then push the twisted section of the bag inside the nozzle to close it off.

2 Fold the top of the bag over your hand to make a "collar". Spoon in the mixture. When the bag is about half full, gently twist the top to remove the air. Holding the top of the bag, push the mixture down.

3 To pipe, hold the twisted end firmly and use the other hand to guide the nozzle. Using firm, steady pressure, pipe the shape. Push down slightly then lift up.

PIPING SHAPES

Viennese cookie mixture can be piped it into all manner of shapes.

VIENNESE COOKIES

Round swirls are the classic shape for Viennese cookies.

Spoon the mixture into a piping (pastry) bag fitted with a 12mm/½in star nozzle. Pipe rosettes 5cm/2in across on to greased baking sheets, spacing them well apart.

VIENNESE WHIRLS

Sandwich two Viennese cookies together with buttercream filling and a little sieved apricot jam.

SWISS FINGERS

Pretty piped fingers are very popular, and very simple to make.

Spoon the mixture into a piping bag fitted with a 1cm/½in star nozzle. Pipe 6cm/2¼in lengths on greased baking sheets, spacing well apart.

OYSTER COOKIES

These pretty, sophisticated cookies resemble oyster shells.

Spoon the mixture into a piping bag fitted with a 1cm/½in star nozzle and pipe about five lines to make shells. Make the shape wide at one end and tapered at the other.

CHOCOLATE VANILLA SWIRLS

These two-colour cookies look lovely piped into paper cake cases.

1 Divide the Viennese cookie mixture into two equal parts and beat 15ml/1 tbsp sifted (unsweetened) cocoa powder into half of it. Spoon the vanilla mixture down one side of a piping bag fitted with a 1cm/½in star nozzle and then spoon the chocolate mixture down the other side.

2 Pipe the mixture into 12 paper cake cases in a bun tray (muffin pan) to make pretty striped swirls.

OTHER PIPED COOKIES

Many other cookie mixtures are piped to give them an even length, width and shape.

LANGUES DE CHATS

These classic French cookies are long, thin ovals with a slightly rough texture (like a cat's tongue).

Makes 18
75g/3oz/6 tbsp unsalted (sweet)
*   butter, softened*
115g/4oz/1 cup icing (confectioners')
*   sugar, sifted, plus extra for dusting*
2 large (US extra large) egg whites
30ml/2 tbsp caster (superfine) sugar
75g/3oz/⅔ cup plain (all-purpose)
*   flour, sifted*

1 Preheat the oven to 200°C/400°F/Gas 6. Grease two baking sheets or line them with baking parchment. Cream the butter and icing sugar together until pale and fluffy.

2 In a separate bowl, whisk the egg whites to soft peaks, then add the caster sugar 15ml/1 tbsp at a time, whisking between each addition. Fold the whites into the butter mixture, then fold in the flour.

3 Spoon the mixture into a piping (pastry) bag fitted with a 1cm/½in plain nozzle and pipe 6cm/2½in lengths on to the prepared baking sheets. Allow 5cm/2in between each cookie for spreading.

4 Bake for 5–7 minutes, or until the edges are lightly browned. Leave to cool on the baking sheets for 5 minutes before transferring to a wire rack to cool completely.

FILIGREE CROWNS

These delicate, shaped cookies are made from finely piped lines of cookie mixture, which are first baked and then moulded into crowns. They make stunning little containers for desserts such as ice cream, sorbet, mousse or fresh fruit.

Makes 6
1 egg white
50g/2oz/¼ cup caster
  (superfine) sugar
25g/1oz/¼ cup plain
  (all-purpose) flour

1 Preheat the oven to 200°C/400°F/ Gas 6. Draw six rectangles, each measuring about 20 x 7.5cm/8 x 3in, on six separate pieces of baking parchment.

2 Whisk the egg white and sugar together in a small mixing bowl until foamy. Sift the flour over the egg mixture and stir in thoroughly.

3 Spoon the cookie mixture into a greaseproof (waxed) paper piping (pastry) bag and snip off the tip to create a small hole. On each rectangle of baking parchment, carefully pipe thin wiggly lines from side to side to fill the marked shape, then pipe a little extra mixture down one of the long edges.

4 Bake the cookies for about 3 minutes. Remove the tray from the oven and immediately roll the cookie around a straight-sided glass.

5 Peel away the paper and stand the crowns upright. Remove the glass. If the mixture hardens before you've moulded the crowns, return to the oven for a few seconds. Cool and store in an airtight container.

SPANISH CHURROS

These little Spanish cake-cookies are made from sweetened choux pastry, which is piped into hot oil and then deep-fried. Serve sprinkled generously with cinnamon sugar.

Makes 25
75g/3oz/6 tbsp butter, diced
250ml/8fl oz/1 cup water
115g/4oz/1 cup plain
  (all-purpose) flour
50g/2oz/4 tbsp caster
  (superfine) sugar
3 eggs, lightly beaten
2.5ml/½ tsp ground cinnamon

1 Heat the butter and water in a small heavy pan until the butter has melted – do not allow the water to boil. Sift the flour and 15ml/1 tbsp of the caster sugar on to a piece of greaseproof (waxed) paper.

2 Once the butter has melted, bring to a boil, then add the flour and sugar. Remove the pan from the heat and beat the mixture vigorously. Leave to cool for 5 minutes, then gradually beat in the eggs until the mixture is smooth and glossy.

3 Half-fill a large, heavy pan or deep-fryer with oil and heat to 190°C/375°F. Spoon the mixture into a piping (pastry) bag with a 1cm/½in star nozzle. Pipe five 10cm/4in lengths of the mixture into the hot oil being careful not to cause the fat to splash or spit. Fry the churros for 2 minutes, or until golden and crisp.

4 Remove the churros from the oil with a slotted spoon and drain on kitchen paper. Repeat until all the mixture has been used. Mix the remaining caster sugar with the ground cinnamon and sprinkle over the churros. Serve warm.

Pressed Cookies

Shaped cookies are amazingly simple to make using a commercial cookie press. The press comes with a range of patterened discs and may have several settings so that a variety of shapes and sizes of cookie can be made. Choose soft-textured cookie doughs that will easily push through the press.

VANILLA FLOWERS

These pretty cookies use vanilla essence for an irresistible flavour.

Makes 25

90g/3½oz/scant ½ cup butter, softened
90g/3½oz/½ cup caster (superfine) sugar
1 egg yolk
165g/5½oz/scant 1½ cups plain
* (all-purpose) flour*
5ml/1 tsp milk
5ml/1 tsp vanilla essence (extract)

1 Cream the butter and sugar together until pale and fluffy. Beat in the egg yolk. Sift the flour over the butter mixture and then fold in with the milk and vanilla essence to make a soft dough. Knead for a few seconds until smooth.

2 Fill the cookie press cylinder almost to the top with the dough and then screw on the plunger. Press out the dough on to greased baking sheets, spacing the cookies well apart.

3 Place the baking sheets in the refrigerator for at least 30 minutes, so that the cookies keep their shape while baking. Decorate with sugar or nuts, if using. Meanwhile, preheat the oven to 180°C/350°F/Gas 4.

4 Bake for 15 minutes, or until very lightly browned. Leave to cool on the baking sheets for 5 minutes, then transfer to a wire rack.

CHOCOLATE DAISIES

This dark chocolate mixture works perfectly in a cookie press.

Makes 12

175g/6oz/¾ cup unsalted (sweet)
* butter, softened*
40g/1½oz/3 tbsp icing (confectioners')
* sugar, sifted*
175g/6oz/1½ cups plain (all-purpose) flour
25g/1oz/2 tbsp cocoa powder
* (unsweetened)*
40g/1½oz/3 tbsp cornflour (cornstarch)

1 Preheat the oven to 180°C/350°F/Gas 4. Grease or line two baking sheets. Cream the butter and icing sugar together until very pale and fluffy.

2 Sift the flour and cornflour together over the butter mixture and mix together until smooth.

3 Put enough of the dough into the press to fill it almost to the top, then screw on the plunger.

4 Press out the dough on to the greased baking sheets. Make sure the shapes are spaced well apart.

5 Bake the cookies for about 12 minutes until just beginning to change colour. Leave the cookies for a few minutes on the baking sheets to firm up slightly before carefully transferring them to a wire rack to cool completely.

PRESSED COOKIE TIPS AND TECHNIQUES

• To achieve a really short texture, thoroughly cream the butter and sugar until very light and fold in the flour gently.
• The dough must be very smooth to go through the fine holes in the cookie discs, so don't add chunky flavouring ingredients, such as chopped nuts, dried fruit, glacé (candied) cherries or chocolate chips.
• The dough must be sufficiently soft to be easily squeezed through the press, but firm enough to hold its shape.
• If the mixture is too firm to press, add a few drops of milk
• If the dough is slightly soft and sticks to the cookie disc, put it in the refrigerator for about 30 minutes until it has firmed.
• Pressed cookies can be decorated with ingredients such as chocolate chips, sugar crystals or nuts before baking.

Moulded Cookies

Shaping cookie dough in a mould gives a professional finish. The dough can be either shaped in a mould, then turned out for baking or baked in the shaped tin (pan) itself. It is not essential to buy special moulds, you can improvise with plain tins for both shaping and baking.

SHAPING SHORTBREAD

Shortbread moulds usually have a carved design of a thistle and are available in different sizes. The mould should be brushed with a flavourless oil the first time it is used, then wiped with kitchen paper.

1 Make one quantity of shortbread mixture and roll out to a 15cm/6in round. Press it firmly into an 18cm/7in shortbread mould. Line a baking sheet with baking parchment.

2 Invert the mould on to the baking sheet, tapping the mould firmly to release the dough. Chill for about 30 minutes until firm.

3 Preheat the oven to 160°C/325°F/ Gas 3. Bake the shortbread for 35–40 minutes, or until pale golden. Sprinkle the top with a little caster (superfine) sugar, then leave to cool.

SHAPING MADELEINES

These French lemon cookies are baked in shell-shaped tins (pans).

Makes 15
1 egg
65g/2½oz/generous ¼ cup caster
(superfine) sugar
65g/2½oz/9 tbsp self-raising
(self-rising) flour
1.5ml/¼ tsp baking powder
finely grated rind of ½ lemon
65g/2½oz/5 tbsp butter, melted
and cooled

1 Preheat the oven to 220°C/425°F/ Gas 7. Brush the tins with melted unsalted (sweet) butter. Chill for 10 minutes, then brush lightly with butter again, dust with flour and shake off any excess.

2 Whisk the egg and sugar until thick and pale. (The mixture should leave a trail when the whisk is lifted.) Sift over half the flour with the baking powder and fold in the lemon rind. Pour half the melted butter around the edge of the bowl and fold in gently.

3 Sift over the remaining flour, then pour in the rest of the melted butter around the edge of the bowl. Fold in gently until combined.

4 Spoon the mixture into the moulds, filling them just to the top. Bake for 10 minutes until golden. Leave for a few moments, then ease out the madeleines with a palette knife or metal spatula and transfer to a wire rack.

MAKING PETTICOAT TAILS

Shortbread is traditionally made into wedge-shaped petticoat tails.

1 Press one quantity of shortbread mixture into an 18cm/7in loose-based fluted flan tin (quiche pan).

2 Prick the surface with a fork and mark the shortbread into eight wedges using a knife. If you do not have a fluted tin, use a straight-sided sandwich tin (layer pan) and press a pattern around the edge.

MAKING SQUARES AND BARS

Cookie dough can be baked in a loose-based square or rectangular tin (pan), then cut into pieces.

1 Press one quantity of shortbread mixture into a 15cm/6in square tin or two quantities into an 18 × 28cm/7 × 11in rectangular tin.

2 To cut into squares, make two cuts lengthways, then two cuts across for the square tin and four for the rectangular tin. To cut into bars, cut in half lengthways first, then cut across widthways into bars.

SMALL MOULDED COOKIES

These can be made in tiny tartlet tins (mini quiche pans) or pretty metal chocolate moulds.

Press shortbread dough into the tins or moulds until level, then bake. Alternatively, turn out the moulded rounds on to greased or lined baking sheets. Chill before baking.

SHAPING COOKIES BY HAND

You can model cookie dough into all manner of shapes. Classic hand-moulded cookies include jumbles and pretzels. Choose a dough that will retain its shape when baked.

FORK COOKIES

These are the simplest moulded cookies, made by rolling dough into balls, then flattening with a fork to make a pretty pattern on the top.

Makes 16
115g/4oz/½ cup butter, softened
50g/2oz/¼ cup caster (superfine) sugar
150g/5oz/1¼ cups self-raising (self-rising) flour, sifted

1 Preheat the oven to 180°C/350°F/ Gas 4. Lightly grease two baking sheets. Beat the butter in a bowl until creamy, then beat in the sugar. Stir in the flour and bring the dough together with your hands.

2 Shape into walnut-size balls and place on the baking sheets, spacing well apart. Dip a fork in cold water and use to flatten the cookies.

3 Bake for 10–12 minutes, until pale brown. Leave to cool on the baking sheets for a few minutes, then transfer to a wire rack to cool.

PRETZELS

These are complicated shapes, so require a more pliable dough.

Makes 40
115g/4oz/½ cup butter, softened
115g/4oz/1 cup icing (confectioners') sugar, sifted
1 egg, lightly beaten
15ml/1 tbsp golden (light corn) syrup
1.5ml/¼ tsp vanilla essence (extract)
250g/9oz/2¼ cups plain (all-purpose) flour, sifted

1 Preheat the oven to 190°C/375°F/ Gas 5. Beat the butter and sugar together until light and creamy. Beat in the egg, syrup and vanilla essence. Add the flour and stir to make a dough. Knead on a floured surface, then wrap and chill for 30 minutes.

2 Divide the dough into 40 pieces and cover the pieces that you aren't working on with clear film (plastic wrap). Roll one piece into a thin strand about 25cm/10in long.

3 Create a loop with the strand, bring the ends together and press them into the top of the circle. Make the rest of the pretzels in the same way. Chill for 30 minutes.

4 Bake for 10 minutes until lightly browned, then cool on wire racks.

Bar Cookies

These are a cross between a cake and a cookie; some are thin and crunchy, others thick and chewy or light and spongy. Some bar cookies, such as brownies and flapjacks, are just a single layer, but many have two or more different layers that combine tastes and textures. Sometimes this base is partially or fully cooked first before the topping is added, then the oven temperature is lowered so that the topping doesn't overcook.

Always make bar cookies in the recommended tin (pan) size; even a small change in size will affect the cooking time and final result.

LAYERED FRUIT AND NUT BAR COOKIE

This indulgent treat combines several flavours and textures.

Makes 15

250g/9oz/2¼ cups plain (all-purpose) flour
175g/6oz/¾ cup chilled butter or
   hard margarine, diced
75g/3oz/scant ½ cup caster (superfine)
   sugar or soft light brown sugar

For the filling

115g/4oz/½ cup glacé (candied) cherries,
   coarsely chopped
50g/2oz/⅓ cup sultanas (golden raisins)
50g/2oz/½ cup almonds, chopped

For the topping

115g/4oz/½ cup butter or hard
   margarine, softened
115g/4oz/generous ½ cup caster
   (superfine) sugar
2 eggs
50g/2oz/½ cup plain (all-purpose) flour
50g/2oz/½ cup ground almonds
icing (confectioners') sugar, for dusting

1 Preheat the oven to 180°C/350°F/ Gas 4. Line the base and grease an 18 × 28 × 2.5cm/7 × 11 × 1in cake tin (pan). To make the base, sift the flour into a bowl. Additional dry flavourings such as ground spices or (unsweetened) cocoa powder (substitute for an equal quantity of flour) can be added at this stage.

2 Rub in the butter or margarine pieces until the mixture resembles breadcrumbs. Stir in the sugar. If you are adding chunky flavourings, such as coconut or chocolate chips, stir them in with the sugar. Mix with your hands until the dough comes together.

3 Press the mixture into the base of the tin. Level with the back of a spoon or a potato masher. Prick the base with a fork to let out the steam and to make sure it remains level as it cooks, then bake for 10 minutes. Remove from the oven.

4 Reduce the temperature to 160°C/325°F/Gas 3. Mix together the filling ingredients, then sprinkle evenly over the base. To make the topping, cream the butter and sugar together until pale and fluffy, then beat in the eggs. Sift over the flour and fold in with the ground almonds. Spread the topping carefully over the fruit and nuts.

5 Bake for 30 minutes, or until a light golden brown colour and firm to the touch. Check the topping is cooked by inserting a wooden cocktail stick (toothpick) into it and leaving for a few seconds; it should come out clean. Leave to cool in the tin for 15 minutes. Lightly dust with icing sugar and cut into bars.

Variations

• *Use chopped dried fruit or spread over a thick layer of jam for the filling.*
• *Try flavouring the sponge cake topping with a little finely grated citrus rind.*

TOPPING IDEAS

There are dozens of different toppings for bar cookies. The base must be fairly firm but the topping can be softer, ranging from sponge cake to caramel, and from sticky meringue to chocolate. The following ideas are sufficient for an 18 x 28cm/7 x 11in tin (pan).

CRUMBLE OR STREUSEL

This works best on top of a slightly soft or sticky base or filling such as jam, fruit purée or soft caramel.

Beat 115g/4oz/½ cup butter until creamy, then mix in 50g/2oz/¼ cup soft light brown sugar. Stir in 115g/4oz/⅔ cup semolina and 115g/4oz/1 cup plain wholemeal (whole-wheat) flour until the mixture resembles breadcrumbs. Add 2.5ml/½ tsp ground ginger. Sprinkle over the base and press down. Bake at 160°C/325°F/Gas 3 for 40 minutes.

COCONUT

This light topping has a delicate flavour and lovely texture. Beat two eggs, then stir in 115g/4oz/generous ½ cup demerara (raw) sugar, 25g/1oz/3 tbsp ground rice, and 150g/5oz/1⅔ cup desiccated (dry unsweetened shredded) coconut. Spread over the base and bake at 180°C/350°F/Gas 4 for 25 minutes.

MERINGUE

This produces a wonderfully light, topping that melts in the mouth,

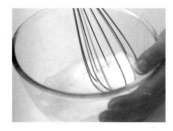

Whisk two egg whites with a pinch of salt in a clean bowl until they form soft peaks. Gradually whisk in 115g/4oz/generous ½ cup caster (superfine) sugar, a spoonful at a time, until the mixture is stiff and glossy. Fold in 2.5ml/½ tsp cornflour (cornstarch) and 5ml/1 tsp lemon juice. Spread over the base and swirl with a metal spatula to form soft peaks. Bake at 140°C/275°F/Gas 1 for 40 minutes until the meringue is set and tinged brown.

GRATED SHORTBREAD

To make this rich, buttery filling, cream together 115g/4oz/½ cup softened butter and 40g/1½oz/3 tbsp soft light brown sugar. Combine 5ml/1 tsp sunflower oil, 5ml/1 tsp vanilla essence (extract) and 1 egg yolk and beat into the butter mixture. Sift over 200g/7oz/1¾ cups plain (all-purpose) flour, 25g/1oz/¼ cup cornflour (cornstarch) and 2.5ml/½ tsp baking powder. Mix well and knead on a lightly floured surface for 30 seconds. Wrap in clear film (plastic wrap) and chill for about 30 minutes. Grate over the base or filling and press down. Bake at 150°C/300°F/Gas 2 for 45 minutes.

CITRUS CHEESECAKE

To make this zesty topping, put the finely grated rind of two lemons and two limes in a bowl with 225g/8oz/1 cup melted butter, 30ml/2 tbsp caster (superfine) sugar and three eggs. Whisk until thick and mousse-like. Sift over 40g/1½oz/⅓ cup plain (all-purpose) flour and 2.5ml/½ tsp baking powder and fold in with 30ml/2 tbsp lemon or lime juice. Pour over the base and bake at 180°C/350°F/Gas 4 for 25 minutes.

NUT CARAMEL

Put 175g/6oz/⅔ cup soft light brown sugar, 30ml/2 tbsp golden (light corn) syrup and 175g/6oz/¾ cup butter in a pan. Heat gently until the sugar has dissolved, then bring to the boil and simmer for 5 minutes, until a rich golden colour. Stir in 175g/6oz/1 cup chopped roasted unsalted peanuts. Immediately spread over base and leave to cool.

CHOCOLATE

This topping is incredibly simple and always produces great results.

Chop 350g/12oz plain (semisweet), milk or white chocolate. Sprinkle over the hot cookie base, then return to the oven for 1 minute until melted. Mark into bars when the chocolate is almost set.

BAKING THE PERFECT BROWNIE

Brownies, named after their dark rich colour, should be moist and chewy; with a sugary crust on the outside, but squidgy on the inside. There are many different recipes for brownies, varying in richness. Plainer ones rely on (unsweetened) cocoa powder alone, others on vast quantities of melted chocolate. Often, a small amount of coffee is added that is barely perceptible to the taste, but cuts through the sweetness a little. True brownies have a very high proportion of sugar and fat and most contain nuts, usually walnuts or pecan nuts.

Light versions and those made from white chocolate are often referred to as blondies. It is important to remove brownies from the oven as soon as the cooking time is up, even though they will still seem quite soft. They will firm up on standing and, if overcooked, the characteristic gooey texture will be ruined.

BROWNIE VARIATIONS

Double chocolate Add chocolate chips in place of the chopped walnuts.
Chunky choc and nut Use coarsely chopped chunks of white chocolate in place of half the walnuts.
Macadamia nut Replace the chopped walnuts with whole macadamia nuts.
Almond brownies Use almond essence and almonds instead of vanilla and walnuts.

CLASSIC CHOCOLATE BROWNIES

Richly coloured and flavoured, these are deliciously gooey and moist.

Makes 24
225g/8oz plain (semisweet) chocolate
225g/8oz/1 cup butter, diced
3 eggs
225g/8oz/generous 1 cup caster
  (superfine) sugar
30ml/2 tbsp strong black coffee
75g/3oz/⅔ cup self-raising
  (self-rising) flour
pinch of salt
150g/5oz/1¼ cups chopped walnuts
5ml/1 tsp vanilla essence (extract)

1 Preheat the oven to 180°C/375°F/ Gas 5. Grease and line a 18 x 28cm/ 7 x 11in tin (pan). Break the chocolate into squares and place in a heatproof bowl with the butter.

2 Set the bowl over a pan of barely simmering water and leave for 5–10 minutes, stirring occasionally until the mixture is melted and smooth. Remove the bowl from the pan and then leave the chocolate mixture to cool for 5 minutes.

3 In a large bowl, beat the eggs, sugar and coffee until smooth, then gradually beat in the cooled melted chocolate mixture.

4 Sift the flour and salt over the mixture, then fold in together with the walnuts and vanilla essence.

5 Spoon the mixture into the prepared tin and bake for about 35 minutes, or until just firm to the touch in the centre. (Don't bake it for any longer than this as the mixture will still be soft under the crust, but will firm up as it cools. Overcooking gives a dry result.)

6 Leave the brownies to cool in the tin then turn out on to a board, trim off the crusty edges and cut into squares, using a serrated knife and a gentle sawing action.

GREASING, LINING AND REDUCING THE SIZE OF TINS

When making bar cookies, it is imporant to line the baking tin (pan) with greaseproof (waxed) paper or baking parchment. This makes it much easier to lift the baked brownies or bars from the tin. If you use greaseproof paper, you will need to brush a little flavourless oil over the paper before pouring in the mixture. If you use baking parchment, the paper does not need to greased.

Base-lining Some recipes only require the base of the tin to be lined. This technique can be used to line any shape of tin, whether rectangular, square or round. Place the tin on a sheet of greaseproof (waxed) paper or baking parchment and, using a pencil, carefully draw around the tin. Using a pair of scissors, cut just inside the drawn line so that it will fit neatly inside the tin.

Using a sheet of buttered paper or a piece of kitchen paper drizzled with a flavourless oil such as sunflower or vegetable oil, grease the inside of the tin and place the lining paper in the base, pressing it into the corners.

Square and rectangular tins
To line both the base and sides of a square or rectangular tin, place the tin on a piece of greaseproof paper or baking parchment that is considerably larger than the tin. Using a pencil, draw around the tin. Cut a straight line from the edge of the paper to each corner of the square or rectangle. Turn the piece of paper over so the side marked with pencil is facing downwards. Fold in each side along its pencil line.

Grease the tin, then fit the paper inside the tin, folding the corners to fit neatly.

Round tins To line a round tin, place the tin on a piece of greaseproof paper or baking parchment and use a pencil to draw around it. Cut out the circle just inside the line. Next cut a long strip of paper about 2cm/¾in wider than the depth of the tin. (It must be long enough to wrap around the outside of the tin with 3cm/1¼in to spare.) Fold up the lower edge by 1cm/½in, then make cuts about 2.5cm/1in apart from the edge to the fold.

Grease the tin, then position the paper strip(s) around the side of the tin, so that the snipped edge sits flat on the base. Place the paper circle in the base of the tin, covering the snipped paper. Lightly grease all the paper if necessary.

Reducing tin size If the tin you are using is larger than the size required, you can reduce its size by fitting a strip of foil across the tin to make it the correct size. Make a long strip of triple thickness foil and cut it to fit three sides of the required tin.

Fold the strip of foil along one of the long edges to make a lap and fit it inside the tin to make it the required size. The weight of the mixture will hold the lap down and keep the divider in place.

Short-cut Cookies

There are occasions when you may want to make cookies in a hurry and you either don't want to turn on the oven just to bake a single batch of cookies or take the time and trouble measuring and mixing. Using ready-made cookie dough that you've either made in advance or bought, baking in a microwave oven or following a no-bake cookie recipe may provide you with the perfect solution.

REFRIGERATOR COOKIES

These are so called because the dough can be made in advance and kept in the refrigerator for up to 2 weeks before being cooked. It means that cookies can be freshly baked on demand. They are ideal for those who enjoy the pleasures of home-baked cookies, but don't always have time to make them from scratch.

The cookie dough is shaped into a log, wrapped in clear film (plastic wrap) and chilled in the refrigerator. Because the dough has a high fat content it should be chilled for at least 1 hour and preferably for longer. This will firm it to make slicing easier and will also ensure that the cookies hold their shape when cooked. The texture of the cookies is partly determined by the thickness of the slices: thinner slices will make fairly crisp cookies, thicker ones will be slightly less crisp. Some cookies such as those with chunks of chocolate or nuts are best cut in thicker slices. When baking thicker cookies, lower the temperature slightly and cook for a few minutes longer to make sure that they're cooked through.

QUICK VANILLA COOKIES

Just a few drops of vanilla essence (extract) is needed for these.

Makes 32

150g/5oz/10 tbsp butter, softened
150g/5oz/¾ cup caster (superfine) sugar
1 egg, lightly beaten
2.5ml/½ tsp vanilla essence (extract)
225g/8oz/2 cups plain (all-purpose) flour, sifted

1 Put the ingredients in a bowl and mix to a smooth dough. Lightly knead on a floured surface then roll the dough into a log shape about 5cm/2in diameter and 20cm/8in long. Wrap the log in clear film (plastic wrap) and chill for at least 1 hour or until firm enough to slice. For mini cookies, divide the dough in half and make two thinner logs.

2 Preheat the oven to 190°C/375°F/Gas 5. Cut the dough into 5mm/¼in slices. You can dip the knife in water and wipe it dry for a clean cut.

3 When you have cut the required number of cookies, re-wrap the remaining dough and put it back in the refrigerator.

4 Place the cookies about 2.5cm/1in apart on ungreased baking sheets. Bake for 12 minutes, or until just golden around the edges. Leave on the baking sheets for 2–3 minutes, then transfer to a wire rack to cool completely. Use the remaining cookie dough within 1 week of making, or double-wrap and freeze for up to 3 months.

BOUGHT COOKIE DOUGH

If you do not have the time to make your own cookie dough, ready-made chilled or frozen dough can be bought instead. This usually comes in tubs and, although several different varieties are available, chocolate chip cookie dough is the most popular. The mixture is ready to be spooned on to greased baking sheets, then baked according to the manufacturer's instructions. Once opened, the dough can be kept in its tub in the refrigerator for several days, so that you can bake fresh batches when required.

NO-BAKE COOKIES

A range of cookies can be made by mixing melted ingredients with dry ingredients and leaving them to set. The setting agent may be chocolate, which sets firm, or syrups and marshmallows, which set to create a chewier cookie. The mixture may be spooned into paper cake cases or into a greased and base-lined shallow tin (pan), then cut into squares, bars or triangles when set.

SETTING COOKIES WITH CHOCOLATE

The simplest no-bake cookies are made with breakfast cereals such as cornflakes combined with melted plain (semisweet) chocolate, golden (light corn) or maple syrup and butter. Others may contain crushed or broken plain cookies, dried fruit and nuts rather than cereal. Always leave the melted chocolate to cool before adding the dry ingredients.

To make a basic mixture, melt 65g/2½oz/5 tbsp unsalted (sweet) butter and 175g/6oz plain chocolate together, then cool. Stir in 75g/3oz broken digestive biscuits (Graham crackers), 50g/2oz/½ cup flaked (sliced) almonds, 50g/2oz/⅓ cup chopped dried fruit and 50g/2oz roughly chopped white chocolate.

SETTING COOKIES WITHOUT CHOCOLATE

No-bake cookies can be set with a mixture of cooked sugar or golden (light corn) syrup combined with melted butter, marshmallows and soft toffees. The most effective mixture uses equal quantities of toffees, butter and marshmallows mixed with puffed rice cereal.

To make a basic mixture, melt 115g/4oz each of butter, marshmallows and toffees in a pan, then stir in 115g/4oz/2 cups puffed rice cereal.

MAKING ROUND COOKIES

Spoon the no-bake cookie mixture on to a sheet of greaseproof (waxed) paper or baking parchment and wrap the mixture, packing it into a fat log-shape roll about 20cm/8in long. Chill until firm, then cut into 1cm/½in slices.

MAKING COOKIE WEDGES

Some cookies are made in a round, then sliced into wedges like cakes.

1 Spoon the cookie mixture into a lightly greased and lined shallow 20cm/7in round or 15cm/6in square tin (pan). Chill for 1–2 hours, or until very firm, but not rock hard.

2 Remove the mixture from the tin, then cut into thin wedges using a sharp knife.

MAKING COOKIE TRIANGLES

Rather than making individual cookies, you can make a triangular block of cookie mixture, then slice it once it has set.

1 Line the base and three sides of a deep, greased 18cm/7in square tin (pan) with clear film (plastic wrap). Prop up one side of the tin on a box so that it is at an angle of about 45 degrees.

2 Spoon the mixture into the tin and level the surface with the back of the spoon. Leave to stand until firm, then chill until completely set. To serve, remove the block from the tin, peel off the clear film and cut into 1cm/½in triangular slices.

LAYERED NO-BAKE COOKIES

Most no-bake cookies are single-layered affairs but some are richer and have two or more layers. Bear in mind that you need to be able to slice through the cookies cleanly; so don't make one layer much more fragile than the others. Canadian nanaimo bars are a classic layered no-bake cookie. The base is made of a non-crumbly cookie and nut mixture, the filling is firm and smooth, and the chocolate topping has a little oil added to it so it doesn't crack when cut.

MICROWAVE COOKIES

Many traditional cookie recipes written with oven-baking in mind need to be adjusted for microwave cooking and there are some that simply cannot be converted successfully. Others, however, will turn out every bit as good but in a fraction of the time.

The key to cooking round cookies in a microwave is to arrange them in circles so that they cook evenly. Don't be tempted to add a cookie to the middle as it will cook more slowly than the rest.

SOFT ALMOND COOKIES

These almond cookies remain soft for some time after cooking.

Makes 12

50g/2oz/¼ cup butter, softened
50g/2oz/¼ cup soft light brown sugar
1 egg yolk
75g/3oz/⅔ cup plain (all-purpose) flour
25g/1oz/¼ cup ground almonds

1 Cream the butter and sugar together in a large mixing bowl until light and fluffy. Beat in the egg yolk. Sift over the flour and gently fold into the mixture together with the ground almonds. If you like, fold in other ingredients such as chopped glacé (candied) cherries, a mixture of dried fruit or chopped nuts.

2 Place six tablespoonfuls of the mixture in a circle on a microwave-proof dish or a piece of baking parchment cut to fit the base of the oven. Cook for 1¾–2½ minutes on high (100 per cent power) or until the surface of the cookies is dry.

3 Remove the cookies carefully from the microwave as the edges will still be soft, leave to stand for 1 minute before lifting them on to a wire rack. They will finish cooking and become firmer as they cool.

BAR MICROWAVE COOKIES

To achieve the best results with bar cookies and traybakes in a microwave, bake them in a round flan dish (quiche pan), or 4cm/1½in-deep pie plate, then cut the cookies into wedges. The centre may be difficult to cook properly in recipes such as shortbread, but this isn't a problem with high-fat, syrupy mixtures such as flapjacks.

STICKY LEMON FLAPJACKS

Made with rolled oats, flapjacks are deliciously thick and chewy.

Makes 8

75g/3oz/6 tbsp butter, diced
60ml/4 tbsp golden (light corn) syrup
115g/4oz/generous ½ cup demerara (raw) sugar
175g/6oz/1½ cups rolled oats
juice and finely grated rind of ½ lemon

1 Put the butter, syrup and sugar in a heatproof bowl. Microwave on medium (50 per cent) power for 3–4 minutes, stirring halfway through.

2 Stir in the oats, lemon rind and juice. Spoon the mixture into a 20cm/8in microwave flan dish and spread out.

3 Cook on full (100 per cent) power for 3–3½ minutes, or until bubbling all over. Remove from the oven and mark into wedges when warm. Leave to cool in the dish.

DIFFERENT-SHAPED COOKIES

Microwave cookies don't have to be round, but whatever the shape, they should still be arranged in a ring. Irregular-shaped cookies should be positioned with the widest part towards the outer edge of the dish. When microwaving finger or stick-shaped cookies, avoid arranging them like the spokes of a wheel; instead, place them around the edge of the dish in one or two rows.

SESAME CHEESE TWISTS

These savoury snacks are perfect to serve with soups or salads.

Makes 36
115g/4oz/1 cup plain (all-purpose) flour
1.5ml/¼ tsp salt
pinch of mustard powder
50g/2oz/¼ cup butter, diced and chilled
50g/2oz/½ cup finely grated strong-
   flavoured cheese, such as Cheddar
1 egg yolk
10ml/2 tsp cold water
30ml/2 tbsp sesame seeds

1 Sift the flour, salt and mustard powder into a bowl. Rub in the butter until the mixture resembles fine breadcrumbs, then stir in the cheese. Mix the egg yolk and water together, sprinkle over the dry ingredients and mix to a firm dough. Lightly knead on a floured surface.

2 Roll out the dough to 5mm/¼in thickness and cut into sticks about 7.5cm/3in long and 5mm/¼in wide.

3 Hold the ends of the sticks and twist them in opposite directions. Sprinkle the sesame seeds on a plate and roll the twists in them until coated. Line a microwave tray with baking parchment and arrange 12 twists in a circle on it.

4 Cook on full (100 per cent) power for 2–2½ minutes, until firm to the touch. Leave to stand for 2 minutes, then transfer to a wire rack to cool. Cook the remaining cheese twists in the same way.

Cook's Tip
There isn't a standard output or name or number for settings used by all microwave manufacturers, so cooking times are only a guide. The recipes given here are for 750-watt microwave ovens.

GETTING GOOD RESULTS

• Always use microwave-proof cookware. Glass and china are suitable, but avoid melamine, plastic and any dishes that contain metal.
• Microwaved cookies don't brown in the same way as conventionally baked ones, so coloured mixtures such as ginger and chocolate work best.
• Improve the look of microwave cookies by icing them after cooking or adding a dusting of sugar.
• Added ingredients such as chocolate, nuts and dried fruit should be cut into small, even-sized pieces.
• Don't cover the cookies during cooking to allow the steam to escape.
• Microwaved cookies continue cooking for a short time after the machine is switched off, so stop microwaving just before they are ready. Open the door during cooking to check progress. The best way to discover whether they are done is to sacrifice one and break it open; if the centre is beginning to change colour, the cookies are ready. Use the same cooking time for subsequent batches.
• Foods with a high fat or sugar content cook very quickly in a microwave and can burn easily. Always cook for the minimum time and watch carefully. Remember, if you reduce the number of cookies, the cooking time must also be reduced.

Baking Cookies

To make perfect cookies, you must take as much care with cooking them as you did with mixing and shaping the dough.

USING THE OVEN

Always allow time to preheat the oven; it will take about 15 minutes to reach the required temperature (although fan-assisted ovens may heat more quickly).

Unless the recipe instructs otherwise, bake cookies in the middle, or just above the middle, of the oven. If you are baking large quantities of cookies, do not put more than two baking sheets in the oven at once because this can cause the oven temperature to drop. This particularly applies to cookies that have been chilled beforehand.

USING BAKING SHEETS

If you are using a new baking sheet, check that it fits into the oven before you arrange the cookies on it; ideally, there should be a small gap at either side and at the back of the baking sheet to allow hot air to circulate. If you need to divide the cookies between two or more baking sheets, put the same number of cookies on each sheet, so the batches cook at the same rate. If you put two baking sheets of cookies in the oven at the same time, switch them around halfway through the cooking time. If you need to cook a second batch of cookies straight away, let the baking sheet cool before placing the next batch of raw cookies on it; a hot baking sheet might make the raw cookies spread, which will result in thin, irregular-sized cookies.

TIME AND TEMPERATURE

Baking times may vary slightly with different ovens, and can depend on how chilled the cookies were when cooking commenced. Get to know your oven. If you feel that it is either too cool or too hot, use an oven thermometer to check the temperature. If it needs adjusting, change your oven temperature dial accordingly to correct this.

Always check cookies a few minutes before the end of the suggested cooking time. Unlike cakes, they will not loose volume or sink if the oven door is opened, although you should avoid doing this too frequently or the temperature will drop and the cookies will be less crisp. Second and subsequent batches of cookies may take slightly less time to cook.

COOKING GUIDELINES

Not all cookies are the same. Different types of cookie need to be cooked in different ways and at different temperatures.

DROP COOKIES

These are baked in a moderate oven, around 180°C/350°F/Gas 4. This gives them a chance to spread out a little before they set. To make cookies that are crisp on the outside, but with a slightly soft and chewy centre, remove from the oven as soon as the edges are dark golden but the middle is still a little pale. For crisp cookies, wait until the whole cookie is lightly browned before removing from the oven. To achieve an even crisper result, spread out the mixture slightly to make a thinner layer before baking.

ROLLED, PIPED AND PRESSED COOKIES

These are usually chilled before baking to prevent them spreading too much during cooking. They are cooked in a moderate to hot oven, between 180°C/350°F/Gas 4 and 200°C/400°F/Gas 6.

1 Place the cookies on a baking sheet, then chill for 30 minutes.

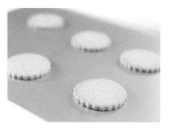

2 Bake until pale golden; do not allow to colour too much.

3 Leave to cool slightly on the baking sheets, then carefully transfer to wire racks to cool completely.

REFRIGERATOR COOKIES

These cookies have a relatively high fat content and so are baked at a moderately high temperature, around 190°C/375°F/Gas 5.

1 Slice the chilled cookie mixture and arrange on ungreased baking sheets. Do not use non-stick sheets or line the sheets with baking parchment because this will make the cookies spread.

2 The cookies must be well chilled before baking, so either cook them as soon as they have been sliced or place the baking sheets in the refrigerator until ready to bake.

BAR COOKIES

This type of cookie is usually baked in a moderate to moderately low oven, between 160°C/325°F/Gas 3 and 180°C/350°F/Gas 4.

1 Bar cookies with a shortbread, pastry or crumb base are often partially baked before the topping is added. This allows the base to be cooked until crisp and firm without the topping becoming overcooked.

2 To test whether sponge or brownie mixtures are cooked, insert a cocktail stick (toothpick) into the mixture. It should come out clean.

COOLING COOKIES

Always follow the instructions in the recipe when cooling cookies. Most cookies are quite delicate so benefit from being left on the baking sheets for a minute or two to firm up, before removing to a wire rack to cool completely.

Use a thin palette knife or metal spatula to transfer cookies to wire racks. Placing them on a wire rack allows air to circulate around the them, and prevents moisture being trapped, which can make them lose their crisp texture. Don't cram too many cookies on the rack at any one time and avoid placing hot cookies on top of each other; they are likely to lose their crispness.

Cookies such as tuiles that are to be moulded into shape should be removed from the baking sheets after 30 seconds, while they are still warm and pliable. Others such as bar cookies may benefit from being allowed to cool in the baking tins (pans). Placing the whole tin on a wire rack can speed the cooling.

BAKING COOKIES AT HIGH ALTITUDE

At 3,000m/9,800ft above sea level, atmospheric pressure becomes lower, which makes liquid boil faster and causes greater evaporation. This affects cookie baking in several ways: flavours, especially sweet ones, are more concentrated; slightly more liquid is necessary; and smaller quantities of raising agents are needed. It also helps if you marginally reduce the amount of fat in recipes and increase the quantity of flour.

	ALTITUDE		
	3,000m/9,800ft	**5,000m/16,350ft**	**7,000/22,900ft**
Sugar For each 115g/4oz/ generous ½ cup, reduce by:	10ml/2 tsp	115ml/1 tbsp	30ml/2 tbsp
Baking powder For each 5ml/1 tsp, reduce by:	0.75ml/⅛ tsp	1.5ml/¼ tsp	1.5ml/¼ tsp
Liquid For each 75ml/5 tbsp, reduce by:	5ml/1 tsp	110ml/2 tsp	30ml/1tbsp
Oven temperature Increase by:	5°C/10°F/Gas ¼	15°C/25°F/Gas ½	20°C/35°F/Gas 1½

Cookie Decoration

Decorating cookies can add the final flourish to home-made cookies and can be one of the most enjoyable aspects of cookie-making. Cookies can be decorated before baking, while the cookies are still warm from the oven, or when they are completely cool.

DECORATING COOKIES BEFORE BAKING

Techniques for decorating unbaked cookies can range from the most simple sprinkling of sugar or nuts to brushing with a glossy glaze or painting intricate designs with edible food colouring.

SUGAR

A crunchy sugar topping is one of the easiest and most effective ways to decorate unbaked cookies. (It is also one of the most popular decorations for baked cookies.) Many different sugars can be used.

Caster (superfine) sugar can be sprinkled straight over raw cookies to give a subtle, crunchy texture. Coarse sugars such as demerara (raw) sugar and irregular-shaped coffee crystals give a crunchier result. Pretty coloured sugars and crushed white and brown sugar lumps also produce a lovely effect when sprinkled over raw cookies.

Moist cookie doughs can simply be sprinkled with sugar; drier cookies such as refrigerator or rolled cookies may benefit from being lightly brushed with a little water or milk before they are sprinkled with sugar. Alternatively, after rolling the dough, sprinkle it with sugar, then roll very lightly before cutting out the cookies.

Cookie dough that is shaped into a log before slicing can be rolled in sugar before the log is chilled and sliced. This will produce cookies with a crisp, sugary edge.

Cookies such as macaroons that produce a cracked surface during baking look particularly attractive dusted with sugar before baking. The sugar helps to accentuate the cracked effect. Flatten the balls of dough slightly, brush each with a little water and sift over a fine and even layer of icing (confectioners') sugar before baking.

NUTS

Chopped and flaked (sliced) nuts can be sprinkled over cookies in the same way as sugar. Nuts brown during baking, so avoid using on cookies that are baked at a high temperature or on cookies that are baked for a long time as the nuts may overcook.

A whole nut can be pressed into the top of each individual cookie. (This technique is best suited to soft cookie doughs.) The nuts may be decorative, or they can be used to indicate the type of cookie. For example, you might want to press a whole hazelnut into a hazelnut cookie, or an almond into an almond flavoured cookie.

Flaked (sliced) almonds look stunning sprinkled over cookies but should be baked for no longer than 10 minutes in a moderately hot oven or they will burn. This is the classic topping for tuiles.

GLAZES

Brushing a glaze over cookies can serve two purposes, either to provide a sticky surface that nuts or sugar can stick to, or simply to give an attractive finish.

To give cookies a rich, glossy finish, use a whole beaten egg or yolk. Brush the glaze lightly and evenly on the top, without it dripping over the edges – this is especially important where raising agents have been used because it will prevent the cookies rising evenly. You can dilute the glaze by adding 15ml/1 tbsp cold water or milk and adding a pinch of caster (superfine) sugar for sweet cookies; salt for savoury ones.

Lightly beaten egg white produces a clear, shiny finish. Brush over the cookies halfway through the baking time, so that it soaks into the cookies slightly and does not set to a crackled glaze. It looks effective sprinkled with a little sugar.

PAINTED COOKIES

Edible food colouring can be painted directly on to unbaked cookies to make pretty patterns. This technique is best suited to drier, firmer cookie doughs such as rolled and refrigerator cookies.

To decorate cookies, cut the dough into shapes, place them on baking sheets and chill for 30 minutes. Beat an egg yolk and mix in a few drops of food colouring. Using a fine paintbrush, paint patterns on to the cookies, and then bake. (Remember that the yellow egg yolk may affect the colour of the food colouring.)

CANDY CENTRES

This technique is very simple to do, yet is extremely effective.

Cut out the centre of each cookie and fill it with crushed boiled sweets (hard candy). The sweets will melt during baking, then harden when cooled to make a colourful centre.

SIMPLE WAYS TO DECORATE COOKIES BEFORE BAKING

• Chopped fudge, toffee and chocolate chunks and chips add a delicious, decorative finish to drop cookies.

• Candy-coated chocolate buttons retain their bright colours when baked in cookies and are especially popular with young children. Mix into the dough or gently press them into the surface of the cookies.

• Halved or sliced glacé (candied) cherries and candied angelica diamonds are effective and colourful decorations.

• Pressing a pattern with the tines of a fork or marking lines on cookies with a knife look great. This also helps to prevent the cookies from rising unevenly.

SIMPLE BAKED COOKIE DECORATIONS

As with unbaked cookies, you can transform simple baked cookies into something really special with just a few simple decorating techniques. A sprinkling of sugar takes just a few seconds, while dusting a design using a stencil or writing a simple message with a food colouring pen takes only a little longer. Food colouring pens work best on refrigerator or rolled cookies that have been only lightly baked, or on firm icing.

DECORATING COOKIES WITH SUGAR

Different types of sugar can be used to give a range of effects on various baked cookies.

Icing/confectioners' sugar A light dusting of icing sugar gives plain cookies a wonderfully professional finish and is a useful way of disguising any imperfections.

Use a fine sieve or sugar dredger to give an even coating. If you want a very light layer, hold the sieve or dredger high and shake gently; for a thicker finish, keep the sieve or dredger closer to the cookies. If you are dusting pairs of cookies sandwiched together, fill them first, then sprinkle with sugar.

Caster/superfine sugar Simply sprinkling freshly baked cookies with a little caster (superfine) sugar is perhaps one of the quickest and easiest decorations to use.

Sprinkle sugar over the cookies while they are still warm so that the sugar sticks to them. (Soft light and dark brown sugars can also be used but, because they are so moist, even sprinkling is very difficult. Push through a medium sieve rather than sprinkling by hand.)

FLAVOURED SUGARS

These are a good alternative to plain caster (superfine) sugar and give cookies a subtle hint more flavour. It is possible to buy flavoured sugars, but it is just as easy to make your own.

Vanilla Put a vanilla pod (bean) in a jar of caster sugar and leave for at least 2 weeks. Refill the jar with sugar as you use it.
Sweet spice Infuse (steep) the sugar for two weeks with whole spices such as cloves. To make instant spiced sugar, use about 2.5ml/½ tsp ground cinnamon or mixed (apple pie) spice for every 30ml/2 tbsp sugar.

Coarse-grained sugars Granulated and demerara (raw) sugar look pretty sprinkled over cookies but, because the grains are so large, they will not stick to the cookie on their own. The easiest way to overcome this problem is to use a glaze such as beaten egg white to stick the sugar to the cookie, then return the cookies to the oven for 2–3 minutes.

Cookies such as sweet pretzels are usually coated with sugar, then grilled (broiled) until the it starts to caramelize. Brush the cooled cookies lightly with egg white and sprinkle generously with demerara sugar. (Sprinkle on plenty of sugar to protect the cookie from the heat.) Place under a hot grill (broiler) for about 1 minute until the sugar is just starting to bubble. Return to wire racks to cool.

Citrus Add a strip of orange or lemon rind to the sugar and leave for 3 days. Shake the sugar before use as it may have become slightly damp from the rind.
Rosemary Add a sprig of fresh rosemary to the sugar and leave for 3–4 days.
Lavender Add lavender (about five heads) to the sugar and leave for 3–4 days.

DECORATING COOKIES WITH SUGAR GLAZES

Cookies such as Lebkuchen are sometimes given a slightly shiny finish with a sugar glaze. These glazes may be clear or opaque and are usually brushed over the cookies while they are still hot or warm.

LEBKUCHEN GLAZE

This semi-opaque glaze gently softens the surface of the cookie, giving it a chewy texture.

Sift 175g/6oz/1½ cups icing (confectioners') sugar into a bowl. Add 2.5ml/½ tsp almond essence (extract), 5ml/1 tsp lemon juice and 30ml/2 tbsp hot water. Mix together until smooth, then brush over the hot Lebkuchen and leave to cool.

CLEAR GLAZE

This simple sugar glaze gives cookies a lovely, glossy finish.

1 Heat 25g/1oz/2 tbsp sugar in 60ml/4 tbsp water until the sugar dissolves. Boil rapidly for 5 minutes, or until reduced by half. (The glaze can be flavoured with a strip of lemon or orange rind if you like).

2 Remove from the heat and leave to cool. Gradually beat in 115g/4oz/1 cup sifted icing sugar, then brush over warm cookies and leave to set.

STENCILLING DESIGNS

This is an easy way to decorate cookies. You can buy stencils that are specially made for cake and cookie decorating, or make your own by drawing a small design on thin cardboard and cutting it out. Make sure there is a contrast between the colour of the cookie and the dusting ingredient; icing sugar works well on chocolate cookies, while (unsweetened) cocoa powder is better on pale cookies. You can also colour icing sugar by blending cake decorator's colouring dust (petal dust) with the sugar.

Place the stencil over the cookie. Dust with icing sugar or cocoa powder through a fine sieve, then carefully remove the cardboard.

Paper doilies can be used to make an attractive lacy pattern. Place a large doily over several cookies at once and dust liberally with icing sugar or cocoa powder.

To create a dramatic light and dark effect on cookies, lightly dust a whole cookie with icing sugar, then cover half of it with a piece of cardboard or a sheet of paper and carefully dust the other half with cocoa powder.

FOOD-COLOURING PENS

These pens look like felt-tipped pens but they are filled with edible food colouring. They come in a range of colours from primary to pastels and some are flavoured.

They can be used directly on to the cookies or on to icing. They are most effective used on rolled and cut cookies that have been baked only until light golden rather than well browned; icing must be dry and firm.

Use the decorating pens in the same way as an ordinary pen. Draw designs, write messages, or use to colour in shapes.

DECORATING COOKIES WITH ICING

Cookies can look lovely decorated with pretty coloured icing. It is important to get the consistency of icing exactly right; too thick and it will be difficult to spread; too thin and it will run off the edges and soak into the cookie.

There are many different types of icing that can be used to decorate cookies and they can range in colour from the palest pastels to vibrant primary colours. Glacé or fondant icings give a smooth, glossy finish and can be used to create simple finishing touches to the cookies, while royal icing can be swirled to give a textured pattern or piped into delicate and intricate designs. Whatever type of icing you use, iced cookies should usually be eaten within 3 or 4 days.

GLACÉ ICING

This is the simplest type of icing to make and use. It is perfect for the tops of cookies, or for drizzling and piping simple designs.

To cover 24 cookies
*115g/4oz/1 cup icing
  (confectioners') sugar
a few drops of vanilla essence
  (extract) (optional)
15ml/1 tbsp hot water
a few drops of food colouring (optional)*

Sift the icing sugar into a bowl, then add the vanilla essence, if using. Gradually stir in the hot water until the mixture is the consistency of thick cream. Add the food colouring, and continue stirring until smooth.

Top coating This is the simplest technique for coating the top of cookies with glacé icing.

Spoon a little icing on to the centre of the cookie, then carefully spread it out almost to the edges using the back of the spoon. (To make a perfect shape, pipe the outline of the shape first. Leave to dry for 1–2 minutes, then spoon in the icing and spread out to fill the shape.)

Feathered glacé icing Spoon a little icing over a cookie to cover it completely, then pipe several thin, straight parallel lines of icing in a contrasting colour across the top of the cookie.

Starting at the middle of the cookie, draw a wooden cocktail stick (toothpick) or fine skewer through the lines in the opposite direction, gently dragging the colour through the icing and creating a feathered effect on the cookie.

Cobweb icing Cover a cookie in icing, then pipe on fine, concentric circles of icing in a contrasting colour, starting from the centre and working outwards.

Draw a cocktail stick (toothpick) from the centre of the cookie to the outside edge, dividing the cookie into quarters, then repeat to divide it into eighths.

Drizzled icing Glacé icing can be drizzled or piped over cookies to give a pretty finish.

Place the cookies on a wire rack. Using a paper piping (pastry) bag or teaspoon, drizzle fine lines of icing over the cookies. You can then drizzle more icing at right angles to these first lines, if you like.

Variation
To make white glacé icing, add a few drops of lemon juice instead of vanilla essence; this enhances the whiteness.

ICING GLAZE

This is similar to glacé icing, but is flavoured with lemon juice and thinned with egg white, giving it a shinier, slightly harder set.

To cover 12 cookies

15ml/1 tbsp lightly beaten egg white
15ml/1 tbsp lemon juice
115g/4oz/1 cup icing (confectioners') sugar, sifted

Mix together the egg white and lemon juice in a bowl. Gradually beat in the icing sugar until the mixture is completely smooth, then place the cookies on a wire rack. Spoon the icing evenly over the cookies and leave to set.

ROYAL ICING

This icing sets hard to give a good finish so is perfect for piping designs and messages on cookies such as gingerbread. It can be coloured with a few drops of food colouring but is better left unflavoured.

To cover 30 cookies

1 egg white, at room temperature or 7.5ml/1½ tsp albumen powder
225g/8oz/2 cups icing (confectioners') sugar, sifted, plus extra if necessary

1 Beat the egg white for a few seconds with a fork. (If using albumen powder, mix according to the instructions.) Mix in the icing sugar a little at a time until the mixture stands in soft peaks and is thick enough to spread. If the icing is for piping, beat in a little more icing sugar until the icing will stand in stiff peaks. Spread or pipe the icing over the cookies. Leave to set.

MAKING AND USING A PAPER ICING BAG

A paper bag for piping is easy to make once you know how.

1 Cut a piece of greaseproof (waxed) paper or baking parchment into a 25cm/10in square, then cut it in half diagonally so that you have two triangles. Hold one triangle with the longest side away from you. Curl the left-hand point over into a cone to meet the point nearest you. Curl the right-hand point over the cone.

2 Bring the points of the folded triangles together to make a neat, narrow cone. Tuck the point of paper inside the cone, fold it over and secure with sticky tape.

3 If using a nozzle, cut off the pointed end of the bag. Position the nozzle so that it fits snugly.

4 Using a palette knife or metal spatula, fill the bag with icing. Take care not to overfill the bag; half to two-thirds full is ideal.

5 Fold the top corners of the bag in towards the centre, then fold over the top, firmly pushing the icing down towards the tip. Fold over the top corner again, making a pad to push with your thumb.

6 If you have not inserted a nozzle into the bag, snip a small, straight piece off the end of the bag for the icing to pass through. (It is better to snip off the small tip first. If the line of icing is too narrow, snip off a little bit more.)

7 Hold the piping bag between your middle and forefingers and push down with your thumb. Place the tip in position over the cookie, then gently push the icing through the bag using your thumb. To stop the flow of icing, release the pressure from your thumb. The icing will continue to flow for a few seconds after the pressure has stopped so you should release your thumb before you reach the end of the line.

DECORATING COOKIES WITH CHOCOLATE

The taste, texture and versatility of chocolate makes it one of the most popular ingredients for decorating cookies. It can be used to coat cookies, pipe or drizzle patterns, or even write short messages.

MELTING CHOCOLATE

For most decorating techniques, chocolate needs to be melted. Take care doing this as overheating will spoil both the texture and flavour. When melting chocolate, choose a variety with a high proportion of cocoa butter as this will melt much more easily and smoothly.

Using a double boiler Break the chocolate into pieces and put it in the top of a double boiler or in a heatproof bowl set over a pan of hot water; the water should not touch the top container. Bring the water to simmering point, then turn down the heat to keep the water at a very gently simmer.

Check the chocolate every few minutes, turning off the heat if necessary. Stir once or twice during melting until the chocolate is completely smooth. Do not cover the bowl once the chocolate has melted or condensation will form.

Using a microwave This is a quick and simple way of melting chocolate. Bear in mind that microwaved chocolate will retain its shape, so you will need to stir the chocolate to see if it has melted.

Break the chocolate into pieces and place in a microwave-safe bowl. Melt in bursts of 30–60 seconds, checking often and reducing the time as the chocolate begins to soften. Stop microwaving before all the chocolate has melted; the residual heat in the chocolate should complete the process.

As a guide, 115g/4oz chocolate will take about 1½ minutes on full (100 per cent) power and 225g/8oz will take 2–2½ minutes. White chocolate should be melted on medium (50 per cent) power.

Using direct heat This method is only suitable for recipes where the chocolate is melted with another liquid such as milk or cream, or with other ingredients such as butter and golden (light corn) syrup.

Put the liquid ingredients in the pan, then add the chopped or broken chocolate and melt slowly over the lowest heat. When the chocolate has started to melt, turn off the heat and stir constantly until the mixture is completely smooth.

Tempering chocolate This technique is used for couverture chocolate, making it easier to work with and giving it a glossy appearance when set.

Melt the chocolate in the usual way, then pour about two-thirds of it on to a marble slab or cold surface. Using a palette knife or metal spatula, move the chocolate back and forth until it is thick and beginning to reach setting point. Return the chocolate to the bowl and melt again, stirring constantly.

USING MELTED CHOCOLATE

When you are decorating cookies with melted chocolate, handle the chocolate as little as possible and use a palette knife or metal spatula to lift and move the decorated cookies around; the warmth of your fingers will leave prints on the chocolate and make the surface dull.

Always leave chocolate-coated cookies to set at room temperature and do not store in the refrigerator unless it is exceptionally warm; chilling will cause the chocolate to lose its glossy appearance. Also make sure that the cookies are at room temperature rather than still warm from the oven or cold (if they have been stored in the refrigerator or freezer).

Coating cookies with
chocolate Before coating cookies in melted chocolate, make sure that the chocolate is just starting to cool; chocolate that is hot or even very warm will soak into the cookies and spoil the texture.

I Place the cookies on a wire rack with a sheet of baking parchment underneath. Spoon cooled melted chocolate over each cookie, then tap the rack to help it run down the sides and to level the top. Leave to set on the rack, then cover with a second coat, if you like. Scrape the chocolate off the baking parchment, return to the bowl and re-melt to coat more cookies.

2 To decorate coated cookies, drizzle or pipe with a contrasting colour of chocolate. For a smooth surface, do this before the first layer of chocolate has set; for a raised surface, wait until the first layer of chocolate has hardened.

Dipping cookies in chocolate
Round or shaped cookies are often half-coated in chocolate and finger cookies sometimes have one or both ends dipped in chocolate. This method is simpler than completely covering cookies in chocolate. If you're planning to sandwich cookies together, they are best dipped in chocolate before filling as the warmth of the chocolate may melt the filling if dipped afterwards.

I Melt the chocolate in a narrow deep bowl. Holding the cookie by the part that you don't want to coat, dip it briefly in the melted chocolate, then allow any excess to drip back into the bowl.

2 Place the cookie on a sheet of baking parchment and leave to set. When the chocolate is firm carefully peel off the paper. If you want to sprinkle chopped nuts or other decorations on the top, do this before the chocolate sets.

Coating florentines with
chocolate The flat underside of florentines is traditionally coated with chocolate.

Holding the florentine between finger and thumb, spread the flat base with chocolate. With the prongs of a fork, create wavy lines in the chocolate. Place the florentine on a wire rack, and leave to set

Piping chocolate Use a small paper piping (pastry) bag with the end snipped off to pipe thin lines of chocolate.

Place cookies on a sheet of baking parchment and pipe over thin lines, first in one direction, then the other.

Colouring white chocolate You can colour melted white chocolate with cake decorator's colouring dust (petal dust). Do not use liquid or paste food colourings as these will spoil the texture of the chocolate.

Cookie Fillings

From smooth custard creams to sticky jammie sweethearts, two cookies sandwiched together are better than one. The key to a good cookie filling is to make the mixture soft enough to spread or pipe but not too moist because this can make the cookies soft and crumbly.

BUTTERCREAM

This simple cookie filling is very easy to make. Once filled, the cookies should be eaten within 3 days.

I To make enough filling for about 12 pairs of average-size cookies, put 50g/2oz/¼ cup softened unsalted (sweet) butter in a bowl and beat with a wooden spoon until very soft, smooth and creamy.

2 Gradually stir in 90g/3½oz/scant 1 cup icing (confectioners') sugar and 5ml/1 tsp vanilla essence (extract). Beat the ingredients well with an electric mixer until they are very light and smooth.

Variations

Orange, lemon or lime buttercream
Add 15ml/1 tbsp finely grated citrus rind and replace the vanilla with juice, beating well to avoid curdling. The buttercream cannot be piped through a small nozzle because of the citrus rind.
Chocolate buttercream *Blend 10ml/ 2 tsp (unsweetened) cocoa powder with 20ml/4 tsp boiling water until smooth Cool, then beat into the buttercream.*
Coffee buttercream *Replace the vanilla essence (extract) with 10ml/2 tsp instant coffee powder dissolved in 15ml/ 1 tbsp near-boiling water. Cool before adding to the mixture.*

CRÈME AU BEURRE

This delicious buttercream has a rich taste and very smooth texture.

I To make enough filling for about 12 pairs of average-size cookies, put 40g/1½oz/3 tbsp caster (superfine) sugar and 30ml/2 tbsp water in a small, heavy pan and heat gently until the sugar has completely dissolved. Bring to the boil and boil steadily for 2–3 minutes, until the syrup reaches 107°C/225°F on a sugar thermometer or when a little syrup pulled apart between two dry teaspoons makes a fine thread.

2 Beat 1 egg yolk in a heatproof bowl for a few seconds. Gradually pour over the syrup in a steady, narrow stream, whisking constantly. Continue whisking until the mixture is thick and cold. Beat 75g/3oz/ 6 tbsp unsalted (sweet) butter until creamy. Gradually add the egg yolk mixture to the butter, whisking well after each addition.

CHOCOLATE GANACHE

This filling is a fairly soft so chill for a few minutes before using to fill cookies. It is rich, so spread thinly.

I To make enough filling for about 20 pairs of average-size cookies. Pour 120ml/4fl oz/½ cup double (heavy) cream into a small pan and bring to the boil. Remove the pan from the heat and add 115g/4oz plain (semisweet) chocolate. Stir until melted and smooth.

2 Return the mixture to the heat and bring back to the boil. Transfer to a bowl and leave to cool. Chill for 10 minutes before using.

FILLING COOKIES WITH JAM

To make a smooth, slightly set jam filling, the jam needs to be boiled briefly to thicken it.

I To makes enough for 16 pairs of cookies, put 120ml/8 tbsp jam in a small, heavy pan. Add 5ml/1 tsp lemon juice. Heat gently until runny, then boil for 3–4 minutes.

2 Remove the pan from the heat and leave to cool slightly, then push the jam through a fine sieve to remove any lumps. Leave the jam until barely warm, then use to sandwich the cookies together.

FILLING BRANDY SNAPS

Whipped cream, sometimes sweetened with a little sugar and flavoured with brandy or a few drops of vanilla essence (extract), makes a simple filling for these crisp rolled cookies. Using a well-chilled bowl for whipping the cream will give a lighter result.

1 To make enough cream to fill about 20 brandy snaps, pour 250ml/ 8fl oz/1 cup whipping cream into a large chilled bowl. Sift 10ml/2 tsp icing (confectioners') sugar over the cream and add about 30ml/2 tbsp brandy. Whip the mixture using an electric mixer or balloon whisk until the cream just forms soft peaks.

2 Spoon the cream into a piping (pastry) bag fitted with a large star nozzle. Push the end of the nozzle into the end of the brandy snap and squeeze gently until the brandy snap is filled to the middle. Repeat with the other end of the brandy snap.

CHOCOLATE-FILLED COOKIES

Chunks of chocolate can be baked inside the cookie to make a delicious surprise filling.

Makes about 16
150g/5oz/10 tbsp butter, softened
150g/5oz/¾ cup caster
  (superfine) sugar
1 egg yolk
15ml/1 tbsp ground almonds
225g/8oz/2 cups self-raising
  (self-rising) flour
25g/1oz/¼ cup (unsweetened)
  cocoa powder
150g/5oz plain (semisweet) chocolate
icing (confectioners') sugar, for dusting

1 Preheat the oven to 190°C/375°F/ Gas 5 and grease or line two baking sheets. Cream the butter and sugar until pale and fluffy. Beat in the egg yolk and ground almonds. Sift over the flour and cocoa powder and fold into the mixture to make a firm dough. Knead for a few seconds, then wrap in clear film (plastic wrap) and chill for 30 minutes.

2 Roll out just over a third of the dough to a thickness of 3mm/⅛in and stamp out 16 rounds using a 4cm/1½in cookie cutter. Break the chocolate into squares and put one in the centre of each cookie round.

3 Roll out the remaining dough and cut into 16 larger rounds using a 5cm/2in cutter. Place these over the chocolate-covered cookie rounds and press the edges together. Bake for 10 minutes until firm. Dust the cookies with icing sugar and transfer to a wire rack. Serve warm while the filling is still soft and melted.

CLASSIC COOKIE FILLINGS

These recipes will make enough to fill 12–15 pairs of cookies.

Custard cream Melt 25g/ 1oz/2 tbsp butter in a small pan, then beat in 225g/8oz/2 cups sifted icing (confectioners') sugar, 30ml/2 tbsp milk and a few drops of vanilla essence (extract) until smooth.

Chocolate bourbon Beat together 50g/2oz/¼ cup of softened butter, 75g/3oz/¾ cup sifted icing (confectioners') sugar, 15ml/1 tbsp sifted (unsweetened) cocoa powder and 5ml/1 tsp golden (light corn) syrup until smooth.

Chocolate and orange Bring 120ml/4fl oz/½ cup whipping cream to the boil. Remove from the heat and stir in 200g/7oz chopped white chocolate until smooth. Stir in 5ml/1 tsp orange essence (extract) or liqueur.

Fudgy mocha Dissolve 10ml/ 2 tsp instant coffee powder in 5ml/1 tsp water in a heatproof bowl set over a pan of boiling water. Add four chopped chocolate-coated fudge fingers. Stir until melted, remove from the heat and whisk in 30ml/ 2 tbsp double (heavy) cream. Chill until firm enough to spread.

Honey and ginger Beat together 75g/3oz/6 tbsp softened butter, 75g/3oz/¾ cup set honey and 75g/3oz/¾ cup icing (confectioners') sugar until light and creamy. Beat in 40g/1½oz finely chopped, preserved stem ginger.

Storing Cookies

With few exceptions, cookies are best eaten on the day that they are made. Some such as American-style soft cookies are delicious when still slightly warm from the oven, but most cookies need to be cooled first to allow them to crisp. If you're not planning to eat them straight away, store them as soon as they have cooled. This will prevent crisp cookies from becoming soft and soft ones from drying out and hardening. Store crisp and soft cookies separately; if kept together, not only will their texture suffer, but the flavours may mingle as well.

SOFT COOKIES

It is essential to keep these cookies in an airtight container and, if possible, they should also be stored in the refrigerator to retain the freshly baked flavour.

Carefully pack cookies into an airtight container and seal. If the lid of the container isn't tight-fitting, put the cookies inside a plastic bag first, or cover the whole container with clear film (plastic wrap) before closing the lid. To restore the texture of soft cookies that have hardened – this may happen very quickly in dry climates – add a slice of brown bread to the container. Replace the bread daily.

CRISP COOKIES

The container for this type of cookie does not need to be absolutely airtight; unless the atmosphere is very humid, a slight flow of air will help them stay crisp.

Glass jars and ceramic containers with cork stoppers are ideal for storing crisp cookies. Place a little crumpled tissue paper in the base of the jar to help absorb any moisture. If cookies become soft, place them on a baking sheet and put in a preheated oven at 150°C/300°F/Gas 2 for about 3 minutes to re-crisp. Remove and cool on a wire rack before storing.

COOKIES IN THE FREEZER

Undecorated baked cookies can be frozen successfully. Freeze the cookies on trays, then pack into an airtight container interleaving with greaseproof (waxed) paper or baking parchment. (Avoid freezing cream-filled cookies such as brandy snaps as these will quickly become soggy.) To thaw, leave at room temperature for about 20 minutes.

Iced cookies can also be frozen in the same way, but they should be removed from the airtight container and thawed on a wire rack – the icing may be spoiled if they are left to thaw while still packed in layers.

CHILLING AND FREEZING COOKIE DOUGH

As long as cookie dough doesn't contain leavening ingredients, it can be stored in the refrigerator overnight or, in some cases, for up to a week. Cookie dough can also be frozen for up to 3 months but the flavours tend to lose their intensity after a month so, for optimum results, the dough is best frozen for just a few weeks.

To store cookie dough in the refrigerator, wrap it in clear film (plastic wrap) or place it in a bowl and cover it tightly with clear film. To freeze, wrap the dough in a double wrapping of clear film, then store in an airtight container.

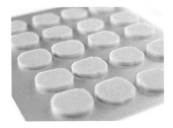

To freeze unbaked cookies, open-freeze them on trays, then pack into airtight containers, interleaving them layers with greaseproof (waxed) paper or baking parchment. Thaw unbaked cookies on baking sheets.

WHAT WENT WRONG AND WHY

Occasionally cookies don't turn out quite as you had hoped. If you have a problem when baking, try to work out why so that you can either remedy it at the time, or at least avoid it next time you bake cookies.

Problem	Cause	Remedy
The dough is very soft and won't hold its shape.	Too much liquid or fat or too little flour, or the dough has become too warm.	Always measure ingredients carefully. Chill the dough for 30 minutes before baking. If it is still too soft, work in a little extra flour.
The dough is dry and crumbly and won't hold together.	Not enough liquid or fat or too much flour, or the dough may not have been kneaded sufficiently.	Try gently kneading the dough; the warmth of your hands may bring it together. If the dough includes egg, check the right size was used. Knead in a little beaten egg, milk or soft butter.
The cookies are not evenly cooked.	The cookies are either of uneven sizes on the baking sheet; or some cookies were placed too near the edge of the sheet.	Make sure that all the cookies on a baking sheet are an even size. Leave at least a 2.5cm/1in gap around the edge of the baking sheet and turn the sheets around halfway through baking.
The cookies stick to the baking sheet.	The baking sheet was not greased or greased unevenly. Alternatively, it may have been greased with salted butter.	Use melted, unsalted (sweet) butter or oil for greasing or line the sheet with baking parchment.
The cookies crumble when removed from baking sheet.	Cookies that have a very high butter content are often more fragile than less rich ones.	Leave fragile cookies to cool on the baking sheet for at least 3 minutes before transferring to a wire rack.
The cookies are dry and too crisp on top.	The oven was too hot or the cookies were baked for too long.	If you have concerns about the temperature of your oven, use an oven thermometer. Check cookies a few minutes before end of cooking time.
The cookies spread out too much on the baking sheet.	The cookies were not chilled before baking, or, the baking sheet was over-greased when the cookies were added.	Most cookies benefit from chilling before baking. Grease baking sheets only lightly. Some cookies such as refrigerator cookies should be baked on ungreased baking sheets. Always use cold baking sheets.
The cookies are burnt on the base but not on the top.	There are a number of possible causes: baking too low down in the oven, or at too low a temperature; the baking sheets may be poor quality, or you may have used salted butter for greasing.	Check the oven temperature and bake cookies on the middle shelf. Avoid thin or very dark baking sheets. Butter burns at a lower temperature, so use oil for cookies baked at high temperatures or for a long time.

Presentation and Packaging

Whether you're making cookies to serve to guests, give as a gift or sell at a fundraising event, it is worth spending a little time on pretty presentation and attractive and elegant packaging.

All cookies should be properly stored as soon as they have cooled or, if iced or decorated, as soon as they have set and hardened. Leave gift wrapping and packaging until the last minute so that the cookies are as fresh as possible. It is often useful to include information about the cookies as well, including a list of ingredients and advice on storing.

GIFT BOXES
You can buy a huge range of pretty storage containers that make perfect packaging for cookies. Stationers and department stores sell a range of beautiful gift boxes and containers in all shapes and sizes, patterns and colours. These are the simplest way to package cookies and look stunning tied with curled ribbon or raffia.

Line the box with either crumpled tissue paper or several layers of greaseproof (waxed) paper. If the cookies are iced or fragile, then shallow boxes that will hold the cookies in one or just a few layers are better than very deep ones.

Certain types of cookie can be individually wrapped in tissue paper or cellophane before packing into the box. Amaretti, for example, are usually wrapped in pairs in twists of fine tissue paper.

JARS, TINS AND OTHER CONTAINERS
Reusable containers such as glass or ceramic storage jars or tins, are more practical than simple cardboard boxes, as they have the advantage of being airtight. They also have the advantage of becoming part of the gift as well.

As well as packaging cookies in more conventional jars and tins, you could also consider packing cookies into a container such as a cup. Wrap the cookies in cellophane and tie with a ribbon, then place in the container. (This form of packaging is not airtight, so the cookies should be wrapped at the last minute.)

MAKING BOXES
It can be great fun making your own boxes or cartons to pack cookies in. It is also much cheaper than buying ready-made gift boxes, which can be surprisingly expensive. All you need is some fine cardboard, a metal ruler and a sharp knife.

MAKING A CUBE BOX
Following the template on the opposite page, draw the outline of the cube box on the back of a piece of coloured, patterned or plain cardboard. Cut out the shape and carefully score along the dotted lines with a sharp craft knife.

1 Fold along the dotted lines, sticking tab A to edge A (keeping the tab inside the box), then tab B to edge B. Repeat with tab C to edge C and tab D to edge D.

2 To create the lid, simply fold in tabs E and tuck the flap inside the box to hold the lid in place.

MAKING A CARTON

Following the template shown below, draw the outline of the carton on the back of a piece of fine cardboard and carefully cut out.

1 Score along the dotted lines using a sharp craft knife and cut out the four slots. You can use a hole punch to make the four holes as marked on the diagram.

2 Fold the carton along the scored lines, tucking tongue A into flaps B and tongue C into flaps D, so that the end of the tongue is on the inside of the carton. Fill the carton with cookies, then you can thread fine ribbon through the punched holes and tie together.

DECORATING BOXES

If you don't have time to make a box, you can cover a used box with coloured paper. Stick on gift wrap or coloured paper, then trim the paper back to the edges of the box.

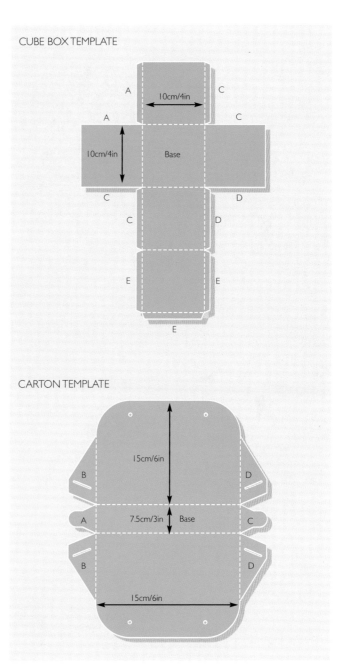

CUBE BOX TEMPLATE

A   10cm/4in   C

A   C

10cm/4in   Base

C   D

C   D

E   E

E

CARTON TEMPLATE

15cm/6in

B   D

A   7.5cm/3in   Base   C

B   D

15cm/6in

BAGS

You can buy pretty ready-made bags made out of paper, cardboard and cellophane, which look very attractive filled with cookies. Fabric bags can also look very pretty. Both are ideal for cookies that are to be given and eaten on the same day.

SIMPLE BAGS

These are best made from clear or coloured cellophane and make a perfect quick and easy wrapping for square or round cookies.

1 Cut a 25cm/10in square of cellophane. Put a pile of about six cookies in the centre.

2 Gather up the edges around the cookies, then tie a ribbon tightly where you've gathered the cellophane together. If you use curling ribbon, pull the ribbon between your thumb and the blade of a pair of scissors to create very pretty corkscrew curls.

POINTED BAGS

These are perfect for wrapping small cookies and long, thin fingers.

1 Cut a 40cm/16in square of cellophane. Fold it in quarters, hold the corner where the folds join and cut a quarter circle.

2 Open out and cut in half. Pull the two points of one half to meet. Slide one of the points behind the other to make a cone. Secure with sticky tape. Half-fill with cookies, then gather and tie with ribbon.

TUBE BAGS

These little packages, tied at both ends, are perfect for wrapping long, thin finger-shaped cookies such as brandy snaps. Simply cut out a sheet of cellophane that is about twice the length of the cookies, then roll a few cookies together to make a little tube-shaped package. Tie each end of the tube with ribbon to keep the cookies in place.

GIFT TAGS

Adding a label or gift tag to gift-wrapped cookies is the final touch. They can either carry a message or information about the ingredients and advice on storing. You can buy ready-made gift tags, make your own from thin cardboard or even bake your own individual cookie gift tags and ice on a message.

EDIBLE GIFT TAGS

These are pretty and fun, and make a really unusual, themed label.

1 Sift 75g/3oz/⅔ cup plain (all-purpose) flour, a pinch of bicarbonate of soda (baking soda) and a pinch of salt into a mixing bowl. Rub in 30g/1¼oz chilled, diced butter until the mixture resembles fine breadcrumbs. Stir in 40g/1½oz/ scant ¼ cup caster (superfine) sugar.

2 Blend together 15ml/1 tbsp golden (light corn) syrup and ½ egg yolk in a separate bowl. Add these to the dry ingredients and mix to a firm dough. Knead the dough lightly, then wrap in clear film (plastic wrap) and chill for 30 minutes.

3 Roll the dough out on a lightly floured surface to a thickness of 5mm/¼in, then stamp out gift tag-size shapes using a cookie cutter.

4 Using a skewer, pierce a hole for the ribbon to thread through about 1cm/½in from the top. Place the cookies on lightly greased baking sheets and bake in a preheated oven at 180°C/350°F/Gas 4 for 12–15 minutes, or until lightly browned. Leave on the baking sheets for 3 minutes, then, using a palette knife or metal spatula, transfer to a wire rack to cool.

5 Put a little royal icing – either white or coloured – in a paper piping (pastry) bag fitted with a writing nozzle. Pipe on your message, then leave the icing to dry. Thread ribbon through the holes made with the skewer and tie on to the cookies' container.

Cook's Tip

If the gift tag hole closes up during baking, gently pierce it again while the cookies are still hot. They will be too brittle once they have cooled.

SENDING COOKIES BY POST

If you choose cookies that are robust, there is no reason why you can't post your gift of cookies as long as you package them carefully and send by next-day delivery. Delicate iced cookies are not ideal for sending via post because they are too likely to be damaged.

1 Line the base and sides of a strong box or tin with bubble wrap or plenty of crumpled tissue paper to stop the cookies moving around.

2 Pack the cookies tightly into a box or tin, interleaving the layers with baking parchment.

3 Cut a piece of corrugated paper or bubblewrap and place between the cookies and the lid, then place the box in a plastic bag. (This will protect the cookies against damp or rain should the package be left on a doorstep or leaking mail box.)

4 Put the wrapped box in a slightly larger box, surrounded by more bubblewrap, foam pieces or crumpled paper to stop the two boxes knocking against each other.

5 Clearly address the package and label it fragile, then take the box to the post office immediately and send it next-day delivery.

Cook's Tip

It is not really practical to send home-made cookies abroad, as the mail is often unreliable and the arrival of stale cookies would be very disappointing for the recipient. In addition, some countries will have very strict rules about the importation and transportation of foodstuffs, even home-baked gifts, to protect their indigenous agriculture and to abide by local health and safety rules.

LISTING INGREDIENTS

When offering cookies as a gift, particularly when you do not give them in person, it is best to include information about the ingredients. Many people suffer from allergies and intolerance to certain foods, and many of the main food culprits are included in cookies. The most common being gluten in flour, dairy products in the form of butter, and eggs and nuts.

Even if you know the person to whom you are giving the cookies has no allergy, it is best to let them know what they contain in case they share them with someone who does have an allergy or intolerance.

Teatime Treats

Whether you are taking a well-earned five-minute break, entertaining friends for afternoon tea – a sadly forgotten custom these days – or attempting to stem the hunger pangs of ravenous children returning from school, this is the chapter to turn to. Tasty cookie treats range from Peanut Butter Cookies – perfect for the kids – to delicious Cappuccino Swirls – ideal for those with more sophisticated tastes.

Butter Cookies

These crunchy, buttery cookies make a delicious afternoon treat served with a cup of tea or a glass of milk. The dough can be made in advance and chilled until you are ready to bake the cookies.

Makes 25–30

175g/6oz/¾ cup unsalted (sweet) butter,
*   at room temperature, diced*
90g/3½oz/½ cup golden caster
*   (superfine) sugar*
250g/9oz/2¼ cups plain
*   (all-purpose) flour*
demerara (raw) sugar, for coating

1 Put the butter and sugar in a bowl and beat until light and fluffy. Add the flour and, using your hands, gradually work it in until the mixture forms a smooth dough. Roll into a sausage shape about 30cm/12in long, then pat the sides flat to form either a square or triangular log.

2 Sprinkle a thick layer of demerara sugar on a piece of greaseproof (waxed) paper. Press each side of the dough into the sugar to coat. Wrap and chill for about 30 minutes until firm. Meanwhile, preheat the oven to 160°C/325°F/Gas 3.

3 When ready to bake, remove the dough from the refrigerator and unwrap. Cut into thick slices and place slightly apart on non-stick baking sheets. Bake for 20 minutes until just beginning to turn brown. Transfer to a wire rack to cool.

Variations
• *To flavour the cookies, add ground cinnamon, grated lemon or orange rind, or vanilla or almond essence (extract) to the butter mixture, or add whole glacé (candied) cherries, chocolate chips, chopped nuts or dried fruit such as chopped apricots to the dough.*
• *As an alternative, coat the outside in granulated sugar or chopped toasted nuts.*

Sugar-crusted Shortbread Rounds

There should always be a supply of shortbread in the cookie jar – it is so moreish. It should melt in the mouth and taste buttery but never greasy.

Makes about 24

450g/1lb/2 cups butter
225g/8oz/generous 1 cup caster
   (superfine) sugar
450g/1lb/4 cups plain (all-purpose) flour
225g/8oz/scant 1½ cups ground rice or
   rice flour
5ml/1 tsp salt
demerara (raw) sugar, to decorate
golden caster (superfine) sugar,
   for dusting

1 Place the butter and sugar in a bowl and cream together until light, pale and fluffy. Alternatively, process them in a food processor, then scrape the mixture into a bowl.

2 Sift together the flour, ground rice or rice flour and salt and stir into the butter and sugar with a wooden spoon, until the mixture resembles fine breadcrumbs.

3 Working quickly, gather the dough together with your hand, then put it on a clean work surface. Knead lightly together until it forms a ball, but take care not to over-knead or the shortbread will be tough and greasy. Lightly roll into a sausage shape, about 7.5cm/3in thick. Wrap the roll of dough in clear film (plastic wrap) and chill until firm.

4 Preheat the oven to 190°C/375°F/Gas 5. Line two baking sheets with baking parchment.

5 Pour the demerara sugar on to a sheet of baking parchment. Unwrap the dough and roll it in the sugar until evenly coated. Using a large, sharp knife, slice the roll into discs about 1cm/½in thick.

6 Place the discs on to the baking sheets, spacing them well apart. Bake for 20–25 minutes until very pale gold in colour.

7 Remove from the oven and sprinkle with golden caster sugar. Leave to cool on the baking sheet for 10 minutes before transferring to a wire rack to cool completely.

Cook's Tip

The rice flour adds a toothsome grittiness and shortness to the dough, which is what distinguishes home-made shortbread from the store-bought variety.

Peanut Butter Cookies

These must come close to the top of the list of America's favourites. For extra crunch, add 50g/2oz/½ cup chopped peanuts with the peanut butter.

Makes 24

115g/4oz/½ cup butter at room
temperature, diced
125g/4½oz/¾ cup firmly packed soft light
brown sugar
1 egg
5ml/1 tsp vanilla essence (extract)
225g/8oz/1 cup crunchy peanut butter
115g/4oz/1 cup plain (all-purpose) flour
2.5ml/½ tsp bicarbonate of soda
(baking soda)
pinch of salt

1 With an electric mixer, cream together the butter and sugar until light and fluffy.

2 In another bowl, mix the egg and vanilla essence, then gradually beat into the butter mixture.

3 Stir in the peanut butter and blend thoroughly. Sift together the flour, bicarbonate of soda and salt and stir into the mixture to form a soft dough. Chill the dough for at least 30 minutes, until firm.

4 Preheat the oven to 180°C/350°F/Gas 4. Lightly grease two baking sheets.

5 Spoon out rounded teaspoonfuls of the dough and roll into balls.

6 Place the balls on the prepared baking sheets and press flat with a fork into rounds about 6cm/2½in in diameter, making a criss-cross pattern. Bake the cookies for about 12 minutes or until lightly coloured. Transfer to a wire rack to cool.

Tollhouse Cookies

Crunchy and delicious, these vanilla-flavoured cookies are packed with chopped walnuts and chocolate chips and are certainly worth an afternoon break in your journey.

Makes 24

115g/4oz/½ cup butter or margarine
ot room temperature, diced
50g/2oz/¼ cup granulated sugar
75g/3oz/½ cup soft dark brown sugar
1 egg
2.5ml/½ tsp vanilla essence (extract)
125g/4½oz/generous 1 cup plain
(all-purpose) flour
2.5ml/½ tsp bicarbonate of soda
(baking soda)
pinch of salt
175g/6oz/1 cup chocolate chips
50g/2oz/½ cup walnuts, chopped

1 Preheat the oven to 180°C/350°F/Gas 4. Grease two baking sheets.

2 With an electric mixer, cream together the butter or margarine and the two sugars until the mixture is light and fluffy.

3 In another bowl, combine the egg and vanilla essence, then gradually beat into the butter mixture. Sift over the flour, bicarbonate of soda and salt. Stir to blend.

4 Add the chocolate chips and chopped walnuts, and mix well to combine thoroughly.

5 Place rounded teaspoonfuls of the dough, spaced about 5cm/2in apart, on the prepared baking sheets. Bake for 10–15 minutes until lightly coloured. With a metal spatula, transfer to a wire rack to cool completely.

Buttermilk Cookies

It was once thought that buttermilk was especially good for children, but don't let them know as that will give them the perfect excuse for not leaving any cookies for the adults in the family. These cookies are particularly good if served warm.

Makes 15
175g/6oz/1½ cups plain
  (all-purpose) flour
pinch of salt
5ml/1 tsp baking powder
2.5ml/½ tsp bicarbonate of soda
  (baking soda)
50g/2oz/4 tbsp cold butter or margarine
175ml/6fl oz/¾ cup buttermilk

1 Preheat the oven to 220°C/425°F/ Gas 7. Grease a baking sheet.

Cook's Tip
Buttermilk is slightly acidic and helps activate the raising agents.

2 Sift the dry ingredients into a large bowl. Rub in the butter or margarine until the mixture resembles coarse breadcrumbs.

3 Gradually pour in the buttermilk, stirring constantly with a fork until the mixture comes together and forms a soft dough.

4 Roll out the dough to about 1cm/½in thick, then stamp out 15 rounds with a 5cm/2in cutter.

5 Place on the prepared baking sheet and bake for 12–15 minutes until golden. Serve warm or cool to room temperature.

Baking Powder Cookies

These all-purpose cookies are delicious served warm, spread with butter and jam or honey as an accompaniment to tea or coffee. Kids will enjoy them as an after-shool snack, perhaps served with hot drinking chocolate, on a chilly winter's afternoon.

Makes 15
165g/5½oz/1⅓ cups plain
  (all-purpose) flour
30ml/2 tbsp granulated sugar
15ml/1 tbsp baking powder
pinch of salt
40g/1½oz/5 tbsp cold
  butter, diced
120ml/4fl oz/½ cup milk

1 Preheat the oven to 220°C/425°F/ Gas 7. Grease one or two baking sheets.

2 Sift together the flour, sugar, baking powder and salt into a bowl. Rub in the butter until the mixture resembles coarse crumbs.

3 Pour in the milk and stir with a fork to form a soft dough.

4 Roll out the dough to about 5mm/¼in thick. Stamp out rounds with a 6cm/2½in cutter.

5 Place well apart on the prepared baking sheets and bake for about 12 minutes until golden. Serve these soft cookies hot or warm, spread with butter for children's teas. To accompany tea or coffee, serve with butter and jam or honey.

Scottish Shortbread

Light, crisp shortbread looks very professional when shaped in a decorative mould. This recipe is sufficient to make two large shortbreads or eight individual ones.

Makes 2

175g/6oz/¾ cup plain
  (all-purpose) flour
50g/2oz/¼ cup cornflour (cornstarch)
50g/2oz/¼ cup caster (superfine) sugar,
  plus extra for sprinkling
115g/4oz/½ cup unsalted (sweet)
  butter, diced

1 Preheat the oven to 160°C/325°F/ Gas 3. Lightly flour the shortbread mould and line two baking sheets with baking parchment. Sift together the flour, cornflour and sugar into a large mixing bowl. Rub in the butter until you can knead the mixture into a soft dough.

2 Place half the dough into the mould and press gently but firmly to fit neatly. Careully invert the mould on to one of the baking sheets and tap firmly to release the dough shape. Mould the remaining dough in the same way.

3 Bake the shortbreads for about 35–40 minutes, until just pale golden in colour. Sprinkle a little caster sugar evenly over the tops of the shortbreads and then leave them to cool on the baking sheets before serving.

Brittany Butter Cookies

These lightly glazed little cookies are similar to shortbread, but are even richer and more like cakes in texture. Traditionally, they are made with lightly salted butter.

Makes 18–20

6 egg yolks, lightly beaten
15ml/1 tbsp milk
250g/9oz/2¼ cups plain
(all-purpose) flour
175g/6oz/¾ cup caster (superfine) sugar
200g/7oz/scant 1 cup butter at room
temperature, diced

1 Preheat the oven to 180°C/350°F/ Gas 4. Grease two heavy baking sheets. Mix 15ml/1 tbsp of the egg yolks with the milk to make a glaze. Set aside.

2 Sift the flour into a bowl. Add the egg yolks, sugar and butter, and work them together until creamy.

3 Using your fingertips, bring in the flour, a little at a time, until it is all incorporated and the mixture forms a slightly sticky dough. Gather it together.

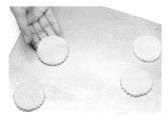

4 Using floured hands, pat out the dough to about 5mm/¼in thick and stamp out rounds using a 7.5cm/3in cutter. Transfer the rounds to the prepared baking sheet, brush each with a little of the reserved egg and milk glaze, then, using the back of a knife, score gently with lines to create a lattice pattern.

5 Bake for about 12 minutes or until golden. Cool on the baking sheet placed on a wire rack for 15 minutes, then carefully remove the cookies with a spatula and leave to cool completely on the rack.

Variation
To make a large Brittany butter cake, pat the dough with well-floured hands into a 23cm/9in loose-based cake tin (pan) or springform tin (pan). Brush with the glaze and score the lattice pattern on top. Bake for 45–60 minutes until firm to the touch and golden brown.

Ladies' Kisses

These old-fashioned cookies from the Piedmont region of Italy are sweet, light and a rare treat, just like their name. They certainly merit the best silver teapot and bone china cups.

Makes 20
150g/5oz/10 tbsp butter, softened
115g/4oz/generous ½ cup caster
(superfine) sugar
1 egg yolk
2.5ml/½ tsp almond essence (extract)
115g/4oz/1 cup ground almonds
175g/6oz/1½ cups plain
(all-purpose) flour
50g/2oz plain (semisweet) chocolate

1 Cream the butter and sugar with an electric mixer until light and fluffy, then beat in the egg yolk, almond essence, ground almonds and flour until evenly mixed. Chill for about 2 hours until firm.

2 Preheat the oven to 160°C/ 325°F/Gas 3. Line several baking sheets with baking parchment.

3 Break off small pieces of dough and roll into balls with your hands, making 40 altogether.

4 Place the balls on the baking sheets, spacing them out as they will spread in the oven.

Cook's Tip
These cookies look extra dainty served in frilly petit fours cases.

5 Bake for 20 minutes or until golden. Remove the baking sheets from the oven, lift off the parchment with the cookies still on it, then place on wire racks. Leave to cool Repeat with the remaining mixture.

6 Lift the cooled cookies off the paper. Melt the chocolate in a bowl over a pan of hot water. Use to sandwich the cookies in pairs, then leave to cool and set before serving.

Tea Biscuits

These cookies are very quick and easy to make. If you don't want to pipe the mixture, simply spoon it on to the baking parchment and press it down with a fork.

Makes 20
150g/5oz/10 tbsp butter, softened
75g/3oz/¾ cup caster (superfine)
sugar, sifted
1 egg, beaten
a few drops almond essence (extract)
225g/8oz/2 cups plain (all-purpose) flour
2–3 large pieces candied peel, cut into
small diamond shapes

Variation
Use 10 halved glacé (candied) cherries instead of the candied peel.

1 Preheat the oven to 230°C/450°F/ Gas 8. Line two baking sheets with baking parchment.

2 Cream the butter and sugar with an electric mixer until light and fluffy, then beat in the egg yolk, almond essence and flour.

3 Spoon the mixture into a piping (pastry) bag fitted with a star nozzle and pipe 10 rosette shapes on each of the baking sheets.

4 Press a candied peel diamond into the centre of each. Bake for 5 minutes until golden. Cool.

Shortbread

You have to use butter to get exactly the right texture and flavour for these rich, melt-in-the-mouth, traditional Scottish cookies. Margarine simply won't do.

Makes 8

175g/6oz/⅔ cup unsalted (sweet) butter at room temperature, diced
115g/4oz/generous ½ cup caster (superfine) sugar
150g/5oz/1¼ cups plain (all-purpose) flour
50g/2oz/⅓ cup rice flour
1.5ml/¼ tsp baking powder
pinch of salt

1 Preheat the oven to 160°C/325°F/ Gas 3. Grease a shallow, loose-based 20cm/8in cake tin (pan).

2 With an electric mixer, cream the butter and sugar together until light and fluffy. Sift over the flours, baking powder and salt and mix well to form a smooth dough.

3 Press the dough into the tin, smoothing the surface with the back of a spoon. Prick all over with a fork, then score into eight wedges using the back of a knife.

4 Bake the shortbread for 40–45 minutes. Leave it in the tin until it is cool enough to handle, then unmould carefully and re-cut the wedges while still hot.

Rolled Oat Wedges

Similar to the ever-popular flapjacks, these scrumptious, chewy wedges have a deeper, richer flavour and darker colour that is derived from using treacle.

Makes 8

50g/2oz/¼ cup butter, plus extra for greasing
25ml/1½ tbsp treacle (molasses)
50g/2oz/¼ cup dark brown soft sugar
175g/6oz/1¾ cups rolled oats
pinch of salt

1 Preheat the oven to 180°C/350°F/ Gas 4. Line a 20cm/8in shallow cake tin (pan) with greaseproof (waxed) paper and then grease the paper with a little butter.

2 Place the butter, treacle and sugar in a pan set over a low heat. Cook, stirring constantly, until melted and thoroughly combined.

3 Remove the pan from the heat and stir in the rolled oats and salt.

4 Spoon into the prepared cake tin and smooth the surface. Bake for 20–25 minutes until golden brown. Leave in the tin until cool enough to handle, then unmould and cut into eight equal wedges while still hot.

Ginger Cookies

These are a supreme treat for ginger lovers – richly spiced cookies packed with chunks of succulent preserved stem ginger. They are sure to give a boost when your energy starts to flag.

Makes 30 small or 20 large cookies

350g/12oz/3 cups self-raising (self-rising) flour

pinch of salt

200g/7oz/1 cup golden caster (superfine) sugar

15ml/1 tbsp ground ginger

5ml/1 tsp bicarbonate of soda (baking soda)

115g/4oz/½ cup unsalted (sweet) butter

90g/3½oz/generous ¼ cup golden (light corn) syrup

1 large (US extra large) egg, beaten

150g/5oz preserved stem ginger in syrup, drained and coarsely chopped

1 Preheat the oven to 160°C/325°F/ Gas 3. Line three baking sheets with baking parchment or lightly greased greaseproof (waxed) paper.

2 Sift the flour into a large mixing bowl, add the salt, caster sugar, ground ginger and bicarbonate of soda and stir to combine.

3 Dice the butter and put it in a small, heavy pan with the syrup. Heat gently, stirring, until the butter has melted. Remove from the heat and set aside to cool until just warm.

4 Pour the butter mixture over the dry ingredients, then add the egg and two-thirds of the ginger. Mix thoroughly, then use your hands to bring the dough together.

5 Shape the dough into 20 large or 30 small balls, depending on the size you require. Place them, spaced well apart, on the baking sheets and gently flatten the balls.

6 Press a few pieces of the remaining preserved stem ginger into the top of each of the cookies.

7 Bake for about 12–15 minutes, depending on the size of your cookies, until light golden in colour. Remove from the oven and leave to cool for 1 minute on the baking sheets to firm up. Using a metal spatula, transfer the cookies to a wire rack to cool completely.

Spiced-nut Palmiers

First created at the beginning of the last century, these dainty French cookies are designed to be served with afternoon tea. They are said to look like the foliage of palm trees.

Makes 40

75g/3oz/¾ cup chopped almonds,
   walnuts or hazelnuts
30ml/2 tbsp caster (superfine) sugar, plus
   extra for sprinkling
2.5ml/½ tsp ground cinnamon
225g/8oz rough-puff or puff pastry,
   thawed if frozen
1 egg, lightly beaten

1 Lightly butter two large baking sheets, preferably non-stick. In a food processor fitted with a metal blade, process the nuts, sugar and cinnamon until finely ground.

2 Sprinkle the work surface with caster sugar and roll out the rough-puff or puff pastry to a rectangle measuring 50 x 20cm/20 x 8in and about 3mm/⅛in thick. Lightly brush the pastry all over with beaten egg and sprinkle evenly with about half of the nut mixture.

3 Fold in the long edges of the pastry to meet in the centre and flatten with the rolling pin. Brush with egg and sprinkle with most of the remaining nut mixture. Fold in the edges to meet in the centre, brush with egg and sprinkle with the remaining nut mixture. Fold one side of the pastry over the other.

4 Cut the pastry crossways into 8mm/⅜in slices and place 2.5cm/1in apart on the baking sheets.

5 Spread the pastry edges apart to form a wedge shape. Chill the palmiers in the refrigerator for at least 15 minutes. Preheat the oven to 220°C/425°F/Gas 7.

6 Bake for about 8–10 minutes until golden. Carefully turn them over halfway through the cooking time using a metal spatula. Keep a careful eye on them as the sugar can easily scorch. Transfer to a wire rack to cool.

Spicy Pepper Cookies

Don't be put off by their peppery name – try these warmly spiced cookies and you are sure to be pleasantly surprised by their fabulous flavour. They are also very quick and easy to make.

Makes 48

200g/7oz/1¾ cups plain
    (all-purpose) flour
50g/2oz/½ cup cornflour (cornstarch)
10ml/2 tsp baking powder
2.5ml/½ tsp ground cardamom
2.5ml/½ tsp ground cinnamon
2.5ml/½ tsp grated nutmeg
2.5ml/½ tsp ground ginger
2.5ml/½ tsp ground allspice
pinch of salt
2.5ml/½ tsp ground black pepper
225g/8oz/1 cup butter or margarine
    at room temperature, diced
90g/3½oz/scant ½ cup soft light
    brown sugar
2.5ml/½ tsp vanilla essence (extract)
5ml/1 tsp finely grated lemon rind
50ml/2fl oz/¼ cup whipping cream
75g/3oz/¾ cup finely ground almonds

1 Preheat the oven to 180°C/350°F/ Gas 4. Sift together the flour, cornflour, baking powder, ground cardamom, cinnamon, nutmeg, ginger, allspice, salt and pepper into a medium bowl. Set aside.

2 With an electric mixer, cream the butter or margarine and brown sugar together until light and fluffy. Beat in the vanilla essence and grated lemon rind.

3 With the mixer on low speed, add the flour mixture alternately with the whipping cream, beginning and ending with flour. Stir in the ground almonds.

4 Shape the dough into 2cm/¾in balls. Place them on ungreased baking sheets, about 2.5cm/1in apart. Bake for 15–20 minutes until golden brown underneath.

5 Leave the cookies on the baking sheets for about 1 minute to firm up slightly before transferring them with a metal spatula to a wire rack to cool completely.

Cinnamon and Treacle Cookies

These treacle-flavoured cookies are slightly moist, spicy and nutty. The white icing sugar zig-zag decoration contrasts appealingly with the dark colour of the cookies.

Makes about 24

30ml/2 tbsp black
   treacle (molasses)
50g/2oz/¼ cup butter or margarine
115g/4oz/1 cup plain
   (all-purpose) flour
1.5ml/¼ tsp bicarbonate of soda
   (baking soda)
2.5ml/½ tsp ground ginger
5ml/1 tsp ground cinnamon
40g/1½oz/3 tbsp soft light brown sugar
15ml/1 tbsp ground almonds
   or hazelnuts
1 egg yolk
115g/4oz/1 cup icing (confectioners')
   sugar, sifted

1 Grease two baking sheets. Heat the treacle and butter or margarine gently until just beginning to melt.

2 Sift the flour into a bowl with the bicarbonate of soda and spices, then stir in the sugar and ground nuts.

3 Beat the treacle mixture and egg yolk briskly into the flour mixture, drawing the ingredients together to form a firm but soft dough.

4 Roll out the dough on a lightly floured surface to 5mm/¼in thick and stamp out shapes, such as stars, hearts or rounds. Re-roll the trimmings and cut more shapes. Place on the prepared baking sheets and chill for 15 minutes.

5 Preheat the oven to 190°C/375°F/Gas 5. Prick the cookies lightly with a fork and bake for 12–15 minutes until just firm. Using a metal spatula, transfer to wire racks and leave until crisp.

6 Mix the icing sugar with a little lukewarm water to make it slightly runny, then drizzle over the cookies.

Cinnamon Refrigerator Cookies

Cookies don't come much easier to make than these. Keep a roll of dough in the rerigerator or freezer so that you can cut slices and bake fresh cookies any afternoon that you fancy them.

Makes 50

225g/8oz/2 cups plain (all-purpose) flour
pinch of salt
10ml/2 tsp ground cinnamon
225g/8oz/1 cup unsalted (sweet) butter
   at room temperature, diced
225g/8oz/1 cup caster (superfine) sugar
2 eggs
5ml/1 tsp vanilla essence (extract)

1 Sift together the flour, salt and cinnamon into a bowl. Set aside.

2 With an electric mixer, cream the butter until soft. Add the sugar and continue beating until the mixture is light and fluffy. Beat together the eggs and vanilla essence, then gradually stir into the butter mixture.

3 Add the dry ingredients to the butter mixture and stir together to form a soft dough.

4 Divide the dough into four parts, then roll each part into a 5cm/2in diameter log. Wrap tightly in foil and chill or freeze until firm.

5 Preheat the oven to 190°C/375°F/ Gas 5. Grease two baking sheets.

6 With a sharp knife, cut the dough into 5mm/¼in slices. Place the slices on the prepared baking sheets and bake for about 10 minutes, or until lightly coloured. With a metal spatula, transfer to a wire rack to cool completely.

Lady Fingers

These long, delicate cookies are named after the pale, slim fingers of highborn gentlewomen. They are also known, much more mundanely, as sponge fingers.

Makes 18

90g/3½oz/generous ¾ cup plain
  (all-purpose) flour
pinch of salt
4 eggs, separated
115g/4oz/½ cup caster (superfine) sugar
2.5ml/½ tsp vanilla essence (extract)
icing (confectioners') sugar,
  for sprinkling

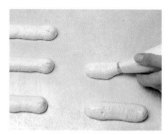

1 Preheat the oven to 150°C/300°F/ Gas 2. Grease two large baking sheets, then dust lightly with flour, and shake off the excess. Sift the flour and salt together twice and set aside.

2 With an electric mixer, beat the egg yolks with half of the sugar until thick enough to leave a ribbon trail when the beaters are lifted.

3 In another grease-free bowl, beat the egg whites to stiff peaks. Beat in the remaining sugar until very glossy.

4 Sift the flour mixture over the yolks and spoon about a quarter of the egg whites over the flour. Carefully fold in with a large metal spoon to slacken, adding the vanilla essence. Then gently fold in the remaining egg whites.

5 Spoon the mixture into a piping (pastry) bag fitted with a large plain nozzle. Pipe 10cm/4in long lines on the prepared baking sheets. Sift over a layer of icing sugar. Tip off any excess sugar.

6 Bake for 20 minutes, until crusty on the outside with soft centres. Cool slightly on the baking sheets before transferring to a wire rack.

Walnut Cookies

Crisp and crunchy, these cookies are great for a mid-afternoon energy boost during a busy day. The recipe makes 60 little cookies, so cook them in batches – two trays at a time.

Makes 60

115g/4oz/½ cup butter or margarine
  at room temperature, diced
175g/6oz/scant 1 cup caster
  (superfine) sugar
115g/4oz/1 cup plain
  (all-purpose) flour
10ml/2 tsp vanilla essence (extract)
115g/4oz/1 cup walnuts,
  finely chopped

1 Preheat the oven to 150°C/300°F/ Gas 2. Grease two baking sheets.

2 With an electric mixer, cream the butter or margarine until soft. Add 50g/2oz/¼ cup of the sugar and continue to beat until light and fluffy. Stir in the flour, vanilla essence and chopped walnuts.

3 Drop teaspoonfuls of the batter on to the prepared baking sheets, spaced about 2.5cm/1in apart, and flatten slightly with the back of the spoon. Bake the cookies for about 25 minutes until golden.

4 Transfer to a wire rack set over a baking sheet and sprinkle with the remaining sugar. Leave to cool.

Pecan Nut Puffs

As they don't keep very well, you have the perfect excuse to enjoy these melt-in-the-mouth, light-as-air cookies as freely as you like.

Makes 24

115g/4oz/½ cup unsalted (sweet) butter
   at room temperature, diced
30ml/2 tbsp granulated sugar
pinch of salt
5ml/1 tsp vanilla essence (extract)
115g/4oz/1 cup pecan nuts
115g/4oz/1 cup plain (all-purpose)
   flour, sifted
icing (confectioners') sugar,
   for dusting

1 Preheat the oven to 150°C/300°F/Gas 2. Grease two baking sheets.

2 Using an electric mixer, cream the butter and sugar in a bowl until light and fluffy. Stir in the salt and vanilla essence.

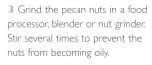

3 Grind the pecan nuts in a food processor, blender or nut grinder. Stir several times to prevent the nuts from becoming oily.

4 Push the ground nuts through a sieve set over a bowl to aerate them. Any pieces that are too large to go through the sieve can be ground again.

5 Stir the nuts and flour into the butter mixture to make a dough. Roll the dough into marble-size balls between the palms of your hands. Place on the prepared baking sheets, spaced well apart, and bake for 45 minutes.

6 Leave the puffs to cool slightly, then, while they are still hot, roll them in icing sugar. Leave to cool completely on a wire rack, then roll once more in icing sugar.

Pecan Tassies

These are a kind of cross between a rich cookie and a sweet tart, although however you describe them, they will accompany a cup of tea to perfection.

Makes 24
115g/4oz/½ cup cream cheese
115g/4oz/½ cup butter, softened
115g/4oz/1 cup plain (all-purpose) flour

For the filling
2 eggs
115g/4oz/½ cup soft dark brown sugar
5ml/1 tsp vanilla essence (extract)
pinch of salt
25g/1oz/2 tbsp butter, melted
115g/4oz/1 cup pecan nuts

1 Place one or two baking sheets in the oven and preheat to 180°C/350°F/Gas 4. Grease 24 mini muffin tins (pans).

2 Chop the cream cheese and butter. Put in a mixing bowl. Sift over the flour and mix to a dough.

3 Roll out the dough thinly. Stamp out 24 rounds using a floured, fluted 7cm/2¾in cutter. Line the muffin tins with the pastry rounds and chill until required.

4 To make the filling, lightly whisk the eggs in a bowl. Whisk in the brown sugar, a few tablespoons at a time, and add the vanilla essence, salt and butter. Set aside.

5 Reserve 24 undamaged pecan nut halves and chop the remainder coarsely with a sharp knife.

6 Place a spoonful of chopped nuts in each pastry case (pie shell) and cover with a little of the filling. Set a pecan half on the top of each.

7 Bake on the hot baking sheets for about 20 minutes until puffed and set. Transfer to a wire rack to cool. Serve at room temperature.

Tuiles d'Amandes

These cookies are named after the French roof tiles they resemble. Making them is a little tricky, so bake only four at a time. With a little practice, you will find them really quite easy.

Makes 24

65g/2½oz/generous ½ cup whole
   blanched almonds, lightly toasted
65g/2½oz/⅓ cup caster
   (superfine) sugar
40g/1½oz/3 tbsp unsalted (sweet) butter
   at room temperature, diced
2 egg whites
2.5ml/½ tsp almond essence (extract)
30g/1¼oz/scant ⅓ cup plain (all-purpose)
   flour, sifted
50g/2oz/½ cup flaked (sliced) almonds

1 Preheat the oven to 200°C/400°F/ Gas 6. Generously butter two heavy baking sheets.

2 Place the almonds and about 30ml/2 tbsp of the caster sugar in a food processor fitted with the metal blade and process until the almonds are finely ground and well combined with the sugar.

3 Using an electric mixer, beat the butter until creamy, then add the remaining sugar and beat until light and fluffy. Gradually beat in the egg whites, then add the almond essence. Sift the flour over the butter mixture, gently fold in with a metal spoon, then fold in the ground almond mixture.

4 Drop tablespoonfuls of the mixture on to the prepared baking sheets about 15cm/6in apart. With the back of a wet spoon, spread each mound into a paper-thin 7.5cm/3in round. (Don't worry if holes appear, they will fill in.) Sprinkle a few flaked almonds evenly over the top.

5 Bake the cookies, one sheet at a time, for 5–6 minutes until the edges are golden. Working quickly, use a spatula to loosen the edges of one cookie. Lift it on the spatula and place over a rolling pin, then press down the sides to curve it. Transfer the cookies to a wire rack as they become firm.

Cook's Tip
If the cookies become too crisp to shape, return the baking sheet to the hot oven for 15–30 seconds, then continue as before. If they flatten or lose their crispness, reheat them on a baking sheet in a moderate oven, until they are completely flat, then reshape.

Flaked Almond Cookies

These attractive, golden cookies have the most wonderful texture and flavour – crisp and nutty in one bite. They're good with afternoon tea, especially a fragrant Chinese variety.

Makes 30

175g/6oz/¾ cup butter or
   margarine, diced
225g/8oz/2 cups self-raising
   (self-rising) flour
150g/5oz/⅔ cup caster (superfine) sugar
2.5ml/½ tsp ground cinnamon
I egg, separated
30ml/2 tbsp cold water
50g/2oz/½ cup flaked (sliced) almonds

I Preheat the oven to 180°C/
350°F/Gas 4. Rub the butter or
margarine into the flour. Reserve
15ml/1 tbsp of the sugar and mix
the rest with the cinnamon. Stir into
the flour and then add the egg yolk
and water and mix to a firm dough.

2 Roll out the dough on a lightly
floured surface to about 1cm/½in
thick. Sprinkle over the almonds.
Continue rolling until the dough is
about 5mm/¼in thick.

3 Using a floured fluted cutter,
stamp out rounds. Lift on a metal
spatula on to an ungreased baking
sheet. Re-form the trimmings and
cut more rounds to use all the
dough. Whisk the egg white lightly,
brush it over the cookies and
sprinkle with the reserved sugar.

4 Bake the cookies for about
10 minutes, or until golden. To
remove from the baking sheet, slide
a palette knife (metal spatula) under
the cookies, which will still seem a
bit soft, but they harden as they
cool. Carefully transfer to a wire
rack and leave until quite cold.

Melting Moments

These cookies are very crisp and light – and they quite simply melt in your mouth. The secret of their wonderful texture lies in using two different kinds of fat to make them.

Makes 16–20

40g/1½oz/3 tbsp butter or margarine
  at room temperature, diced
65g/2½oz/5 tbsp lard or white cooking
  fat at room temperature, diced
75g/3oz/⅓ cup caster (superfine) sugar
½ egg, beaten
a few drops of vanilla or almond
  essence (extract)
150g/5oz/1¼ cups self-raising
  (self-rising) flour
rolled oats, for coating
4–5 glacé (candied) cherries,
  cut into quarters

1 Preheat the oven to 180°C/350°F/ Gas 4. Grease two baking sheets. Cream together the butter or margarine, lard or white cooking fat and sugar until light and fluffy, then gradually beat in the egg and vanilla or almond essence.

2 Stir the flour into the beaten mixture to form a soft dough.

Cook's Tip

To halve an egg, beat a whole egg in a measuring jug (cup), then pour off half.

3 Roll the dough into 16–20 small balls in your hands.

4 Spread the rolled oats on a sheet of greaseproof (waxed) paper and roll the balls in them to coat evenly.

5 Place the balls, spaced well apart, on the baking sheets, place a piece of cherry on top of each ball and bake for 15–20 minutes until lightly browned. Leave to cool for a few minutes before transferring to a wire rack using a spatula.

Sugar-topped Vanilla Cookies

Buttery, crumbly vanilla cookies with an irresistible crunchy sugar topping, these are great with a cup of tea for adults or a glass of milk or even a milkshake for children.

Makes about 24
115g/4oz/½ cup unsalted (sweet) butter,
* at room temperature, diced*
50g/2oz/¼ cup vanilla caster
* (superfine) sugar*
1 egg, beaten
1.5ml/¼ tsp vanilla essence (extract)
200g/7oz/1¾ cups self-raising
* (self-rising) flour*
45ml/3 tbsp cornflour (cornstarch)

For the topping
1 egg white
15ml/1 tbsp vanilla caster
* (superfine) sugar*
75g/3oz sugar cubes, crushed

1 Preheat the oven to 180°C/350°F/ Gas 4. Put the butter and sugar in a bowl and beat until the mixture is light and fluffy. Beat in the egg and vanilla essence. Sift together the flour and cornflour over the mixture and mix to a soft but not sticky dough.

2 Roll the mixture out on a lightly floured surface. Using a flower cookie cutter or ring cutter, stamp out cookies and place on a non-stick baking sheet. Re-roll any trimmings and stamp out more cookies until you have used up all the dough.

3 To make the topping, put the egg white in a small bowl and whisk until foamy. Whisk in the vanilla sugar. Using a pastry brush, spread generously on each cookie. Sprinkle with the crushed sugar cubes.

4 Bake for about 15 minutes or until the topping is just beginning to turn golden brown. Remove from the oven and transfer to a wire rack to cool.

Cook's Tip
To make your own vanilla sugar, take a vanilla pod (bean) and split it open down one side. Place in a jar of sugar and use as necessary. If you don't have any vanilla sugar, increase the quantity of vanilla essence (extract) to 2.5ml/½ tsp.

Traditional Sugar Cookies

Always a popular choice, these cookies are often baked in more interesting shapes than the rounds shown here. Stamp out hearts, moons and stars if you have the right shaped cutters.

Makes about 36

350g/12oz/3 cups plain
  (all-purpose) flour
5ml/1 tsp bicarbonate of soda
  (baking soda)
10ml/2 tsp baking powder
2.5ml/½ tsp grated nutmeg
115g/4oz/½ cup butter or margarine
  at room temperature, diced
225g/8oz/1 cup caster (superfine) sugar
2.5ml/½ tsp vanilla essence (extract)
1 egg
115g/4oz/½ cup milk
coloured or demerara (raw) sugar,
  for sprinkling

1 Sift the flour, bicarbonate of soda, baking powder and nutmeg into a small bowl. Set aside.

2 With an electric mixer, cream together the butter or margarine, caster sugar and vanilla essence until the mixture is light and fluffy. Add the egg and beat to mix well.

3 Add the flour mixture alternately with the milk to make a soft dough. Wrap in clear film (plastic wrap) and chill for at least 30 minutes.

4 Preheat the oven to 180°C/350°F/ Gas 4. Roll out the dough on a lightly floured surface to 3mm/⅛in thick. Stamp out rounds or other shapes of your choice with lightly floured cutters.

5 Transfer to ungreased baking sheets. Sprinkle with coloured or demerara sugar. Bake for about 10 minutes or until golden brown. Using a spatula, transfer the cookies to a wire rack to cool.

Cappuccino Swirls

A melt-in-the-mouth, mocha-flavoured cookie drizzled with white and dark chocolate is just the thing to have with that mid-morning café latte, as well as with afternoon tea with friends.

Makes 18

10ml/2 tsp instant coffee powder
10ml/2 tsp boiling water
150g/5oz/1¼ cups plain
   (all-purpose) flour
115g/4oz/½ cup cornflour (cornstarch)
15ml/1 tbsp (unsweetened)
   cocoa powder
225g/8oz/1 cup unsalted (sweet) butter,
   at room temperature, diced
50g/2oz/¼ cup golden caster
   (superfine) sugar

For the decoration

50g/2oz white chocolate
25g/1oz dark (bittersweet) chocolate

1 Preheat the oven to 190°C/375°F/ Gas 5. Line two baking sheets with baking parchment. Put the coffee powder in a cup, add the boiling water and stir until dissolved. Set aside to cool. Sift together the flour, cornflour and cocoa powder.

2 Put the butter and sugar in a bowl and beat until creamy. Add the coffee and the sifted flour and mix well. Spoon into a piping (pastry) bag fitted with a plain nozzle.

3 Pipe 18 spirals, slightly apart, on to the prepared baking sheets.

4 Bake for 10–15 minutes, or until firm but not browned. Remove from the oven and leave on the baking sheets for 1 minute, then transfer to a wire rack to cool.

5 Melt the white and dark chocolate separately in heatproof bowls set over a pan of hot water.

6 Place the cooled cookies close together on kitchen paper. Using a teaspoon, take some white chocolate and flick over the cookies, moving your hand speedily from left to right to create small lines of chocolate drizzle over them.

7 When all the white chocolate has been used, repeat the process with the dark chocolate, flicking it over the cookies so the dark chocolate is at an angle to the white chocolate. Leave until the chocolate has set and then remove the cookies from the paper.

Golden Ginger Macaroons

Macaroons are classic no-fuss cookies – easy to whisk up in minutes from the minimum ingredients and always appreciated. A hint of ginger makes this recipe excitingly different.

Makes 18–20
1 egg white
75g/3oz/scant ½ cup soft light
  brown sugar
115g/4oz/1 cup ground almonds
5ml/1 tsp ground ginger

Variation
Other ground nuts, such as hazelnuts or walnuts, are good alternatives to the almonds. Ground cinnamon or mixed (apple pie) spice can be used instead of the ginger, if you like.

1 Preheat the oven to 180°C/ 350°F/Gas 4. Line two baking sheets with baking parchment.

2 Whisk the egg white in a large, clean, grease-free bowl until stiff and standing in peaks, but not dry and crumbly, then gradually whisk in the brown sugar.

3 Sprinkle the ground almonds and ginger over the whisked egg white and gently fold them together.

4 Using two teaspoons, place spoonfuls of the mixture on the baking sheets, spaced apart. Bake for about 20 minutes until golden.

5 Leave to cool slightly on the baking sheets before transferring to a wire rack to cool completely.

Nutty Nougat

Nougat is an almost magical sweetmeat that emerges from honey-flavoured meringue made with boiled syrup. However, any other nuts or candied fruits can be used instead of almonds.

Makes about 500g/1¼lb
225g/8oz/generous 1 cup granulated
  sugar
225g/8oz/⅔ cup cup clear honey
1 large (US extra large) egg white
115g/4oz/1 cup flaked (sliced)
  almonds or chopped pistachio
  nuts, roasted

1 Line a 17.5cm/7in square cake tin (pan) with rice paper. Place the sugar and honey together with 60ml/4 tbsp water in a large, heavy pan and heat gently, stirring frequently, until the sugar has completely dissolved.

2 Bring the syrup to the boil and boil gently, without stirring, to the soft crack stage (when the syrup is dropped into cold water, it separates into hard but not brittle threads) or until it registers 151°C/ 304°F on a sugar thermometer. remove the syrup from the heat and leave to cool slightly.

3 Meanwhile, using an electric mixer, whisk the egg white in a large, clean, grease-free bowl until very stiff, but not dry and crumbly, then gradually drizzle in the syrup while whisking constantly.

4 Quickly stir in the almonds or pistachio nuts. Pour the mixture into the tin. Leave to cool completely but, before the nougat becomes too hard, cut it into squares. Store in an airtight container.

Chocolate Macaroons

The Italians claim to have invented these little cookies during the Renaissance and this classic combination of almonds and chocolate certainly suggests that this is true.

Makes 20

50g/2oz plain (semisweet) chocolate, chopped into small pieces
115g/4oz/1 cup ground almonds
2 egg whites
200g/7oz/1 cup caster (superfine) sugar
2.5ml/½ tsp vanilla essence (extract)
1.5ml/¼ tsp almond essence (extract)
icing (confectioners') sugar, for dusting

1 Preheat the oven to 150°C/300°F/ Gas 2. Line two baking sheets with baking parchment.

2 Melt the chocolate in the top of a double boiler or in a heatproof bowl placed over a pan of barely simmering water.

3 In a clean, grease-free mixing bowl, whisk the egg whites until they form soft peaks. Gently fold in the sugar, vanilla and almond essence, and ground almonds along with the cooled melted chocolate. The mixture should just hold its shape. If it is too soft, chill in the refrigerator for 15 minutes.

4 Place mounded teaspoonfuls of the mixture, spaced well apart, on the prepared baking sheets and flatten slightly. Brush each ball with a little water and sift over a thin layer of icing sugar.

5 Bake the macaroons for 20–25 minutes until just firm. Transfer to a wire rack to cool.

Cook's Tip
To make Chocolate Pine Nut Macaroons, spread 75g/3oz/¾ cup pine nuts in a shallow dish. Press the balls of chocolate macaroon dough into the nuts to cover one side of each ball and place them, nut side up, on lined baking sheets, then bake as above.

Coconut Macaroons

The French also claim to have invented macaroons, and recipes – almost all from monasteries and convents – date back many centuries. This is a little surprising considering their richness.

Makes 24

40g/1½oz/⅓ cup plain (all-purpose) flour
pinch of salt
215g/7½oz/2½ cups desiccated (dry unsweetened shredded) coconut
150ml/¼ pint/⅔ cup sweetened condensed milk
5ml/1 tsp vanilla essence (extract)

1 Preheat the oven to 180°C/350°F/ Gas 4. Line two baking sheets with greaseproof (waxed) paper and grease the paper or line with non-stick baking parchment.

2 Sift the flour and salt into a large bowl. Stir in the desiccated coconut.

3 Pour in the milk. Add the vanilla and stir together from the centre to form a very thick batter.

4 Drop mounded tablespoonfuls of batter 2.5cm/1in apart on the prepared baking sheets. Bake the macaroons for about 20 minutes or until golden brown. Transfer to a wire rack to cool.

Cook's Tip
For a very rich, sweet and tempting petit four, make the macaroons smaller and, when cooked, coat them in melted plain (semisweet) chocolate. Place them on greaseproof (waxed) paper and leave to set. Serve with small cups of strong, black coffee after a dinner party.

Macaroons

Freshly ground almonds, lightly toasted beforehand to intensify the flavour, give these cookies their rich taste and texture so, for best results, avoid using ready-ground almonds as a shortcut.

Makes 12

115g/4oz/1 cup blanched
   almonds, toasted
165g/5½oz/¾ cup caster
   (superfine) sugar
2 egg whites, lightly beaten
2.5ml/½ tsp almond or vanilla
   essence (extract)
icing (confectioners') sugar,
   for dusting

1 Preheat the oven to 180°C/350°F/ Gas 4. Lightly grease a large baking sheet.

2 Reserve 12 of the toasted almonds for decorating the macaroons. In a food processor, grind the rest of the almonds with the sugar.

3 With the machine running, slowly pour in enough of the lightly beaten egg whites to form a soft dough. Add the almond or vanilla essence and pulse to mix.

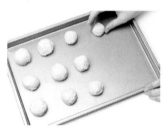

4 Remove the mixture from the machine and, with moistened hands, shape into walnut-size balls and arrange on the baking sheet.

5 Press one of the reserved almonds on to each ball, flattening the balls slightly, and dust lightly with icing sugar.

6 Bake the macaroons for about 12 minutes or until the tops are golden and feel slightly firm. Transfer to a wire rack and leave to cool completely.

Cook's Tip

To toast the almonds, spread them out on a baking sheet and bake in the preheated oven, at 180°C/350°F/Gas 4, for 10–15 minutes or until golden. Leave to cool before grinding.

Madeleines

These little tea cakes were made famous by Marcel Proust, who referred to them in his novel, *Remembrance of Things Past*. They are best eaten on the day they are made.

Makes 12

165g/5½oz/generous 1¼ cups plain
   (all-purpose) flour
5ml/1 tsp baking powder
2 eggs
75g/3oz/¾ cup icing (confectioners')
   sugar, plus extra for dusting
grated rind of 1 lemon or orange
15ml/1 tbsp lemon or orange juice
75g/3oz/6 tbsp unsalted (sweet) butter,
   melted and slightly cooled

1 Preheat the oven to 190°C/375°F/ Gas 5. Generously butter a 12-cup madeleine tin (pan). If you don't have one, use a bun tin (muffin pan). Sift together the flour and baking powder.

2 Using an electric mixer, beat together the eggs and icing sugar in a bowl for 5–7 minutes, until thick and creamy and the mixture leaves a ribbon trail when the beaters are lifted. Gently fold in the lemon or orange rind and juice using a rubber spatula or metal spoon.

3 Beginning with the flour mixture, alternately fold in the flour and melted butter in four batches with a rubber spatula. Leave the mixture to stand for 10 minutes, then carefully spoon into the tin. Tap gently to release any air bubbles.

4 Bake for 12–15 minutes, rotating the tin halfway through cooking, until a skewer or cake tester inserted in the centre comes out clean. Tip the madeleines on to a wire rack to cool completely and dust with icing sugar before serving.

Snickerdoodles

An irresistible name for irresistible cookies – two very good reasons why you will find everyone asking for more. Not only do they have a deliciously nutty flavour, but with their dusting of cinnamon sugar, they look attractive too.

Makes 20

115g/4oz/½ cup butter at room
  temperature, diced
115g/4oz/generous ½ cup caster
  (superfine) sugar
5ml/1 tsp vanilla essence (extract)
2 eggs
50ml/2fl oz/¼ cup milk
400g/14oz/3½ cups plain
  (all-purpose) flour
5ml/1 tsp bicarbonate of soda
  (baking soda)
50g/2oz/½ cup walnuts, finely chopped

For the coating

75ml/5 tbsp caster (superfine) sugar
30ml/2 tbsp ground cinnamon

1 With an electric mixer, beat the butter until light and creamy. Add the sugar and vanilla essence and continue to beat until fluffy. Beat in the eggs, then the milk.

2 Sift the flour and bicarbonate of soda over the butter mixture and stir to blend. Stir in the nuts. Chill for 15 minutes. Preheat the oven to 190°C/375°F/Gas 5. Lightly grease two baking sheets.

3 To make the coating, mix the sugar and ground cinnamon in a shallow plate or bowl. Roll tablespoonfuls of the dough into walnut-size balls between the palms of your hands, then roll the balls in the sugar mixture. You may need to work in batches.

4 Place the balls, spaced about 5cm/2in apart, on the prepared baking sheets and flatten slightly with the back of a spoon or your fingers. Bake for about 10 minutes or until golden. Using a spatula, transfer to a wire rack to cool.

Chewy Chocolate Cookies

The texture of these dark and delicious cookies is sublime – soft on the inside with a crisper, crunchier outside – matched only by their subtle mocha flavour.

Makes 18

4 egg whites
300g/11oz/2½ cups icing
  (confectioners') sugar
115g/4oz/1 cup (unsweetened)
  cocoa powder
30ml/2 tbsp plain (all-purpose) flour
5ml/1 tsp instant coffee powder
15ml/1 tbsp water
115g/4oz/1 cup walnuts, finely chopped

1 Preheat the oven to 180°C/350°F/ Gas 4. Line two or three baking sheets with greaseproof (waxed) paper and grease the paper well. Whisk the egg whites until frothy.

2 Sift the sugar, cocoa powder, flour and coffee into the egg whites. Add the water and continue beating on low speed to blend, then on high for a few minutes until the mixture thickens. Fold in the walnuts.

3 Place spoonfuls of the mixture 2.5cm/1in apart on the baking sheets. Bake in batches for 12–15 minutes until firm and cracked on top but soft inside. Transfer to a wire rack to cool.

Coffee Biscotti

These crisp cookies are made twice as delicious with both freshly roasted ground coffee beans and strong aromatic brewed coffee in the mixture. They are great for perking you up when you need a morale boost in the middle of the afternoon.

Makes about 30

25g/1oz/⅓ cup espresso-roasted
  coffee beans
115g/4oz/1 cup blanched almonds
200g/7oz/scant 2 cups plain
  (all-purpose) flour
7.5ml/1½ tsp baking powder
1.5ml/¼ tsp salt
75g/3oz/6 tbsp unsalted (sweet)
  butter, cubed
150g/5oz/¾ cup caster (superfine) sugar
2 eggs, beaten
25–30ml/1½–2 tbsp strong
  brewed coffee
5ml/1 tsp ground cinnamon, for dusting

1 Preheat the oven to 180°C/350°F/Gas 4. Put the espresso coffee beans in a single layer on one side of a large baking sheet and the almonds on the other. Roast for 10 minutes, then remove from the oven and leave to cool.

2 Process the coffee beans in a food processor or blender until fairly finely ground. Tip out into a bowl and set aside. Add the almonds to the food processor or blender and process until finely ground, but not oily.

3 Sift the flour, baking powder and salt into a bowl. Rub in the butter, then stir in the caster sugar, ground coffee and almonds. Add the beaten eggs and just enough brewed coffee to make a fairly firm dough.

4 Lightly knead for a few seconds until smooth and then shape into two rolls about 7.5cm/3in in diameter. Place on a greased baking sheet and dust with cinnamon. Bake for 20 minutes.

5 Using a sharp knife, cut the rolls into 4cm/1½in slices on the diagonal. Arrange the slices on the baking sheet, return to the oven and bake for a further 10 minutes, or until lightly browned. Transfer to a wire rack to cool.

Toffee Cookies

Sheer – if slightly sticky – joy. The deliciously chewy base of these irresistible squares is topped with a luscious layer of chocolate and chopped nuts. Children might prefer milk or white chocolate instead of plain, or use a mixture and swirl the two colours together.

Makes 36

175g/6oz/¾ cup unsalted (sweet)
   butter, melted
200g/7oz/1¾ cups rolled oats
115g/4oz/packed ½ cup soft light
   brown sugar
120ml/4fl oz/½ cup golden (light
   corn) syrup
30ml/2 tbsp vanilla essence (extract)
large pinch of salt
175g/6oz/¾ cup plain (semisweet)
   chocolate, grated
40g/1½oz/⅓ cup chopped walnuts

1 Preheat the oven to 200°C/400°F/ Gas 6. Grease a shallow 37.5 x 25cm/ 15 x 10in baking tin (pan).

2 Mix together the butter, oats, sugar, syrup, vanilla essence and salt and press into the prepared tin. Bake for about 15–18 minutes, until the mixture is brown and bubbly.

3 Remove from the oven and immediately sprinkle on the chocolate. Set aside for 10 minutes, then spread the chocolate over the base. Sprinkle on the nuts. Transfer to a wire rack to cool. Cut into squares.

Rose Water Thins

These light, crunchy cookies are easy to make and bake in minutes. For an unusual tea party, serve them with North African mint tea – the two flavours are made for each other. The mixture makes about 60 cookies, so bake them in batches, two trays at a time.

Makes 60

225g/8oz/1 cup slightly salted butter
225g/8oz/1 cup caster
   (superfine) sugar
1 egg
15ml/1 tbsp single (light) cream
300g/11oz/2⅔ cups plain
   (all-purpose) flour
pinch of salt
5ml/1 tsp baking powder
15ml/1 tbsp rose water
caster (superfine) sugar, for sprinkling

1 Preheat the oven to 190°C/375°F/ Gas 5. Line two baking sheets with baking parchment.

2 Soften the butter and mix with all the other ingredients to make a firm dough. Mould the mixture into an even roll and wrap in greaseproof (waxed) paper.

3 Chill until it is firm enough to slice very thinly. This will take 1–1½ hours.

4 Arrange the cookies on the prepared baking sheets allowing enough space for them to spread during cooking. Sprinkle with a little caster sugar and bake for about 10 minutes, until they are just turning brown at the edges.

Fruity Corn Meal Cookies

These little yellow cookies come from the Veneto region in the north of Italy, where they would probably be served with a glass of wine. However, they make excellent teatime treats.

Makes 48

75g/3oz/½ cup sultanas (golden raisins)
115g/4oz/1 cup finely ground yellow corn meal
175g/6oz/1½ cups plain (all-purpose) flour
7.5ml/1½ tsp baking powder
pinch of salt
225g/8oz/1 cup butter, softened
225g/8oz/1 cup granulated sugar
2 eggs
15ml/1 tbsp Marsala or 5ml/1 tsp vanilla essence (extract)

1 Soak the sultanas in warm water for 15 minutes. Drain well. Preheat the oven to 180°C/350°F/Gas 4. Lightly grease two baking sheets.

2 Sift the corn meal, flour, baking powder and salt together into a mixing bowl. Set aside.

3 Cream the butter and sugar until light and fluffy. Beat in the eggs, one at a time. Beat in the Marsala or vanilla essence.

4 Add the dry ingredients to the butter mixture, beating until well blended. Stir in the sultanas.

5 Drop mounded teaspoonfuls of the mixture on to the prepared baking sheets in rows about 5cm/2in apart. Bake for 7–8 minutes or until the cookies are golden brown at the edges. With a metal spatula transfer to a wire rack to cool.

Cook's Tip
If you can find them, buy sun-dried sultanas (golden raisins) for the best flavour. They may not even need soaking to plump them up.

Amaretti

These ever-popular Italian almond cookies are very more-ish and great with afternoon tea, although they are equally delicious served with a sweet white dessert wine later in the day.

Makes 36

200g/7oz/1¾ cups almonds
plain (all-purpose) flour, for dusting
225g/8oz/generous 1 cup caster (superfine) sugar
2 egg whites
2.5ml/½ tsp almond essence (extract) or 5ml/1 tsp vanilla essence (extract)
icing (confectioners') sugar, for dusting

1 Preheat the oven to 160°C/325°F/Gas 3. Peel the almonds by dropping them into a pan of boiling water for 1–2 minutes. Drain well, then rub the almonds in a clean dishtowel to remove the skins.

2 Spread out the sweet and bitter almonds on a baking sheet and let them dry out in the oven for 10–15 minutes but do not allow them to turn brown. Remove them from the oven and leave to cool. Turn the oven off. Dust the almonds with a little flour.

3 Grind the almonds with half of the sugar in a food processor.

4 Use an electric beater or wire whisk to whisk the egg whites in a grease-free bowl until they form soft peaks.

5 Gradually add half the remaining sugar and whisk until stiff peaks form. With a metal spoon gently fold in the remaining sugar, the almond or vanilla essence and the almonds.

6 Spoon the almond mixture into a piping (pastry) bag and, using a plain nozzle, pipe the mixture in walnut-size rounds on to a baking sheet. Sprinkle lightly with the icing sugar and leave to stand for 2 hours.

7 Preheat the oven to 180°C/350°F/Gas 4. Bake for 15 minutes, until pale gold. Remove from the oven and cool on a wire rack.

Citrus Drops

These soft, cake-like treats are deliciously tangy, with a zesty, crumbly base filled with sweet, sticky lemon or orange curd. The crunchy topping of almonds makes the perfect finish.

Makes about 20

175g/6oz/¾ cup unsalted (sweet) butter, at room temperature, diced
150g/5oz/¾ cup caster (superfine) sugar
finely grated rind of 1 large lemon
finely grated rind of 1 orange
2 egg yolks
50g/2oz/½ cup ground almonds
225g/8oz/2 cups self-raising (self-rising) flour
lemon and/or orange curd
milk, for brushing
flaked (sliced) almonds, for sprinkling

1 Preheat the oven to 160°C/325°F/ Gas 3. Line two baking sheets with baking parchment. Beat the butter and sugar together until light and fluffy, then stir in the citrus rinds.

2 Stir the egg yolks into the butter mixture, then add the ground almonds and flour and mix well.

3 Divide the mixture into 20 pieces and shape into balls. Place on the baking sheets. Using the handle of a wooden spoon, make a hole in the centre of each cookie. Put 2.5ml/ ½ tsp lemon or orange curd into each hole and pinch the opening to semi-enclose the curd.

4 Brush the tops of each cookie with milk and sprinkle with flaked almonds. Bake for about 20 minutes until pale golden brown. Leave to cool slightly on the baking sheets to firm up, then transfer to a wire rack to cool completely.

Fig and Date Ravioli

These melt-in-the-mouth cushions of sweet pastry are filled with a delicious mixture of figs, dates and walnuts and dusted with icing sugar. They are ideal for serving with tea.

Makes about 20

375g/13oz packet sweet
   shortcrust pastry
milk, for brushing
icing (confectioners') sugar, sifted,
   for dusting

For the filling

115g/4oz/²⁄₃ cup ready-to-eat dried figs
50g/2oz/¹⁄₃ cup stoned (pitted) dates
15g/½oz/1 tbsp chopped walnuts
10ml/2 tsp lemon juice
15ml/1 tbsp clear honey

1 Preheat the oven to 180°C/350°F/ Gas 4. To make the filling, put all the ingredients into a food processor and blend to a paste.

2 Roll out just under half of the shortcrust pastry on a lightly floured surface to a square. Place spoonfuls of the fig paste on the pastry in neat rows at equally spaced intervals, as when making ravioli.

3 Roll out the remaining pastry to a slightly larger square. Dampen all around each spoonful of filling, using a pastry brush dipped in cold water. Place the second sheet of pastry on top and press together around each mound of filling.

4 Using a zigzag pastry wheel or a pizza cutter, cut squares between the mounds of filling. Place the cookies on non-stick baking sheets and lightly brush the top of each with a little milk. Bake for 15–20 minutes until golden.

5 Using a palette knife (metal spatula), transfer the cookies to a wire rack to cool. When cool, dust with icing sugar.

Baked Sweet Ravioli

These delicious sweet ravioli are made with a rich pastry flavoured with lemon and filled with the traditional ingredients used in Sicilian cassata.

Serves 4

225g/8oz/2 cups plain (all-purpose) flour
65g/2½oz/⅓ cup caster (superfine) sugar
90g/3½oz/scant ½ cup butter
1 egg
5ml/1 tsp finely grated lemon rind
icing (confectioners') sugar and grated
   chocolate, for sprinkling

For the filling

175g/6oz/¾ cup ricotta cheese
50g/2oz/¼ cup caster (superfine) sugar
4ml/¾ tsp vanilla essence (extract)
1 egg yolk
15ml/1 tbsp mixed candied fruits or
   mixed (candied) peel
25g/1oz dark (bittersweet) chocolate,
   finely chopped or grated
1 small (US medium) egg, beaten

1 Put the flour and sugar into a food processor and, working on full speed, add the butter in pieces until fully worked into the mixture. With the food processor running, add the egg and lemon rind. The mixture should form a dough which just holds together. Scrape the dough on to a sheet of clear film (plastic wrap), cover with another sheet, flatten and chill until needed.

2 To make the filling, push the ricotta through a sieve into a bowl. Stir in the sugar, vanilla essence, egg yolk, candied fruits or peel and chocolate until combined.

3 Remove the dough from the refrigerator and leave to come to room temperature. Divide the dough in half and roll out each half between sheets of clear film to make strips, measuring 15 x 56cm/ 6 x 22in. Preheat the oven to 180°C/350°F/Gas 4.

4 Arrange heaped tablespoons of the filling in two rows along one of the dough strips, making sure that there is a 2.5cm/1in clear space around each spoonful. Brush the dough between the heaps of filling with beaten egg. Place the second strip of dough on top and press down between each mound to seal.

5 Using a 6cm/2½in plain cutter, cut around each mound to make circular ravioli. Lift each one and, with your fingertips, seal the edges. Place on a greased baking sheet and bake for 15 minutes until golden brown. Serve warm sprinkled with icing sugar and grated chocolate.

Spicy Fruit Cake from Siena

This is a delicious flat cake with a wonderful spicy flavour. This cake is very rich, so it should be cut into small wedges. Serve with tea or a glass of sparkling wine on special occasions.

Serves 12–14

butter for greasing
175g/6oz/1 cup hazelnuts,
   coarsely chopped
75g/3oz/½ cup whole almonds,
   coarsely chopped
225g/8oz/1⅓ cups mixed candied
   fruits, diced
1.5ml/¼ tsp ground coriander
5ml/1 tsp ground cinnamon
1.5ml/¼ tsp ground cloves
1.5ml/¼ tsp grated nutmeg
50g/2oz/½ cup plain (all-purpose) flour
115g/4oz/⅓ cup honey
115g/4oz/½ cup granulated sugar
icing (confectioners') sugar, for dusting

1 Preheat the oven to 180°C/ 350°F/Gas 4. Grease a 20cm/8in round cake tin (pan) with the butter. Line the base of the tin with non-stick baking parchment.

2 Spread the nuts on a baking tray and place in the oven for about 10 minutes until lightly toasted. Set aside. Lower the oven temperature to 150°C/300°F/Gas 2.

3 Combine the candied fruits, all the spices and the flour in a bowl and stir together. Add the nuts and stir in thoroughly.

4 In a small heavy pan, stir together the honey and sugar and bring to the boil. Cook the mixture until it reaches 138°C/280°F on a sugar thermometer or when a small piece forms a hard ball when pressed between fingertips in iced water. Take care when doing this and use a teaspoon to remove a little mixture out of the pan for testing.

5 At this stage immediately pour the sugar syrup into the dry ingredients and stir in well until evenly coated. Pour into the prepared tin. Dip a spoon into water and use the back of the spoon to press the mixture evenly into the tin. Bake in the preheated oven for 1 hour.

6 When the cake is ready, it will still feel quite soft, but it will firm up as it cools. Leave to cool completely in the tin and then turn out on to a serving plate. Dust with icing sugar before serving.

Cook's Tip
This will store in an airtight container for up to 2 weeks.

Orange Shortbread Fingers

These delicately scented cookies are a real teatime treat and they would be the perfect choice for a leisurely summer afternoon sitting in the shade in the garden.

Makes 18

115g/4oz/½ cup unsalted (sweet) butter
  at room temperature, diced
50g/2oz/4 tbsp caster (superfine) sugar,
  plus extra for sprinkling
finely grated rind of 2 oranges
175g/6oz/1½ cups plain (all-purpose) flour

1 Preheat the oven to 190°C/375°F/ Gas 5. Grease a large baking sheet. Beat together the butter and sugar until soft and creamy. Beat in the orange rind.

2 Gradually add the flour and gently pull the dough together to form a soft ball. Roll out the dough on a lightly floured surface to about 1cm/½in thick.

3 Cut into narrow bars, sprinkle over a little extra caster sugar and place on the baking sheet. Prick the surface with a fork and bake for about 20 minutes, until the cookies are a light golden colour. Transfer the cookies to a wire rack and leave to cool.

Cook's Tip
Store the cookies in plastic bags or an airtight container for up to 2 weeks.

Variation
Use the rind of 1 or 2 lemons in place of the orange rind. Remember to use unwaxed fruit and wash thoroughly before use.

Coconut and Lime Macaroons

These pretty pistachio nut topped cookies are crunchy on the outside and soft and gooey in the centre. The zesty lime topping contrasts wonderfully with the sweet coconut.

Makes 12–14

4 large (US extra large) egg whites

250g/9oz/3 cups sweetened desiccated (dry shredded) coconut

150g/5oz/¾ cup granulated sugar

10ml/2 tsp vanilla essence (extract)

25g/1oz/¼ cup plain (all-purpose) flour

115g/4oz/1 cup icing (confectioners') sugar, sifted

grated rind of 1 lime

15–20ml/3–4 tsp lime juice

about 15g/½oz/1 tbsp pistachio nuts, chopped

1 Preheat the oven to 180°C/350°F/ Gas 4. Line two baking sheets with baking parchment. Put the egg whites, desiccated coconut, sugar, vanilla essence and flour in a large, heavy pan. Mix well.

2 Place over a low heat and cook for 6–8 minutes, stirring constantly to make sure it does not stick. When the mixture becomes the consistency of thick porridge (oatmeal), remove from the heat.

3 Place spoonfuls of the mixture in rocky piles on the lined baking sheets. Bake for 12–13 minutes until golden brown. Remove from the oven and leave to cool completely on the baking sheets.

4 To make the topping, put the icing sugar and lime rind into a bowl and add enough lime juice to give a thick pouring consistency. Place a spoonful of icing on each macaroon and allow it to drip down the sides. Sprinkle over the pistachio nuts and serve.

Variation
If you prefer, make Coconut and Lemon Macaroons by substituting grated lemon rind and juice.

Shape and Bake Cookies

The mixture for these simple Maryland-style cookies can be made and stored in the refrigerator. It's so easy to cook some each day – and there's nothing like a warm, freshly baked cookie.

**Makes about 12 giant or
20 standard size cookies**

115g/4oz/½ cup unsalted (sweet) butter, at room temperature, diced
115g/4oz/generous ½ cup granulated sugar
115g/4oz/generous ½ cup light muscovado (brown) sugar
1 large (US extra large) egg
5ml/1 tsp vanilla essence (extract)
200g/7oz/1¾ cups self-raising (self-rising) flour
150g/5oz/scant 1 cup chocolate chips
50g/2oz/½ cup chopped toasted hazelnuts or walnuts
50g/2oz/scant ½ cup raisins

1 Preheat the oven to 180°C/350°F/Gas 4. Line two baking sheets with baking parchment. Put the butter, granulated sugar and muscovado sugar in a large mixing bowl and beat together well until light and fluffy. Add the egg and vanilla essence and beat again until the mixture is well combined.

2 Add the flour, chocolate chips, chopped toasted hazelnuts or walnuts and raisins, and mix together until the ingredients have just blended. The dough will now have a slightly crumbly consistency.

3 Depending on whether you want giant or standard size cookies, place tablespoonfuls or teaspoonfuls of the mixture, spaced well apart, on the prepared baking sheets. Bake for 15 minutes until golden brown.

4 Leave the cookies on the baking sheets for 5 minutes, then use a palette knife (metal spatula) to transfer to a wire rack to cool.

Cook's Tip

If you don't want to bake the mixture all at once, simply spoon it into a plastic container, cover the surface with clear film (plastic wrap) to prevent it from drying out and replace the lid. Keep in the refrigerator for up to 1 week. When required, remove the dough from the refrigerator 15 minutes before you want to bake the cookies to soften slightly, and shape and bake as before.

Apple and Elderflower Stars

These delicious, crumbly apple cookies are topped with a sweet yet very sharp icing. Packaged in a pretty box, they would make a delightfully festive gift for someone special.

Makes about 18

115g/4oz/½ cup unsalted (sweet) butter,
  at room temperature, diced
75g/3oz/scant ½ cup caster
  (superfine) sugar
2.5ml/½ tsp mixed (apple pie) spice
1 large (US extra large) egg yolk
25g/1oz dried apple rings, finely chopped
200g/7oz/1¾ cups self-raising
  (self-rising) flour
5–10ml/1–2 tsp milk, if necessary

For the topping

200g/7oz/1¾ cups icing (confectioners')
  sugar, sifted
60–90ml/4–6 tbsp elderflower cordial
granulated sugar, for sprinkling

1 Preheat the oven to 190°C/375°F/ Gas 5. Cream together the butter and sugar until light and fluffy. Beat in the mixed spice and egg yolk. Add the chopped apple and flour and stir together well. The mixture should form a stiff dough but if it is too dry, add some milk.

2 Roll the dough out on a floured surface to 5mm/¼in thick. Draw a five-pointed star on cardboard. Cut out and use as a template for the cookies. Alternatively, use a star biscuit (cookie) cutter.

3 Place the cookies on non-stick baking sheets and bake for about 10–15 minutes or until just beginning to brown around the edges. Using a palette knife (metal spatula), carefully transfer the cookies to a wire rack to cool.

4 To make the topping, sift the icing sugar into a bowl and add just enough elderflower cordial to mix to a fairly thick but still pourable consistency.

5 When the cookies are completely cool, trickle the icing randomly over the stars. Immediately sprinkle with granulated sugar and leave to set.

Greek Honey Crunch Creams

With its scent of liquorice and aniseed, Greek honey lends a wonderful flavour to these cookies. If you like your honey less strong, try using orange blossom or lavender instead.

Makes 20

250g/9oz/2¼ cups self-raising
  (self-rising) flour
10ml/2 tsp bicarbonate of soda
  (baking soda)
50g/2oz/¼ cup caster (superfine) sugar
115g/4oz/½ cup unsalted (sweet)
  butter, diced
finely grated rind of 1 large orange
115g/4oz/½ cup Greek honey
25g/1oz/¼ cup pine nuts or
  chopped walnuts

For the filling

50g/2oz/¼ cup unsalted (sweet) butter,
  at room temperature, diced
115g/4oz/1 cup icing (confectioners')
  sugar, sifted
15ml/1 tbsp Greek honey

1 Preheat the oven to 200°C/400°F/ Gas 6. Line three or four baking sheets with baking parchment. Sift the flour, bicarbonate of soda and caster sugar into a bowl. Add the butter and rub in until the mixture resembles breadcrumbs. Stir in the orange rind.

2 Put the honey in a small pan and heat until just runny but not hot. Pour over the dry mixture and mix to a firm dough.

3 Divide the dough in half and shape one half into 20 small balls about the size of a hazelnut in its shell. Place the balls on the baking sheets, spaced well apart, and gently flatten. Bake for 6–8 minutes, until golden brown. Leave to cool and firm up on the baking sheets. Use a palette knife (metal spatula) to transfer the cookies to a wire rack and leave them to cool completely.

4 Shape the remaining dough into 20 balls and dip one side of each one into the pine nuts or walnuts. Place the cookies, nut sides up, on the baking sheets, gently flatten and bake for 6–8 minutes, until golden brown. Leave to cool and firm up slightly on the baking sheets before carefully transferring the cookies to a wire rack, still nut sides up, to cool completely.

5 To make the filling, put the butter, sugar and honey in a bowl and beat together until light and fluffy. Use the mixture to sandwich the cookies together in pairs using a plain cookie for the base and a nut-coated one for the top.

Cook's Tip

Greek honey is also called Hymettus honey, named after the mountain. It is very dark and aromatic, with a unique taste, and is one of the most expensive honeys in the world.

Cookies for Kids

There's nothing quite like coming home from school to a plate of freshly baked cookies and a glass of milk. This chapter is packed with fabulous, fun ideas that kids will love, from simple cookies with pretty sugar icing to utterly adorable puppy faces and indulgent ice cream sandwiches.

Orange Biscotti

These crisp, crunchy cookies are based on a traditional Italian recipe in which the cookies are packed with nuts and twice baked. This version is flavoured with orange instead of the nuts and shaped into long, thin sticks. They are a little softer than the classic biscotti, which are very hard.

3 Bake the dough for 25 minutes, then remove from the oven and leave to stand for about 5 minutes until slightly cooled.

4 Using a sharp knife, carefully cut the mixture widthways into thin sticks, about 1cm/½in wide.

5 Space the cookies out slightly on the baking sheet so there's a gap in between each one allowing air to circulate, then return to the oven and bake for a further 20 minutes until crisp. Transfer the biscotti to a wire rack and leave to cool. Serve dusted with a little icing sugar.

Makes about 20

50g/2oz/¼ cup unsalted (sweet) butter, at room temperature, diced
90g/3½oz/½ cup light muscovado (brown) sugar
1 egg
finely grated rind of 1 small orange, plus 10ml/2 tsp juice
175g/6oz/1½ cups self-raising (self-rising) flour
7.5ml/1½ tsp baking powder
good pinch of ground cinnamon
50g/2oz/½ cup polenta
icing (confectioners') sugar, for dusting

1 Preheat the oven to 160°C/325°F/Gas 3. Grease a large baking sheet. In a large bowl, beat together the butter and sugar until smooth and creamy. Beat in the egg, then the orange rind and juice, flour, baking powder, cinnamon and polenta.

2 Tip the mixture on to a lightly floured surface and knead. Place the dough on the baking sheet and flatten out with the palm of your hand to make a rectangle about 25 × 18cm/10 × 7in.

Five-spice Fingers

These light, crumbly cookies have an unusual Chinese five-spice flavouring. Pipe them into finger shapes, then arrange them on cut-out paper hand shapes and add a bracelet or watch stamped out from citrus rind.

Makes 28

115g/4oz/½ cup butter or margarine
  at room temperature, diced
50g/2oz/½ cup icing
  (confectioners') sugar
115g/4oz/1 cup plain
  (all-purpose) flour
10ml/2 tsp Chinese five-spice powder
grated rind and juice of ½ orange

1 Preheat the oven to 180°C/350°F/ Gas 4. Lightly grease two baking sheets. Put the butter or margarine and half the icing sugar in a bowl and beat well with a wooden spoon, until the mixture is smooth and creamy.

2 Add the flour and five-spice powder and beat again until thoroughly mixed. Spoon the mixture into a large piping (pastry) bag fitted with a large star nozzle.

3 Pipe short lines of mixture, about 7.5cm/3in long, on the prepared baking sheets. Leave enough room for them to spread.

4 Bake for 15 minutes, until lightly browned. Leave to cool slightly, before transferring to a wire rack using a metal spatula.

5 Sift the remaining icing sugar into a small bowl and stir in the orange rind. Add enough juice to make a thin icing. Brush over the cookies while they are still warm.

Cook's Tip
These cookies are delicious served with ice cream or creamy desserts.

Variation
Use mixed (apple pie) spice instead of five-spice, if you prefer.

Pink Sugared Hearts

Pretty and pink, these delightful cookies are always a hit with Barbie-loving girls. Rolling the edges of the cookies in coloured sugar to accentuate their shape really adds to the fun of decorating.

Makes 32

225g/8oz/2 cups plain
  (all-purpose) flour
175g/6oz/¾ cup unsalted (sweet)
  butter, chilled and diced
130g/4½oz/⅔ cup caster
  (superfine) sugar
1 egg yolk

For the decoration

50g/2oz/¼ cup granulated sugar
pink food colouring
225g/8oz/2 cups icing
  (confectioners') sugar
30–45ml/2–3 tbsp lemon juice

1 Preheat the oven to 180°C/350°F/Gas 4. Grease two baking sheets.

2 Put the flour and diced butter into a food processor, then process until the mixture resembles fine breadcrumbs. Add the sugar and egg yolk to the food processor and process until the mixture begins to form a ball.

3 Turn the dough out on to a lightly floured surface and knead until smooth. Shape the dough into a ball, wrap in clear film (plastic wrap) and chill for at least 30 minutes.

4 Working in batches, roll out the dough thinly on a lightly floured surface and cut out heart shapes using a 5cm/2in cutter. Transfer to the baking sheets, spacing them slightly apart. Bake for 10 minutes or until pale golden. Transfer to a wire rack to cool.

5 To decorate, put the granulated sugar in a bowl and add a small dot of pink food colouring. Using the back of a teaspoon, work the food colouring into the sugar until it is completely pink.

6 Put the icing sugar in a separate bowl and add 30ml/2 tbsp of the lemon juice, stirring until smooth but spreadable. If the paste is too thick add a little more lemon juice and stir until well combined.

Cook's Tip
To make festive cookies, try cutting out tree shapes and use green food colouring instead of pink. Alternatively, cut out star shapes and use silver or gold food colouring to tint the sugar. Children will love these festive shapes and will enjoy leaving a plate of cookies and a glass of milk out for Santa.

7 Using a palette knife (metal spatula) spread a little icing on to each cookie, to within 5mm/¼in of the edge.

8 Turn each iced cookie on its side and gently roll in the coloured sugar so that the edges of the icing become coated in pink sugar. Leave the cookies to set for about 1 hour.

Jammie Bodgers

These buttery cookies are an absolute classic. Sandwiched with buttercream and a generous spoonful of strawberry jam, they make a perfect snack served with a glass of milk at teatime, or are equally good wrapped tightly, and popped in a lunchbox as a post-sandwich treat.

Makes 20

225g/8oz/2 cups plain (all-purpose) flour
175g/6oz/¾ cup unsalted (sweet) butter,
   chilled and diced
130g/4½oz/⅔ cup caster
   (superfine) sugar
1 egg yolk

For the filling

50g/2oz/¼ cup unsalted (sweet)
   butter, at room temperature, diced
90g/3½oz/scant 1 cup icing
   (confectioners') sugar
60–75ml/4–5 tbsp strawberry jam

Cook's Tip

If you don't have a small cutter for the cookie centres, use a sharp knife to cut out triangles or squares instead.

1 Put the flour and butter in a food processor and process until the mixture resembles breadcrumbs. Add the sugar and egg yolk and process until the mixture starts to form a dough.

2 Turn out on to a floured surface and knead until smooth. Shape into a ball, wrap in clear film (plastic wrap) and chill for at least 30 minutes. Preheat the oven to 180°C/350°F/ Gas 4. Grease two baking sheets.

3 Roll out the dough thinly on a lightly floured surface and cut out rounds using a 6cm/2½in cookie cutter. Re-roll the trimmings and cut out more rounds until you have 40.

4 Place half the cookie rounds on a prepared baking sheet. Using a small heart-shaped cutter, about 2cm/¾in in diameter, cut out the centres of the remaining rounds. Place these rounds on the second baking sheet.

5 Bake the cookies for about 12 minutes until pale golden, then transfer to a wire rack and leave to cool completely.

6 To make the buttercream, beat together the butter and sugar until smooth and creamy.

7 Using a palette knife (metal spatula), spread a little buttercream on to each whole cookie. Spoon a little jam on to the buttercream, then gently press the cut-out cookies on top, so that the jam fills the heart-shaped hole.

Applesauce Cookies

These soft and chewy, fruit-flavoured cookies are a favourite with children and ideal to make if you have a glut of apples in the autumn. They're best eaten within a day or two of baking, or they can be frozen and then thawed as you need them.

Makes 36

450g/1lb cooking apples, peeled, cored
* and chopped*
45ml/3 tbsp water
115g/4oz/generous ½ cup caster
* (superfine) sugar*
115g/4oz/½ cup butter or margarine
* at room temperature, diced*
115g/4oz/1 cup plain (all-purpose) flour
2.5ml/½ tsp baking powder
1.5ml/¼ tsp bicarbonate of soda
* (baking soda)*
pinch of salt
2.5ml/½ tsp ground cinnamon
50g/2oz/½ cup chopped walnuts

1 Cook the apples with the water in a covered pan over a low heat until tender. Purée in a blender, then measure out 175ml/6fl oz/¾ cup.

2 Preheat the oven to 190°C/375°F/ Gas 5. Grease two baking sheets. Cream together the sugar and butter or margarine until well mixed. Beat in the apple purée.

3 Sift the flour, baking powder, bicarbonate of soda, salt and ground cinnamon into the mixture and stir to blend thoroughly. Fold in the chopped walnuts.

4 Drop teaspoonfuls of the dough on to the prepared baking sheets, spacing them about 5cm/2in apart.

5 Bake the cookies for about 10 minutes or until they are golden brown. With a spatula, transfer to a wire rack and leave to cool. Store in an airtight container for up to 2 days or freeze for up to 4 months.

Lemony Peanut Pairs

These simple-to-make cookies are filled with peanut butter, but you could use buttercream or chocolate-and-nut spread instead. Make a selection with different fillings and let the kids choose.

Makes 8–10

40g/1½oz/3 tbsp soft light brown sugar
50g/2oz/¼ cup soft margarine
5ml/1 tsp grated lemon rind
75g/3oz/¾ cup wholemeal
   (whole-wheat) flour
50g/2oz/¼ cup chopped crystallized
   (candied) pineapple
25g/1oz/2 tbsp smooth peanut butter
sifted icing (confectioners') sugar,
   for dusting

I Preheat the oven to 190°C/375°F/ Gas 3. Grease a baking sheet.

2 Cream the sugar, margarine and lemon rind together. Work in the flour and knead until smooth then roll out thinly.

3 Stamp out rounds. Place on the baking sheet. Press on the pineapple. Bake for 20 minutes. Cool. Sandwich with peanut butter. Dust with sugar.

Iced Ginger Cookies

If your children enjoy cooking with you, mixing and rolling the dough and cutting out all sorts of different shapes, this is the ideal recipe to let them practise on.

Makes 16

115g/4oz/½ cup soft brown sugar
115g/4oz/½ cup soft margarine
pinch of salt
a few drops of vanilla essence (extract)
175g/6oz/1¼ cups wholemeal
   (whole-wheat) flour
15ml/1 tbsp (unsweetened) cocoa
   powder, sifted
10ml/2 tsp ground ginger
glacé icing and glacé (candied) cherries,
   to decorate

I Preheat the oven to 190°C/375°F/ Gas 5. Lightly grease one or two large baking sheets.

2 Cream together the sugar, margarine, salt and vanilla essence until very soft and light.

3 Work in the flour, cocoa powder and ginger, adding a little water, if necessary, to bind the mixture. Knead lightly on a floured surface until smooth.

4 Roll out the dough to about 5mm/¼in thick. Stamp out shapes using floured cookie cutters and place on the baking sheet.

5 Bake the cookies for about 10–15 minutes until just firm to a light touch. Leave to cool on the baking sheets until completely firm, then transfer to a wire rack to cool completely. Decorate the tops with glacé icing and pieces of glacé cherries.

Gingerbread Family

You can have great fun with these cookies by creating characters with different features. By using an assortment of different gingerbread cutters you can make a gingerbread family of all shapes and sizes. If you want to make decorating the cookies simpler, use just one colour of chocolate rather than three. Coloured writer icing and candy are also good for decorating.

Makes about 12

350g/12oz/3 cups plain
  (all-purpose) flour
5ml/1 tsp bicarbonate of soda
  (baking soda)
5ml/1 tsp ground ginger
115g/4oz/½ cup unsalted (sweet)
  butter, chilled and diced
175/6oz/scant 1 cup light muscovado
  (brown) sugar
1 egg
30ml/2 tbsp black treacle (molasses)
  or golden (light corn) syrup
50g/2oz each plain (semisweet), milk and
  white chocolate, to decorate

1 Preheat the oven to 180°C/350°F/Gas 4. Grease two large baking sheets.

2 Put the flour, bicarbonate of soda, ginger and diced butter into the food processor. Process until the mixture begins to resemble fine breadcrumbs.

3 If necessary, scrape down the sides of the food processor bowl with a wooden spoon or spatula to remove any crumbs that have become stuck to the sides.

4 Add the sugar, egg and black treacle or golden syrup to the food processor and process the mixture until it begins to form into a ball.

5 Turn the dough out on to a lightly floured surface, and knead until smooth and pliable.

6 Roll out the dough on a lightly floured surface (you might find it easier to roll half of the dough out at a time). Cut out figures using people-shaped cutters, then transfer to the baking sheets. Re-roll any trimmings and cut out more figures.

7 Bake for 15 minutes until slightly risen and starting to colour around the edges. Leave for 5 minutes, then transfer to a wire rack to cool.

8 To decorate the cookies, break each type of chocolate into a separate bowl. One at a time, set a bowl over a pan of simmering water and heat, stirring frequently, until melted. Spoon the melted chocolate into paper piping (pastry) bags, snip off the merest tip, then pipe faces and clothes on to the cookies. Leave to set.

Cook's Tip
You can use any colour of sugar for these cookies: the darker the sugar, the darker the final cookies will be. Similarly, treacle (molasses) will produce a darker cookie than golden (light corn) syrup will.

Peanut Crunch Cookies

These delicious sweet and nutty cookies are so easy to make. They puff up into lovely domed rounds during baking, giving them a really professional look. If you prefer cookies with a slightly less "nutty" texture, use smooth peanut butter rather than the crunchy variety.

Makes 25

115g/4oz/½ cup unsalted (sweet)
   butter, at room temperature, diced
115g/4oz/generous ½ cup light
   muscovado (brown) sugar
1 egg
150g/5oz/1¼ cups self-raising
   (self-rising) flour
2.5ml/½ tsp baking powder
150g/5oz/generous ½ cup crunchy
   peanut butter
icing (confectioners') sugar, for dusting

1 Preheat the oven to 190°C/375°F/
Gas 5. Grease two baking sheets.

2 Put the butter and sugar in a mixing bowl and beat until pale and creamy. Beat in the egg, then add the flour, baking powder and peanut butter. Beat until the ingredients are thoroughly mixed.

3 Place heaped teaspoonfuls of the mixture on to the greased baking sheets; space well apart to allow the cookies to spread while baking. (If necessary, spoon the dough on to the baking sheets in batches.)

4 Bake the cookies for about 20 minutes until risen; they will still be quite soft to the touch.

5 Leave the cookies on the baking sheets for about 5 minutes, then transfer to a wire rack to cool. To serve, lightly dust with icing sugar.

Ice Cream Sandwiches

Home-made wafer cookies have a flavour unlike anything you can buy at the supermarket. These crisp, nutty cookies make perfect ice cream sandwiches for a summertime treat. They're also fun to make and are a good accompaniment to almost any fruity or creamy dessert.

Makes 6 sandwiches

50g/2oz/¼ cup unsalted (sweet) butter

2 egg whites

75g/3oz/scant ½ cup caster (superfine) sugar

50g/2oz/½ cup plain (all-purpose) flour

40g/1½oz/scant ½ cup ground almonds

30ml/2 tbsp flaked (sliced) almonds (optional)

raspberry ripple or vanilla ice cream, to serve

icing (confectioners') sugar, for dusting

1 Preheat the oven to 200°C/400°F/Gas 6. Line two large baking sheets with baking parchment. Put the butter in a small pan and melt over a very low heat.

2 Put the egg whites and sugar in a bowl and whisk lightly with a fork until the egg whites are broken up. Add the flour, melted butter and ground almonds and mix until evenly combined.

3 Drop 6 level tablespoonfuls of mixture on to each baking sheet, spacing them well apart. Spread the mixture to rounds about 7cm/2¾in in diameter. Sprinkle with almonds, if using, and bake for 10–12 minutes until golden around the edges. Peel away the paper and transfer to a wire rack to cool.

4 Place a scoop of slightly softened ice cream on to one cookie and top with another, gently pressing them together. Dust with sugar and serve.

Cook's Tip

Don't be tempted to use greaseproof (waxed) paper instead of baking parchment as the cookies may stick to it.

Flower Power Cookies

Look out for little piped sugar flower decorations in the supermarket. Some are in pretty pale colours, while others are much brighter and more vibrant. The latter are best for these colourful cookies as they contrast better with the pretty pastel-coloured icing.

Makes 28

225g/8oz/2 cups plain (all-purpose) flour
175g/6oz/¾ cup unsalted (sweet)
    butter, chilled and diced
finely grated rind of 1 orange
130g/4¼oz/⅔ cup light muscovado
    (brown) sugar
1 egg yolk

For the decoration

30ml/2 tbsp orange juice
200g/7oz/1¾ cups icing
    (confectioners') sugar
green, yellow and orange food colourings
multi-coloured sugared flowers, to decorate

1 Put the flour, butter and orange rind into a food processor. Process until the mixture resembles fine breadcrumbs. Add the sugar and egg yolk to the food processor and process until the mixture starts to bind together.

2 Turn the mixture out on to a lightly floured surface and knead until it forms a dough. Shape the dough into a ball, wrap tightly in clear film (plastic wrap) and chill in the refrigerator for at least 30 minutes.

3 Preheat the oven to 180°C/350°F/Gas 4. Grease two baking sheets. Roll out the dough thinly on a floured surface and cut out rounds using a fluted cookie cutter about 6cm/2½in in diameter.

4 Transfer the cookies to the baking sheets, spacing them slightly apart. Bake for 12–15 minutes until pale golden, then transfer to a wire rack to cool completely.

5 To decorate the cookies, put the orange juice in a bowl and gradually stir in the icing sugar until the mixture has the consistency of thick pouring cream. Divide the mixture among three bowls and stir a few drops of a different food colouring into each bowl.

6 Spoon a little green icing on to one third of the cookies, spreading it to within 1cm/½in of the cookie edges. Top each one with a sugared flower (ideally of a contrasting colour). Decorate the remaining cookies in the same way, using the yellow icing on half the cookies and the orange icing on the remaining half. Leave to set for about 1 hour.

Alphabetinis

These funny little letters are great for kids – and might even be a good way to encourage them to practise their spelling. They are great fun to make and even better to eat.

Makes about 30

2 egg whites
15ml/1 tbsp cornflour (cornstarch)
50g/2oz/½ cup plain (all-purpose) flour
150g/5oz/¾ cup caster (superfine) sugar
10ml/2 tsp vanilla essence (extract)
90g/3½oz milk chocolate

1 Preheat the oven to 180°C/350°F/Gas 4. Line two large baking sheets with baking parchment.

2 In a clean glass bowl, whisk the egg whites until peaking. Sift the cornflour and plain flour over the egg whites and add the sugar and vanilla essence. Fold in using a large metal spoon.

3 Spoon half the mixture into a plastic bag and gently squeeze it into a corner of the bag. Snip off the tip of the corner so that the cookie mixture can be squeezed out in a thin line, 1cm/½in wide.

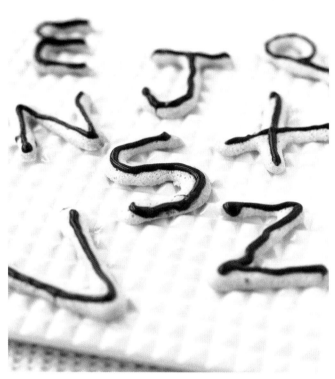

4 Very carefully, pipe letters on to one of the lined baking sheets, making each letter about 6cm/2½in tall. Spoon the remaining cookie mixture into the bag and pipe more letters on to the second lined baking sheet.

5 Bake the cookies for 12 minutes, or until crisp and golden. Carefully transfer to a wire rack to cool.

6 Break the chocolate into pieces and put in a heatproof bowl set over a pan of simmering water. Heat, stirring frequently, until melted.

7 Spoon the melted chocolate into a small paper piping (pastry) bag (or use a smaller plastic bag) and snip off the merest tip.

8 Pipe the chocolate in lines over the cookies to highlight the shape of each letter. Leave to set for at least 1 hour.

Puppy Faces

Children of any age can have fun making these little pups – you could even use the family pet as a model. These cookies are decorated with the widely available, white "ready-to-roll" icing, but you can knead in a little black, brown or yellow food colouring to make different coloured dogs.

Makes 10

100g/3½oz/scant 1 cup plain
  (all-purpose) flour
50g/2oz/½ cup rolled oats
2.5ml/½ tsp mixed (apple pie) spice
50g/2oz/¼ cup unsalted (sweet) butter,
  chilled and diced
100g/3½oz/½ cup caster
  (superfine) sugar
1 egg yolk

For the decoration

60ml/4 tbsp apricot jam
250g/9oz white ready-to-roll icing
10 round coloured sweets (candies)
black and red writer icing tubes
icing (confectioners') sugar, for dusting

1 Put the flour, rolled oats, mixed spice and butter into the food processor. Process until the mixture resembles fine breadcrumbs.

2 Add the sugar, egg yolk and 5ml/1 tsp water to the food processor and blend until the mixture begins to form a ball.

3 Turn the dough out on to a lightly floured surface and knead until smooth. Wrap in clear film (plastic wrap) and chill for 30 minutes.

4 Preheat the oven to 200°C/400°F/Gas 6. Grease a large baking sheet.

5 Roll out the dough on a floured surface and cut out rounds using a 6cm/2½in cutter. Transfer to the baking sheet, spacing slightly apart. Bake for 12 minutes until pale golden. Transfer to a wire rack to cool.

6 Press the jam through a sieve. Brush a little jam over each cookie to within 5mm/¼in of the edge.

7 Roll out half the icing as thinly as possible on a surface dusted with icing sugar. Cut out 10 rounds using the 6cm/2½in cutter and lay one over each cookie. To make the eyes, halve the coloured sweets, brush the icing lightly with water and press the sweets into the cookies.

8 Use the black writer tube to pipe the noses and mouths, finishing with little red tongues.

9 To make the ears, divide the remaining icing into 20 pieces. Roll each piece into a ball and flatten between the thumb and forefinger to make a flat pear shape. Lightly brush the icing with water and secure the ears. Arrange the cookies in a single layer on a tray.

Tree Cookies

These cookies look really effective with their chocolate "trunks" and brightly coloured "fruits". Kids will love helping to decorate them. Arrange the cookies in a line on the tea table (preferably on a multi-coloured cloth if you have one).

Makes 10

50g/2oz/¼ cup unsalted (sweet) butter,
    at room temperature, diced
115g/4oz/½ cup light muscovado
    (brown) sugar
1 egg
150g/5oz/1¼ cups self-raising
    (self-rising) flour
2.5ml/½ tsp bicarbonate of soda
    (baking soda)
finely grated rind of 1 lemon

For the decoration

50g/2oz/½ cup icing
    (confectioners') sugar
10ml/2 tsp lemon juice
10 milk chocolate fingers
brightly coloured sweets (candies),
    such as m&ms

1 Preheat the oven to 180°C/350°F/ Gas 4. Grease two baking sheets.

2 In a large bowl, beat together the butter and sugar until smooth and creamy. Beat in the egg. Add the flour, bicarbonate of soda and lemon rind and mix until smooth.

3 Place 5 large spoonfuls of the mixture on to each baking sheet, spacing them well apart. Bake for 15 minutes until the cookies have risen. Leave on the baking sheet for 5 minutes to firm up, then transfer to a wire rack to cool.

Variation

To create pretty blossoming trees, attach pastel-coloured sugar flowers to the cookies instead of coloured sweets.

4 To decorate the cookies, mix together the icing sugar and lemon juice to make a thick paste. Use a little paste to secure one end of a chocolate finger to each cookie.

5 Attach the coloured sweets in the same way, securing each one with a little paste. Leave the cookies to set for at least 1 hour. (Handle the decorated cookies with care.)

Butter Gems

These tiny shortbread-based cookies are topped with rosettes of soft buttercream and a pretty sprinkling of brightly coloured sugar. They make a great treat for even the smallest of mouths.

Makes about 40

115g/4oz/½ cup unsalted (sweet)
    butter, at room temperature, diced
50g/2oz/¼ cup caster (superfine) sugar
175g/6oz/1½ cups plain
    (all-purpose) flour

For the decoration

50g/2oz/4 tbsp unsalted (sweet) butter,
    at room temperature, diced
5ml/1 tsp vanilla essence (extract)
90g/3½oz/scant 1 cup icing
    (confectioners') sugar
25g/1oz/2 tbsp granulated sugar
green, lilac or pink food colourings

1 Put the diced butter and the sugar in a large bowl and beat together until smooth and creamy. Add the flour to the creamed butter and mix well to form a thick paste.

2 Turn the dough on to a lightly floured surface and knead until smooth. Wrap the dough in clear film (plastic wrap) and chill for at least 30 minutes.

3 Preheat the oven to 180°C/350°F/Gas 4. Grease two baking sheets.

4 Roll out the dough on a lightly floured surface and cut out rounds using a 3.5cm/1¼in cookie cutter. Space slightly apart on the baking sheets and bake for 10 minutes, or until pale golden. Transfer to a wire rack to cool completely.

5 To decorate the cookies, beat the butter with the vanilla essence and icing sugar until smooth and creamy. Spoon the buttercream into a piping (pastry) bag fitted with a star-shaped nozzle, then pipe a rosette on to each cookie.

6 Put the granulated sugar into a small bowl and add several drops of the food colouring. Using the back of a teaspoon work the colouring into the sugar until it is deeply coloured. Sprinkle a little of the sugar over the cookies.

Dolly Cookies

These pretty cookies look like they belong at a doll's tea party and are great fun for kids to make and decorate. The cookies are made by simply chilling a roll of dough, then slicing off pieces on to a baking sheet so you don't even need cookie cutters. Baking doesn't get much easier than this.

Makes 14

115g/4oz/½ cup unsalted (sweet)
  butter, at room temperature, diced
50g/2oz/¼ cup caster
  (superfine) sugar
pink food colouring
5ml/1 tsp vanilla essence (extract)
175g/6oz/1½ cups plain
  (all-purpose) flour
90g/3½oz white chocolate
75g/3oz multi-coloured
  sweets (candies)

1 Put the butter and sugar in a bowl with a dash of pink food colouring and the vanilla essence. Beat together until smooth and creamy.

2 Add the flour to the butter and sugar mixture and stir well until thoroughly combined. Turn the dough out on to a lightly floured surface and knead until smooth.

3 Using your hands, roll the dough into a thick sausage shape, about 12cm/4½in long and 5cm/2in in diameter. Wrap the dough in clear film (plastic wrap) and chill for at least 30 minutes.

4 Preheat the oven to 180°C/350°F/ Gas 4. Grease two large baking sheets.

5 Cut the dough into 5mm/¼in slices and space them slightly apart on the baking sheets. Bake for 15–18 minutes, or until the cookies begin to colour. Transfer to a wire rack to cool completely.

6 Break the chocolate into pieces and put in a heatproof bowl set over a pan of simmering water. Heat, stirring frequently, until the chocolate has melted. Using a sharp knife, cut the sweets in half.

7 Using a small palette knife (metal spatula) swirl a little chocolate on to each cookie and decorate with a ring of sweets. Leave to set.

Marshmallow Toasties

These soft cookie squares topped with a layer of strawberry jam and melted marshmallow make a sweet, sticky treat for kids of all ages. When you're toasting the marshmallows, watch them very closely because once they start to colour, they brown extremely quickly.

Makes 12

130g/4½oz/generous ½ cup unsalted
  (sweet) butter, at room temperature,
  diced
75g/3oz/scant ½ cup caster
  (superfine) sugar
finely grated rind of 1 lemon
10ml/2 tsp vanilla essence (extract)
75g/3oz/¾ cup ground almonds
1 egg
115g/4oz/1 cup self-raising
  (self-rising) flour
150g/5oz/½ cup strawberry jam
200g/7oz pink and white marshmallows
icing (confectioners') sugar, for dusting

1 Preheat the oven to 180°C/350°F/ Gas 4. Grease the base and sides of a 23cm/9in square baking tin (pan) and line with baking parchment.

2 Put the butter, sugar and lemon rind in a bowl and beat until creamy. Beat in the vanilla essence, ground almonds and egg, then add the flour and stir well.

3 Turn the mixture into the tin and spread in an even layer. Bake for 20 minutes until pale golden and just firm. Leave to cool in the tin for 10 minutes.

4 Spread the cookie base with jam. Using scissors, cut the marshmallows in half, then arrange them, cut sides down, in an even layer over the jam. Preheat the grill (broiler) to medium.

5 Put the tin under the grill for about 2 minutes until the marshmallows are melted and pale golden. Remove from the heat and gently press down each marshmallow with the back of a spoon to create an even layer of melted marshmallow. Return to the grill for a further minute until the surface is very toasted. Leave to cool.

6 To serve, dust lightly with icing sugar, cut into 12 squares or bars and remove from the tin.

Chocolate Cookies on Sticks

Let your imagination run riot when decorating these fun chocolate cookies. Use plenty of brightly coloured sweets or create a real chocolate feast by using only chocolate decorations. Whichever you choose, these cookies are very sweet, so should be kept as a real treat for special occasions.

3 Spoon the milk chocolate into the outlines on the paper, reserving one or two spoonfuls of chocolate. Using the back of a spoon, carefully spread the chocolate to the edges to make neat shapes.

4 Press the end of a wooden ice lolly stick into each of the shapes, and spoon over a little more melted milk chocolate to cover the stick. Sprinkle the chocolate shapes with the crumbled cookies.

Makes 12

125g/4¼oz milk chocolate
75g/3oz white chocolate
50g/2oz chocolate-coated sweetmeal cookies, crumbled into chunks
a selection of small coloured sweets (candies), chocolate chips or chocolate-coated raisins
12 wooden ice lolly (popsicle) sticks

1 Break the milk and white chocolate into pieces and put in separate heatproof bowls. Place each bowl in turn over a pan of gently simmering water and heat, stirring frequently, until melted.

2 Meanwhile, draw six 7cm/2 ¾in rounds on baking parchment and six 9 x 7cm/3½ x 2¾in rectangles. Invert the paper on to a large tray.

5 Pipe or drizzle the cookies with the melted white chocolate, then sprinkle the cookies with the coloured sweets, chocolate chips or chocolate-coated raisins, pressing them gently to make sure they stick.

6 Chill for about 1 hour until set, then carefully peel away the paper.

Marshmallow Crispie Cakes

This is a delicious variation of a perennially popular childhood cookie, which even very young children will love to help make. The marshmallows make them wonderfully sticky.

Makes 45

250g/9oz bag of toffees
50g/2oz/¼ cup butter
45ml/3 tbsp milk
115g/4oz/1 cup marshmallows
175g/6oz/6 cups crisped rice cereal

1 Lightly brush a 20 × 33cm/ 8 × 13in roasting pan with a little oil. Put the toffees, butter and milk in a pan and heat gently, stirring until the toffees have melted.

2 Add the marshmallows and crisped rice cereal and stir until well mixed and the marshmallows have melted.

Variation

Instead of using toffees, try using plain (semisweet) chocolate instead. Melt the chocolate by putting it into a heatproof bowl set over a pan of hot water on a low heat. Do not allow the water to touch the base of the bowl or the chocolate may become too hot.

3 Spoon the mixture into the prepared roasting pan, level the surface and leave to set.

4 When cool and hard, cut into squares, remove from the pan, and put into paper cases to serve.

Sweet Peanut Wafers

Delicate wafers filled with a sweet, peanut-flavoured buttercream make a fun, no-bake recipe that kids of any age can help with. Just remember to chill the wafer sandwiches after they have been assembled, otherwise they will be almost impossible to cut.

Makes 12

65g/2½oz/4 tbsp unsalted (sweet)
  butter, at room temperature, diced
65g/2½oz/generous ½ cup icing
  (confectioners') sugar
115g/4oz/½ cup crunchy peanut butter
12 fan-shaped wafers
50g/2oz plain (semisweet) chocolate

1 Put the butter and sugar in a bowl and beat with a hand-held electric whisk until very light and creamy. Beat in the peanut butter.

2 Using a small palette knife (metal spatula), spread a thick layer of the mixture on to a wafer and spread to the edges.

3 Place another wafer on top of the peanut buttercream and press it down very gently. Spread the top wafer with more buttercream, then place another wafer on top and press down gently.

4 Use the remaining buttercream and wafers to assemble three more fans in the same way. Spread any remaining buttercream around the sides of the fans. Chill for at least 30 minutes until firm.

5 Using a serrated knife, carefully slice each fan into three equal wedges and arrange in a single layer on a small tray.

6 Break the chocolate into pieces and put in a heatproof bowl placed over a pan of gently simmering water. Stir frequently until melted.

7 Remove the bowl from the heat and leave to stand for a few minutes to cool slightly.

8 Drizzle lines of chocolate over the wafers, then leave to set in a cool place for at least 1 hour.

Peanut Butter and Jelly Cookies

These cookies are a twist on the original American peanut butter cookie and are a real hit with kids and adults alike. **Give them a try – you'll love the crunchy nuts and sweet raspberry centres.**

Makes 20–22

227g/8oz jar crunchy peanut butter
  (with no added sugar)
75g/3oz/6 tbsp unsalted (sweet) butter,
  at room temperature, diced
90g/3½oz/½ cup golden caster
  (superfine) sugar
50g/2oz/¼ cup light muscovado
  (brown) sugar
1 large (US extra large) egg, beaten
150g/5oz/1¼ cups self-raising
  (self-rising) flour
250g/9oz/scant 1 cup seedless
  raspberry jam

1 Preheat the oven to 180°C/350°F/ Gas 4. Line three or four baking sheets with baking parchment. Put the peanut butter and unsalted butter in a large bowl and beat together until well combined and creamy.

2 Add the caster and muscovado sugars and mix. Add the beaten egg and blend well. Sift in the flour and mix to a stiff dough.

3 Roll the dough into walnut-size balls between the palms of your hands. Place the balls on the prepared baking sheets and gently flatten each one with a fork to make a rough-textured cookie with a ridged surface. (Don't worry if the dough cracks slightly.)

4 Bake for 10–12 minutes, or until cooked but not browned. Using a palette knife (metal spatula), transfer to a wire rack to cool.

5 Spoon jam on to one cookie and top with a second. Continue to sandwich the cookies in this way.

Old-fashioned Ginger Cookies

As these spicy cookies bake, the kitchen will be filled with a wonderfully tempting aroma. Children love them as a mid-morning snack with a glass of ice cold milk.

Makes 60

300g/11oz/2½ cups plain
  (all-purpose) flour
5ml/1 tsp bicarbonate of soda
  (baking soda)
7.5ml/1½ tsp ground ginger
1.5ml/¼ tsp ground cinnamon
1.5ml/¼ tsp ground cloves
115g/4oz/½ cup butter or margarine
  at room temperature, diced
350g/12oz/1¾ cups caster
  (superfine) sugar
1 egg
60ml/4 tbsp black treacle (molasses)
5ml/1 tsp fresh lemon juice

1 Preheat the oven to 160°C/325°F/ Gas 3. Grease three baking sheets.

2 Sift the flour, bicarbonate of soda and spices into a small bowl. Set aside.

3 Place the butter or margarine and two-thirds of the sugar in a bowl and cream together with an electric mixer until light and fluffy. Lightly beat the egg and stir it in.

4 Stir in the treacle and lemon juice. Add the flour mixture and mix in thoroughly with a wooden spoon to make a soft dough.

5 Shape the dough into 2cm/¾in balls. Roll the balls in the remaining sugar to coat and place them on the prepared baking sheets, spaced about 5cm/2in apart to allow for the dough spreading.

6 Bake for about 12 minutes, or until the cookies are just firm to the touch. With a spatula, transfer the cookies to a wire rack and leave to cool.

Cook's Tip
You'll need to cook trays of these cookies in batches. It is best not to put more than two trays in the oven at one time.

Raspberry Sandwich Cookies

Children will love these sweet, sticky treats, so the chances are there will be none left to store. If you need to keep them, layer with greaseproof paper in an airtight container.

Makes 32

115g/4oz/1 cup blanched almonds
175g/6oz/1½ cups plain (all-purpose) flour
175g/6oz/¾ cup butter
115g/4oz/generous ½ cup caster
  (superfine) sugar
grated rind of 1 lemon
5ml/1 tsp vanilla essence (extract)
1 egg white
pinch of salt
40g/1½oz/⅓ cup flaked (sliced)
  almonds, chopped
350g/12oz/1¼ cups raspberry jam
15ml/1 tbsp lemon juice

1 Finely grind the almonds with 45ml/3 tbsp of the flour.

2 Cream together the butter and sugar until light and fluffy. Stir in the lemon rind and vanilla. Add the ground almonds and remaining flour and mix to form a dough. Gather it into a ball, wrap in greaseproof (waxed) paper and chill for 1 hour.

3 Preheat the oven to 160°C/325°F/ Gas 3. Line two baking sheets with greaseproof paper.

4 Divide the dough into four. Roll out on a lightly floured surface to 3mm/⅛in thick. With a floured 6cm/ 2½in cutter, stamp out rounds, then stamp out the centres from half of them with a piping nozzle. Check that you have equal numbers of rings and rounds, then place them 1cm/½in apart on the baking sheets.

5 Whisk the egg white with the salt until just frothy. Brush only the rings with the egg white, then sprinkle over the chopped almonds. Bake for 12–15 minutes, until lightly browned. Cool for 2–3 minutes on the sheets before transferring to a wire rack.

6 In a small, heavy pan, heat the jam with the lemon juice until it melts and comes to a simmer. Brush the jam over the cookie rounds and sandwich together with the rings.

Toffee Apple and Oat Crunchies

An unashamedly addictive mixture of chewy oats, soft apple and wonderfully crunchy toffee, this cookie won't win large prizes in the looks department but is top of the class for flavour.

Makes about 16

150g/5oz/10 tbsp unsalted
  (sweet) butter
175g/6oz/scant 1 cup light muscovado
  (brown) sugar
90g/3½oz/½ cup granulated sugar
1 large (US extra large) egg, beaten
75g/3oz/⅔ cup plain (all-purpose) flour
2.5ml/½ tsp bicarbonate of soda
  (baking soda)
pinch of salt
250g/9oz/2½ cups rolled oats
50g/2oz/scant ½ cup sultanas
  (golden raisins)
50g/2oz dried apple rings,
  coarsely chopped
50g/2oz chewy toffees, coarsely chopped

1 Preheat the oven to 180°C/350°F/ Gas 4. Line two or three baking sheets with baking parchment. In a large bowl, beat together the butter and both sugars until creamy. Add the beaten egg and stir well until thoroughly combined.

2 Sift together the flour, bicarbonate of soda and salt. Add to the butter, sugar and egg mixture and mix in well. Finally add the oats, sultanas, chopped apple rings and toffee pieces and stir gently until just combined.

3 Using a small ice cream scoop or large tablespoon, place heaps of the mixture well apart on the prepared baking sheets. Bake for about 10–12 minutes, or until lightly set in the centre and just beginning to brown at the edges.

4 Remove from the oven and leave to cool on the baking sheets for a few minutes. Using a palette knife (metal spatula), transfer the cookies to a wire rack to cool completely.

Celebration Cookies

Food and festivals go together – from China to America and from January to December, you cannot have a celebration without cooking something special to eat. Of course, you don't have to wait for Diwali to enjoy Neuris, Hanukkah to feast on Rugelach or Easter to bake a batch of Simnel Cookies. Making any of the cookies in this chapter will turn an ordinary day into a special occasion and an international celebration.

Almond Orange Cookies

The combination of lard and almonds gives these traditional cookies a lovely short texture, so that they melt in the mouth, but you could use white cooking fat if you like. Serve them whenever you have guests – they are perfect with coffee or hot chocolate.

Makes 36
250g/9oz/generous 1 cup lard, softened
125g/4½oz/generous ½ cup caster
  (superfine) sugar
2 eggs, beaten
grated rind and juice of 1 small orange
300g/11oz/2¾ cups plain (all-purpose)
  flour, sifted with 5ml/1 tsp
  baking powder
200g/7oz/1¾ cups ground almonds

For dusting
50g/2oz/½ cup icing (confectioners')
  sugar mixed with 5ml/1 tsp
  ground cinnamon

1 Preheat the oven to 200°C/ 400°F/Gas 6. Place the lard in a large bowl and beat with an electric whisk until light and aerated. Gradually beat in the caster sugar.

2 Whisk in the eggs, orange rind and juice. Whisk for 3–4 minutes more, then stir in the flour mixture and almonds to form a dough.

3 Roll out on a lightly floured surface to 1cm/½in thick. Stamp out 36 rounds with a plain cutter. Lift the rounds on to baking sheets and bake for about 10 minutes until golden. Leave on the baking sheets for 10 minutes to cool and firm slightly. Sift the icing sugar mixture evenly over the cookies and leave to cool completely.

Mexican Wedding Cookies

Almost hidden beneath their veil of icing sugar, these little shortbread cookies are traditionally served at weddings and are absolutely delicious. Serve them after dinner with coffee or, perhaps, a glass of the Mexican coffee liqueur – Kahlúa.

Makes 30
225g/8oz/1 cup butter, softened
175g/6oz/1½ cups icing
  (confectioners') sugar
5ml/1 tsp natural vanilla
  essence (extract)
300g/11oz/2¾ cups plain
  (all-purpose) flour
pinch of salt
150g/5oz/1¼ cups pecan nuts,
  finely chopped

1 Preheat the oven to 190°C/ 375°F/Gas 5. Beat the butter in a large bowl until it is light and fluffy, then beat in 115g/4oz/1 cup of the icing sugar, with the vanilla essence.

2 Gradually add the flour and salt to the creamed mixture, beating well after each addition, until it starts to form a dough. Add the finely chopped pecans with the remaining flour. Knead the dough lightly until combined.

3 Divide the dough into 30 equal pieces and roll them into balls. Space about 5mm/¼in apart on baking sheets. Press each ball lightly with your thumb, to flatten it slightly.

4 Bake for 10–15 minutes until the cookies are starting to brown. Cool on the baking sheets for 10 minutes, then, using a metal spatula, transfer to wire racks to cool completely.

5 Put the remaining icing sugar in a bowl. Add a few cookies at a time, shaking them gently until they are heavily coated. Serve immediately or store in an airtight container.

Cinnamon and Orange Tuiles

The tempting aroma of cinnamon and orange evokes a feeling of Christmas and, served with coffee, these chocolate-dipped tuiles are perfect for festive occasions.

Serves 15

2 egg whites
90g/3½oz/½ cup caster (superfine) sugar
7.5ml/1½ tsp ground cinnamon
finely grated rind of 1 orange
50g/2oz/½ cup plain (all-purpose) flour
75g/3oz/6 tbsp butter, melted

For the dipping chocolate

75g/3oz Belgian plain (continental semisweet) chocolate
45ml/3 tbsp milk
75–90ml/5–6 tbsp double (heavy) or whipping cream

1 Preheat the oven to 200°C/ 400°F/Gas 6. Line two or three large baking sheets with non-stick baking parchment.

2 Whisk the egg whites until softly peaking, then whisk in the sugar until smooth and glossy. Add the cinnamon and orange rind, sift over the flour and fold in with the melted butter. When well blended, add 15ml/1 tbsp of recently boiled water to thin the mixture.

3 Place 4–5 teaspoons of the mixture on each tray, well apart. Flatten out and bake, one sheet at a time, for 7 minutes until just golden. Cool for a few seconds then remove from the sheet with a metal spatula and immediately roll around the handle of a wooden spoon. Place on a rack to cool.

4 Melt the chocolate in the milk, then stir in the cream. Dip one or both ends of the cookies in the chocolate and leave to cool.

Lavender Heart Cookies

In folklore, lavender has always been linked with love, as has food, so make some heart-shaped cookies and serve them on Valentine's Day or any other romantic anniversary.

Makes about 18

115g/4oz/½ cup unsalted (sweet) butter at room temperature, diced
50g/2oz/¼ cup caster (superfine) sugar
175g/6oz/1½ cups plain (all-purpose) flour
30ml/2 tbsp fresh lavender florets or 15ml/1 tbsp dried culinary lavender, coarsely chopped
30ml/2 tbsp caster (superfine) sugar, for sprinkling

1 Using an electric mixer, cream together the butter and caster sugar until fluffy. Stir in the flour and lavender and bring the mixture together in a soft ball. Cover with clear film (plastic wrap) and chill for about 15 minutes.

Cook's Tip
If you are using fresh lavender, make sure that it has not been sprayed with any chemicals or subjected to traffic pollution.

2 Preheat the oven to 200°C/400°F/Gas 6. Roll out the dough on a lightly floured surface and stamp out about 18 cookies, using a 5cm/2in heart-shaped cookie cutter. Place on a heavy baking sheet and bake for about 10 minutes until golden.

3 Leave the cookies standing for 5 minutes to set. Using a metal spatula, transfer carefully from the baking sheet on to a wire rack to cool completely. The cookies can be stored in an airtight container for up to 1 week.

Double Gingerbread Cookies

Packed in little bags, these festive two-tone cookies would make a lovely Christmas gift. They are easy to make, but will have everyone wondering how you did it.

Makes 25

For the golden gingerbread
175g/6oz/1½ cups plain
  (all-purpose) flour
1.5ml/¼ tsp bicarbonate of soda
  (baking soda)
pinch of salt
5ml/1 tsp ground cinnamon
65g/2½oz/5 tbsp unsalted (sweet) butter,
  cut into pieces
75g/3oz/scant ½ cup caster
  (superfine) sugar
30ml/2 tbsp maple syrup
1 egg yolk, beaten

For the chocolate gingerbread
175g/6oz/1½ cups plain
  (all-purpose) flour
pinch of salt
10ml/2 tsp mixed (apple pie) spice
2.5ml/½ tsp bicarbonate of soda
  (baking soda)
25g/1oz/¼ cup (unsweetened)
  cocoa powder
75g/3oz/⅓ cup unsalted (sweet)
  butter, chopped
75g/3oz/⅓ cup light muscovado
  (brown) sugar
1 egg, beaten

1 To make the golden gingerbread mixture, sift together the flour, bicarbonate of soda, salt and cinnamon into a large bowl. Rub the butter into the flour mixture with your fingertips until the mixture resembles fine breadcrumbs. Add the sugar, syrup and egg yolk and mix to a firm dough. Knead lightly. Wrap in clear film (plastic wrap) and chill in the refrigerator for 30 minutes before shaping.

2 To make the chocolate gingerbread mixture, sift together the flour, salt, spice, bicarbonate of soda and cocoa powder. Knead the butter into the flour in a large bowl. Add the sugar and egg and mix to a firm dough. Knead lightly. Wrap in clear film and chill for 30 minutes.

3 Roll out half of the chocolate dough on a floured surface to a 28 × 4cm/11 × 1½in rectangle, 1cm/½in thick. Repeat with half of the golden gingerbread dough. Using a knife, cut both lengths into seven long, thin strips. Lay the strips together, side by side, alternating the chocolate and golden dough.

4 Roll out the remaining golden gingerbread dough with your hands to a long sausage, 2cm/¾in wide and the length of the strips. Lay the sausage of dough down the centre of the striped dough.

Cook's Tip
As the shaping and combining of the two gingerbread doughs is crucial to the success of these cookies and because you will have to handle them quite a lot, it is important to chill the doughs thoroughly before you start shaping.

5 Carefully bring the striped dough up around the sausage and press it gently in position, to enclose the sausage completely.

6 Roll the remaining chocolate dough to a 28 × 13cm/11 × 5in rectangle. Bring the chocolate dough up around the striped dough, to enclose it. Press gently into place. Wrap and chill for 30 minutes.

7 Preheat the oven to 180°C/350°F/ Gas 4. Grease a large baking sheet. Cut the gingerbread roll into thin slices and place them, slightly apart, on the prepared baking sheet.

8 Bake for about 12–15 minutes until just beginning to colour around the edges. Leave on the baking sheet for 3 minutes, then transfer to a wire rack to cool completely.

Simnel Cookies

Enjoy these mini variations on the sweet, marzipan-covered simnel cake that is traditionally eaten at Easter and, originally, Mothering Sunday in Britain. Children will enjoy decorating them.

Makes about 18

175g/6oz/¾ cup unsalted (sweet) butter,
    at room temperature, diced
115g/4oz/generous ½ cup caster
    (superfine) sugar
finely grated rind of 1 lemon
2 egg yolks
225g/8oz/2 cups plain (all-purpose) flour
50g/2oz/¼ cup currants

For the topping

400g/14oz/¾ cup marzipan
200g/7oz/1¾ cups icing (confectioners')
    sugar, sifted
2–3 shades of food colouring
mini sugar-coated chocolate Easter eggs

1 Preheat the oven to 180°C/350°F/ Gas 4. Put the butter, sugar and lemon rind in a bowl and cream with a wooden spoon or electric mixer until light and fluffy. Beat in the egg yolks, then stir in the flour and currants and mix to a firm dough. If it is a little soft, chill in the refrigerator until firm.

2 Roll the dough out on a sheet of baking parchment to just under 5mm/¼in thickness. Using a 9cm/ 3½in fluted cutter, stamp out rounds and place, spaced slightly apart, on two non-stick baking sheets.

3 To make the topping, roll out the marzipan to just under 5mm/¼in thickness and use a 6cm/2½in plain or fluted cutter to stamp out the same number of rounds as there are cookies. Place a marzipan round on top of each cookie and press down very gently to fix the marzipan to the cookie dough.

4 Bake the cookies for about 12 minutes, or until just golden. Remove from the oven and leave to cool on the baking sheets.

5 Put the icing sugar in a bowl and add just enough water to mix to a smooth, soft, spreadable consistency. Divide the icing among two or three bowls and add a few drops of different food colouring to each one. Stir until evenly mixed.

6 Divide the cooled cookies into three batches and spread each batch with icing of a different colour. While the icing is still wet, gently press a few sugar-coated eggs on top of each cookie and leave to set.

Sweet Hearts

These cookies are for Valentine's Day or an anniversary, but you could use different-shaped cutters in the same way to make cookies for other occasions – stars and bells for Christmas, perhaps, or fluted "flowers" for a special birthday or Mother's Day present.

Makes 12–14

50g/2oz/¼ cup unsalted (sweet)
  butter, softened
75g/3oz/scant ½ cup caster (superfine) sugar
1 egg yolk
150g/5oz/1¼ cups plain (all-purpose) flour
25g/1oz dark (bittersweet) chocolate,
  melted and cooled
25–50g/1–2oz dark (bittersweet)
  chocolate, to decorate

1 Preheat the oven to 180°C/350°F/ Gas 4. Line two baking sheets with baking parchment. Put the butter, sugar and egg yolk in a mixing bowl and beat well. Stir in the flour and then knead until smooth.

2 Divide the dough in half, then knead the melted chocolate into one half until it is evenly coloured.

3 Roll out the chocolate dough between two sheets of baking parchment, to a thickness of about 3mm/⅛in. Then roll out the plain dough in the same way.

4 Cut out hearts from both doughs using a 7.5cm/3in biscuit (cookie) cutter. Place the hearts on the prepared baking sheets.

5 Using a smaller heart-shaped cutter, stamp out the centres from all the hearts. Place a light-coloured heart in the centre of a larger chocolate heart and vice versa.

6 Bake the cookies for about 10 minutes, or until just beginning to turn brown. Remove from the oven and leave to cool.

7 To decorate, melt the chocolate in a microwave or in a heatproof bowl set over a pan of hot water. Put into a disposable piping (pastry) bag. Leave the chocolate to cool slightly.

8 Snip the end off the piping bag and carefully pipe dots directly onto the outer part of the large chocolate hearts (with the plain centres). Then pipe zigzags on the pale part of the large plain hearts (with the chocolate centres). Put the cookies aside in a cool place and leave until they are set.

Variation
For a tasty variation, make chocolate and orange hearts by kneading 10ml/2 tsp very finely grated orange rind into the plain dough.

Rugelach

Jewish cookies, traditionally served during the eight-day festival of Hanukkah, these little crescents have a spicy fruit-and-nut filling. They can, of course, be enjoyed at any time of the year.

3 Divide the dough into four. Take one piece and leave the rest in the refrigerator, as it is important to keep the dough as cold as possible because it is very sticky and therefore difficult to roll out. Sprinkle a sheet of baking parchment with flour and quickly roll out the dough to a round as thin as possible. Cut into six wedges; sprinkle with a quarter of the filling.

Makes about 24

115g/4oz/½ cup unsalted (sweet) butter,
  chilled and diced
115g/4oz/½ cup cream cheese
120ml/4fl oz/½ cup sour cream
250g/9oz/2¼ cups plain
  (all-purpose) flour
beaten egg, to glaze

For the filling

50g/2oz/¼ cup caster
  (superfine) sugar
10ml/2 tsp ground cinnamon
60ml/4 tbsp raisins, chopped
60ml/4 tbsp ready-to-eat dried
  apricots, chopped
75g/3oz/¾ cup walnuts, finely chopped

1 To make the dough, put the butter, cream cheese and sour cream into a food processor and process until just creamy and combined. Add the flour and process briefly, using the pulse button, until the mixture just comes together, taking care not to overmix. Remove, wrap in clear film (plastic wrap) and chill for at least 6 hours.

2 Preheat the oven to 180°C/350°F/ Gas 4. Line two large baking sheets with baking parchment. To make the filling, put all the filling ingredients in a bowl and mix until thoroughly combined.

4 Starting at the wide end, roll each triangle up towards the point. Curve each roll into a crescent and place, the pointed side down, on the prepared baking sheets. Repeat with the remaining dough and filling.

5 Brush with beaten egg and bake for about 15–20 minutes, or until golden brown. Transfer to a wire rack and leave to cool.

Oznei Haman

These little cookies, shaped like tricorns – three-cornered hats – are eaten at the Jewish feast called Purim, which celebrates the Jews' deliverance from the scheming Haman.

Makes about 20

115g/4oz/½ cup unsalted (sweet) butter,
   at room temperature, diced
115g/4oz/generous ½ cup caster
   (superfine) sugar
2.5ml/½ tsp vanilla essence (extract)
3 egg yolks
250g/9oz/2¼ cups plain (all-purpose) flour
beaten egg to seal and glaze

For the filling

40g/1½oz/3 tbsp poppy seeds
15ml/1 tbsp clear honey
25g/1oz/2 tbsp caster (superfine) sugar
finely grated rind of 1 lemon
15ml/1 tbsp lemon juice
40g/1½oz/⅓ cup ground almonds
1 small (US medium) egg, beaten
25g/1oz/scant ¼ cup raisins

1 Beat the butter with the sugar until light and creamy. Beat in the vanilla and egg yolks. Sift over the flour, stir in, then work into a dough with your hands. Knead until smooth. Wrap in clear film (plastic wrap) and chill.

2 For the filling, put the poppy seeds, honey, sugar, lemon rind and juice into a pan with 60ml/4 tbsp water and bring to the boil, stirring. Remove from the heat and beat in the almonds, egg and raisins. Cool.

3 Preheat the oven to 180°C/350°F/ Gas 4. Line two large baking sheets with baking parchment. Roll out the dough on a lightly floured surface to 3mm/⅛in thickness. Using a plain round 7.5cm/3in cutter, stamp out rounds. Place a heaped teaspoon of filling on each round. Brush the edges with beaten egg, then bring the sides to the centre to form a tricorne shape. Seal the edges well together and place on the prepared baking sheets, spaced slightly apart.

4 Brush with beaten egg and bake for 20–30 minutes, or until golden brown. Transfer to a wire rack and leave to cool.

Hamantashen

These triangular-shaped pastries are eaten at Purim, the Jewish festival celebrating the story of Esther, Mordecai and Haman. Their shape represents the hat of Haman, whose plot to exterminate all the Jews of Persia was foiled. They can be made with a cookie or yeast dough.

Makes about 24

115g/4oz/½ cup unsalted (sweet) butter,
   at room temperature
250g/9oz/generous 1 cup sugar
30ml/2 tbsp milk
1 egg, beaten
5ml/1 tsp vanilla or almond
   essence (extract)
pinch of salt
200–250g/7–9oz/1½–2¼ cups plain
   (all-purpose) flour
icing (confectioners') sugar, for
   dusting (optional)

For the apricot filling

250g/9oz/generous 1 cup dried apricots
1 cinnamon stick
45ml/3 tbsp sugar

For the poppy seed filling

130g/4½oz/1 cup poppy seeds,
   coarsely ground
120ml/4fl oz/½ cup milk
75g/3oz/½ cup sultanas (golden raisins),
   coarsely chopped
45–60ml/3–4 tbsp sugar
30ml/2 tbsp golden (light corn) syrup
5–10ml/1–2 tsp grated lemon rind
5ml/1 tsp vanilla essence (extract)

For the prune filling

250g/9oz/generous 1 cup pitted
   ready-to-eat prunes
hot, freshly brewed tea or water, to cover
60ml/4 tbsp plum jam

Cook's Tip

Every Jewish family has its own favourite filling for this hefty little pastry-cake. Their size can also vary, from small and dainty to the size of a hand.

1 Cream the butter and sugar in a large bowl until pale and fluffy. Mix together the milk, egg, vanilla or almond essence and salt in another bowl. Sift the flour into a third bowl.

2 Beat the butter mixture with one-third of the flour. Gradually add the remaining flour, alternating with the milk mixture. If the dough is too stiff, add a little extra milk. Cover and chill for 1 hour.

3 To make the apricot filling, put the apricots, cinnamon and sugar in a pan and add enough water to cover. Simmer for 15 minutes or until the apricots are tender and most of the liquid has evaporated. Remove the cinnamon stick, then purée the fruit in a food processor or blender with a little of the cooking liquid to the consistency of thick jam.

4 To make the poppy seed filling, put all the ingredients, except the vanilla, in a pan and simmer for 5–10 minutes until the mixture has thickened and most of the milk has been absorbed. Stir in the vanilla.

5 To make the prune filling, put the prunes in a bowl and add enough hot tea or water to cover. Cover and set aside for 30 minutes, or until the prunes have absorbed the liquid. Drain, then purée in a food processor or blender with the jam.

6 Preheat the oven to 180°C/ 350°F/Gas 4. Roll out the dough on a lightly floured surface to 3–5mm/ ⅛–¼in thick. Stamp out 7.5cm/3in rounds with a plain cutter.

7 Place 15–30ml/1–2 tbsp of filling in the centre of each round, then pinch the pastry together to form three corners, leaving a little of the filling showing in the middle.

8 Place the pastries on a baking sheet and bake for 15 minutes, or until pale golden. Serve the pastries warm or cold, dusted with icing sugar, if you like.

Coconut Pyramids

These delightful, moist and chewy coconut cookies are sold in Israeli street markets during Passover, but are also popular in many other countries, too.

Makes 15

225g/8oz/1 cup desiccated (dry unsweetened shredded) coconut
115g/4oz/generous ½ cup caster (superfine) sugar
2 egg whites

1 Preheat the oven to 190°C/375°F/ Gas 5. Grease a large baking sheet with a little oil.

2 Mix together the desiccated coconut and sugar. Lightly whisk the egg whites. Fold enough egg white into the coconut to make a fairly firm mixture. You may not need quite all the egg whites.

3 Form the mixture into pyramids by taking a teaspoonful and rolling it first into a ball. Flatten the base and press the top into a point. Arrange the pyramids on the baking sheet.

4 Bake for 12–15 minutes on a low shelf. The tips should begin to turn golden and the pyramids should be just firm, but still soft inside.

5 Slide a palette knife (metal spatula) underneath to loosen them. Leave to cool, then transfer to a wire rack.

Easter Cookies

These are enjoyed as a traditional part of the Christian festival of Easter. Traditionally, butter could not be eaten during the Lenten fast, so these cookies were a welcome treat.

Makes 16–18

115g/4oz/½ cup butter at room
    temperature, diced
75g/3oz/scant ½ cup caster (superfine)
    sugar, plus extra for sprinkling
1 egg, separated
200g/7oz/1¾ cups plain
    (all-purpose) flour
2.5ml/½ tsp mixed (apple pie) spice
2.5ml/½ tsp ground cinnamon
50g/2oz/¼ cup currants
15ml/1 tbsp chopped mixed
    (candied) peel
15–30ml/1–2 tbsp milk

1 Preheat the oven to 200°C/400°F/ Gas 6. Lightly grease two baking sheets. Beat together the butter and sugar in a bowl until light and fluffy, then beat in the egg yolk.

2 Sift together the flour, mixed spice and cinnamon over the creamed mixture, then, using a metal spoon, gently fold in with the currants and peel, adding sufficient milk to mix to a fairly soft dough.

3 Turn out the dough on to a floured surface, knead lightly until just smooth, then roll out using a floured rolling pin, to about 5mm/ ¼in thick. Stamp the dough into rounds using a 5cm/2in fluted cutter. Carefully transfer the rounds to the prepared baking sheets and bake for 10 minutes.

Cook's Tip
Cinnamon is one of the exceptions to the rule that you should, if possible, buy spices whole and grind them freshly when you need them. Although cinnamon sticks are widely available, they are difficult – almost impossible – to grind yourself.

4 Beat the egg white, then brush over the cookies. Sprinkle with caster sugar and return to the oven for a further 10 minutes, or until golden. Using a metal spatula, transfer to a wire rack to cool.

Kourabiedes

Lightly spiced and delicately flavoured with orange flower water and almonds, these crisp little crescents are perfect for parties and festive occasions such as christenings and weddings.

Makes about 20

115g/4oz/½ cup unsalted (sweet)
   butter, softened
pinch of ground nutmeg
10ml/2 tsp orange flower water
50g/2oz/½ cup icing (confectioners')
   sugar, plus extra for dusting
90g/3½oz/¾ cup plain
   (all-purpose) flour
115g/4oz/1 cup ground almonds
25g/1oz/¼ cup whole almonds, toasted
   and chopped

1 Preheat the oven to 160°C/325°F/ Gas 3. Line two large baking sheets with baking parchment. Beat the butter in a large bowl until soft and creamy.

2 Beat in the nutmeg and orange flower water. Add the icing sugar and beat until fluffy.

3 Add the flour, ground and chopped almonds and mix well, then use your hands to bring the mixture together to form a dough, being careful not to overwork it.

4 Shape pieces of dough into sausages about 7.5cm/3in long. Curve each one into a crescent shape and place, spaced well apart, on the prepared baking sheets. Bake for about 15 minutes, or until firm but still pale in colour. Cool for about 5 minutes, then dust with a little icing sugar.

Spicy Hearts and Stars

These soft, sweet cookies have a wonderfully chewy texture and a deliciously warm, fragrant flavour. Serve with coffee at the end of a festive meal, or make them as a gift on a special occasion.

Makes about 25

115g/4oz/½ cup unsalted (sweet)
  butter, softened
115g/4oz/generous ½ cup light
  muscovado (brown) sugar
1 egg
50g/2oz/1½ tbsp golden
  (light corn) syrup
50g/2oz/1½ tbsp black treacle
  (molasses)
400g/14oz/3½ cups self-raising
  (self-rising) flour
10ml/2 tsp ground ginger

For the toppings

200g/7oz plain (semisweet) or
  milk chocolate
150g/5oz/1¼ cups icing (confectioners')
  sugar, sifted

1 Beat together the butter and sugar until creamy. Beat in the egg, syrup and treacle together. Sift in the flour and ginger and mix to form a firm dough. Chill for 20 minutes. Meanwhile, preheat the oven to 180°C/350°F/Gas 4 and line two large baking sheets with a layer of baking parchment.

2 Roll out the dough on a lightly floured surface to just under 1cm/ ½in thick and use biscuit (cookie) cutters to stamp out heart and star shapes. Place, spaced slightly apart, on the prepared baking sheets and bake for about 10 minutes, or until risen. Cool on a wire rack.

3 To make the toppings, melt the chocolate in a microwave or in a heatproof bowl set over a pan of barely simmering water. Use the melted chocolate to coat the heart-shaped cookies. Put the icing sugar into a bowl and mix with enough warm water to make a coating consistency, then use this to glaze the star-shaped cookies.

Italian Pastry Twists

Deep-fried pastry twists, hearts or knots, traditionally flavoured with vin santo, a sherry-like Italian wine, are served hot, dusted with icing sugar, at Italian carnival time.

Makes 40

250g/9oz/2¼ cups plain
  (all-purpose) flour
1 egg
pinch of salt
25g/1oz/2 tbsp granulated sugar
2.5ml/½ tsp vanilla essence (extract)
25g/1oz/2 tbsp butter, melted
45–60ml/3–4 tbsp sherry
oil, for deep-frying
icing (confectioners') sugar,
  for dusting

1 Sift the flour into a large mixing bowl and make a well in the centre. Add the egg, salt, sugar, vanilla essence and melted butter.

2 Mix with your hands until the mixture starts to come together. When the dough becomes stiff, add enough sherry to make the dough soft and pliable. Knead until smooth and then wrap in clear film (plastic wrap) and chill for about 1 hour.

3 Roll out the pastry thinly on a lightly floured surface and cut into 40 strips each about 18 × 1cm/ 7 × ½in . Tie each strip loosely into a knot.

4 Heat the oil in a pan to 190°C/ 375°F and deep-fry the knots, in batches, for 2–3 minutes, until puffed up and golden.

5 Drain the pastry twists on kitchen paper, dust generously with icing sugar and serve either hot or cold.

Variation
If you prefer the flavour, you could use Marsala instead of sherry.

Cook's Tip
Fry the cookies in flavourless oil, such as vegetable or sunflower.

Apricot Meringue Bars

Whenever you serve them, these unusual meringue-topped cookies make any occasion special. They would be lovely served, Mediterranean style, with a glass of chilled white wine.

Makes 16

50g/2oz/½ cup plain (all-purpose) flour
50g/2oz/¼ cup butter, softened
2.5ml/½ tsp vanilla essence (extract)
large pinch of salt
1 large (US extra large) egg, separated
115g/4oz/generous ½ cup caster
   (superfine) sugar
50g/2oz/½ cup chopped walnuts
50g/2oz/½ cup chopped pecan nuts
115g/4oz/⅓ cup apricot jam

1 Preheat the oven to 180°C/350°F/ Gas 4. Grease a 20cm/9in square baking tin (pan). Beat together the flour, butter, vanilla essence, salt, egg yolk and 50g/2oz/¼ cup of the sugar. Spread the mixture in the base of the baking tin, prick it all over with a fork and bake for 10 minutes.

2 Beat the egg white until stiff. Gradually beat in the remaining sugar until the mixture is smooth and glossy. Gently fold in the chopped walnuts and pecan nuts, but do not over-mix.

3 Remove the tin from the oven, spread the apricot jam over the base and spread the meringue mixture to cover it evenly.

4 Return to the oven and bake for 20 minutes, until the meringue is crisp and light brown. Cool on a wire rack, then cut into bars.

Cook's Tip

Apricot Meringue Bars may be stored in an airtight container for up to 3 days.

Moravian Tarts

These birthday cookies are irresistible when freshly baked, so don't be surprised if there aren't any left over. They need to be thoroughly chilled, so make the dough the day before you need them.

Makes 35

115g/4oz/½ cup unsalted
   (sweet) butter
2.5ml/½ tsp vanilla essence (extract)
large pinch of salt
150g/5oz/¾ cup caster
   (superfine) sugar
1 egg, beaten
115g/4oz/1 cup plain (all-purpose) flour
1.5ml/¼ tsp bicarbonate of soda
   (baking soda)
7.5ml/1½ tsp ground cinnamon
1 egg white, lightly beaten
35 pecan nut halves

1 Cream the butter, vanilla essence, salt and 115g/4oz/½ cup of the sugar until light and fluffy. Gradually add the egg, beating constantly.

2 Sift the flour, bicarbonate of soda and 2.5ml/½ tsp of the cinnamon into another bowl and stir a little at a time into the creamed mixture. Form the mixture into a dough, wrap in clear film (plastic wrap) and chill overnight. Remove from the refrigerator 30 minutes before using.

3 Preheat the oven to 180°C/ 350°F/Gas 4. Lightly grease a baking sheet. Roll out the dough until it is about 3mm/⅛in thick. Stamp out rounds with a 5cm/2in cutter.

4 Place the rounds on the prepared baking sheet and brush the tops with the egg white. Mix the remaining ground cinnamon with the remaining caster sugar. Sprinkle over the rounds and press a pecan nut half into each centre. Bake for 8–10 minutes until golden brown.

Mexican Aniseed Biscochitos

It is time to revive the tradition of baking cookies flavoured with aniseed, as they are absolutely delicious. There are versions of this recipe served at fiestas in many other countries as well.

Makes 24

175g/6oz/1½ cups plain
 (all-purpose) flour
5ml/1 tsp baking powder
pinch of salt
115g/4oz/½ cup unsalted (sweet) butter
 at room temperature, diced
115g/4oz/½ cup caster (superfine) sugar
1 egg
5ml/1 tsp whole aniseed
15ml/1 tbsp brandy
50g/2oz/¼ cup caster (superfine) sugar
 mixed with 2.5ml/½ tsp ground
 cinnamon, for sprinkling

I Sift together the flour, baking powder and salt. Set aside.

2 Beat the butter with the sugar until soft and fluffy. Add the egg, aniseed and brandy and beat until incorporated. Fold in the dry ingredients until just blended to a dough. Chill for 30 minutes.

3 Preheat the oven to 180°C/ 350°F/Gas 4. Lightly grease two baking sheets.

4 On a lightly floured surface, roll out the chilled dough to about 3mm/⅛in thick.

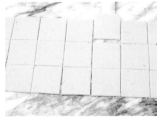

5 With a lightly floured cutter, pastry wheel or knife, stamp out or cut out the dough into squares, diamonds, stars or other shapes. The traditional shape for biscochitos is a fleur-de-lis, but you might find this a little too ambitious.

6 Place the cookies on the prepared baking sheets, spaced apart, and sprinkle lightly with the cinnamon sugar.

7 Bake for about 10 minutes, or until just barely golden. Cool on the baking sheet for 5 minutes before transferring to a wire rack, with a metal spatula, and leave to cool completely. The cookies can be stored in an airtight container for up to 1 week.

Fourth of July Blueberry Softbakes

These are simply wonderful when eaten still warm from the oven. However, they are also good if left to cool and then packed for a traditional Independence Day picnic.

Makes 10

150g/5oz/1¼ cups plain
   (all-purpose) flour
7.5ml/1½ tsp baking powder
5ml/1 tsp ground cinnamon
50g/2oz/¼ cup unsalted (sweet) butter,
   at room temperature, diced
50g/2oz/¼ cup demerara (raw) sugar,
   plus extra for sprinkling
120ml/4fl oz/½ cup sour cream
90g/3½oz/1 cup fresh blueberries
50g/2oz/½ cup semi-dried cranberries

Variation

For Hallowe'en or Thanksgiving, substitute fresh cranberries for the blueberries and chopped preserved stem ginger for the semi-dried cranberries.

1 Preheat the oven to 190°C/375°F/ Gas 5. Line two baking sheets with baking parchment. Sift together the flour, baking powder and cinnamon into a large mixing bowl. Add the diced butter and rub in with your fingers until the mixture resembles fine breadcrumbs. Stir in the demerara sugar.

2 Add the sour cream, blueberries and cranberries and stir until just combined. Spoon ten mounds of the mixture, spaced well apart, on to the prepared baking sheets. Sprinkle with the extra demerara sugar and bake for about 20 minutes, or until golden and firm in the centre. Serve warm.

Cinnamon Balls

These almond balls should be soft inside, with a strong cinnamon flavour. Great for parties, they also harden with keeping, so it is a good idea to freeze some and use them when required.

Makes 16

oil, for greasing
175g/6oz/1½ cups ground almonds
75g/3oz/scant ½ cup caster
  (superfine) sugar
15ml/1 tbsp ground cinnamon
2 egg whites
icing (confectioners') sugar, for dredging

1 Preheat the oven to 180°C/350°F/ Gas 4. Oil a large baking sheet. Mix together the ground almonds, sugar and cinnamon. Whisk the egg whites in a grease-free bowl until they begin to stiffen and fold enough into the almonds and sugar to make a fairly firm mixture.

2 Dampen your hands and roll small spoonfuls of the mixture into balls. Place on the baking sheet and bake for about 15 minutes.

3 Slide a metal spatula under the balls to release them from the baking sheet and leave to cool.

4 Sift a few tablespoonfuls of icing sugar on to a plate. When the cinnamon balls are completely cold slide them on to the plate. Roll the cinnamon balls gently over the plate to cover completely in sugar. Store in an airtight container or in the freezer.

Baklava

This, the queen of all pastries, is enjoyed all year but is specially associated with the Persian New Year on 21 March, celebrating the first day of spring. Leave the baklava to cool in the tin.

Makes about 30

350g/12oz/3 cups ground pistachio nuts
150g/5oz/1¼ cups icing
   (confectioners') sugar
15ml/1 tbsp ground cardamom
150g/5oz/⅔ cup unsalted (sweet)
   butter, melted
450g/1lb filo pastry

For the syrup

450g/1lb/2 cups granulated sugar
300ml/½ pint/1¼ cups water
30ml/2 tbsp rose water

Variation

Baklava may also be made with flaked (sliced) almonds and drizzled with honey instead of syrup.

1 To make the syrup, place the sugar and water in a pan, bring them to the boil and simmer for 10 minutes, until syrupy. Stir in the rose water. Mix together the nuts, icing sugar and cardamom. Preheat the oven to 160°C/325°F/Gas 3. Brush a baking tin (pan) with butter.

2 Taking one sheet of filo pastry at a time, and keeping the remainder covered with a damp cloth, brush with melted butter and lay in the base of the tin. Continue until you have six buttered layers in the tin. Spread half of the nut mixture over, pressing down with a spoon.

3 Take another six sheets of filo pastry, brush with butter and lay over the nut mixture. Sprinkle over the remaining nuts and top with a final layer of six filo sheets.

4 Cut the pastry into small lozenge shapes. Pour the remaining butter over the top. Bake for 20 minutes, increase the heat to 200°C/400°F/Gas 6 and bake for 15 minutes. Drizzle most of the syrup over the pastry, reserving the rest for serving.

Persian Rice Flour Cookies

These prettily decorated cookies are traditionally served on special occasions with black tea. However, they taste as good with coffee or even a glass of chilled dry white wine.

Makes about 22

75g/3oz/⅔ cup icing (confectioners')
sugar, sifted
225g/8oz/1 cup unsalted (sweet)
butter, softened
300g/10oz/2½ cups rice flour
75g/3oz/⅔ cup self-raising
(self-rising) flour
1 egg yolk
15ml/1 tbsp rose water

For the topping

150g/5oz/1¼ cups icing (confectioners')
sugar, sifted
rose water
pink food colouring
crystallized rose petals or violets
or pink sugar balls or
sugar vermicelli

1 Mix together the sugar, butter, flours, egg yolk and rose water and gather into a ball. Wrap and chill. Meanwhile, preheat the oven to 160°C/325°F/Gas 3. Line two baking sheets with baking parchment.

2 Shape the mixture into balls. Place well apart on the prepared baking sheets and flatten each one slightly.

3 Bake for 15–20 minutes until firm but still quite pale in colour. Leave to cool completely on the baking sheets.

4 To make the topping, put the icing sugar into a bowl and add just enough rose water to mix to a thick, flowing consistency. Add just a light touch of pink food colouring to make a very pale shade.

5 Drizzle the icing in random squiggles and circles over all the cookies. Place a few crystallized rose petals or violets or pink sugar balls on top, or sprinkle with a little sugar vermicelli. Leave to set completely before serving the cookies.

Neuris

These melt-in-the-mouth sweet and spicy samosas are traditionally eaten during the Hindu festival of Diwali and are also given as little gifts to friends and family at this time.

Makes 12

75g/3oz/1 cup desiccated (dry
   unsweetened shredded) coconut
50g/2oz/¼ cup light muscovado
   (brown) sugar
25g/1oz/¼ cup cashew nuts, chopped
50g/2oz/⅓ cup seedless raisins
250ml/8fl oz/1 cup evaporated
   (unsweetened condensed) milk
large pinch grated nutmeg
2.5ml/½ tsp ground cinnamon
12 sheets filo pastry, about 28 x 18cm/
   11 x 7in each
sunflower oil, for brushing

For the topping

15ml/1 tbsp evaporated (unsweetened
   condensed) milk
15ml/1 tbsp caster (superfine) sugar
desiccated coconut

1 To make the filling, put the coconut, muscovado sugar, cashews, raisins and evaporated milk into a small pan. Bring to the boil, stirring occasionally. Reduce the heat to very low and cook for about 10 minutes, stirring, until the milk has been absorbed. Stir in the nutmeg and cinnamon, then set aside to cool.

2 Preheat the oven to 180°C/350°F/ Gas 4. Line two baking sheets with baking parchment.

3 Brush one sheet of filo pastry with a little sunflower oil. Fold the sheet in half lengthways, then brush with more oil and fold widthways. Brush the edges of the folded pastry with water.

4 Place a spoonful of the cooled filling on one half of the folded pastry sheet. Fold the other half of the sheet over the filling, then press together the edges to seal. Trim off the rough edges and place on the baking sheet. Continue making neuris in this way until all the pastry and filling has been used up.

5 To make the topping, put the evaporated milk and sugar into a small pan and heat gently, stirring constantly until the sugar has completely dissolved.

6 Brush the topping over the neuris and sprinkle them with the coconut. Bake for about 20 minutes, until crisp and golden brown. Transfer to a wire rack and leave to cool before serving.

Jewelled Elephants

These delightful, stunningly robed elephants make a lovely gift for young animal-lovers, or make a perfect edible decoration for a special occasion. If you make holes in them before baking, you could use them as original Christmas tree decorations.

Makes 10

1 quantity Lebkuchen mixture
1 quantity icing glaze
red food colouring
225g/8oz ready-to-roll sugar paste
a little royal icing
small candy-covered chocolates or chews
gold dragees

1 Preheat the oven to 180°C/ 350°F/Gas 4. Grease two large baking sheets.

2 Make a paper template for the elephant. Roll out the lebkuchen mixture. Use the template and a sharp knife to cut out elephant shapes. Space them, slightly apart, on the baking sheet and bake for 3 minutes. Then transfer the elephants to a wire rack to cool.

3 Put a little icing glaze in a greaseproof (waxed) paper piping (pastry) bag fitted with a fine nozzle. Alternatively, cut off the tip of the bag.

4 Knead some red food colouring into half of the sugar paste. Roll a little red sugar paste on a work surface with your fingertips to make ropes. Secure them around the feet and tips of the trunks, using icing from the bag. Shape more red sugar paste into flat oval shapes, about 2cm/¾in long, and stick them to the elephants' heads. Shape smaller ovals and secure them at the top of the trunks with icing glaze.

5 Roll out the white sugar paste. Stamp out rounds, using a 6cm/ 2½in cookie cutter. Secure to the elephants' backs with royal icing so that the edge of the sugar paste is about 2.5cm/1in above the top of the legs. Trim off the excess paste around the top of the white sugar paste shapes.

6 Pipe 1cm/½in tassels around the edges of the flat ovals. Pipe dots of white icing at the tops of the elephants' trunks, around their necks and at the tops of their tails and also use it to draw small eyes. Halve the small sweets (candies) and press them into the sugar paste, above the tassels. Decorate the headdress, sweets and white sugar paste with gold dragees, securing them with dots of icing. Leave for several hours to harden.

Variation
If you have the time and you want to make these charming cookies even more special, you could colour the sugar paste for their decorations in a variety of brilliant, jewel-like colours, so that each one is different.

Cook's Tip
If you are artistic, you can draw the elephant template freehand. Otherwise, you could trace around a picture. If you cannot find a picture the right size, enlarge or reduce it on a photocopier and then trace around it.

Almond Cigars

These simple, Moroccan-inspired pastries can be prepared in minutes. They are perfect served with strong black coffee or as an after-dinner treat and are great with sweet Moroccan mint tea.

Makes 8–12
250g/9oz/1⅓ cups marzipan
1 egg, lightly beaten
8–12 sheets filo pastry
melted butter, for brushing

1 Knead the marzipan until soft and pliable, then put it in a mixing bowl and mix in the lightly beaten egg. Cover and chill in the refrigerator for 1–2 hours.

2 Preheat the oven to 190°C/375°F/Gas 5. Lightly grease a baking sheet. Place a sheet of filo pastry on a piece of greaseproof (waxed) paper, keeping the remaining pastry covered with a damp cloth. Brush the first sheet of filo with some of the melted butter.

3 Shape 30–45ml/2–3 tbsp of the almond paste into a cylinder and place at one end of the pastry. Fold the pastry over to enclose the ends of the paste, then roll up to form a cigar shape. Place on the baking sheet and make 7–11 more cigars in the same way.

4 Bake the pastries for about 15 minutes, or until golden brown in colour. Transfer to a wire rack to cool before serving.

Variation
Similar pastries are made throughout North Africa. In Tunisia, they are coated in syrup and sesame seeds after baking. To make the syrup, heat 150g/5oz/⅔ cup sugar with 300ml/½ pint/1¼ cups water, stirring until dissolved. Add 15ml/1 tbsp lemon juice, bring to the boil and boil until syrupy. Remove from the heat and stir in 15ml/1 tbsp orange flower water. Soak the cigars in the hot syrup for 2–3 minutes, then sprinkle with sesame seeds. Cool before serving.

Honey and Nut Clusters

These are popular at all family celebrations in Italy. To serve, cut in squares or small bars and keep in the refrigerator. They are delightfully sticky and taste fabulous.

Makes 48

115g/4oz/1 cup almonds
115g/4oz/1 cup shelled hazelnuts
2 egg whites
115g/4oz/½ cup clear honey
115g/4oz/generous ½ cup caster
   (superfine) sugar

1 Preheat the oven to the lowest temperature. Line a 20cm/8in square tin (pan) with non-stick baking parchment.

2 Spread out the almonds and hazelnuts on separate baking sheets and toast in the oven for about 30 minutes. Tip on to a clean dishtowel and rub off the skins. Coarsely chop both types of nut.

3 Whisk the egg whites in a clean bowl until stiff, then gently stir in the chopped nuts.

4 Put the honey and sugar into a small, heavy pan and bring to the boil. Stir in the nut mixture and cook over a medium heat for 10 minutes.

5 Turn the mixture into the tin and level the top. Cover with another piece of baking parchment, put weights (such as food cans) on top and chill for at least 2 days.

Cook's Tip

If you like, you can use blanched almonds, so you don't have to rub off their skins. They will still taste more intense if toasted in the oven first.

Christmas Tree Angels

Why not make these charming edible decorations to brighten your Yuletide? However, don't hang them on the tree until Christmas Eve or they'll all be gone by Christmas Day.

Makes 20–30

90g/3½oz/scant ½ cup demerara
  (raw) sugar
200g/7oz/scant1 cup golden
  (light corn) syrup
5ml/1 tsp ground ginger
5ml/1 tsp ground cinnamon
1.5ml/¼ tsp ground cloves
115g/4oz/½ cup unsalted (sweet) butter,
  cut into pieces
10ml/2 tsp bicarbonate of soda
  (baking soda)
1 egg, beaten
500g/1¼lb/4½ cups plain (all-purpose)
  flour, sifted

For the decoration

1 egg white
175–225g/6–8oz/1½–2 cups icing
  (confectioners') sugar, sifted
silver and gold balls
fine ribbon

1 Preheat the oven to 160°C/325°F/ Gas 3. Line two large baking sheets with baking parchment. Put the sugar, syrup, ginger, cinnamon and cloves into a heavy pan and bring to the boil over a low heat, stirring constantly. Once the mixture has boiled, remove the pan from the heat.

2 Put the pieces of butter in a large heatproof bowl and pour over the hot sugar and syrup mixture. Add the bicarbonate of soda and stir well until the butter has completely melted. Beat the egg into the mixture, then stir in the flour. Mix thoroughly and then knead to form a smooth dough.

3 Divide the dough into four pieces and roll out, one at a time, between sheets of baking parchment, to a thickness of about 3mm/⅛in. Keep the unrolled dough in a plastic bag until needed to prevent it from drying out. Stamp out festive shapes, such as Christmas trees, using biscuit (cookie) cutters, or make angels, as follows.

4 To make simple angels, stamp out rounds of dough of any size you like, using a plain cutter. Don't make them too big or they might be too heavy to hang on the Christmas tree. As shown in the photograph, cut off two segments from either side of the round to give a body and two wings. Place the wings, rounded side facing down, behind the body and press lightly together with your fingers.

5 Roll a small piece of dough for the head, place at the top of the body and flatten with your fingers. Using a skewer, make a wide hole in the cookies through which ribbon can be threaded when they are cooked. Place on the baking sheets. Bake the cookies for 10–15 minutes until golden brown. Transfer to a wire rack to cool.

6 To make the decoration, beat the egg white with a fork. Whisk in icing sugar until you have an icing of soft-peak consistency.

7 Put the icing in a piping (pastry) bag fitted with a plain writing nozzle and decorate the cookies with simple designs. Add silver and gold balls before the icing has set. Finally, thread fine ribbon through the holes in the cookies.

Brandy Snaps

Eat these on high days and holidays as an indulgent treat. They look incredibly tempting and are very easy to make, so long as you work quickly and in small batches.

Makes 18
50g/2oz/¼ cup butter
150g/5oz/⅔ cup caster
   (superfine) sugar
7.5ml/1½ tbsp golden (corn) syrup
40g/1½oz/⅓ cup plain (all-purpose) flour
2.5ml/½ tsp ground ginger

For the filling
250ml/8fl oz/1 cup whipping cream
30ml/2 tbsp brandy

1 With an electric mixer, cream together the butter and sugar until light and fluffy, then beat in the golden syrup. Sift over the flour and ginger and mix to a coarse dough.

2 Transfer the dough to a lightly floured work surface and knead until smooth. Cover with clear film (plastic wrap) and chill in the refrigerator for 30 minutes. Preheat the oven to 190°C/375°F/Gas 5. Grease a baking sheet.

3 Working in batches of four, form walnut-size balls of dough. Place well apart on the prepared baking sheet and flatten slightly. Bake for about 10 minutes, until golden.

4 Remove from the oven and leave to cool for a few moments. Working quickly, slide a metal spatula under each cookie, turn over, and wrap around the handle of a wooden spoon. When firm, slide off the snaps and place on a wire rack to cool completely.

5 To make the filling, whip the cream and brandy together with a hand-held electric mixer until soft peaks form. Spoon the flavoured cream into a piping (pastry) bag fitted with a star nozzle and pipe into each end of the brandy snaps just before serving.

Glazed Ginger Cookies

These also make good hanging cookies for decorating trees and garlands. For this, make a hole in each one with a skewer and thread with fine ribbon.

Makes about 20

1 quantity Golden Gingerbread mixture
2 quantities Icing Glaze
red and green food colourings
175g/6oz white almond paste

1 Preheat the oven to 180°C/ 350°F/Gas 4. Grease a large baking sheet. Roll out the gingerbread dough on a floured surface and, using a selection of floured cutters, cut out a variety of shapes, such as trees, stars, crescents and bells. Transfer to the prepared baking sheet and bake for 8–10 minutes, until just beginning to colour around the edges. Leave the cookies on the baking sheet for 3 minutes.

2 Transfer the cookies to a wire rack and leave to cool completely. Place the wire rack over a large tray or plate. Using a dessertspoon, spoon the icing glaze over the cookies until they are completely covered. Leave in a cool place to dry for several hours.

3 Knead red food colouring into half of the almond paste and green into the other half. Roll a thin length of each coloured paste and then twist the two together into a rope.

4 Secure a rope of almond paste around a cookie, dampening the icing with a little water, if necessary, to hold it in place. Repeat on about half of the cookies. Dilute a little of each food colouring with water. Using a fine paintbrush, paint festive decorations over the plain cookies. Leave to dry completely and then wrap in tissue paper to give as a gift or store in an airtight container until required.

Decorated Chocolate Lebkuchen

Wrapped in paper or cellophane, or beautifully boxed, these decorated cookies make a lovely Christmas present. Don't make them too far in advance as the chocolate will gradually discolour.

Makes 40

1 quantity Lebkuchen mixture
* (see Chocolate Fruit and Nut Cookies)*
115g/4oz plain (semisweet)
* chocolate, chopped*
115g/4oz milk chocolate, chopped
115g/4oz white chocolate, chopped
chocolate vermicelli, for sprinkling
(unsweetened) cocoa powder or icing
* (confectioners') sugar, for dusting*

Variation

Traditionally, Lebkuchen contains other spices as well as ginger and cloves – star anise, cinnamon, nutmeg and black pepper, so you can add a pinch of each of these, to the basic mixture if you like. The treacle (molasses) can also be replaced by clear honey.

1 Grease two baking sheets. Roll out just over half the Lebkuchen mixture to 5mm/¼in thick. Stamp out 20 heart shapes with a 4.5cm/1¾in heart-shaped cutter. Transfer to one of the prepared baking sheets. Gather the trimmings together with the remaining dough and cut into 20 pieces. Roll into balls and place on the second baking sheet. Flatten each ball slightly with your fingers.

2 Chill both sheets for 30 minutes. Preheat the oven to 180°C/350°F/Gas 4. Bake for 8–10 minutes. Cool on a wire rack.

3 Melt the plain chocolate in a heatproof bowl set over a small pan of hot water. Melt the milk and white chocolate, in turn, in separate bowls over hot water.

4 Make three small paper piping (pastry) bags out of greaseproof (waxed) paper. Spoon a little of each chocolate into the three paper piping bags.

5 Spoon a little plain chocolate over one-third of the cookies, spreading it to cover completely.

Cook's Tip

If the chocolate in the bowls starts to set before you have finished decorating, put the bowls back over the heat for about 1–2 minutes. If the chocolate in the piping bags starts to harden, microwave briefly or put in a clean bowl over a pan of simmering water until soft.

6 Snip the merest tip from the bag of white chocolate and drizzle it over some of the coated cookies, to give a decorative zig-zag finish.

7 Sprinkle the chocolate vermicelli over the plain chocolate-coated cookies that have not been decorated. Coat the remaining cookies with the melted milk and white chocolate and decorate some of these with more chocolate from the piping bags, contrasting the colours. Sprinkle more undecorated cookies with vermicelli. Leave the cookies to set.

8 Transfer the undecorated cookies to a plate or tray and dust lightly with sifted cocoa powder or icing sugar.

Christmas Cookies

You don't have to be a talented artist to produce these little edible masterpieces. They are amazingly easy to make and decorate. Use whatever shape of cutter you have to hand.

Makes 30

175g/6oz/¾ cup unsalted (sweet) butter
    at room temperature, diced
300g/11oz/generous 1½ cups caster
    (superfine) sugar
1 egg
1 egg yolk
5ml/1 tsp vanilla essence (extract)
grated rind of 1 lemon
pinch of salt
300g/11oz/2⅔ cups plain
    (all-purpose) flour

For the decoration (optional)

coloured glacé icing and small sweets
    (candies) such as silver balls and
    coloured sugar crystals

1 Preheat the oven to 190°C/375°F/ Gas 5. With an electric mixer, cream the butter until soft. Add the sugar gradually and continue beating until light and fluffy.

2 Gradually stir in the egg and egg yolk. Add the vanilla essence, lemon rind and salt. Stir to mix well.

3 Sift the flour over the mixture and stir to blend. Gather the dough into a ball, wrap in clear film (plastic wrap) and chill for 30 minutes.

4 On a lightly-floured surface, roll out the dough until about 3mm/ ⅛in thick.

5 Stamp out shapes or rounds with floured cutters and place on a non-stick baking sheet.

6 Bake for about 8 minutes, until lightly coloured. Transfer to a wire rack and leave to cool completely before decorating, if you like, with icing and sweets.

Jewelled Christmas Trees

These attractive and unusual cookies make an appealing gift. They look wonderful hung on a Christmas tree or in front of a window where they will catch the light.

Makes 12

175g/6oz/1½ cups plain
  (all-purpose) flour
75g/3oz/6 tbsp butter, diced
40g/1½oz/3 tbsp caster
  (superfine) sugar
1 egg white
30ml/2 tbsp orange juice
225g/8oz coloured fruit sweets (candies)
coloured ribbons, to decorate

1 Preheat the oven to 180°C/350°F/ Gas 4. Line two baking sheets with non-stick baking parchment. Sift the flour into a mixing bowl.

2 Add the butter and rub it into the flour with your fingertips until the mixture resembles fine breadcrumbs. Stir in the sugar, egg white and enough orange juice to form a soft dough. Knead on a lightly floured surface until smooth.

3 Roll out thinly and stamp out as many shapes as possible using a floured Christmas tree cutter. Transfer the shapes to the baking sheets, spacing them well apart. Knead the trimmings together, cover and set aside or if there is still room on the baking sheets, stamp out more trees.

4 Using a 1cm/½in round cookie cutter or the end of a large plain piping nozzle, stamp out and remove six rounds from each tree shape. Cut each sweet into three and place a piece in each hole. Make a small hole at the top of each tree to thread through the ribbon.

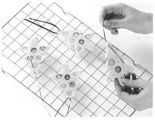

5 Bake for 15–20 minutes, until the cookies are golden and the sweets have melted and filled the holes. Cool on the baking sheets. Repeat until you have used up the rest of the dough and sweets. Thread short lengths of ribbon through the holes so that the cookies can be hung up.

Speculaas

These Dutch cookies are made from a spicy dough wrapped around a wonderfully rich marzipan filling. They are eaten in Holland around the Feast of St Nicholas on 6 December.

Makes about 35

175g/6oz/1½ cups ground hazelnuts
175g/6oz/1½ cups ground almonds
175g/6oz/scant 1 cup caster (superfine) sugar
175g/6oz/1½ cups icing (confectioners') sugar
1 egg, beaten
10–15ml/2–3 tsp lemon juice
250g/9oz/2¼ cups self-raising (self-rising) flour
5ml/1 tsp mixed (apple pie) spice
75g/3oz/⅓ cup light muscovado (brown) sugar
115g/4oz/½ cup unsalted (sweet) butter, at room temperature, diced
2 eggs
15ml/1 tbsp milk
15ml/1 tbsp caster (superfine) sugar
about 35 blanched almond halves

1 For the filling, put the ground hazelnuts, almonds, caster sugar, icing sugar, beaten egg and 10ml/2 tsp lemon juice in a bowl and mix to a firm paste, adding more lemon juice if needed. Divide the mixture in half and roll each piece into a sausage shape about 25cm/10in long. Wrap in clear film (plastic wrap) and chill in the refrigerator.

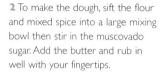

2 To make the dough, sift the flour and mixed spice into a large mixing bowl then stir in the muscovado sugar. Add the butter and rub in well with your fingertips.

3 Beat one of the eggs, add to the mixture and mix together to form a dough. Knead lightly, then wrap in clear film and chill in the refrigerator for 15 minutes. Meanwhile, preheat the oven to 180°C/350°F/Gas 4 and line a large baking sheet with baking parchment.

4 Roll out the pastry on a lightly floured surface to a 30cm/12in square and cut in half to make two equal rectangles. Beat the remaining egg and brush some all over the pastry rectangles.

5 Place a roll of filling on each piece of pastry and roll the pastry to enclose the filling. Place, join side down, on the baking sheet.

6 Beat the remains of the egg with the milk and caster sugar and brush over the rolls. Press almond halves along the top. Bake for 35 minutes until golden brown. Leave to cool before cutting diagonally into slices.

Chinese Fortune Cookies

Whether you're a rabbit or a dragon, a snake or a tiger, these charming cookies are sure to delight and are a wonderful way to celebrate the **Chinese New Year** with family and friends.

Makes about 35

2 egg whites
50g/2oz/½ cup icing (confectioners')
    sugar, sifted, plus extra for dusting
5ml/1 tsp almond or vanilla
    essence (extract)
25g/1oz/2 tbsp unsalted (sweet)
    butter, melted
50g/2oz/½ cup plain (all-purpose) flour
25g/1oz/⅓ cup desiccated (dry
    unsweetened shredded) coconut,
    lightly toasted
tiny strips of paper with "good luck",
    "health, wealth and happiness" and
    other appropriate messages typed or
    written on them, to decorate

1 Preheat the oven to 190°C/375°F/ Gas 5. Prepare two or three sheets of baking parchment (they can be used more than once) by cutting them to the size of a baking sheet. Draw two or three circles of about 7.5cm/3in diameter, with a little distance between them, on each sheet of parchment. Place one of these sheets of parchment on the baking sheet and set aside.

2 Put the egg whites into a clean, grease-free bowl and whisk until foamy and white. Whisk in the icing sugar, a little at a time. Beat in the almond or vanilla essence and the butter. Stir in the flour and mix lightly until smooth.

Cook's Tip

You need to work quickly to shape the cookies. Placing the hot cookies on the rim of wine glasses sets them with a curve in the centre.

3 Place a teaspoonful of mixture into the centre of each marked circle on the prepared parchment and spread out evenly to fit the circle. Sprinkle with a little coconut. Bake one sheet at a time (as you will only have enough time to shape one sheetful of cookies before they set) for about 5 minutes, or until very lightly brown on the edges.

4 Remove the cookies from the oven, immediately loosely fold in half and place on the rim of a glass. Leave until firm, then transfer to a wire rack. Continue baking one sheet of cookies at a time.

5 Tuck the messages into the side of each cookie. Dust very lightly with icing sugar before serving.

Kids' Party Pieces

There's nothing quite like an extra-special cookie to make a kids' party go with a swing. This chapter is packed with fun ideas that kids will love, including cookie bracelets to slip around the wrist, novelty cookies that look like mini pizzas or a giant birthday cookie studded with candles to take the place of the more traditional birthday cake.

Gingerbread Jungle

These snappy biscuits in animal shapes are always popular at birthday parties and on picnics. Children will love helping to make and ice them.

Makes 14

175g/6oz/1½ cups self-raising (self-rising) flour
2.5ml/½ tsp bicarbonate of soda (baking soda)
2.5ml/½ tsp ground cinnamon
10ml/2 tsp caster (superfine) sugar
50g/2oz/¼ cup butter
45ml/3 tbsp golden (light corn) syrup
50g/2oz/½ cup icing (confectioners') sugar
5–10ml/1–2 tsp water

1 Preheat the oven to 190°C/375°F/Gas 5. Lightly oil two large baking sheets.

2 Put the flour, bicarbonate of soda, cinnamon and caster sugar in a bowl and mix together.

3 Place the butter and syrup in a pan and melt over a low heat, stirring occasionally. Pour over the dry ingredients.

4 Mix together well with a wooden spoon and then use your hands to pull the mixture together to make a smooth dough.

5 Turn the mixture out on to a lightly floured surface and roll out to about 5mm/¼in thick.

6 Use lightly-floured animal cutters to stamp out shapes from the cookie dough. Arrange them on the prepared baking sheets, leaving enough room between the cookies to allow space for them to rise.

7 Press the trimmings back into a ball, roll it out again and stamp out more animal shapes. Continue until all the dough has been used. Bake the cookies for 8–12 minutes, until lightly browned.

8 Leave on the baking sheets to cool slightly, before carefully transferring to a wire rack with a palette knife or metal spatula to cool completely.

9 Sift the icing sugar into a small bowl and add enough water to make a fairly soft icing, stirring well to mix smoothly.

10 Spoon the icing into a piping (pastry) bag fitted with a small, plain nozzle and pipe decorations on the cookies. Leave to set before serving.

Cook's Tip
You don't have to be especially artistic to decorate the cookies. It is simple to pipe a letter of the alphabet, for example, which could be either the initial of each child's name or that of the type of animal – L for lion, E for elephant and so on. If you like, mix a little liquid edible food colouring with the icing.

Variation
Any cutters can be used with the same mixture. Obviously, the smaller the cutters, the more cookies you will make.

Gingerbread Teddies

These endearing teddies, dressed in striped pyjamas, would make a perfect gift for friends of any age. If you can't get a large cutter, make smaller teddies or use a traditional gingerbread-man cutter. Children love to help make them, but might need a hand with the decorating.

Makes 6

75g/3oz white chocolate, chopped
175g/6oz ready-to-roll white sugar paste
blue food colouring
25g/1oz plain (semisweet) or
  milk chocolate

For the gingerbread

175g/6oz/1½ cups plain
  (all-purpose) flour
1.5ml/¼ tsp bicarbonate of soda
  (baking soda)
pinch of salt
5ml/1 tsp ground ginger
5ml/1 tsp ground cinnamon
65g/2½oz/⅓ cup unsalted (sweet)
  butter, diced
75g/3oz/scant ½ cup caster
  (superfine) sugar
30ml/2 tbsp maple or golden (light
  corn) syrup
1 egg yolk, beaten

1 To make the gingerbread, sift together the flour, bicarbonate of soda, salt, ginger and cinnamon into a large bowl. Add the butter and rub it into the flour with your fingertips until the mixture resembles fine breadcrumbs.

2 Stir in the sugar, syrup and egg yolk and mix to a firm dough with a wooden spoon. Knead lightly on a floured surface. Wrap in clear film (plastic wrap) and chill in the refrigerator for 30 minutes.

3 Preheat the oven to 180°C/ 350°F/Gas 4. Grease two large baking sheets.

4 Unwrap the gingerbread dough and roll out on a floured surface, then stamp out teddies, using a floured 13cm/5in shaped cutter.

5 Carefully transfer the teddies to the prepared baking sheets and bake for 10–15 minutes until just beginning to colour around the edges. Leave on the baking sheets for 3 minutes, then transfer to a wire rack to cool.

6 Melt half the white chocolate in a heatproof bowl set over a pan of hot water. Spoon the melted chocolate into a paper piping (pastry) bag and snip off the tip. Make a neat template for the teddies' clothes: draw an outline of the cutter on to paper, finishing at the neck, halfway down the arms and around the legs.

7 Thinly roll the sugar paste on a surface dusted with icing sugar. Use the template to cut out the clothes, and secure them to the cookies with the melted chocolate.

8 Use the sugar paste trimmings to add ears, eyes and snouts.

9 Dilute the blue colouring with a little water and use to paint the striped pyjamas using a fine-tipped paint brush.

10 Melt the remaining white chocolate and the plain or milk chocolate in separate heatproof bowls set over pans of hot water. Put in separate paper piping bags and snip off the tips. Use the white chocolate to pipe a decorative outline around the pyjamas and use the plain or milk chocolate to pipe the teddies' faces.

Gingerbread House Cookies

For a party of young children, these gingerbread house cookies provide plenty of entertainment. You could incorporate a house decorating session as one of the party games, allowing the children to design their own houses and take them home after the party.

Makes 10

115g/4oz/½ cup unsalted (sweet)
   butter, at room temperature, diced
115g/4oz/generous ½ cup light
   muscovado (brown) sugar
1 egg
115g/4oz/scant ⅓ cup black treacle
   (molasses) or golden (light corn) syrup
400g/14oz/3½ cups self-raising
   (self-rising) flour
5ml/1 tsp ground ginger (optional)

For the decoration

1 tube white decorating icing
1 tube pastel-coloured decorating icing
selection of small multi-coloured sweets
   (candies), sugar flowers and silver balls

1 Put the butter and sugar in a large bowl and beat together until pale and creamy. Beat in the egg and treacle or syrup, then add the flour and ginger, if using. Mix together to make a thick paste.

2 Turn the mixture on to a lightly floured surface and knead until smooth. Wrap in clear film (plastic wrap) and chill for 30 minutes.

3 Preheat the oven to 180°C/350°F/Gas 4. Grease three baking sheets. On a piece of cardboard, draw an 11 x 8cm/4¼ x 3¼in rectangle. Add a pitched roof. Cut out the shape to use as a template.

4 Roll out the dough on a lightly floured surface. (It might be easier to roll out half the quantity of dough at a time.)

5 Using the template, cut out house shapes. Transfer to the baking sheets and re-roll the trimmings to make more. Bake for 12–15 minutes until risen and golden. Transfer the cookies to a wire rack to cool.

6 Use the icing in the tubes to pipe roof tiles, window and door frames and other decorative touches. Secure sweets and decorations to finish, cutting them into smaller pieces if preferred.

Secret Message Cookies

These fortune cookies are light and wafery, and what they lack in substance, they certainly make up for in their fun factor. These are great for older kids who can prepare birthday messages, jokes or predictions to tuck into the cookies as soon as they're baked.

Makes 18

3 egg whites
50g/2oz/⅓ cup icing
  (confectioners') sugar
40g/1½oz/3 tbsp unsalted (sweet)
  butter, melted
50g/2oz/½ cup plain (all-purpose) flour

1 Preheat the oven to 200°C/400°F/ Gas 6. Line two baking sheets with baking parchment and grease. Cut a piece of paper into 18 small strips, measuring 6 × 2cm/2½ × ¾in. Write a message on each one.

2 Lightly whisk the egg whites and icing sugar until the whites are broken up. Add the melted butter and flour and beat until smooth.

3 Using a 10ml/2 tsp measure, spoon a little of the paste on to one baking sheet and spread to a 7.5cm/3in round with the back of a spoon. Add two more spoonfuls of mixture to the baking sheet and shape in the same way.

4 Bake for 6 minutes until the cookies are golden. Meanwhile, prepare three more cookies on the second baking sheet.

5 Remove the first batch of cookies from the oven and replace with the second batch.

6 Working quickly, peel a hot cookie from the paper and fold it in half, tucking a message inside the fold. Rest the cookie over the rim of a glass or bowl and, very gently, fold again. (It probably won't fold over completely.) Fold the remaining two cookies in the same way.

7 Continue to bake and shape the remaining cookies in the same way until all the batter and messages have been used.

Cook's Tips
• *The secret to success is to spread the batter as thinly as possible on the paper. This will give a really crisp, light result.*
• *Don't be tempted to bake more than three cookies at once or they'll harden before you can shape them.*

Giant Birthday Cookie

This enormous cookie is one for cookie-lovers of any age. Complete with candles, it makes the perfect party centrepiece. To personalize the cookie, write the recipient's name on top in icing.

Makes one 28cm/11in cookie

175g/6oz/¾ cup unsalted
  (sweet) butter, at room
  temperature, diced
125g/4¼oz/⅔ cup light muscovado
  (brown) sugar
1 egg yolk
175g/6oz/1½ cups plain
  (all-purpose) flour
5ml/1 tsp bicarbonate of soda
  (baking soda)
finely grated rind of 1 orange
  or lemon
75g/3oz/scant 1 cup rolled oats

For the decoration

125g/4¼oz/generous ½ cup
  cream cheese
225g/8oz/2 cups icing
  (confectioners') sugar
5–10ml/1–2 tsp lemon juice
birthday candles
white and milk chocolate-coated
  raisins or peanuts
cocoa powder, for dusting
gold or silver balls, for sprinkling

1 Preheat the oven to 190°C/375°F/ Gas 5. Grease a 28cm/11in metal flan tin (tart pan) and place on a large baking sheet.

2 Put the diced butter and the sugar in a large bowl and beat together until pale and creamy.

3 Add the egg yolk to the butter and sugar mixture and stir well to mix. Add the flour, bicarbonate of soda, grated orange or lemon rind and rolled oats and stir thoroughly until evenly combined.

4 Turn the mixture into the tin and flatten with a wet wooden spoon.

5 Bake for 15–20 minutes until risen and golden. Leave to cool in the tin. (If any of the mixture has seeped under the ring during baking, trim it off with a knife while still warm.)

6 Carefully slide the cookie from the tin on to a large, flat serving plate or board.

7 To decorate, beat the cream cheese in a bowl, then add the icing sugar and 5ml/1 tsp of the lemon juice. Beat until smooth and peaking, adding more juice if required.

8 Spoon the mixture into a piping (pastry) bag and pipe swirls around the edge of the cookie. Press the candles into the frosting. Sprinkle with chocolate raisins or peanuts and dust with cocoa powder. Finish by sprinkling with gold or silver balls.

Mini Party Pizzas

These cute little cookie confections look amazingly realistic and older children will love them. They're fun to make and are simply a basic cookie topped with icing, marzipan and dark cherries.

Makes 16

90g/3½oz/7 tbsp unsalted (sweet)
  butter, at room temperature, diced
90g/3½oz/½ cup golden caster
  (superfine) sugar
15ml/1 tbsp golden (light corn) syrup
175g/6oz/1½ cups self-raising
  (self-rising) flour

For the topping

150g/5oz/1¼ cups icing
  (confectioners') sugar
20–25ml/4–5 tsp lemon juice
red food colouring
90g/3½oz yellow marzipan,
  grated (shredded)
8 dark glacé (candied) cherries, halved
a small piece of angelica, finely chopped

1 Preheat the oven to 180°C/350°F/ Gas 4. Grease two baking sheets.

2 In a bowl, beat together the butter and sugar until creamy. Beat in the syrup, then add the flour and mix to a smooth paste.

3 Turn the mixture on to a lightly floured surface and cut into 16 even-size pieces. Roll each piece into a ball, then space well apart on the baking sheets, slightly flattening each one.

4 Bake for about 12 minutes, or until pale golden. Leave on the baking sheets for 3 minutes, then transfer to a wire rack to cool.

5 To make the topping, put the icing sugar in a bowl and stir in enough lemon juice to make a fairly thick, spreadable paste. Beat in enough food colouring to make the paste a deep red colour.

Cook's Tip

Make sure you use a red food colouring rather than cochineal, which will colour the icing pink. Red food colouring is more readily available in paste form.

6 Spread the icing to within 5mm/ ¼in of the edges of the cookies. Sprinkle with the shredded marzipan and place a halved cherry in the centre. Arrange a few pieces of chopped angelica on top so that the cookies resemble little cheese and tomato pizzas.

Jelly Bean Cones

Chocolate-dipped cookie cones filled with jelly beans make great treats for kids of all ages. The filled cones look very pretty arranged in glasses or other small containers to keep them upright. This way they can double as a tasty treat and a delightful table decoration.

Makes 10

3 egg whites

90g/3½oz/½ cup caster (superfine) sugar

25g/1oz/2 tbsp unsalted (sweet) butter, melted

40g/1½oz/⅓ cup plain (all-purpose) flour

30ml/2 tbsp single (light) cream

90g/3½oz plain (semisweet) chocolate

jelly beans or other small sweets (candies)

1 Preheat the oven to 190°C/375°F/ Gas 5. Line two baking sheets with baking parchment and lightly grease.

2 Put the egg whites and sugar in a bowl and whisk lightly with a fork until the egg whites are broken up. Add the melted butter, flour and cream and stir well to make a smooth batter.

3 Using a 15ml/1 tbsp measure, place a rounded tablespoon of the mixture on one side of a baking sheet. Spread to a 9cm/3½in round with the back of the spoon. Spoon more mixture on to the other side of the baking sheet and spread out to make another round.

4 Bake for about 8–10 minutes until the edges are deep golden. Meanwhile, spoon two more rounds of cookie mixture on to the second baking sheet.

5 Remove the first batch of cookies from the oven and replace with the second batch. Peel away the paper from the baked cookies and roll them into cone shapes. Leave to set. Continue in this way until you have made 10 cones.

6 Break the chocolate into a heatproof bowl set over a pan of simmering water and stir until melted. Dip the wide ends of the cookies in the chocolate and prop them inside narrow glasses to set, then fill with jelly beans or sweets.

Chocolate Flake Cookies

You don't need a special cutter to make these party cookies. They're shaped using an ordinary round cutter to which you add a V-shaped cone when cutting them out – quite simple once you've made one or two. Children will find these fun cookies irresistible.

Makes 15
150g/5oz/1¼ cups self-raising
   (self-rising) flour
90g/3½oz/7 tbsp unsalted (sweet)
   butter, diced
50g/2oz/¼ cup light muscovado
   (brown) sugar
1 egg yolk
5ml/1 tsp vanilla essence (extract)

For the decoration
75g/3oz/6 tbsp unsalted (sweet) butter,
   softened
5ml/1 tsp vanilla essence (extract)
115g/4oz/1 cup icing (confectioners')
   sugar
2 chocolate flakes

1 Put the flour and butter in a food processor and process until the mixture resembles fine breadcrumbs. Add the sugar, egg yolk and vanilla and blend to a smooth dough. Wrap in clear film (plastic wrap) and chill for 30 minutes.

2 Preheat the oven to 200°C/400°F/Gas 6. Grease a large baking sheet. Roll the dough out thinly on a floured surface. Lay a 5cm/2in round biscuit (cookie) cutter on the dough. Using a ruler mark a point 5cm/2in away from the edge of the cutter, then cut two lines from either side of the cutter to the point, to make cornet shapes. Cut around the rest of the cutter and transfer the cornet shape to the baking sheet. Make 14 more in the same way, re-rolling the trimmings to make the full quantity.

3 Using a sharp knife, make shallow cuts 5mm/¼in apart across the cone area of each cookie, then make more cuts diagonally across the first to create a "wafer" effect. Be careful not to cut all the way through the biscuit.

4 Bake for 8–10 minutes until pale golden. Leave for 2 minutes then transfer to a wire rack to cool.

5 For the buttercream, beat together the butter, vanilla and icing sugar until smooth. Add 5ml/1 tsp hot water and beat again until the mixture is very light and airy. Place in a piping (pastry) bag fitted with a large plain nozzle. Pipe swirls on to the tops of the biscuits so that they look like swirls of ice cream.

6 Cut the flakes across into 5cm/2in lengths. Carefully cut each piece lengthways into four small lengths. Push a flake piece into each biscuit.

Cook's Tip
The biscuits and buttercream can be made ahead, but assemble them on the day they're served as the cream will gradually soften the biscuits.

Stained Glass Windows

Baking coloured sweets inside a cookie frame creates a stunning stained glass effect, particularly if you hang the cookies in front of a window or near a lamp or wall light where the light can shine through. The translucent cookie centre will stay brittle for a day or so before softening and finally melting, so don't be tempted to hang them up for too long.

Makes 12–14

175g/6oz/1½ cups plain
(all-purpose) flour
2.5ml/½ tsp bicarbonate of soda
(baking soda)
2.5ml/½ tsp ground cinnamon
75g/3oz/6 tbsp unsalted (sweet)
butter, chilled and diced
75g/3oz/scant ½ cup caster
(superfine) sugar
30ml/2 tbsp golden (light
corn) syrup
1 egg yolk
150g/5oz brightly coloured, clear
boiled sweets (hard candies)

1 Put the flour, bicarbonate of soda, cinnamon and butter into a food processor. Process until the mixture resembles breadcrumbs.

2 Add the sugar, syrup and egg yolk to the food processor, then process again until the mixture starts to cling together in a dough.

3 Turn the dough out on to a lightly floured surface and knead until smooth. Wrap in clear film (plastic wrap) and chill in the refrigerator for at least 30 minutes.

4 Preheat the oven to 180°C/350°F/ Gas 4. Line two large baking sheets with baking parchment.

5 Roll out the dough thinly on a lightly floured surface. Cut into 6cm/ 2½in wide strips, then cut diagonally across the strips to create about 12 diamond shapes.

6 Carefully transfer the diamond shapes to the lined baking sheets, spacing them slightly apart.

7 Using a sharp knife, cut out a smaller diamond shape from the centre of each cookie and remove to leave a 1cm/½in frame.

8 Using a skewer, make a hole at one end of each cookie (large enough to thread fine ribbon).

9 Bake the cookie diamonds for about 5 minutes. Meanwhile, lightly crush the sweets (still in their wrappers) by tapping them gently with the end of a rolling pin.

10 Remove the cookies from the oven and quickly fill the centre of each one with about two crushed sweets of the same colour.

11 Return the cookies to the oven for a further 5 minutes until the sweets have melted. Remove from the oven and use a skewer to re-mark the skewer holes if they have shrunk during baking.

12 If the sweets haven't spread to fill the cookie centre during baking, while still hot, carefully spread the melted sweets with the tip of a skewer.

13 Leave the cookies on the baking parchment until the melted sweets have hardened. Once the centres are hard, gently peel away the paper from the cookies.

14 Thread fine ribbon of different lengths through the holes in the cookies, then hang as decorations around the home.

Cook's Tip
Make sure you re-mark the skewer holes while the cookies are still hot as they'll probably break if you try to make the holes once they've cooled.

Silly Faces

These funny little characters can be made using almost any type of cookie mix, as long as the baked cookies are quite big and not too craggy. Silly faces are great fun for kids to decorate.

5 Bake the cookies for 10–12 minutes until just turning golden around the edges. Transfer to a wire rack to cool.

6 To decorate, beat together the butter and icing sugar in a bowl until smooth and creamy.

7 Using a small palette knife (metal spatula) spread a little buttercream along the top edge of each cookie, then secure the strawberry, apple or liquorice strands. Either snip the strands to make straight hair, or twist the strands to make curly hair.

8 Use a dot of buttercream to secure a glacé cherry to the middle of each cookie for a nose. Pipe eyes and mouths using the writer icing, then add halved sweets, attached with buttercream, for the centres of the eyes.

Makes 14

115g/4oz/½ cup unsalted (sweet) butter, at room temperature, diced
115g/4oz/generous ½ cup golden caster (superfine) sugar
1 egg
115g/4oz/scant ⅓ cup golden (light corn) syrup
400g/14oz/3½ cups self-raising (self-rising) flour

For the decoration

75g/3oz/6 tbsp unsalted (sweet) butter, at room temperature, diced
150g/5oz/1¼ cups icing (confectioners') sugar
strawberry, apple or liquorice strands
glacé (candied) cherries, halved
red and black writer icing
small multi-coloured sweets (candies)

1 Put the butter and sugar in a large bowl and beat together until pale and creamy. Beat in the egg and golden syrup, then add the flour and mix together to make a thick paste.

2 Turn the mixture on to a lightly floured surface and knead until smooth. Wrap in clear film (plastic wrap) and chill for 30 minutes.

3 Preheat the oven to 180°C/350°F/ Gas 4. Grease two baking sheets.

4 Roll out the chilled dough on a lightly floured surface and cut out rounds using a 9cm/3½in cookie cutter. Transfer the rounds to the baking sheets, re-rolling the trimmings to make more cookies.

Train Cookies

These simple party cookies are so easy, yet incredibly effective, particularly if you let them trail across the party table. The quantity makes enough for two trains, but double it if required.

Makes 10
150g/5oz/1¼ cups plain
  (all-purpose) flour
90g/3½oz/7 tbsp unsalted (sweet) butter,
  chilled, diced
50g/2oz/½ cup golden icing
  (confectioners') sugar
1 egg yolk
5ml/1 tsp vanilla essence (extract)

For the decoration
40g/1½oz/3 tbsp butter, softened
75g/3oz/⅓ cup golden icing
  (confectioners') sugar
blue food colouring
large bag of liquorice allsorts

1 Put the flour and butter in a food processor. Process until the mixture resembles fine breadcrumbs. Add the sugar, egg yolk and vanilla; blend to a smooth dough. Wrap in clear film (plastic wrap) and chill for 30 minutes.

2 Preheat the oven to 200°C/400°F/Gas 6. Grease a large baking sheet. Roll out the dough and cut 7.5 × 4cm/3 × 1½in rectangles, re-rolling the scraps to make more cookies. Cut two 3 × 2cm/1¼ × ¾in rectangles and secure to the top of the larger rectangles for the engines.

3 Place on the baking sheet and bake for about 10 minutes until pale golden around the edges. Leave for 2 minutes on the baking sheet, then transfer to a wire rack to cool completely.

4 To decorate the biscuits, put the butter and icing sugar in a bowl with a dash of blue food colouring and beat until smooth and creamy. Chop plenty of the liquorice pieces into small dice.

Cook's Tip
If you don't want to use liquorice, try other colourful sweets (candies) or even chocolate. Round chocolates make good wheels and chopped chocolate or polka dots make good "cargo".

5 Spread a little buttercream along one long side of all the biscuits except the engines and press the chopped sweets into the buttercream. Halve some square sweets and secure to the engines for windows and another piece on the front of the engine for the funnel. Secure two wheels on all the biscuits. Arrange the biscuits in a trail across the table.

Gold Medals

These cookies are great for kids' parties. You can present each child with a huge cookie medal when they sit down at the table, or hand them out to winners of party games.

Makes 10

50g/2oz/¼ cup unsalted (sweet) butter,
   at room temperature, diced
115g/4oz/generous ½ cup caster
   (superfine) sugar
1 egg
150g/5oz/1¼ cups self-raising
   (self-rising) flour
1.5ml/¼ tsp bicarbonate of soda
   (baking soda)

For the decoration

1 egg white
200g/7oz/1¾ cups icing
   (confectioners') sugar
small brightly coloured sweets (candies)

1 Preheat the oven to 180°C/350°F/ Gas 4. Grease two baking sheets with a little butter.

2 In a bowl, beat together the butter and sugar until smooth and creamy, then beat in the egg. Add the flour and bicarbonate of soda and mix well to combine.

3 Place large spoonfuls of the mixture on the baking sheets, spacing them well apart to allow room for spreading. Bake for about 15 minutes, or until pale golden and slightly risen.

4 Using a skewer, make quite a large hole in the cookie, 1cm/½in from the edge. Transfer to a wire rack and leave to cool.

5 To make the icing, beat the egg white in a bowl using a wooden spoon. Gradually beat in the icing sugar to make a thick paste that just holds its shape. Spoon the icing into a small plastic bag and snip off the merest tip.

6 Write icing numbers in the centre of the cookies. Secure a circle of sweets around the edge of each cookie with a little more of the icing, then leave to set.

7 Once the icing has hardened, carefully thread each cookie with a piece of ribbon.

Chocolate Dominoes

A recipe for children to eat rather than make, these fun bars are ideal for birthday parties, when you can match the spots on the dominoes to the children's ages.

Makes 16

175g/6oz/¾ cup soft margarine
175g/6oz/generous ¾ cup caster
  (superfine) sugar
150g/5oz/1¼ cups self-raising
  (self-rising) flour
25g/1oz/¼ cup (unsweetened) cocoa
  powder, sifted
3 eggs

For the topping

175g/6oz/¾ cup butter
25g/1oz/¼ cup (unsweetened)
  cocoa powder
300g/11oz/2¾ cups icing
  (confectioners') sugar
a few liquorice strips and 115g/4oz
  packet candy-coated chocolate drops,
  to decorate

1 Preheat the oven to 180°C/350°F/ Gas 4. Lightly brush an 18 × 28cm/ 7 × 11in rectangular baking tin (pan) with a little oil and line the base with greaseproof (waxed) paper.

2 Put all the cake ingredients into a large bowl and beat until smooth.

3 Spoon the cake mixture evenly into the prepared cake tin and level the surface with a palette knife or metal spatula.

4 Bake for 30 minutes, or until the cake springs back when pressed with the fingertips.

5 Cool in the tin for 5 minutes, then loosen the edges with a knife and transfer to a wire rack. Peel off the lining paper and leave the cake to cool completely. When cold, turn it out on to a chopping board.

6 To make the topping, place the butter in a bowl. Sift together the cocoa and icing sugar into the bowl and beat until smooth. Spread the topping evenly over the cake with a palette knife or metal spatula.

7 Cut the cake into 16 bars. Place a strip of liquorice, across the middle of each bar, then decorate with candy-coated chocolate drops to make the domino spots.

Variation

To make Traffic Light Cakes, omit the cocoa and add an extra 45ml/3 tbsp plain (all-purpose) flour. Omit cocoa from the icing and add an extra 60ml/4 tbsp icing (confectioners') sugar and 2.5ml/ ½ tsp vanilla essence (extract). Spread over the cakes and decorate with a row of red, yellow and green glacé (candied) cherries.

Name Cookies

You could decorate these cookies for children coming to a party, either in vibrant, bright colours or in more delicate pastels. It can be a fun idea to prop a name cookie up against the glass at each place setting around the tea table and let the children find their own seats.

Makes 20

200g/7oz/scant 1 cup unsalted (sweet) butter, chilled and diced
300g/10oz/2½ cups plain (all-purpose) flour
finely grated rind of 1 orange
90g/3½oz/scant 1 cup icing (confectioners') sugar
2 egg yolks

For the decoration
1 egg white
200g/7oz/1¼ cups icing sugar
2 different food colourings
jelly beans or silver balls

1 Put the butter, flour and orange rind in a food processor and process until the mixture resembles fine breadcrumbs. Add the icing sugar and egg yolks and blend until smooth. Wrap in clear film (plastic wrap) and chill for 30 minutes.

2 Preheat the oven to 200°C/400°F/Gas 6. Grease two baking sheets.

3 Roll out the dough on a floured surface and cut out cookies in a variety of shapes, such as squares, hearts and rounds. Make sure each cookie is at least 7.5cm/3in across.

4 Transfer the cookies to the baking sheets, spacing them slightly apart, and bake for 10–12 minutes until pale golden around the edges.

5 Leave the cookies on the baking sheet for about 2 minutes to firm up, then transfer to a wire rack to cool completely.

6 To make the icing, put the egg white and icing sugar in a bowl and beat together until smooth, and the icing only just holds its shape.

7 Divide the icing between two bowls, then beat a few drops of food colouring into each bowl to make two different colours.

8 Spoon the two different icings into separate small plastic bags and gently squeeze into one corner.

Variation
If you prefer, add food colouring to only one of the bowls of icing, leaving the second bowl of icing white. This can look very pretty, particularly if you choose a pastel colour for the second bowl of icing and decorate with silver balls.

9 Cut off the merest tip from each bag so the icing can be piped in a very thin line, then write the names or initials of party guests on the cookies. Pipe decorative borders around the edges of the cookies using both colours of icing. Use either straight lines, flutes, dots of icing or squiggled lines of piping to decorate.

10 Chop the jelly beans, if using, into small pieces. Secure the jelly beans or the silver balls on to the icing on the cookies to finish. Leave the cookies to set for at least 1 hour.

Peanut Cookies

Packing up a party picnic? Got another kind of birthday party coming up? Make sure that some of these fabulous nutty cookies are on the menu. Remember to make sure that none of the children have a nut allergy.

Makes 25

225g/8oz/1 cup butter
30ml/2 tbsp smooth peanut butter
115g/4oz/1 cup icing
  (confectioners') sugar
50g/2oz/¼ cup cornflour (cornstarch)
225g/8oz/2 cups plain (all-purpose) flour
115g/4oz/1 cup unsalted peanuts

1 Put the butter and peanut butter in a bowl and beat together. Add the icing sugar, cornflour and plain flour and mix together to make a soft dough.

2 Preheat the oven to 180°C/350°F/ Gas 4. Lightly oil two baking sheets. Roll the mixture into 25 small balls, using the palms of your hands, and place on the baking sheets. Leave plenty of room for the cookies to spread.

3 Press the tops of the balls of dough flat, using either the back of a fork or your fingertips.

4 Press a few of the peanuts into each of the cookies. Bake for about 15–20 minutes, until lightly browned. Leave to cool for a few minutes before lifting them carefully on to a wire rack with a palette knife or metal spatula.

Cook's Tip
For a party, make really monster cookies by rolling bigger balls of dough. Remember to leave plenty of room on the baking sheets for them to spread during cooking.

Party Bracelets

These tiny cookies are threaded on to fine ribbon along with an assortment of brightly coloured sweets that have a ready-made hole in the middle. Make the cookies a day or two in advance and simply thread together with the sweets on the day of the party.

Makes 10

50g/2oz/¼ cup unsalted (sweet) butter,
   at room temperature, diced
115g/4oz/generous ½ cup caster
   (superfine) sugar
5ml/1 tsp vanilla essence (extract)
pink or green food colouring
1 egg
200g/7oz/1¾ cups self-raising
   (self-rising) flour

For the decoration

2 large bags of boiled sweets (hard
   candies) with holes in the centre
narrow pastel-coloured ribbon,
   for threading

1 Preheat the oven to 180°C/350°F/ Gas 4. Grease two baking sheets.

2 In a bowl, beat together the butter, sugar and vanilla essence until pale and creamy. Add a dash of pink or green food colouring, then beat in the egg. Add the flour and mix well to form a dough.

3 Turn the dough on to a lightly floured surface and roll out under the palms of your hands into two long, thin sausage shapes, each about 40cm/16in long.

4 Cut each roll across into 5mm/¼in lengths and space them slightly apart on the baking sheets. Place the baking sheets in the refrigerator for about 30 minutes.

5 Bake the cookies for about 8 minutes until slightly risen and beginning to colour. Remove from the oven and, using a skewer, immediately make holes for the ribbon to be threaded through. (You may find it easier to bake one sheet of cookies at a time.) Transfer the cookies to a wire rack to cool.

6 Thread the cookies on to 55cm/ 22in lengths of narrow ribbon, alternating with the sweets. (You should end up with about seven cookies on each ribbon.) Tie the ends of the ribbons together in bows to finish.

Cook's Tip
When you make the holes in the cookies, you will need to work quickly. If the cookies start to harden before you have time to make holes in all of them, pop the remaining cookies back in the oven very briefly to re-soften.

Sweet Necklaces

These are too awkward for really young children to make but ideal as novelty Christmas or birthday party presents. Arrange in a pretty, tissue-lined box or other container for presentation.

Makes 12
1 quantity Lebkuchen mixture
  (see Chocolate Fruit and Nut Cookies)
200g/7oz royal icing
pink food colouring
selection of small sweets (candies)
6m/6 yards fine pink, blue or
  white ribbon

I Preheat the oven to 180°C/350°F/ Gas 4. Grease two large baking sheets. Roll out slightly more than half of the Lebkuchen mixture on a lightly-floured surface to a thickness of 5mm/¼in.

2 Stamp out stars using a lightly floured 2.5cm/1in star cutter. Carefully transfer to a prepared baking sheet, spacing them evenly and allowing room for them to rise. Taking care not to distort the shape of the stars, make a large hole in the centre of each, using a metal or wooden skewer.

Variation
You can adapt this technique to use with other kinds of cookie dough for children who don't like ginger. However, Lebkuchen is ideal because it is quite substantial and firm, so holds its shape. It is traditionally used for threaded shapes.

3 Gather the trimmings together with the remaining dough. Roll the dough under the palms of your hands, to make a thick, even sausage about 2.5cm/1in in diameter. Cut into 1cm/½in thick slices. Using the skewer, carefully make a hole in the centre of each round. Place on the second baking sheet.

4 Bake for about 8 minutes, or until slightly risen and just beginning to colour. Remove from the oven and, while still warm, re-make the skewer holes as the gingerbread will have spread slightly during baking. Leave to cool on a wire rack.

5 Put half the royal icing in a paper piping (pastry) bag and snip off the tip. Use to pipe neat outlines all around the edges of each of the gingerbread stars.

6 Colour the remaining icing with the pink colouring. Spoon into another paper piping bag fitted with a star nozzle.

7 Cut the sweets into smaller pieces and use to decorate the cookies, attaching them with icing. Leave to harden.

8 Cut the ribbon into 50cm/20in lengths. Thread a selection of the cookies on to each ribbon.

Variation
To make edible tinsel to drape on your Christmas tree, string stars together decorated with green, red and white icing.

Chocolate Heaven

This has to be a favourite chapter for almost everyone – chocolate cookies are universally popular, loved by young and old alike. This is hardly surprising, with such mouthwatering recipes as Chunky Chocolate Drops and Giant Triple Chocolate Cookies. Some, such as Rich Chocolate Cookie Slice, are astonishingly simple to make, while others, such as Mini Chocolate Marylands, take a little more time and effort, but they're certainly worth it.

Chocolate Thumbprint Cookies

Chunky, chocolatey and gooey all at the same time, these gorgeous cookies are filled with a spoonful of chocolate spread after baking to really add to their indulgent feel.

Makes 16

115g/4oz/ ½ cup unsalted (sweet)
  butter, at room temperature, diced
115g/4oz/generous ½ cup light
  muscovado (brown) sugar
1 egg
75g/3oz/ ⅔ cup plain (all-purpose) flour
25g/1oz/ ¼ cup cocoa powder
  (unsweetened)
2.5ml/ ½ tsp bicarbonate of soda
  (baking soda)
115g/4oz/generous 1 cup rolled oats
75–90ml/5–6 tbsp chocolate spread

1 Preheat the oven to 180°C/350°F/ Gas 4. Grease a large baking sheet. In a bowl, beat together the butter and sugar until creamy.

2 Add the egg, flour, cocoa powder, bicarbonate of soda and rolled oats to the bowl and mix well.

3 Using your hands, roll spoonfuls of the mixture into balls. Place the balls on the baking sheet, spacing them well apart to allow room for spreading. Flatten slightly.

4 Dip a thumb in flour and press into the centre of each cookie to make an indent. Bake the cookies for 10 minutes. Leave for 2 minutes, then transfer to a wire rack to cool.

5 Spoon a little chocolate spread into the centre of each cookie.

Chocolate Treacle Snaps

These elegantly thin, treacle-flavoured snap cookies have a delicate hint of spice and a decorative lick of chocolate on top. They are particularly good with a steaming cup of hot coffee.

Makes about 35

90g/3½oz/7 tbsp unsalted (sweet) butter, diced
175ml/6fl oz/¾ cup golden (light corn) syrup
50ml/2fl oz/¼ cup black treacle (molasses)
250g/9oz/2¼ cups plain (all-purpose) flour
150g/5oz/¾ cup golden caster (superfine) sugar
5ml/1 tsp bicarbonate of soda (baking soda)
1.5ml/¼ tsp mixed (apple pie) spice
100g/3½oz milk chocolate
100g/3½oz white chocolate

1 Preheat the oven to 180°C/350°F/ Gas 4. Line two or three baking sheets with baking parchment. Put the butter, syrup and treacle in a small pan. Heat gently, stirring constantly, until the butter has melted. Remove from the heat and set aside until required.

2 Sift the flour into a large mixing bowl. Add the sugar, bicarbonate of soda and mixed spice, and mix well using a wooden spoon. Slowly pour in the butter and treacle mixture and stir to combine well.

3 Place large teaspoonfuls of the mixture well apart on the prepared baking sheets. Bake the cookies for 10–12 minutes until just beginning to brown around the edges. Leave them to cool for a few minutes on the baking sheets. When firm enough to handle, transfer the cookies to a wire rack to cool completely.

4 Melt the milk chocolate and white chocolate separately in the microwave or in heatproof bowls set over pans of hot water. Swirl a little of each into the centre of each cookie and leave to set.

Mini Chocolate Marylands

These tasty little cookies are perfect for any age group. They're easy to make and even young children can get involved with helping to press the chocolate chips into the unbaked dough.

Makes 40–45

125g/4¼oz/generous ½ cup
   unsalted (sweet) butter, at room
   temperature, diced
90g/3½oz/⅓ cup caster
   (superfine) sugar
1 egg
1 egg yolk
5ml/1 tsp vanilla essence (extract)
175g/6oz/1½ cups self-raising
   (self-rising) flour
90g/3½oz/generous ½ cup milk
90g/3½oz/generous ½ cup
   chocolate chips

1 Preheat the oven to 180°C/350°F/ Gas 4. Grease two baking sheets.

2 In a large bowl, beat together the butter and sugar until pale and creamy. Add the egg, egg yolk, vanilla essence, flour, milk and half the chocolate chips and stir well until thoroughly combined.

3 Using two teaspoons, place small mounds of the mixture on the baking sheets, spacing them slightly apart to allow room for spreading.

4 Press the remaining chocolate chips on to the mounds of cookie dough and press down gently.

5 Bake for 10–15 minutes until pale golden. Leave the cookies on the baking sheet for 2 minutes to firm up, then transfer to a wire rack to cool completely.

Cook's Tip

This recipe makes quite a large quantity. If you like, you can freeze half of the cookies for another time. Simply thaw, then return to the oven for a few minutes to re-crisp before serving.

Chocolate Pretzels

These scrumptious snacks look so charming twisted into little knots that it is tempting to take "just one more". Sweet pretzels are a speciality of Germany and Austria.

Makes 28
115g/4oz/1 cup plain (all-purpose) flour
pinch of salt
45ml/3 tbsp (unsweetened)
    cocoa powder
115g/4oz/½ cup butter
150g/5oz/⅔ cup caster
    (superfine) sugar
1 egg
1 egg white, lightly beaten,
    for glazing
sugar crystals, for sprinkling

1 Sift together the flour, salt and cocoa powder. Set aside. Grease two baking sheets.

2 With an electric mixer, cream the butter until light. Add the sugar and continue beating until light and fluffy. Beat in the egg. Add the dry ingredients and stir to blend. Gather the dough into a ball, wrap in greaseproof (waxed) paper and chill for 1 hour, or freeze for 30 minutes.

5 Brush the pretzels with the egg white. Sprinkle sugar crystals over the tops to decorate and bake for 10–12 minutes until firm. Transfer to a wire rack to cool.

3 Roll the dough into 28 small balls. If the dough is sticky, lightly flour your hands first. Chill the dough balls until needed. Preheat the oven to 190°C/375°F/Gas 5.

4 Roll each ball into a rope about 25cm/10in long. With each rope, form a loop with the two ends facing you. Twist the ends and fold back on to the circle, pressing in, to make a pretzel shape. Place on the prepared baking sheets.

Cook's Tip
To make mocha-flavoured pretzels, replace 10ml/2 tsp of the cocoa with instant coffee powder.

Chocolate Box Cookies

These prettily decorated, bitesize cookies look as though they've come straight out of a box of chocolates. They're great for a special tea or for wrapping as gifts, and older children will love getting thoroughly absorbed in making and decorating them.

Makes about 50

175g/6oz/1½ cups self-raising (self-rising) flour
25g/1oz/¼ cup cocoa powder (unsweetened)
5ml/1 tsp mixed (apple pie) spice
50g/2oz/¼ cup unsalted (sweet) butter, at room temperature, diced
115g/4oz/generous ½ cup caster (superfine) sugar
1 egg
1 egg yolk

For the decoration

150g/5oz milk chocolate
150g/5oz white chocolate
100g/3¾oz plain (semisweet) chocolate
whole almonds or walnuts
cocoa powder, for dusting

1 Preheat the oven to 180°C/350°F/ Gas 4. Grease two baking sheets.

2 Put the flour, cocoa powder, spice and butter into a food processor. Process until the ingredients are thoroughly blended. Add the sugar, egg and egg yolk and mix to a smooth dough.

3 Turn the dough out on to a lightly floured surface and knead gently. Cut the dough in half and roll out each piece under the palms of your hands to form two long logs, each 33cm/13in long.

4 Cut each log into 1cm/½in slices. Place the slices on the prepared baking sheet, spacing slightly apart, and chill for at least 30 minutes.

5 Bake for 10 minutes until slightly risen. Transfer to a wire rack to cool.

6 To decorate, break the chocolate into three separate heatproof bowls. Place each bowl, in turn, over a pan of gently simmering water and stir frequently until melted.

7 Divide the cookies into six batches. Using a fork, dip one batch, a cookie at a time, into the milk chocolate to coat completely. Place on a sheet of baking parchment.

8 Taking the next batch of cookies, half-dip in milk chocolate and place on the baking parchment.

9 Continue with the next two batches of cookies and the white chocolate. Completely coat one batch, then half-coat the second.

10 Continue with the remaining cookies, completely coating one batch in the plain chocolate and half-dipping the other. Press a whole nut on to the tops of the plain chocolate-coated cookies.

11 Put the leftover white chocolate in a small plastic bag and squeeze it into one corner. Snip off the tip, then drizzle lines of chocolate over the milk chocolate-coated cookies.

12 Dust the white chocolate-coated cookies with a little cocoa powder. Store all the cookies in a cool place until ready to serve.

Cook's Tip
Once you have mastered the art of decorating the cookies, vary the combinations. Try drizzling milk or dark chocolate over the different cookies.

Chocolate Florentines

These big, flat, crunchy cookies are just like traditional florentines but use tiny seeds instead of nuts. Rolling the edges in milk or white chocolate makes them feel like a real treat.

Makes 12

50g/2oz/¼ cup unsalted (sweet) butter
50g/2oz/¼ cup caster (superfine) sugar
15ml/1 tbsp milk
25g/1oz/scant ¼ cup pumpkin seeds
40g/1½oz/generous ¼ cup
   sunflower seeds
50g/2oz/scant ½ cup raisins
25g/1oz/2 tbsp multi-coloured glacé
   (candied) cherries, chopped
30ml/2 tbsp plain (all-purpose) flour
125g/4¼oz milk or white chocolate

1 Preheat the oven to 180°C/350°F/ Gas 4. Line two baking sheets with baking parchment and grease the paper well.

2 In a pan, melt the butter with the sugar, stirring, until the sugar has dissolved, then cook until bubbling. Remove the pan from the heat and stir in the milk, pumpkin and sunflower seeds, raisins, glacé cherries and flour. Mix well.

3 Spoon 6 teaspoonfuls of the mixture on to each baking sheet, spacing them well apart. Bake for 8–10 minutes until the cookies are turning dark golden. Using a palette knife (metal spatula), push back the edges of the cookies to neaten. Leave on the baking sheets for about 5 minutes to firm up, then transfer to a wire rack to cool.

4 Break up the chocolate and put in a heatproof bowl set over a pan of gently simmering water. Heat, stirring frequently, until melted. Roll the edges of the cookies in the chocolate and leave to set on a clean sheet of baking parchment for about 1 hour.

Variation
If you prefer, use plain (semisweet) chocolate to decorate the cookies.

Chocolate Refrigerator Cookies

The dough must be chilled thoroughly before it can be sliced and baked. Keep a "log" of dough, wrapped in foil, in the freezer ready for baking whenever you need a chocolate boost.

Makes about 50

225g/8oz/2 cups plain (all-purpose) flour
pinch of salt
50g/2oz plain (semisweet)
   chocolate, chopped
225g/8oz/1 cup unsalted (sweet) butter
   at room temperature, diced
225g/8oz/1 cup caster (superfine) sugar
2 eggs
5ml/1 tsp vanilla essence (extract)
115g/4oz/1 cup walnuts, finely chopped

1 Sift together the flour and salt into a small bowl. Set aside. Melt the chocolate in the top of a double boiler, or in a heatproof bowl set over a pan of hot water. Set aside.

2 With an electric mixer, cream the butter until soft. Add the sugar and continue beating until the mixture is light and fluffy.

3 Mix the eggs with the vanilla essence, then gradually stir into the butter mixture.

4 Stir in the melted chocolate, then the flour mixture followed by the nuts and mix to form a firm dough.

5 Divide the dough into four pieces and roll each into 5cm/2in diameter logs. Wrap tightly in foil or clear film (plastic wrap) and chill in the refrigerator or place in the freezer until firm.

6 Preheat the oven to 190°C/375°F/ Gas 5. Grease two or three baking sheets. Cut the dough into 5mm/¼in slices. Place on the baking sheets and bake for 10 minutes. Transfer to a wire rack to cool.

Variation

To make two-tone cookies, make half chocolate and half plain dough. Roll out the plain dough. Roll out the chocolate dough, place on top of the plain dough and roll up. Wrap and chill, then cut and bake as above.

Chocolate Marzipan Cookies

These crisp little cookies are deliciously sweet and have a delightful almond surprise inside. Piped with zig-zag lines of white chocolate, they make a perfect party treat.

Makes 36

200g/7oz/scant 1 cup unsalted (sweet)
* butter at room temperature, diced*
200g/7oz/scant 1 cup light muscovado
* (brown) sugar*
1 egg
300g/11oz/2⅔ cups plain
* (all-purpose) flour*
60ml/4 tbsp (unsweetened)
* cocoa powder*
200g/7oz white almond paste
115g/4oz white chocolate, chopped

1 Preheat the oven to 190°C/375°F/ Gas 5. Lightly grease two large baking sheets. Cream the butter with the sugar in a bowl until pale and fluffy.

2 Add the egg and beat well. Sift the flour and cocoa powder over the mixture. Stir in, first with a wooden spoon, then with clean hands, pressing the mixture together to make a fairly soft dough. If the dough seems rather sticky and might be difficult to roll, wrap it in clear film (plastic wrap) and chill for about 30 minutes.

3 Roll out about half the dough on a lightly floured surface to a thickness of about 5mm/¼in. Using a 5cm/2in cutter, stamp out rounds, re-rolling the dough as required until you have about 36 rounds.

4 Cut the almond paste into about 36 equal pieces. Roll into balls, flatten slightly and place one on each dough round. Roll out the remaining dough, stamp out more rounds, then place on top of the almond paste. Press the dough edges to seal. Bake the cookies for 10–12 minutes until well risen.

5 Transfer the cookies to a wire rack, using a spatula, and leave to cool completely. Melt the white chocolate, spoon into a paper piping (pastry) bag and pipe zig-zag lines on to the cookies. Leave to set before serving.

Chunky Chocolate Drops

Do not allow these cookies to cool completely on the baking sheet or they will become too crisp and will break when you try to lift them.

Makes 18

175g/6oz plain (semisweet)
  chocolate, chopped
115g/4oz/½ cup unsalted (sweet)
  butter, diced
2 eggs
90g/3½oz/½ cup granulated sugar
50g/2oz/¼ cup soft light brown sugar
40g/1½oz/⅓ cup plain (all-purpose) flour
25g/1oz/¼ cup (unsweetened)
  cocoa powder
5ml/1 tsp baking powder
10ml/2 tsp vanilla essence (extract)
pinch of salt
115g/4oz/1 cup pecan nuts, toasted and
  coarsely chopped
175g/6oz/1 cup plain (semisweet)
  chocolate chips
115g/4oz good quality white chocolate,
  chopped into 5mm/¼in pieces
115g/4oz good quality milk chocolate,
  chopped into 5mm/¼in pieces

1 Preheat the oven to 160°C/325°F/ Gas 3. Grease two large baking sheets. Melt the plain chocolate and butter in a pan over a low heat, stirring constantly until smooth. Remove from the heat and set aside to cool slightly.

2 In a large mixing bowl, using an electric mixer, beat the eggs and sugars for 2–3 minutes until pale and creamy. Gradually pour in the melted chocolate mixture, beating until well blended.

3 Beat in the flour, cocoa powder, baking powder, vanilla essence and salt until just blended. Stir in the nuts, chocolate chips and chocolate pieces.

4 Drop mounded tablespoonfuls of the mixture on to the prepared baking sheets, 10cm/4in apart. Gently flatten each to 7.5cm/3in rounds with the back of the spoon. Bake for 8–10 minutes, until the tops are shiny and cracked and the edges look crisp; do not over-bake or the cookies will become fragile.

5 Remove the baking sheets to a wire rack to cool for 2 minutes, then transfer the cookies to the rack to cool completely.

Chocolate Wands

Shaping these long, wafery chocolate cookies is fun, but you need to work quickly so it might take a few attempts to get the technique just right. Bake only two cookies at a time; any more and they will become brittle before you have time to shape them into wands.

Makes 10–12

3 egg whites
90g/3½oz/½ cup caster (superfine) sugar
25g/1oz/2 tbsp unsalted (sweet)
*   butter, melted*
30ml/2 tbsp plain (all-purpose) flour
15ml/1 tbsp cocoa powder
*   (unsweetened)*
30ml/2 tbsp single (light) cream
90g/3½oz milk chocolate and
*   multi-coloured sprinkles, to decorate*

1 Preheat the oven to 180°C/350°F/Gas 4. Line two large baking sheets with baking parchment and grease the paper well.

2 In a bowl, briefly beat together the egg whites and sugar until the whites are broken up.

3 Add the melted butter, flour, cocoa powder and cream to the egg whites and beat with a wooden spoon until smooth.

Cook's Tip

These cookies look best when the wands are really slender. Use a wooden spoon with a thin handle for shaping the cookies around. Alternatively, use a chunky pencil wrapped in kitchen foil.

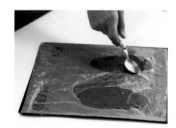

4 Place 2 teaspoonfuls of the mixture to one side of a baking sheet and spread the mixture into an oval shape, about 15cm/6in long. Spoon more mixture on to the other side of the baking sheet and shape in the same way.

5 Bake for 7–8 minutes until the edges begin to darken. Meanwhile, prepare two more cookies on the second baking sheet so you can put them in the oven while shaping the first batch into wands.

6 Leave the baked cookies on the paper for 30 seconds, then carefully lift one off and wrap it around the handle of a wooden spoon. As soon as it starts to hold its shape ease it off the spoon and shape the second cookie in the same way.

7 Continue baking and shaping the cookies in this way until all the mixture has been used up.

8 Break the chocolate into pieces and place in a heatproof bowl set over a pan of gently simmering water. Heat, stirring occasionally, until the chocolate has melted.

9 Dip the ends of the cookies in the chocolate, turning them until the ends are thickly coated.

10 Sprinkle the chocolate-coated ends of the cookies with coloured sprinkles and place on a sheet of baking parchment. Leave for about 1 hour until the chocolate has set.

Chocolate Kisses

These rich little cookies look attractive mixed together on a plate and dusted with icing sugar. Serve them with ice cream or simply with a cup of coffee.

Makes 24

75g/3oz plain (semisweet)
  chocolate, chopped
75g/3oz white chocolate, chopped
115g/4oz/½ cup butter at room
  temperature, diced
115g/4oz/generous ½ cup caster
  (superfine) sugar
2 eggs, beaten
225g/8oz/2 cups plain
  (all-purpose) flour
icing (confectioners') sugar, to decorate

1 Put the plain and white chocolate into separate small, heatproof bowls and melt the chocolates, in turn, over a pan of hot, but not boiling water, stirring until smooth. Remove the bowls from the heat and set them aside to cool slightly.

2 Beat together the butter and caster sugar until pale and fluffy. Beat in the eggs a little at a time, beating well after each addition.

3 Sift the flour over the butter, sugar and egg mixture and mix in lightly and thoroughly.

4 Halve the mixture and divide it between the two bowls of chocolate. Mix each chocolate in well. Knead the doughs until smooth, wrap in clear film (plastic wrap) and chill for 1 hour. Preheat the oven to 190°C/375°F/Gas 5. Grease two baking sheets.

5 Take rounded teaspoonfuls of the doughs and shape them roughly into balls. Roll the balls between the palms of your hands to make neater ball shapes. Arrange the balls on the prepared baking sheets and bake for about 12 minutes. Dust with sifted icing sugar and then transfer to a wire rack to cool.

Chocolate Cinnamon Tuiles

These crisp French cookies acquired their name because their shape is said to resemble that of a curved tile. Classically plain, this special version is flavoured with cocoa and cinnamon.

Makes 12

1 egg white
50g/2oz/¼ cup caster (superfine) sugar
30ml/2 tbsp plain (all-purpose) flour
40g/1½oz/3 tbsp butter, melted
15ml/1 tbsp (unsweetened) cocoa powder
2.5ml/½ tsp ground cinnamon

1 Preheat the oven to 200°C/ 400°F/Gas 6. Lightly grease two large baking sheets. Whisk the egg white in a clean, grease-free bowl until it forms soft peaks. Gradually whisk in the sugar to make a smooth, glossy mixture.

2 Sift the flour over the mixture and fold in evenly. Stir in the butter. Transfer about 45ml/3 tbsp of the mixture to a small bowl and set aside.

3 In a separate small bowl, mix together the cocoa and ground cinnamon. Stir them into the larger quantity of mixture.

Cook's Tip

Work as quickly as possible when removing the tuiles from the baking sheets – if they firm up too quickly, pop the baking sheet back in the switched-off oven for a minute and try again.

4 Leaving room for spreading, drop spoonfuls of the chocolate-flavoured mixture on to the prepared baking sheets, then spread each gently with a palette knife or metal spatula to make a neat round.

5 Using a small spoon, carefully drizzle the reserved unflavoured mixture over the rounds to create a marbled effect.

6 Bake for 4–6 minutes until just set. Using a palette knife or spatula, lift each cookie carefully and quickly drape it over a rolling pin, to give a curved shape as it hardens.

7 Leave the tuiles to cool until set, then remove them gently and place on a wire rack to cool completely. Serve on the same day.

Triple Chocolate Sandwiches

Chocolate shortbread is a brilliant base for sandwiching or coating in lashings of melted chocolate. Kids of any age can enjoy making them as they don't need to be perfectly uniform.

Makes 15

125g/4¼oz/generous ½ cup unsalted (sweet) butter, chilled and diced
150g/5oz/1¼ cups plain (all-purpose) flour
30ml/2 tbsp cocoa powder (unsweetened)
50g/2oz/¼ cup caster (superfine) sugar
75g/3oz white chocolate
25g/1oz/2 tbsp unsalted (sweet) butter
115g/4oz milk chocolate

1 Put the butter, flour and cocoa in a food processor. Process until the mixture resembles breadcrumbs. Add the sugar and process again until the mixture forms a dough.

2 Transfer the dough to a clean surface and knead lightly. Wrap in clear film (plastic wrap) and chill for 30 minutes.

3 Preheat the oven to 200°C/400°F/ Gas 6. Grease a large baking sheet.

4 Roll out the chilled dough on a floured surface to a 33 × 16cm/ 13 × 6¼in rectangle. Lift on to the baking sheet and trim the edges.

5 Cut the dough in half lengthways, then cut across at 2cm/¾in intervals to make 30 small bars.

6 Prick each bar with a fork and bake for 12–15 minutes until just beginning to darken around the edges. Remove from the oven and cut between the bars again while the cookies are still warm. Leave for 2 minutes, then transfer to a wire rack to cool.

7 To make the filling, break the white chocolate into a heatproof bowl. Add half the butter and set the bowl over a pan of gently simmering water and stir frequently until melted.

8 Spread a little of the filling evenly on to one of the bars. Place another bar on top and push together to sandwich the cookies. Continue in the same way with the remaining cookies and filling.

9 To make the topping, break the milk chocolate into a heatproof bowl. Add the remaining butter and set over a pan of simmering water, stirring frequently until melted. Using a teaspoon, drizzle the chocolate over the top of the cookies, then leave to set.

Chocolate Crackle-tops

Older children will enjoy making these distinctive-looking cookies and everyone will love eating them. The dough needs to be chilled for an hour, but then is easy to handle and roll.

Makes 38

200g/7oz plain (semisweet)
  chocolate, chopped
90g/3½oz/scant ½ cup unsalted
  (sweet) butter
115g/4oz/generous ½ cup caster
  (superfine) sugar
3 eggs
5ml/1 tsp vanilla essence (extract)
215g/7½oz/scant 2 cups plain
  (all-purpose) flour
25g/1oz/¼ cup (unsweetened)
  cocoa powder
2.5ml/½ tsp baking powder
pinch of salt
175g/6oz/1½ cups icing (confectioners')
  sugar, for coating

1 In a pan set over a low heat, melt the chocolate and butter together until smooth, stirring frequently.

2 Remove the pan from the heat. Stir in the sugar, and continue stirring for 2–3 minutes until the sugar dissolves. Add the eggs, one at a time, beating well after each addition. Stir in the vanilla essence.

3 Sift the flour, cocoa powder, baking powder and salt into a bowl. Gradually stir into the chocolate mixture in batches, until blended.

4 Cover the dough, cool and chill for at least 1 hour, until the dough is cold and is able to hold its shape.

5 Preheat the oven to 160°C/ 325°F/Gas 3. Grease two or more large baking sheets.

6 Place the icing sugar in a deep bowl. Using a small ice-cream scoop or teaspoon, scoop out the cold dough and, between the palms of your hands, roll into 4cm/1½in balls.

7 Drop each ball into the icing sugar and roll until heavily coated. Remove with a slotted spoon and tap against the side of the bowl to remove excess sugar. Place on the prepared baking sheets about 4cm/1½in apart.

8 Bake for 10–15 minutes, until the tops feel slightly firm when touched. Remove the baking sheet to a wire rack for 2–3 minutes, then with a metal spatula or palette knife, place the cookies on the wire rack to cool completely.

Marbled Caramel Chocolate Slice

The classic millionaire's slice is made even more special here with a decorative and tasty marbled chocolate topping – guaranteed to make you feel like a lottery winner.

Makes about 24

For the base

250g/9oz/2¼ cups plain
  (all-purpose) flour
75g/3oz/scant ½ cup caster
  (superfine) sugar
175g/6oz/¾ cup unsalted (sweet)
  butter, softened

For the filling

90g/3½oz/7 tbsp unsalted (sweet)
  butter, diced
90g/3½oz/scant ½ cup light muscovado
  (brown) sugar
2 x 397g/14oz cans sweetened
  condensed milk

For the topping

90g/3½oz plain (semisweet) chocolate
90g/3½oz milk chocolate
50g/2oz white chocolate

I Preheat the oven to 180°C/350°F/ Gas 4. Line and lightly grease a 33 x 23cm/13 x 9in Swiss roll tin (jelly roll pan). Put the flour and caster sugar in a bowl and rub in the butter until the mixture resembles fine breadcrumbs. Work with your hands until the mixture forms a dough.

2 Put the dough into the prepared tin and press it out with your hand to cover the base. Then use the back of a tablespoon to smooth it evenly into the tin. Prick all over with a fork and bake for about 20 minutes, or until firm to the touch and very light brown. Set aside and leave in the tin to cool.

3 To make the filling, put the butter, muscovado sugar and condensed milk into a pan and heat gently, stirring, until the sugar has dissolved. Stirring constantly, bring to the boil. Reduce the heat and simmer the mixture very gently, stirring constantly, for about 5–10 minutes, or until it has thickened and has turned a caramel colour. Take care that the mixture does not burn on the base of the pan, as this will spoil the flavour. Remove from the heat.

4 Pour the filling mixture over the cookie base, spread evenly, then leave until cold.

5 To make the topping, melt each type of chocolate separately in a microwave or in a heatproof bowl set over a pan of hot water. Spoon lines of plain and milk chocolate over the set caramel filling.

6 Add small spoonfuls of white chocolate. Use a skewer to form a marbled effect on the topping.

Chocolate Fudge Triangles

These delightful white-chocolate fudge sandwiches are surprisingly easy to make and perfect for a children's party, although chocolate-loving adults will enjoy them, too.

Makes 48

600g/1lb 5oz good quality white
   chocolate, chopped
400ml/14fl oz/1¾ cups sweetened
   condensed milk
15ml/1 tbsp vanilla essence (extract)
7.5ml/1½ tsp lemon juice
pinch of salt
215g/7½oz/scant 2 cups hazelnuts or
   pecan nuts, chopped (optional)
175g/6oz plain (semisweet)
   chocolate, chopped
40g/1½oz/3 tbsp unsalted (sweet)
   butter, chopped
50g/2oz plain (semisweet) chocolate,
   melted, to decorate

1 Line a 20cm/8in square cake tin (pan) with foil. Melt the white chocolate with the condensed milk in a pan over a low heat, stirring frequently. Remove from the heat and stir in the vanilla essence, lemon juice, salt, and nuts, if using. Spread half the mixture in the tin. Chill in the refrigerator for 15 minutes.

2 Melt the plain chocolate with the butter in a pan over a low heat, stirring until smooth. Remove from the heat, cool slightly, then pour over the chilled white layer and chill for 15 minutes.

3 Gently reheat the remaining white chocolate and condensed milk mixture until melted and pour it over the set plain chocolate layer. Smooth the top with a palette knife or metal spatula, then chill in the refrigerator for 2–4 hours, until set.

4 Using the foil to lift it, remove the fudge from the tin and turn on to a chopping board. Remove the foil and, using a sharp knife, cut into 24 squares. Cut each square into two triangles. To decorate, drizzle with melted chocolate.

Chocolate, Maple and Walnut Swirls

Gloriously sticky and richly flavoured, these swirls are like a cross between cookies and slices of cake. Serve them as a weekend coffee-time treat when you've had a busy morning.

Makes 12

450g/1lb/4 cups strong white
  bread flour
2.5ml/½ tsp ground cinnamon
50g/2oz/¼ cup unsalted (sweet)
  butter, diced
50g/2oz/¼ cup caster
  (superfine) sugar
1 sachet easy-blend (rapid-rise)
  dried yeast
1 egg yolk
100ml/4fl oz/½ cup water
60ml/4 tbsp milk
10g/1½oz/3 tbsp unsalted (sweet)
  butter, melted
45ml/3 tbsp maple syrup, to finish

For the filling
50g/2oz/¼ cup light muscovado
  (brown) sugar
175g/6oz/1 cup plain (semisweet)
  chocolate chips
75g/3oz/¾ cup chopped walnuts

1 Grease a deep 23cm/9in springform cake tin (pan). Sift the flour and cinnamon into a bowl, then rub in the butter until the mixture resembles breadcrumbs.

2 Stir in the sugar and yeast. In a separate bowl, beat the egg yolk, with the measured water and milk, then stir the mixture into the dry ingredients to make a soft dough.

3 Knead until smooth, then roll out to about 40 x 30cm/16 x 12in. Brush evenly with melted butter.

4 To make the filling, sprinkle the dough evenly with the muscovado sugar, then the plain chocolate chips and, finally, the chopped walnuts.

5 Roll up the dough from a long side like a Swiss (jelly) roll, then cut into 12 thick even-size slices.

6 Pack the slices closely together in the prepared cake tin. Cover and leave in a warm place for 1½ hours, until well risen and springy to the touch. Preheat the oven to 220°C/425°F/Gas 7.

7 Bake for 30–35 minutes until well risen, golden brown and firm. Remove from the tin and transfer to a wire rack. To finish, spoon the maple syrup over the top. Pull the pieces apart to serve.

Cook's Tip
Make sure you use easy-blend (rapid-rise) yeast, as other kinds need dissolving first.

Chocolate Salami

This after-dinner sweetmeat resembles a salami in shape, hence its curious name – although, of course, the flavour is somewhat different. It is very rich and will serve a lot of people. Slice it very thinly and serve with espresso coffee and amaretto liqueur.

Serves 8–12

24 Petit Beurre cookies, broken
   into pieces
350g/12oz bittersweet or plain chocolate,
   broken into squares
225g/8oz/1 cup unsalted (sweet)
   butter, softened
60ml/4 tbsp amaretto liqueur
2 egg yolks
50g/2oz/½ cup flaked (sliced) almonds,
   lightly toasted and thinly
   shredded lengthways
25g/1oz/¼ cup ground almonds

Variation

If you like, substitute pistachio nuts for the flaked (sliced) almonds.

1 Place the cookies in a food processor and process until crushed into coarse crumbs.

2 Place the chocolate in a large heatproof bowl. Place the bowl over a pan of barely simmering water, add a small knob (pat) of the butter and all the liqueur and heat until the chocolate melts, stirring occasionally.

3 Remove the bowl from the heat, leave the chocolate to cool for a minute or two, then stir in the egg yolks, followed by the remaining butter, a little at a time. Tip in most of the crushed cookies, leaving behind a good handful, and stir well to mix. Stir in the shredded almonds. Leave the mixture in a cold place for about 1 hour until it begins to soften.

4 Process the remaining crushed cookies in the food processor until they are very finely ground. Tip into a bowl and mix with the ground almonds. Cover and set aside until you are ready to serve.

5 Turn the chocolate and cookie mixture on to a sheet of lightly oiled greaseproof (waxed) paper, then shape into a 35cm/14in long sausage with a palette knife or metal spatula, tapering the ends slightly so that the roll looks like a salami. Wrap securely in the paper and freeze the roll for at least 4 hours until solid.

6 To serve, unwrap the "salami". Spread the finely ground cookies and almonds out on a clean sheet of greaseproof paper and roll the salami in them until evenly coated. Transfer to a board and leave to stand for about 1 hour before serving in slices.

Cook's Tip

Take care when melting chocolate that it does not overheat. The base of the bowl must not touch the water, and the chocolate must be melted very gently. If you think the water is getting too hot, remove the pan from the heat.

Choc-tipped Cookies

Get those cold hands wrapped around a steaming hot drink and tuck into these tasty cookies. They're delightfully easy to make and quite delicious to eat.

Makes 22

115g/4oz/½ cup butter or margarine
   at room temperature, diced
45ml/3 tbsp icing (confectioners')
   sugar, sifted
150g/5oz/1¼ cups plain
   (all-purpose) flour
few drops vanilla essence (extract)
75g/3oz plain (semisweet)
   chocolate, chopped

1 Preheat the oven to 180°C/350°F/ Gas 4. Lightly grease two baking sheets. Put the butter or margarine and icing sugar in a mixing bowl and cream together until very soft.

2 Add the flour and vanilla essence to the creamed mixture and mix until thoroughly combined.

3 Spoon the mixture into a large piping (pastry) bag fitted with a large star nozzle and pipe 10–13cm/ 4–5in lines on the prepared baking sheets, leaving space for expansion.

4 Cook for 15–20 minutes, until pale golden brown. Leave on the baking sheets to cool slightly before lifting on to a wire rack. Leave the cookies to cool completely.

5 Put the chocolate in a small heatproof bowl and melt over a pan of hot, but not boiling water.

6 Dip both ends of each cookie into the melted chocolate, return the cookies to the wire rack as they are diped and leave them to set. Serve the cookies with mugs of hot chocolate topped with swirls of whipped cream and dusted with chocolate powder.

Variation
Make round cookies if you prefer, and dip each cookie into the melted chocolate to half coat.

Fruity Chocolate Cookie-cakes

The combination of spongy cookie, fruity preserve and dark chocolate makes irresistible eating for kids of all ages. As cookies go, these are a little time consuming, but that's all part of the fun.

Makes 18

90g/3½oz/½ cup caster
  (superfine) sugar
2 eggs
50g/2oz/½ cup plain (all-purpose) flour
75g/3oz/6 tbsp apricot-orange
  marmalade or apricot jam
125g/4¼oz plain (semisweet) chocolate

1 Preheat the oven to 190°C/375°F/ Gas 5. Grease 18 patty tins (muffin pans), preferably non-stick. (If you don't have that many patty tins, you'll need to bake the cookies in batches.)

2 Stand a mixing bowl in very hot water for a couple of minutes to heat through, keeping the inside of the bowl dry. Put the sugar and eggs in the bowl and whisk with a hand-held electric mixer until light and frothy and the beaters leave a ribbon trail when lifted. Sift the flour over the mixture and stir in gently using a large metal spoon.

3 Divide the mixture among the patty tins. Bake for 10 minutes until just firm and pale golden around the edges. Using a palette knife (metal spatula), lift from the tins and transfer to a wire rack to cool.

4 Press the marmalade or jam through a sieve to remove any rind or fruit pieces. Spoon a little of the smooth jam on to the centre of each cookie.

5 Break the chocolate into pieces and place in a heatproof bowl set over a pan of gently simmering water. Heat, stirring frequently, until melted and smooth.

6 Spoon a little chocolate on to the top of each cookie and spread gently to the edges with a palette knife. Once the chocolate has just started to set, very gently press it with the back of a fork to give a textured surface. Leave to set for at least 1 hour.

Chocolate Caramel Nuggets

Inside each of these buttery cookies lies a soft-centred chocolate-coated caramel. They're at their most delicious served an hour or so after baking, so you might want to shape them in advance, then put the baking sheet of uncooked nuggets in the refrigerator until you are ready to bake them.

Makes 14

150g/5oz/1¼ cups self-raising
  (self-rising) flour
90g/3½oz/7 tbsp unsalted (sweet) butter,
  chilled and diced
50g/2oz/¼ cup golden caster
  (superfine) sugar
1 egg yolk
5ml/1 tsp vanilla essence (extract)
14 soft-centred chocolate caramels
icing (confectioners') sugar and cocoa
  powder (unsweetened), for dusting

1 Put the flour and diced butter in a food processor and process until the mixture resembles fairly fine breadcrumbs.

2 Add the sugar, egg yolk and vanilla essence to the food processor and process to a smooth dough. Wrap the dough in clear film (plastic wrap) and chill for 30 minutes.

3 Preheat the oven to 200°C/400°F/ Gas 6. Grease a large baking sheet.

4 Roll out the dough thinly on a lightly floured surface and cut out 28 rounds using a 5cm/2in cutter.

5 Place one chocolate caramel on a cookie round, then lay a second round on top. Pinch the edges of the dough together so that the chocolate caramel is completely enclosed, then place on the baking sheet. Make the remaining cookies in the same way. Bake for about 10 minutes until pale golden.

6 Transfer to a wire rack and leave to cool. Serve lightly dusted with icing sugar and cocoa powder.

Chocolate Whirls

These cookies are so easy that you don't even have to make any dough. They're made with ready-made puff pastry rolled up with a chocolate filling. They're not too sweet and are similar to Danish pastries, so you could even make them as a special treat for breakfast.

Makes about 20

75g/3oz/⅓ cup golden caster (superfine) sugar
40g/1½oz/6 tbsp cocoa powder (unsweetened)
2 eggs
500g/1lb 2oz puff pastry
25g/1oz/2 tbsp butter, softened
75g/3oz/generous ½ cup sultanas (golden raisins)
90g/3½oz milk chocolate

I Preheat the oven to 220°C/425°F/ Gas 7. Grease two baking sheets.

2 Put the sugar, cocoa powder and eggs in a bowl and mix to a paste.

3 Roll out the pastry on a lightly floured surface to make a 30cm/ 12in square. Trim off any rough edges using a sharp knife.

4 Dot the pastry all over with the softened butter, then spread with the chocolate paste and sprinkle the sultanas over the top.

Cook's Tip
Use a sharp knife to cut the cookie slices from the pastry roll, and wipe the blade clean with a cloth every few slices.

5 Roll the pastry into a sausage-shape, then cut the roll into 1cm/ ½in slices. Place the slices on the baking sheets, spacing them apart.

6 Bake the cookies for 10 minutes until risen and pale golden. Transfer to a wire rack and leave to cool.

7 Break the milk chocolate into pieces and put in a heatproof bowl set over a pan of gently simmering water. Heat, stirring frequently until melted and smooth.

8 Spoon or pipe lines of melted chocolate over the cookies, taking care not to completely hide the swirls of chocolate filling.

Chocolate Truffle Cookies

Deeply decadent, these melt-in-the-mouth cookies are given a wicked twist by the addition of cherry brandy – the perfect way to end a dinner party.

Makes 18

50g/2oz/½ cup plain
   (all-purpose) flour
25g/1oz/¼ cup (unsweetened)
   cocoa powder
2.5ml/½ tsp baking powder
90g/3½oz/½ cup caster
   (superfine) sugar
25g/1oz/2 tbsp butter, diced
1 egg, beaten
5ml/1 tsp cherry brandy or fresh
   orange juice
50g/2oz/½ cup icing
   (confectioners') sugar

1 Preheat the oven to 200°C/400°F/ Gas 6. Line two baking sheets with baking parchment.

2 Sift the flour, cocoa and baking powder into a bowl and stir in the sugar. Rub in the butter until the mixture resembles breadcrumbs. Mix together the beaten egg and cherry brandy or orange juice and stir into the flour mixture. Cover with clear film (plastic wrap) and chill in the refrigerator for 30 minutes.

3 Put the icing sugar into a bowl. Shape walnut-size pieces of dough roughly into a ball and drop into the icing sugar. Toss until thickly coated then place on the baking sheets.

4 Bake for about 10 minutes, or until just set. Transfer to a wire rack to cool completely.

White Chocolate Brownies

These scrumptious brownies are best served cut into very small portions – not only because they are incredibly rich, but also because kids find tiny, bitesize cookies utterly irresistible.

Makes 18

75g/3oz/6 tbsp unsalted (sweet)
  butter, diced
400g/14oz white chocolate, chopped
3 eggs
90g/3½oz/½ cup golden caster
  (superfine) sugar
10ml/2 tsp vanilla essence (extract)
90g/3½oz/¾ cup sultanas
  (golden raisins)
coarsely grated rind of 1 lemon, plus
  15ml/1 tbsp juice
200g/7oz/1¾ cups plain
  (all-purpose) flour

1 Preheat the oven to 190°C/375°F/ Gas 5. Grease and line a 28 × 20cm/ 11 × 8in shallow baking tin (pan) with baking parchment.

2 Put the butter and 300g/11oz of the chocolate in a bowl and melt over a pan of gently simmering water, stirring frequently.

3 Remove the bowl from the heat and beat in the eggs and sugar, then add the vanilla essence, sultanas, lemon rind and juice, flour and the remaining chocolate.

4 Tip the mixture into the tin and spread into the corners. Bake for about 20 minutes until slightly risen and the surface is only just turning golden. The centre should still be slightly soft. Leave to cool in the tin.

5 Cut the brownies into small squares and then carefully remove them from the tin.

Rich Chocolate Cookie Slice

These rich, dark chocolate refrigerator cookies are perfect served with strong coffee, either as a mid-morning treat or even in place of dessert. They are always very popular.

Makes about 10

275g/10oz fruit and nut plain
(semisweet) chocolate

130g/4½oz/½ cup unsalted (sweet)
butter, diced

90g/3½oz digestive biscuits
(graham crackers)

90g/3½oz white chocolate

1 Grease and line the base and sides of a 450g/1lb loaf tin (pan) with baking parchment. Break the fruit and nut chocolate into even-size pieces and place in a heatproof bowl along with the diced unsalted butter.

2 Set the bowl over a pan of simmering water and stir gently until melted. Cool for 20 minutes.

3 Break the digestive biscuits into small pieces with your fingers. Finely chop the white chocolate.

4 Stir the broken biscuits and white chocolate into the cooled, melted fruit and nut chocolate until combined. Turn the mixture into the prepared tin and pack down gently. Chill for 2 hours, or until set.

5 To serve, turn out the mixture and remove the lining paper. Cut into slices with a sharp knife.

Variation
You can use this simple, basic recipe for all kinds of variations. Try different kinds of chocolate, such as ginger, hazelnut, honey and almond, peanut or mocha.

Giant Triple Chocolate Cookies

Here is the ultimate cookie, packed full of chocolate and macadamia nuts. You will have to be patient when they come out of the oven, as they are too soft to move until completely cold.

Makes 12 large cookies

90g/3½oz milk chocolate
90g/3½oz white chocolate
300g/11oz dark (bittersweet) chocolate
   (minimum 70 per cent cocoa solids)
90g/3½oz/7 tbsp unsalted (sweet) butter,
   at room temperature, diced
5ml/1 tsp vanilla essence (extract)
150g/5oz/¾ cup light muscovado
   (brown) sugar
150g/5oz/1¼ cups self-raising
   (self-rising) flour
100g/3½oz/scant 1 cup macadamia
   nut halves

1 Preheat the oven to 180°C/350°F/ Gas 4. Line two baking sheets with baking parchment. Coarsely chop the milk and white chocolate and put them in a bowl.

2 Chop 200g/7oz of the dark chocolate into very large chunks, at least 2cm/¾in in size. Set aside.

3 Break up the remaining dark chocolate and place in a heatproof bowl set over a pan of barely simmering water. Stir until melted and smooth. Remove from the heat and stir in the butter, then the vanilla essence and muscovado sugar.

4 Add the flour and mix gently. Add half the dark chocolate chunks, all the milk and white chocolate and the nuts and fold together.

5 Spoon 12 mounds on to the baking sheets. Press the remaining dark chocolate chunks into the top of each cookie. Bake for about 12 minutes until just beginning to colour. Cool on the baking sheets.

Chocolate Chip Oat Cookies

Easy to make and delicious to eat. These vanilla-flavoured cookies are exceedingly moreish, so you'll need to keep the cookie jar or biscuit barrel well stocked up with this family favourite.

Makes 60

115g/4oz/1 cup plain (all-purpose) flour
2.5ml/½ tsp bicarbonate of soda
  (baking soda)
1.5ml/¼ tsp baking powder
pinch of salt
115g/4oz/½ cup butter or margarine
  at room temperature, diced
115g/4oz/generous ½ cup caster
  (superfine) sugar
90g/3½oz/½ cup soft light brown sugar
1 egg
2.5ml/½ tsp vanilla essence (extract)
75g/3oz/scant 1 cup rolled oats
175g/6oz/1 cup plain (semisweet)
  chocolate chips

1 Preheat the oven to 180°C/350°F/ Gas 4. Lightly grease three or four baking sheets.

2 Sift the flour, bicarbonate of soda, baking powder and salt into a mixing bowl. Set aside.

3 With an electric mixer, cream together the butter or margarine and the sugars. Add the egg and vanilla and beat until light and fluffy.

4 Add the flour mixture and beat on low speed until thoroughly blended. Stir in the rolled oats and chocolate chips. The dough should be crumbly. Drop heaped teaspoonfuls on to the prepared baking sheets, spacing the dough about 2.5cm/1in apart.

5 Bake for about 15 minutes until just firm around the edge but still soft to the touch in the centre. Transfer the cookies to a wire rack and leave to cool.

Variation

For an elegant look, melt plain (semisweet) chocolate over a pan of hot, but not boiling water, stirring until smooth. Dip the baked cookies into the chocolate to cover one half of the cookie.

Double Chocolate Cookies

Keep these scrumptious treats under lock and key unless you're feeling especially generous. With two types of chocolate, they would certainly make a special gift for a good friend.

Makes 18–20

115g/4oz/½ cup unsalted (sweet) butter
  at room temperature, diced
115g/4oz/½ cup light muscovado
  (brown) sugar
1 egg
5ml/1 tsp vanilla essence (extract)
150g/5oz/1¼ cups self-raising
  (self-rising) flour
75g/3oz/scant 1 cup rolled oats
115g/4oz plain (semisweet) chocolate,
  coarsely chopped
115g/4oz white chocolate,
  coarsely chopped

3 Place small spoonfuls of the mixture in 18–20 rocky heaps on the prepared baking sheets, leaving space for spreading.

4 Bake for 15–20 minutes until beginning to turn pale golden brown. Cool for 2–3 minutes on the baking sheets, then, using a spatula, transfer the cookies to wire racks to cool completely.

Variation

If you're short of time when making these cookies, substitute chocolate chips for the chopped chocolate. Chopped preserved stem ginger would make a delicious addition as well.

1 Preheat the oven to 190°C/375°F/ Gas 5. Lightly grease two baking sheets. Cream the butter with the sugar in a bowl until pale and fluffy. Add the egg and vanilla essence and beat well.

2 Sift the flour over the mixture and fold in lightly with a metal spoon, then add the oats and chopped plain and white chocolate and stir well until evenly mixed.

Cook's Tip

Rolled oats are also known as oatflakes and porridge oats. Fine oatmeal is also excellent for making cookies.

Chocolate Chip Hazelnut Cookies

Hazelnuts impart a delicious nutty flavour to these little cookies. They would make a wonderful late night snack with a steaming mug of hot chocolate, topped with whipped cream.

Makes 36

115g/4oz/1 cup plain (all-purpose) flour
5ml/1 tsp baking powder
pinch of salt
75g/3oz/⅓ cup butter or margarine
   at room temperature, diced
115g/4oz/generous ½ cup caster
   (superfine) sugar
50g/2oz/¼ cup soft light brown sugar
1 egg
5ml/1 tsp vanilla essence (extract)
125g/4½oz/⅔ cup chocolate chips
50g/2oz/½ cup hazelnuts, chopped

1 Preheat the oven to 180°C/350°F/ Gas 4. Grease two or three baking sheets. Sift the flour, baking powder and salt into a small bowl. Set aside.

2 With an electric mixer, cream together the butter or margarine and the sugars. Beat in the egg and vanilla essence. Add the flour mixture and beat well with the mixer on low speed.

3 Stir in the chocolate chips and half of the chopped hazelnuts.

4 Drop teaspoonfuls of the mixture on to the prepared baking sheets, to form 2cm/¾in mounds. Space the cookies 2.5–5cm/1–2in apart.

5 Flatten each cookie lightly with a wet fork. Sprinkle the remaining hazelnuts on top of the cookies and press lightly into the surface.

6 Bake for 10–12 minutes, until golden. With a metal spatula, transfer the cookies to a wire rack and leave to cool completely.

Cook's Tip

If you need to skin the hazelnuts yourself, spread them out on a baking sheet and toast lightly under the grill (broiler) or in a preheated oven, at 180°C/350°F/Gas 4, then tip into a clean dishtowel. Rub with the dishtowel and the skins should slip off easily. Pick off any obstinate pieces.

Chocolate-coated Nut Brittle

Equal amounts of pecan nuts and almonds set in crisp caramel, then coated in dark chocolate, make a sensational gift – if you can bear to give them away.

Makes 20–24

115g/4oz/1 cup mixed pecan nuts and
   whole almonds
115g/4oz/generous ½ cup caster
   (superfine) sugar
60ml/4 tbsp water
200g/7oz plain (semisweet)
   chocolate, chopped

4 Quickly remove the pan from the heat and tip the mixture on to the prepared baking sheet, spreading it evenly. Leave until completely cold and set hard.

5 Break the nut brittle into pieces. Melt the chocolate and dip the nut brittle to half-coat them. Leave on a sheet of baking parchment to set, then store in an airtight container.

1 Lightly grease a baking sheet. Mix the nuts, sugar and water in a heavy pan. Cook over a low heat, stirring until the sugar has dissolved.

2 Bring to the boil, then lower the heat to medium and cook without stirring until the mixture turns a rich golden brown and registers 148°C/300°F on a sugar thermometer.

3 To test without a thermometer, drop a small amount of the mixture into iced water. It should become brittle enough to snap.

Cook's Tip

This brittle looks best in coarse chunks, so don't worry if the pieces break unevenly, or if there are few small gaps in the chocolate coating.

Indulgent Cookies

In case all the previous recipes haven't spoilt you for choice, here is a superb collection of mouthwatering treats that will prove totally irresistible – from blissful Tiramisu Cookies to light-as-air Praline Pavlova Cookies. There is something special to indulge everyone, whether your tastes are for the rich and creamy, fresh and fruity or dark and chocolatey. There are even breakfast cookies that cook overnight while you sleep.

Florentine Cookies

These are not your traditional Florentines but an utterly yummy cookie version with a soft crumbly base and a wonderfully sticky chewy topping.

Makes 24

115g/4oz/½ cup unsalted (sweet) butter,
   at room temperature, diced
115g/4oz/generous ½ cup caster
   (superfine) sugar
1 egg
a few drops of almond essence
   (extract) (optional)
225g/8oz/2 cups self-raising
   (self-rising) flour

For the topping

175g/6oz/1½ cups ready-to-eat dried
   apricots, chopped
50g/2oz/½ cup dried mango pieces,
   chopped
100g/3½oz/scant 1 cup flaked
   (sliced) almonds
60ml/4 tbsp plain (all-purpose) flour
50g/2oz/¼ cup unsalted (sweet) butter
50g/2oz/¼ cup golden caster
   (superfine) sugar
60ml/4 tbsp golden (light corn) syrup

1 Preheat the oven to 190°C/375°F/ Gas 5. Lightly grease two baking sheets. Cream together the butter and sugar until the mixture is light and fluffy, then beat in the egg, making sure it is well combined. Stir in the almond essence, if using, and the flour and mix to a firm yet soft dough, working it together with your hands.

Variation

For an even more self-indulgent treat, make the topping using maple, rather than golden syrup. Make sure you buy the pure syrup that has not been blended with other cheaper syrups, as it has an incomparable flavour.

2 Roll the dough out on a floured surface and, using a 7.5cm/3in plain round biscuit (cookie) cutter, stamp out 24 rounds. Place them on the prepared baking sheets, spaced slightly apart to allow for spreading.

3 To make the topping, put the apricots, mango pieces, almonds and flour in a bowl and toss gently together to mix. Put the butter, sugar and syrup in a small pan and heat gently until the butter has melted and the mixture is smooth and combined. Pour the butter mixture over the fruit and nuts and mix thoroughly.

4 Spoon the mixture on top of the cookies, spreading it right to the edges. Bake for 12–14 minutes until golden brown and crisp on top. Leave the cookies on the baking sheets for 5 minutes to firm up slightly, then transfer to a wire rack to cool completely.

Candied Peel Crumble Cookies

Crumbly, melt-in-the-mouth cookies, these incorporate candied peel, walnuts and white chocolate chips and are coated with a zingy lemon glaze.

Makes about 24

175g/6oz/¾ cup unsalted (sweet) butter,
   at room temperature, diced
90g/3½oz/½ cup caster (superfine) sugar
1 egg, beaten
finely grated rind of 1 lemon
200g/7oz/1¾ cups self-raising
   (self-rising) flour
90g/3½oz/generous ½ cup
   candied peel, chopped
75g/3oz/¾ cup chopped walnuts
50g/2oz/⅓ cup white chocolate chips

For the glaze

50g/2oz/½ cup icing (confectioners')
   sugar, sifted
15ml/1 tbsp lemon juice
thin strips of candied peel, to
   decorate (optional)

1 Preheat the oven to 180°C/350°F/ Gas 4. Grease two baking sheets or line them with baking parchment. Put the butter and sugar in a large bowl and cream together. Add the egg and beat thoroughly. Add the lemon rind and flour and stir together gently. Finally, fold the candied peel, walnuts and chocolate chips into the mixture.

2 Place tablespoonfuls of mixture, spaced slightly apart, on the baking sheets and bake for 12–15 minutes, until cooked but still pale in colour. Transfer the cookies to a wire rack.

3 For the glaze, put the icing sugar in a bowl and stir in the lemon juice. Spoon glaze over each cookie. Decorate with candied peel, if using.

Midnight Cookies

These cookies are so called because you can make them up before you go to bed and leave them to bake slowly in the switched-off oven. Hey presto – there they are in the morning, lightly crunchy on the outside and deliciously soft in the middle. A wonderfully indulgent way to start the day.

Makes 9

1 egg white
90g/3½oz/½ cup caster
  (superfine) sugar
50g/2oz/½ cup ground almonds
90g/3½oz/generous ½ cup milk
  chocolate chips
90g/3½oz/scant ½ cup glacé (candied)
  cherries, chopped
50g/2oz/⅔ cup sweetened,
  shredded coconut

1 Preheat the oven to 220°C/425°F/ Gas 7. Line a baking sheet with baking parchment. Put the egg white in a large, clean, grease-free bowl and whisk until stiff peaks form.

2 Add the caster sugar to the whisked egg white, a spoonful at a time, whisking well between each addition until the sugar is fully incorporated. The mixture should be completely smooth and glossy in appearance. Use an electric mixer for speed.

3 Fold in the almonds, chocolate chips, cherries and coconut. Place 9 spoonfuls on the baking sheet. Place in the oven, close the door then turn the oven off. Leave overnight (or at least 6 hours during the day) and don't open the door. Serve the cookies for breakfast.

Banana Cream Cookies

These delicious cookies are inspired by the classic childhood dessert bananas and cream. The warm banana cookies are coated in crisp, sugar-frosted cornflakes and, for the ultimate indulgence, are delicious served warm drizzled with clear honey.

Makes about 24

2 eggs
250g/9oz/1¼ cups soft light
   brown sugar
5ml/1 tsp vanilla essence (extract)
100ml/3½fl oz/scant ½ cup
   sunflower oil
90g/3½oz/scant ½ cup crème fraîche
200g/7oz/1¾ cups plain
   (all-purpose) flour
200g/7oz/1¾ cups self-raising
   (self-rising) flour
50g/2oz/2½ cups frosted cornflakes
125g/4¼oz dried small bananas,
   chopped, or 2 bananas, peeled
   and chopped
icing (confectioners') sugar, sifted,
   for dredging

1 Preheat the oven to 180°C/350°F/ Gas 4. Line two or three baking sheets with baking parchment. Put the eggs and brown sugar in a large bowl and whisk together until well blended. Stir in the vanilla essence. Add the oil and crème fraîche and stir in well. Add the flour and mix well. (The mixture will be quite runny at this stage.) Cover with clear film (plastic wrap) and chill in the refrigerator for about 30 minutes.

2 Put the frosted cornflakes in a large bowl. Remove the cookie dough from the refrigerator and stir in the bananas. Using a tablespoon, drop heaps into the flakes. Lightly toss so each cookie is well coated, then remove and place on the prepared baking sheets. Flatten very slightly with your fingertips.

3 Bake for 15–20 minutes, or until risen and golden brown and crispy. Transfer the cookies to a wire rack and dredge with sifted icing sugar. Serve while still warm.

Praline Pavlova Cookies

Crisp, melt-in-the-mouth meringue with a luxurious velvety chocolate filling is topped with nutty praline – just the thing for a special tea party or simply when you feel in need of a treat.

Makes 14

2 large (US extra large)
  egg whites
large pinch of ground cinnamon
90g/3½oz/½ cup caster
  (superfine) sugar
50g/2oz/½ cup pecan nuts,
  finely chopped

For the filling

50g/2oz/¼ cup unsalted (sweet) butter,
  at room temperature, diced
100g/3½oz/scant 1 cup icing
  (confectioners') sugar, sifted
50g/2oz plain (semisweet) chocolate

For the praline

60ml/4 tbsp caster (superfine) sugar
15g/½oz/1 tbsp finely chopped
  toasted almonds

2 Place 14 spoonfuls of meringue on the prepared baking sheets, spaced well apart. Using the back of a wetted teaspoon, make a small hollow in the top of each meringue so it looks like a little nest. Bake in the oven for 45–60 minutes until dry and just beginning to colour. Remove from the oven and set aside to cool.

4 To make the praline, put the sugar in a small non-stick frying pan. Heat gently until the sugar melts to form a clear liquid. When the mixture begins to turn brown, stir in the nuts. When the mixture is a golden brown, remove from the heat and pour immediately on to a lightly oiled or non-stick baking sheet. Leave to cool completely and then break into small pieces. Sprinkle over the meringues and serve.

Cook's Tip
These cookies should be eaten immediately once they have been assembled. To make them ahead of time, store the unfilled meringues in an airtight container and place the filling in a covered container in a cool place. Make the praline on the day itself.

Variation
Use toasted hazelnuts, instead of almonds, to make the praline.

1 Preheat the oven to 140°C/275°F/Gas 1. Line two baking sheets with baking parchment. Put the egg whites in a bowl and whisk until stiff. Stir the cinnamon into the sugar. Add a spoonful of sugar to the egg whites and whisk well. Continue adding the sugar, a spoonful at a time, whisking well until the mixture is thick and glossy. Stir in the chopped pecan nuts.

3 To make the filling, beat together the butter and icing sugar until light and creamy. Break the chocolate into even-size pieces and place in a heatproof bowl. Set over a pan of barely simmering water and stir occasionally until melted. Remove from the heat and leave to cool slightly. Add the chocolate to the butter mixture and stir well. Divide the filling among the meringues, putting a little in each hollow.

Tiramisu Cookies

These delicate cookies taste like the wonderful Italian dessert with its flavours of coffee, chocolate, rum and rich creamy custard. Serve with coffee or cups of frothy hot chocolate.

Makes 14

50g/2oz/¼ cup butter, at room
  temperature, diced
90g/3½oz/½ cup caster
  (superfine) sugar
1 egg, beaten
50g/2oz/½ cup plain (all-purpose) flour

For the filling

150g/5oz/⅔ cup mascarpone cheese
15ml/1 tbsp dark rum
2.5ml/½ tsp instant coffee powder
15ml/1 tbsp light muscovado
  (molasses) sugar

For the topping

75g/3oz white chocolate
15ml/1 tbsp milk
30ml/2 tbsp crushed chocolate flakes

1 To make the filling, put the mascarpone cheese in a bowl. Mix together the rum and coffee powder, stirring well until the coffee has dissolved. Add the rum and coffee mixture and the sugar to the cheese and mix together well. Cover with clear film (plastic wrap) and chill until required.

2 Preheat the oven to 200°C/400°F/ Gas 6. Line two or three baking sheets with baking parchment. To make the cookies, cream together the butter and sugar in a bowl until light and fluffy. Add the beaten egg and mix well. Stir in the flour and mix thoroughly again until well combined.

3 Put the mixture into a piping (pastry) bag fitted with a 1.5cm/⅝in plain nozzle and pipe 28 small blobs on to the baking sheets, spaced slightly apart. Cook for about 6–8 minutes until firm in the centre and just beginning to brown on the edges. Remove from the oven and set aside to cool.

4 When ready to assemble, spread a little of the filling on to half the cookies and place the other halves on top. Put the chocolate and milk in a heatproof bowl and melt over a pan of hot water. Take care not to overheat. When the chocolate has melted, stir vigorously to make a smooth spreadable consistency. Spread the chocolate topping evenly over the cookies, then sprinkle with crushed chocolate flakes to finish.

Chocolate and Prune Cookies

When freshly baked, these cookies have a deliciously gooey centre. As they cool down the mixture hardens slightly to form a firmer, fudge-like consistency. Try these with a glass of brandy.

Makes 18

150g/5oz/⅔ cup butter, at room
    temperature, diced
150g/5oz/¾ cup caster (superfine) sugar
1 egg yolk
250g/9oz/2¼ cups self-raising
    (self-rising) flour
25g/1oz/¼ cup (unsweetened)
    cocoa powder
about 90g/3½oz plain (semisweet)
    chocolate, coarsely chopped

For the topping

50g/2oz plain (semisweet) chocolate
9 ready-to-eat prunes, halved

1 Preheat the oven to 190°C/375°F/ Gas 5. Line two baking sheets with baking parchment. Cream the butter and sugar together until light and creamy. Beat in the egg yolk. Sift over the flour and cocoa powder and stir in to make a firm yet soft dough.

2 Roll out about a third of the dough on baking parchment. Using a 5cm/2in round biscuit (cookie) cutter, stamp out 18 rounds and place them on the baking sheets.

3 Sprinkle the chopped chocolate in the centre of each cookie.

4 Roll out the remaining dough in the same way as before and, using a 7.5cm/3in round biscuit cutter, stamp out 18 "lids". Carefully lay the lids over the cookie bases and press the edges well together to seal. Don't worry if the lids crack slightly when you do this.

5 Bake for about 10 minutes until the cookies have spread a little and are just firm to a light touch. Leave them on the baking sheets for about 5 minutes to firm up slightly, then, using a palette knife (metal spatula), transfer to a wire rack to cool completely.

6 For the topping, melt the chocolate in a heatproof bowl set over a pan of hot water. Dip the cut side of the prunes in the chocolate then place one on top of each cookie. Spoon any remaining chocolate over the prunes.

Chocolate Fruit and Nut Cookies

These simple, chunky gingerbread cookies make a delicious gift, especially when presented in a decorative box. The combination of walnuts, almonds and cherries is very effective, but you can use any other mixture of glacé or candied fruits and nuts.

Makes 20

50g/2oz/4 tbsp caster (superfine) sugar
75ml/5 tbsp water
225g/8oz plain (semisweet)
  chocolate, chopped
40g/1½oz/⅓ cup walnut halves
75g/3oz/⅓ cup glacé (candied) cherries,
  chopped into small wedges
115g/4oz/1 cup whole blanched almonds

For the Lebkuchen

115g/4oz/½ cup unsalted (sweet) butter
115g/4oz/½ cup light muscovado
  (brown) sugar
1 egg, beaten
115g/4oz/⅓ cup black treacle (molasses)
400g/14oz/3½ cups self-raising
  (self-rising) flour
5ml/1 tsp ground ginger
2.5ml/½ tsp ground cloves
1.5ml/¼ tsp chilli powder

1 To make the Lebkuchen, cream together the butter and sugar until pale and fluffy. Beat in the egg and black treacle.

2 Sift the flour, ginger, cloves and chilli powder into the bowl. Using a wooden spoon, gradually mix the ingredients together to make a stiff paste. Turn on to a lightly floured surface and knead lightly until smooth. Wrap and chill for 30 minutes.

3 Shape the dough into a roll, about 20cm/8in long. Chill for 30 minutes. Preheat the oven to 180°C/350°F/ Gas 4. Grease two baking sheets.

4 Cut the dough roll into 20 slices and space them on the baking sheets. Bake for 10 minutes. Leave on the baking sheets for 5 minutes, then transfer to a wire rack and leave to cool.

5 Put the sugar and water in a small, heavy pan. Heat gently, stirring constantly until the sugar has completely dissolved. Bring to the boil and boil without stirring for 1 minute, until slightly syrupy.

6 Remove the pan from the heat and leave for 3 minutes, to cool slightly, and then stir in the chocolate until it has completely melted and made a smooth sauce.

7 Place the wire rack of cookies over a large tray or board. Spoon a little of the chocolate mixture over the cookies, spreading it to the edges with the back of the spoon.

8 Gently press a walnut half into the centre of each cookie. Arrange pieces of glacé cherry and almonds alternately around the nuts. Leave to set in a cool place.

Cook's Tip

Carefully stack the cookies in a pretty box or tin, lined with tissue paper, or tie in cellophane bundles.

Variation

If you prefer, make simpler chocolate-covered Lebkuchen. Simply omit the walnuts, cherries and almonds and sprinkle the cookies with (unsweetened) cocoa powder before serving.

Cranberry and Chocolate Squares

There is no doubt that the contrasting flavours of tangy, sharp cranberries and sweet chocolate were made for each other – and make fabulous cream-topped squares.

Makes 12

115g/4oz/½ cup unsalted (sweet) butter

60ml/4 tbsp (unsweetened)
  cocoa powder

215g/7½oz/scant 1 cup light muscovado
  (brown) sugar

150g/5oz/1¼ cups self-raising
  (self-rising) flour

2 eggs, beaten

115g/4oz/1 cup fresh or thawed
  frozen cranberries

For the topping

150ml/¼ pint/⅔ cup sour cream

75g/3oz/6 tbsp caster (superfine) sugar

30ml/2 tbsp self-raising (self-rising) flour

50g/2oz/4 tbsp soft margarine

1 egg, beaten

2.5ml/½ tsp vanilla essence (extract)

75ml/5 tbsp coarsely grated plain
  (semisweet) chocolate, for sprinkling

1 Preheat the oven to 180°C/350°F/ Gas 4. Grease an 18 x 25cm/ 7 x 10in cake tin (pan) and dust lightly with flour. Combine the butter, cocoa powder and sugar in a pan and stir over a low heat until melted and smooth.

2 Remove from the heat and stir in the flour and eggs. Stir in the cranberries, then spread the mixture in the prepared cake tin.

3 To make the topping, mix all the ingredients, except the chocolate, in a bowl. Beat until smooth, then spread over the mixture in the tin.

4 Sprinkle evenly with the coarsely grated chocolate and bake for about 40 minutes, or until risen and firm. Leave to cool completely in the tin, then cut into 12 squares. Store in an airtight container.

Chocolate-dipped Crescents

A very simple idea, but these hazelnut-flavoured cookies do look special. Walnuts or pecan nuts can be used instead of hazelnuts, but they must be finely ground.

Makes 35

300g/11oz/2⅔ cups plain
   (all-purpose) flour
pinch of salt
225g/8oz/1 cup unsalted (sweet) butter
   at room temperature, diced
50g/2oz/¼ cup caster (superfine) sugar
15ml/1 tbsp hazelnut liqueur or water
5ml/1 tsp vanilla essence (extract)
75g/3oz plain (semisweet) chocolate,
   finely grated
65g/2½oz/⅔ cup hazelnuts, toasted and
   finely chopped
icing (confectioners') sugar, for dusting
350g/12oz plain (semisweet) chocolate,
   melted, for dipping

1 Preheat the oven to 160°C/325°F/ Gas 3. Grease two large baking sheets. Sift the flour and salt into a small bowl.

2 In a large bowl, using an electric mixer, beat the butter until creamy. Add the sugar and beat until fluffy, then beat in the hazelnut liqueur or water and vanilla essence. Using a wooden spoon, gently stir in the flour mixture, until just blended, then fold in the grated chocolate and chopped hazelnuts.

3 With floured hands, shape the dough into 5 x 1cm/2 x ½in crescent shapes. Place on the prepared baking sheets, 5cm/2in apart. Bake for 20–25 minutes, until the edges are set and the cookies slightly golden. Remove the baking sheets to a wire rack to cool for 10 minutes. Transfer the cookies to wire racks to cool completely.

4 Line the baking sheets with baking parchment. Dust the cooled cookies with icing sugar. Using a pair of kitchen tongs, or your fingers, dip half of each crescent into the melted chocolate. Place on the prepared baking sheets. Leave in a cool place until the chocolate has set firmly.

Viennese Whirls

**These crisp, melt-in-the-mouth piped cookies are filled with a creamy coffee buttercream.
Needless to say, they are delicious served with Viennese coffee or hot chocolate.**

Makes 20

175g/6oz/¾ cup butter
50g/2oz/½ cup icing
   (confectioners') sugar
2.5ml/½ tsp vanilla essence (extract)
115g/4oz/1 cup plain
   (all-purpose) flour
50g/2oz/½ cup cornflour (cornstarch)
icing (confectioners') sugar and
   (unsweetened) cocoa powder, to dust

For the filling

15ml/1 tbsp ground coffee
60ml/4 tbsp single (light) cream
75g/3oz/6 tbsp butter, softened
115g/4oz/1 cup icing (confectioners')
   sugar, sifted

Cook's Tip

*For mocha Viennese whirls, substitute
25g/1oz/¼ cup (unsweetened) cocoa
powder for 25g/1oz/¼ cup of the flour.*

1 Preheat the oven to 180°C/
350°F/Gas 4. Grease two baking
sheets. Cream together the butter,
icing sugar and vanilla essence until
light. Stir in the flour and cornflour
and mix until smooth.

2 Using two tablespoons, spoon the
mixture into a piping (pastry) bag
fitted with a 1cm/½in fluted nozzle.

3 Pipe small rosettes, spaced well
apart, on the prepared baking
sheets. Bake for 12–15 minutes until
golden. Using a metal spatula,
transfer to a wire rack to cool.

4 To make the filling, put the ground
coffee in a heatproof bowl. Heat the
cream in a small pan to just below
boiling point and then pour it over
the coffee. Leave to infuse (steep)
for 4 minutes, then strain through a
fine sieve into a clean bowl.

5 Beat together the butter, icing
sugar and coffee-flavoured cream
until light and thoroughly combined.
Use to sandwich the cooled cookies
together in pairs. Dust the whirls
lightly with a little icing sugar and
cocoa powder.

Pecan Toffee Shortbread

Coffee shortbread is topped with pecan-studded toffee – what could be more scrumptious? Cornflour gives it a crunchy light texture, but all plain flour can be used if you like.

Makes 20

15ml/1 tbsp ground coffee
15ml/1 tbsp near-boiling water
115g/4oz/½ cup butter, softened
30ml/2 tbsp smooth peanut butter
75g/3oz/scant ½ cup caster
  (superfine) sugar
75g/3oz/⅔ cup cornflour (cornstarch)
185g/6½oz/1⅔ cups plain
  (all-purpose) flour

For the topping

175g/6oz/¾ cup butter
175g/6oz/¾ cup soft light brown sugar
30ml/2 tbsp golden (light corn) syrup
175g/6oz/1 cup shelled pecan nuts,
  halved

1 Preheat the oven to 180°C/
350°F/Gas 4. Grease and line a
18 × 28cm/7 × 11in tin (pan) with
greaseproof (waxed) paper.

2 Put the ground coffee in a small
heatproof bowl and pour the hot
water over it. Leave to steep for
4 minutes. Strain through a sieve
into a bowl. Discard the grounds.

3 Cream the butter, peanut butter,
sugar and coffee until light. Sift the
cornflour and flour together and
mix in to make a smooth dough.

4 Press into the base of the tin and
prick all over with a fork. Bake for
20 minutes. To make the topping,
put the butter, sugar and syrup in a
pan and heat until melted. Bring the
mixture to the boil.

5 Simmer for 5 minutes, then stir
in the pecan nuts. Spread the
topping evenly over the base. Leave
in the tin until cold, then cut into
squares or bars. Remove from the
tin and serve.

Mocha Viennese Swirls

Sophisticated cookies that look elegant and taste superb, these swirls can be served with morning coffee to impress your guests or just please your friends.

Makes 20

250g/9oz plain (semisweet)
  chocolate, chopped
200g/7oz/scant 1 cup unsalted (sweet)
  butter at room temperature, diced
50g/2oz/½ cup icing
  (confectioners') sugar
30ml/2 tbsp strong black coffee
200g/7oz/1¾ cups plain
  (all-purpose) flour
50g/2oz/½ cup cornflour (cornstarch)
about 20 blanched almonds

1 Preheat the oven to 190°C/375°F/
Gas 5. Lightly grease two large
baking sheets.

2 Melt 115g/4oz of the chocolate
in a heatproof bowl set over a pan
of hot water, then remove from the
heat and leave to cool slightly.
Cream the butter with the icing
sugar in a bowl until smooth and
pale. Beat in the melted chocolate,
then the black coffee.

3 Sift the flour and cornflour over
the mixture. Fold in lightly and
evenly to make a soft mixture.

4 Spoon the mixture into a piping
(pastry) bag fitted with a large star
nozzle and pipe 20 swirls on the
prepared baking sheets, allowing
room for spreading during baking.

5 Gently press an almond into the
centre of each swirl. Bake for about
15 minutes, until the cookies are
firm and just beginning to brown.
Leave to cool for about 10 minutes
on the baking sheets, then, using a
metal spatula, transfer carefully to a
wire rack to cool completely.

6 Melt the remaining chocolate in a
heatproof bowl over a pan of hot
water. Dip the base of each swirl
into the chocolate to coat. Place on
a sheet of baking parchment and
leave to set.

Cook's Tip
*If the mixture is too stiff to pipe, soften it
with a little more black coffee.*

Chocolate Amaretti

Although it is always said that chocolate does not go with wine, make an exception with these scrumptious little cookies and serve them, Italian style, with a glass of chilled champagne.

Makes 24

150g/5oz/1¼ cups blanched
    whole almonds
90g/3½oz/½ cup caster (superfine) sugar
15ml/1 tbsp (unsweetened)
    cocoa powder
30ml/2 tbsp icing (confectioners') sugar
2 egg whites
pinch of cream of tartar
5ml/1 tsp almond essence (extract)
24 flaked (sliced) almonds, to decorate

1 Preheat the oven to 180°C/350°F/ Gas 4. Spread out the almonds on a baking sheet and bake for 10–12 minutes until golden brown. Leave to cool. Reduce the oven temperature to 160°C/325°F/Gas 3. Line a large baking sheet with baking parchment.

2 Process the almonds with half the sugar in a food processor until they are finely ground. Transfer to a bowl and sift in the cocoa and icing sugar. Set aside.

3 Using an electric mixer, beat the egg whites and cream of tartar until stiff peaks form. Sprinkle in the remaining sugar, a tablespoon at a time, and continue beating until the whites are glossy and stiff. Beat in the almond essence.

4 Sprinkle over the almond-sugar mixture and gently fold into the beaten egg whites until just blended. Spoon the mixture into a large piping (pastry) bag fitted with a plain 1cm/½in nozzle. Pipe 4cm/1½in rounds about 2.5cm/1in apart on the prepared baking sheet. Gently press a flaked almond into the centre of each.

5 Bake the cookies for about 12–15 minutes, or until crisp and golden. Remove the baking sheets to a wire rack and leave to cool for about 10 minutes. With a metal palette knife or spatula, transfer the amaretti to the wire rack to cool completely. Wrap individually in tissue paper before packing in a box if giving as a gift.

Chocolate Almond Torrone

The name of this log-shaped cookie is usually translated as nougat, but this is a reference to its nutty flavour rather than its texture. Serve this Italian speciality in thin slices.

Makes 20

115g/4oz plain (semisweet)
  chocolate, chopped
50g/2oz/4 tbsp unsalted (sweet) butter
1 egg white
115g/4oz/generous ½ cup caster
  (superfine) sugar
50g/2oz/½ cup ground almonds
75g/3oz/¾ cup chopped toasted almonds
75ml/5 tbsp chopped candied peel

For the coating

175g/6oz white chocolate, chopped
25g/1oz/2 tbsp unsalted (sweet) butter
115g/4oz/1 cup flaked (sliced)
  almonds, toasted

1 Melt the chocolate with the butter in a heatproof bowl set over a pan of hot water, stirring until the mixture is smooth.

2 In a clean, grease-free bowl, whisk the egg white with the sugar until stiff. Gradually beat in the melted chocolate, then stir in the ground almonds, chopped toasted almonds and candied peel.

Cook's Tip

The mixture can be shaped into a simple round roll instead of the triangular shape, if you prefer.

3 Tip the mixture on to a large sheet of baking parchment and, using your hands, shape it into a thick roll.

4 As the mixture cools, use the baking parchment to press the roll firmly into a triangular shape. Twist the baking parchment over the triangular roll and chill in the refrigerator until completely set.

5 To make the coating, melt the white chocolate with the butter in a heatproof bowl set over a pan of hot water. Unwrap the chocolate roll and spread the white chocolate quickly over the surface. Press the almonds in a thin even coating over the chocolate, working quickly.

6 Chill again until firm, then cut the torrone into thin slices to serve.

Chocolate Hazelnut Galettes

There's stacks of sophistication in these triple-tiered chocolate rounds sandwiched with a light creamy filling. They are elegant enough to serve for dessert.

Makes 4

175g/6oz plain (semisweet)
  chocolate, chopped
45ml/3 tbsp single (light) cream
30ml/2 tbsp flaked (sliced) hazelnuts
115g/4oz white chocolate, chopped
175g/6oz/¾ cup fromage frais or
  ricotta cheese
15ml/1 tbsp dry sherry
60ml/4 tbsp finely chopped
  hazelnuts, toasted
physalis, dipped in white chocolate,
  to decorate

1 Melt the plain chocolate in a heatproof bowl set over a pan of hot water, then remove from the heat and stir in the cream.

2 Draw 12 circles about 7.5cm/3in in diameter on sheets of baking parchment. Turn the parchment over and spread the plain chocolate over each marked circle, covering in a thin, even layer. Sprinkle flaked hazelnuts over four of the circles, then leave until set.

Cook's Tip

The chocolate could be spread over heart shapes instead, for a special Valentine's Day dessert.

3 Melt the white chocolate in a heatproof bowl set over a pan of hot water. Remove the bowl from the heat, then stir in the fromage frais or ricotta cheese and dry sherry. Fold in the chopped, toasted hazelnuts. Leave to cool until the mixture holds its shape.

4 Remove the chocolate rounds from the baking parchment and sandwich them together in stacks of three, spooning the white chocolate cream between each layer and using the hazelnut-covered rounds on top. Chill before serving with chocolate-dipped physalis.

Rocky Road Chocolate Bars

This is a dream to make with kids. They love smashing up the cookies, and can do most of the rest, apart from melting the chocolate and lining the tin. However, when it comes to flavour, the contrast of melting chocolate, crunchy cookies and soft marshmallows is not just kid's stuff.

Makes 16 bars

225g/8oz/1 cup butter
115g/4oz dark (bittersweet) chocolate
  with more than 60% cocoa solids,
  coarsely broken up
30ml/2 tbsp caster (superfine) sugar
30ml/2 tbsp golden (light corn) syrup
30ml/2 tbsp good quality (unsweetened)
  cocoa powder
350g/12oz mixed digestive biscuits
  (graham crackers) and ginger nut
  biscuits (gingersnaps)
50g/2oz mini marshmallows
75g/3oz mixed white and milk
  chocolate chips
icing (confectioners') sugar, for
  dusting (optional)

1 Line a 20cm/8in square cake tin (pan), measuring about 2.5cm/1in deep, with baking parchment. Put the butter in a pan with the chocolate, sugar, syrup and cocoa powder. Place over a gentle heat until completely melted.

2 Put the biscuits into a large plastic bag and smash to coarse chunks with a rolling pin. Stir these into the chocolate mixture, followed by the marshmallows and chocolate chips. Mix well together.

3 Spoon the mixture into the tin, but don't press down too much – it should look like a rocky road. Chill for at least 1 hour or until firm.

4 Remove from the tin and cut into 16 bars. If you like, dust the bars with icing sugar before serving.

Late Night Cookies

Take a pile of these to bed with you and all that will be left next morning will be the crumbs in the duvet. These are dangerous cookies. Crisp yet crumbly and packed with chocolate chips, they are a must with tall glasses of ice-cold milk or stacked with an obscene amount of ice cream.

Makes about 12 large or 20 regular cookies

75g/3oz/6 tbsp butter, softened
75g/3oz/6 tbsp golden caster (superfine) sugar
75g/3oz/6 tbsp soft light brown sugar, sifted
1 large (US extra large) egg, beaten
2.5ml/½ tsp vanilla essence (extract)
150g/5oz/1¼ cups self-raising (self-rising) flour
25g/1oz/¼ cup (unsweetened) cocoa powder
1.5ml/¼ tsp salt
100g/4oz chopped plain (semisweet) chocolate or chocolate chips
ice cream or milk, to serve

1 Preheat the oven to 180°C/350°F/Gas 4. Butter two heavy, non-stick baking sheets. Cream the butter and both sugars together until pale and fluffy. Beat in the egg and vanilla essence.

2 Sift the flour with the cocoa and salt. Gently fold into the egg mixture with the chopped chocolate or chocolate chips. Place four heaped tablespoonfuls of the mixture, spaced well apart, on each baking sheet. Press down and spread out with the back of a wet spoon.

3 Bake for 12 minutes. Cool on the baking sheet for 1 minute, then remove to a cooling rack. Repeat with the remaining mixture. Store in an airtight container when cold. Serve with ice cream sandwiched between, or eat on their own with a glass of ice-cold milk.

Ice Cream Sandwich Cookies

These are great when you get those midnight munchies – either keep the cookies in an airtight container and sandwich together each time with the softened ice cream of your choice or make the sandwiches complete with ice cream and coating and freeze until required.

Makes 12

115g/4oz/½ cup unsalted (sweet) butter, at room temperature, diced
115g/4oz/generous ½ cup caster (superfine) sugar
1 egg, beaten
200g/7oz/1¾ cups plain (all-purpose) flour
25g/1oz/¼ cup (unsweetened) cocoa powder, sieved
ice cream, to fill
toasted nuts, biscuit (cookie) crumbs, chocolate flakes or demerara (raw) sugar, to coat

1 Preheat the oven to 180°C/350°F/Gas 4. Cream the butter and sugar together until light and fluffy, then beat in the egg. Stir in the flour and cocoa powder to make a firm dough.

2 Roll the dough out to a thickness of 6mm/¼in on baking parchment. Using a 7.5cm/3in plain round biscuit (cookie) cutter, stamp out 24 rounds and place on the prepared baking sheets. Alternatively cut into squares or rectangles of equal size. Bake the cookies for about 15 minutes. Set aside on the baking sheets to cool.

3 To make the ice cream cookies, spread 2 good spoonfuls of softened ice cream on a cookie and press a second on top. Squeeze so the filling reaches the edges.

4 Put your chosen coating on a plate and roll the cookies in it to coat the sides. Either eat straight away or wrap individually in foil and freeze. The cookies may be kept for up to 2 weeks in the freezer.

Cook's Tip

For super deluxe cookies, half-dip the ice cream cookies in melted chocolate. Shake off the excess, place on a sheet of baking parchment and freeze at once. When the chocolate has set, either eat or wrap in foil and freeze for later.

Nut Bar Cookies

If you love chocolate, condensed milk, nuts and crumb crust then these are the cookies for you. It's fortunate that they are incredibly easy to make because they are even easier to eat and are sure to become firm favourites with all the family. Children enjoy helping to make them.

Makes 16–18

250g/9oz digestive biscuits
   (graham crackers)
115g/4oz/½ cup butter, melted
150g/5oz/scant 1 cup milk
   chocolate chips
200g/7oz mixed whole nuts, such as
   pecan nuts, hazelnuts, brazil nuts,
   walnuts and almonds
200ml/7fl oz/scant 1 cup can sweetened
   condensed milk

Cook's Tip

If you prefer, use a shallow 20cm/8in cake tin (pan) instead, and cut the cookies into squares.

1 Preheat the oven to 180°C/350°F/ Gas 4. Crush the biscuits in a plastic bag with a rolling pin.

2 Put the biscuit crumbs in a bowl and stir in the melted butter. Mix well. Press the mixture evenly into the base of a 10 x 36cm/4 x 14in cake tin (pan).

3 Sprinkle the chocolate chips over the biscuit base. Arrange the nuts on top and pour the condensed milk over the top evenly.

4 Bake for 25 minutes, or until bubbling and golden. Cool in the tin, loosen from the sides, then cool completely and slice into thin bars.

Apple Crumble and Custard Slice

These luscious apple slices are easy to make using ready-made sweet pastry and custard. Just think, all the ingredients of one of the world's most popular desserts – in a cookie.

Makes 16

350g/12oz ready-made sweet pastry
1 large cooking apple, about 250g/9oz
30ml/2 tbsp caster (superfine) sugar
60ml/4 tbsp ready-made thick custard

For the crumble topping
115g/4oz/1 cup plain (all-purpose) flour
2.5ml/½ tsp ground cinnamon
60ml/4 tbsp granulated sugar
90g/3½oz/7 tbsp unsalted (sweet) butter, melted

I Preheat the oven to 190°C/375°F/ Gas 5. Roll out the pastry and use to line the base of a 28 × 18cm/ 11 × 7in shallow cake tin (pan). Prick the pastry with a fork, line with foil and baking beans and bake blind for about 10–15 minutes. Remove the foil and baking beans and return the pastry to the oven for a further 5 minutes until cooked and golden brown.

2 Meanwhile, peel, core and chop the apple evenly. Place in a pan with the sugar. Heat gently until the sugar dissolves, then cover with a lid and cook gently for 5–7 minutes until a thick purée is formed. Beat with a wooden spoon and set aside to cool.

3 Mix the cold apple with the custard. Spread over the pastry.

4 To make the crumble topping, put the flour, cinnamon and sugar into a bowl and pour over the melted butter. Stir thoroughly until the mixture forms small clumps. Sprinkle the crumble over the filling.

5 Return to the oven and bake for about 10–15 minutes until the crumble topping is cooked and a golden brown. Leave to cool in the tin, then slice into bars to serve.

Creamy Fig and Peach Squares

A sweet cream cheese and dried fruit filling with a hint of mint makes these cookies really special. They are ideal for quietening hunger pangs after school or work.

Makes 24

350g/12oz/3 cups plain (all-purpose) flour
200g/7oz/scant 1 cup unsalted
  (sweet) butter, diced
1 egg, beaten
caster (superfine) sugar,
  for sprinkling

For the filling

500g/1¼lb/2½ cups ricotta cheese
115g/4oz/generous ½ cup
  caster (superfine) sugar
5ml/1 tsp finely chopped fresh mint
50g/2oz/⅓ cup ready-to-eat dried
  figs, chopped
50g/2oz/⅓ cup ready-to-eat dried
  peaches, chopped

1 Preheat the oven to 190°C/375°F/ Gas 5. And then lightly grease a 33 x 23cm/13 x 9in Swiss roll tin (jelly roll pan) or shallow cake tin (pan). Put the flour and butter into a bowl. Rub in the butter until the mixture resembles fine breadcrumbs. Add the egg and enough water to mix to a firm but not sticky dough.

2 Divide the pastry into two and roll out one piece to fit the base of the prepared tin. Place in the tin and trim.

3 To make the filling, put all the ingredients in a bowl and mix together. Spread over the pastry base. Roll out the remaining pastry and place on top of the filling. Prick lightly all over with a fork then sprinkle with caster sugar.

4 Bake for about 30 minutes until light golden brown. Remove from the oven and sprinkle more caster sugar thickly over the top. Cool and cut into slices to serve.

White Chocolate Macadamia Nut Slices

Keep these luxury slices for a celebratory afternoon tea. Not only do they have a superbly rich flavour. but their crunchy texture will also make them a firm favourite among your guests. For a special occasion serve with a spoonful of whipped cream.

Makes 16

150g/5oz/1¼ cups macadamia nuts
400g/14oz white chocolate
50g/2oz/¼ cup ready-to-eat
  dried apricots
75g/3oz/⅓ cup unsalted
  (sweet) butter
5ml/1 tsp vanilla essence (extract)
3 eggs
150g/5oz/⅔ cup light muscovado
  (brown) sugar
115g/4oz/1 cup self-raising
  (self-rising) flour

1 Preheat the oven to 190°C/375°F/ Gas 5. Lightly grease two 20cm/8in sandwich cake tins (layer cake pans) and line the base of each with greaseproof (waxed) paper or baking parchment.

2 Coarsely chop the nuts and half the white chocolate, making sure that the pieces are more or less the same size, then cut the apricots into similar-size pieces.

3 Place the remaining white chocolate and the butter in the top of a double boiler or a heatproof bowl set over a pan of hot water. Melt over a gentle heat, stirring occasionally until smooth. Remove the bowl from the heat and leave to cool slightly.

4 Stir in the vanilla essence. Whisk the eggs and sugar in a mixing bowl until thick and pale, then whisk in the melted chocolate mixture.

5 Sift the flour over the mixture and fold in gently and evenly. Stir in the nuts, chopped white chocolate and apricots.

6 Spoon the mixture into the prepared tins, smooth the top level with a spatula and bake for 30–35 minutes, until golden brown. Leave in the tins to cool slightly then turn out the cakes and leave to cool completely on a wire rack. Serve cut into slices or wedges, with a spoonful of fresh whipped cream, if you like.

Cook's Tip
You might find it easier to use sharp kitchen scissors rather than a knife to snip the apricots into small pieces.

Variation
Use blanched almonds or hazelnuts in place of the macadamia nuts, if you prefer.

Florentines with Grand Marnier

Orange liqueur adds a note of glorious luxury to these ever-popular nut and dried fruit cookies. These mini versions would be delicious with dessert or after-dinner coffee and liqueurs.

Makes about 24

50g/2oz/¼ cup soft light brown sugar

15ml/1 tbsp clear honey

15ml/1 tbsp Grand Marnier

50g/2oz/¼ cup butter

40g/1½oz/3 tbsp plain
  (all-purpose) flour

25g/1oz/¼ cup hazelnuts,
  coarsely chopped

50g/2oz/½ cup flaked (sliced)
  almonds, chopped

50g/2oz/¼ cup glacé (candied)
  cherries, chopped

115g/4oz dark (bittersweet) chocolate,
  melted, for coating

1 Preheat the oven to 180C/350F/ Gas 4. Line three or four baking sheets with baking parchment. Combine the sugar, honey, Grand Marnier and butter in a small pan and melt over a low heat.

2 Remove the pan from the heat and tip in the flour, hazelnuts, almonds and cherries. Stir well.

Variation

For an extra decoration, pour melted milk, plain (semisweet) or white chocolate into a paper piping (pastry) bag, snip off the end and pipe zig-zag lines over the plain side of each Florentine.

3 Spoon small heaps of the mixture on to the baking sheets. Bake for about 10 minutes until golden brown. Leave the cookies on the baking sheets until the edges begin to harden a little, then remove and cool on a wire rack.

4 Spread the melted chocolate over the underside of each Florentine with a round-bladed knife or metal spatula. When the chocolate is just beginning to set, drag a fork through to give wavy lines. Leave to set completely.

Cointreau Chocolate Colettes

Small chocolate cases, filled with swirled chocolate and Cointreau cream, make indulgent treats.
Serve them with a glass of the liqueur at the end of a special meal.

Makes 14

115g/4oz dark (bittersweet) chocolate,
  broken into squares
icing (confectioners') sugar, for dusting

For filling

65g/2½ oz dark (bittersweet) chocolate
25g/1oz/2 tbsp unsalted (sweet) butter
30ml/2 tbsp Cointreau
60ml/4 tbsp double (heavy)
  cream, whipped

1 Put the chocolate in a heatproof bowl. Stand the bowl over a pan of hot water and heat gently until the chocolate has melted.

2 Using a small, clean paintbrush, brush the insides of 14 petit four cases with a thin coating of melted chocolate and leave to set completely. Repeat three or four times. When finally set, carefully peel off the paper cases.

3 Make the filling. Melt the chocolate and butter in a heatproof bowl set over a pan of simmering water, stirring until smooth.

4 Remove from the heat. When cool (but still liquid), stir in the Cointreau and fold in the whipped double cream.

5 Chill this mixture until firm, then pipe into the chocolate cases. Dust with icing sugar.

Cook's Tip

When making the cases, it is best to make several thin layers of chocolate.

Two-tone Chocolate Florentines

Fruit and nut florentines make a deliciously sticky treat to serve with coffee. Store them in an airtight container in the refrigerator. They'll keep for up to 1 week – unless, of course, they're eaten sooner, which is highly likely.

Makes about 30

*120ml/4fl oz/½ cup double
   (heavy) cream*
50g/2oz/¼ cup unsalted (sweet) butter
90g/3½oz/½ cup granulated sugar
30ml/2 tbsp clear honey
*150g/5oz/1¼ cups flaked
   (sliced) almonds*
*40g/1½oz/⅓ cup plain
   (all-purpose) flour*
2.5ml/½ tsp ground ginger
*50g/2oz/⅓ cup diced candied
   orange peel*
*65g/2½oz/½ cup diced preserved
   stem ginger*
*200g/7oz plain (semisweet)
   chocolate, chopped*
*150g/5oz good quality white
   chocolate, chopped*

1 Preheat the oven to 180°C/350°F/ Gas 4. Lightly grease two large baking sheets. Heat the cream, butter, sugar and honey in a pan over a medium heat, stirring constantly until the sugar has dissolved. Bring the mixture to the boil, stirring constantly.

2 Remove from the heat and stir in the almonds, flour and ground ginger until thoroughly blended. Stir in the orange peel, preserved stem ginger and 50g/2oz/⅓ cup chopped plain chocolate.

3 Drop teaspoonfuls of the mixture on to the prepared baking sheets at least 7.5cm/3in apart. Spread each round as thinly as possible with the back of the spoon.

4 Bake in batches for 8–10 minutes, until the edges are golden brown and the cookies are bubbling. Do not under-bake or they will be sticky, but be careful not to over-bake as they burn easily.

5 If you wish, use a 7.5cm/3in biscuit (cookie) cutter to neaten the edges of the florentines while on the baking sheet.

6 Remove the baking sheet to a wire rack to cool for 10 minutes. Using a palette knife or metal spatula, transfer the florentines to the wire rack to cool completely.

7 In a bowl set over a small pan of hot water, melt the remaining plain chocolate. Cool slightly.

8 In a separate bowl, melt the white chocolate in the same way. Remove the bowl from the pan and cool for about 5 minutes, stirring occasionally until the chocolate is slightly thickened.

9 Using a small palette knife or metal spatula, spread the flat side of half the florentines with the plain chocolate, swirling it to create a decorative pattern. Place on a wire rack, chocolate side up.

10 Coat the remaining florentines with the melted white chocolate in the same way. Leave in a cool place for about 10 minutes to set.

Variation
Use glacé (candied) cherries in place of half or all of the orange peel, if you prefer.

Cook's Tip
Dip the spoon in water to prevent it from sticking when you are spreading out the mixture on the baking sheets.

Coffee Sponge Drops with Cheese and Ginger Filling

These little cookies are delicious with a filling of low-fat soft cheese and chopped preserved stem ginger, but if you like, you can serve them on their own.

Makes 12

50g/2oz/½ cup plain (all-purpose) flour
15ml/1 tbsp instant coffee powder
2 eggs
75g/3oz/scant ½ cup caster
  (superfine) sugar

For the filling

115g/4oz/½ cup low-fat soft cheese
40g/1½oz/¼ cup chopped preserved
  stem ginger

1 Preheat the oven to 190°C/375°F/ Gas 5. Line two baking sheets with baking parchment. Sift the flour and coffee powder together. To make the filling, beat together the soft cheese and stem ginger. Chill.

2 Whisk the eggs and sugar in a bowl until thick.

3 Carefully add the sifted flour and coffee powder to the egg mixture and gently fold in with a metal spoon, being careful not to knock out any air.

4 Spoon into a piping (pastry) bag with a 1cm/½in plain nozzle. Pipe 4cm/1½in rounds on to the baking sheets. Bake for 12 minutes. Cool. Sandwich together with the filling.

Sablés with Goat's Cheese and Strawberries

Sablés are little French cookies, made from egg yolk and butter. Crisp and slightly sweet, they contrast perfectly with the tangy goat's cheese and juicy strawberries.

Makes 24

75g/3oz/1/3 cup butter
150g/5oz/1¼ cups plain
   (all-purpose) flour
75g/3oz/¾ cup blanched hazelnuts, lightly
   toasted and ground
30ml/2 tbsp caster (superfine) sugar
2 egg yolks, beaten with 30–45ml/
   2–3 tbsp water
115g/4oz goat's cheese
4–6 large strawberries, cut into
   small pieces
hazelnuts and fresh mint, to decorate

1 Put the butter, flour, ground hazelnuts, sugar and beaten egg yolks into a food processor and process to a smooth dough. Scrape out the dough. Shape into a log about 4cm/1½in thick. Wrap in clear film (plastic wrap) and chill.

Variation

These sablés are ideal served with fruit. Beat 75g/3oz/⅓ cup cream cheese with 15ml/1 tbsp icing (confectioners') sugar and a little lemon or orange rind. Spread a little on the sablés and top with a few pieces of sliced kiwi fruit, peach, nectarine and a few raspberries.

2 Preheat the oven to 200°C/ 400°F/Gas 6. Line a large baking sheet with baking parchment. With a sharp knife, slice the dough into 5mm/¼in thick rounds and arrange on the prepared baking sheet. Bake for 7–10 minutes, until golden brown. Transfer to a wire rack to cool and crisp slightly.

3 Crumble the goat's cheese with your fingers into small pieces on a plate. Mound a little goat's cheese on to each sablé, top with a piece of strawberry and sprinkle with a few hazelnuts. Transfer to a platter or individual plates, decorate with mint leaves and serve the sablés while still warm.

Dessert Cookies

Mousses, sorbets, ice creams and fresh fruit salads are among the many desserts complemented by delicate, elegant or richly flavoured cookies – and, of course, there is nothing so delicious as special little nibbles served with coffee and liqueurs. The recipes in this chapter will be an inspiration for those who love to entertain, as they provide that professional finishing touch that turns a good meal into a truly memorable occasion.

Biscotti

These lovely Italian cookies are part-baked, sliced to reveal a feast of mixed nuts and then baked again until crisp and golden. Traditionally they're served dipped in vin santo, a sweet, sherry-like dessert wine, but they would also go well with zabaglione or creamy chocolate mousse.

Makes 24

50g/2oz/¼ cup unsalted (sweet) butter
   at room temperature, diced
115g/4oz/generous ½ cup caster
   (superfine) sugar
175g/6oz/1½ cups self-raising
   (self-rising) flour
pinch of salt
10ml/2 tsp baking powder
5ml/1 tsp ground coriander
finely grated rind of 1 lemon
50g/2oz/scant ½ cup polenta
1 egg, lightly beaten
10ml/2 tsp brandy or orange-
   flavoured liqueur
50g/2oz/½ cup unblanched almonds
50g/2oz/½ cup pistachio nuts

1 Preheat the oven to 160°C/325°F/ Gas 3. Lightly grease a baking sheet. Cream together the butter and sugar in a bowl.

2 Sift the flour, salt, baking powder and coriander into the bowl. Add the lemon rind, polenta, egg and brandy or liqueur and mix together to make a soft dough.

3 Stir in the nuts until evenly combined. Halve the mixture. Shape each half into a flat "sausage" about 23cm/9in long and 6cm/2½in wide. Bake for about 30 minutes, or until risen and firm. Remove the "sausages" from the oven.

4 When cool, cut each "sausage" diagonally into 12 thin slices. Return to the baking sheet and cook for a further 10 minutes, or until crisp.

5 Transfer to a wire rack to cool completely. Store in an airtight container for up to 1 week.

Cook's Tip
Use a sharp, serrated knife to slice the cooled cookies, otherwise they will crumble and break.

All Butter Cookies

Crisp, buttery cookies are perfect with strawberries and cream or any creamy dessert or fruit compote. These are refrigerator cookies as the mixture is chilled until it is firm enough to cut neatly into thin slices. The dough can be frozen and when thawed enough to slice, can be baked, but do allow a little extra cooking time.

Makes 28–30
275g/10oz/2½ cups plain
  (all-purpose) flour
200g/7oz/scant 1 cup unsalted
  (sweet) butter
90g/3½oz/scant 1 cup icing
  (confectioners') sugar, plus extra
  for dusting
10ml/2 tsp vanilla essence (extract)

1 Put the flour in a food processor. Add the butter and process until the mixture resembles coarse breadcrumbs. Add the icing sugar and vanilla essence and process again until the mixture comes together to form a dough.

2 Turn out the dough on to a lightly floured surface. Knead lightly and then shape into a thick sausage, 30cm/12in long and 5cm/2in in diameter. Wrap in clear film (plastic wrap) or foil and chill for at least 1 hour, until firm.

Cook's Tip
Do make sure that you use a sharp knife for cutting the dough roll into individual cookies. Not only is it safer, but also the results will be neater.

3 Preheat the oven to 200°C/ 400°F/Gas 6. Grease two baking sheets. Using a sharp knife, cut 5mm/¼in thick slices from the dough and space them slightly apart on the baking sheets.

4 Bake for 8–10 minutes, alternating the position of the baking sheets in the oven halfway through cooking, if necessary, until the cookies have turned pale golden around the edges. Leave for 5 minutes, then transfer to a wire rack to cool. Serve dusted with icing sugar.

Cinnamon Pinwheels

These impressive sweet pastries make a superb and attractive accompaniment to ice cream, sorbets, mousses and other creamy desserts. Cinnamon has a deliciously fragrant aroma and gives these simple-to-make pinwheels a warm spicy flavour. If you find they turn slightly soft during storage, re-crisp them briefly in the oven.

Makes 20–24

50g/2oz/¼ cup caster (superfine) sugar, plus a little extra for sprinkling

10ml/2 tsp ground cinnamon

250g/9oz puff pastry

beaten egg, to glaze

1 Preheat the oven to 220°C/425°F/Gas 7. Thoroughly grease a large baking sheet. Put the caster sugar and ground cinnamon in a small bowl and mix well. Set the bowl aside until required.

2 Roll out the pastry on a lightly floured surface to a 20cm/8in square and sprinkle with half the sugar mixture. Roll out the pastry to a 25cm/10in square so that the sugar is pressed into it.

3 Brush with the beaten egg and then sprinkle with the remaining sugar mixture. Loosely roll up the pastry into a log, brushing the end of the pastry with a little more egg to secure the edge in place.

4 Using a large sharp knife, cut the log into fairly thin slices and transfer them to the prepared baking sheet. Bake for about 10 minutes, or until golden and crisp. Sprinkle with a little more sugar and transfer to a wire rack to cool.

Spanish Churros

These sugar-coated deep-fried bites are sold from roadside stalls all over Spain and are eaten from paper cones while piping hot. For a special treat serve with a lemon sorbet.

Makes 24

250ml/8fl oz/1 cup water
15ml/1 tbsp granulated sugar, plus extra
    for coating
pinch of salt
175g/6oz/1½ cups plain
    (all-purpose) flour
1 egg
oil, for deep-frying
½ lime or lemon

1 Pour the measured water into a heavy pan, add the sugar and salt and bring to the boil over a low heat, stirring until the sugar has dissolved. Remove from the heat, tip in the flour and beat until smooth.

2 Beat in the egg until the mixture is smooth and satiny. Set aside.

3 Heat 5cm/2in depth of oil, with the lime or lemon, in a deep frying pan to 190°C/375°F or until a cube of bread browns in 30–60 seconds.

4 Pour the batter into a large piping (pastry) bag with a fluted nozzle. Pipe 7.5cm/3in strips of batter and then add to the oil, a few at a time. Fry for 3–4 minutes until golden. Remove, drain on kitchen paper and roll in granulated sugar.

Golden Pillows

These tasty little Mexican snacks are delicious served warm with syrup or honey, but they can also be sprinkled with sugar and cinnamon if you prefer. They are lovely with ice cream.

Makes 30

225g/8oz/2 cups plain (all-purpose)
    flour, sifted
15ml/1 tbsp baking powder
pinch of salt
30ml/2 tbsp lard, white cooking fat
    or margarine
175ml/6fl oz/¾ cup water
corn oil, for frying
syrup or clear honey, to serve

1 Put the flour, baking powder and salt into a large bowl. Add the lard, white cooking fat or margarine, and then lightly rub in, using just your fingertips, until the mixture resembles coarse breadcrumbs.

2 Gradually stir in the water, using a fork, until the mixture clings together to form a soft dough.

3 Shape the dough into a ball, then turn on to a lightly floured surface and knead very gently until smooth. Roll out thinly to a rectangle measuring about 46 x 35cm/ 18 x 15in. Using a sharp knife, cut about 30 x 7.5cm/3in squares. For a decorative edge, use a fluted pastry wheel to cut out the squares.

4 Heat the oil to 190°C/375°F or until a cube of day-old bread browns in 30–60 seconds.

5 Deep-fry the squares, a few at a time, in the oil. As they brown and puff up, turn them over to cook the other side. Remove with a slotted spoon and drain well on kitchen paper. Serve the pillows warm, with syrup or honey.

Tea Finger Cookies

The unusual ingredient in these cookies is Lady Grey tea – similar to Earl Grey but with the addition of Seville orange and lemon peel – which imparts a subtle flavour.

3 Using your hands, roll the dough on a lightly floured surface into a long cylinder, about 23cm/9in long.

4 Gently press down on the top of the dough cylinder with the palm of your hand to flatten slightly. Wrap the dough in clear film (plastic wrap) and chill for about 1 hour until the dough is firm enough to slice.

5 Using a sharp knife, cut the dough cylinder widthways into 5mm/¼in slices and place, slightly apart, on the prepared baking sheets.

6 Sprinkle the cookies with a little demerara sugar, then bake for 10–15 minutes until lightly browned. Using a palette knife (metal spatula), transfer the cookies to a wire rack and leave to cool.

Makes about 36

150g/5oz/10 tbsp unsalted (sweet)
   butter, at room temperature, diced
115g/4oz/generous ½ cup light
   muscovado (brown) sugar
15–30ml/1–2 tbsp Lady Grey tea leaves
1 egg, beaten
200g/7oz/1¾ cups plain
   (all-purpose) flour
demerara (raw) sugar, for sprinkling

1 Preheat the oven to 190°C/375°F/ Gas 5. Line two or three baking sheets with baking parchment.

2 Beat the butter and sugar until light and creamy. Stir in the Lady Grey tea leaves until well combined. Beat in the egg, then carefully fold in the flour.

Variation
You could use other exotic types of tea for making these cookies. Try Earl Grey, flavoured with bergamot, or aromatic flower or fruit teas, such as jasmine, rose congou or pouchong, chrysanthemum, passion fruit or strawberry.

Rosemary-scented Citrus Tuiles

These delicious crisp cookies are flavoured with tangy orange and lemon rind, and made beautifully fragrant with fresh rosemary – an unusual but winning combination.

Makes 18–20

50g/2oz/¼ cup unsalted (sweet) butter, diced
2 egg whites
115g/4oz/generous ½ cup caster (superfine) sugar
finely grated rind of ½ lemon
finely grated rind of ½ orange
10ml/2 tsp finely chopped fresh rosemary
50g/2oz/½ cup plain (all-purpose) flour

1 Preheat the oven to 190°C/375°F/ Gas 5. Line a baking sheet with baking parchment. Melt the butter in a pan over a low heat. Leave to cool. Whisk the egg whites until stiff, then gradually whisk in the sugar.

2 Fold in the lemon and orange rinds, rosemary and flour and then the melted butter. Place 2 large tablespoonfuls of mixture on the baking sheet. Spread each to a thin disc about 9cm/3½in in diameter. Bake for 5–6 minutes until golden.

3 Remove from the oven and lift the tuiles using a palette knife (metal spatula) and drape over a rolling pin. Transfer to a wire rack when set in a curved shape. Continue baking the rest of the mixture in the same way.

Striped Cylinder Cookies

These cookies can be made in different flavours and colours and look wonderful tied in bundles or packed into decorative jars or boxes. Eat them with ice cream or light desserts.

Makes 25

25g/1oz white chocolate, melted
red and green food colouring dusts
2 egg whites
90g/3½oz/½ cup caster (superfine) sugar
50g/2oz/½ cup plain (all-purpose) flour
50g/2oz/¼ cup unsalted (sweet)
*   butter, melted*

1 Preheat the oven to 190°C/375°F/ Gas 5. Line two baking sheets with baking parchment. Divide the melted chocolate in half and add a little food colouring dust to each half. Using two greaseproof (waxed) paper piping (pastry) bags, fill each with coloured chocolate and fold down the tops. Snip off the tips.

2 Place the egg whites in a bowl and whisk until stiff. Add the sugar gradually, whisking well after each addition. Add the flour and melted butter and whisk until smooth.

3 Drop four separate teaspoonfuls of the mixture on to the prepared baking sheets and spread into thin rounds. Pipe lines or zigzags of green and red chocolate over each round.

4 Bake one sheet at a time for about 3 minutes, until pale golden in colour. Loosen the rounds with a metal spatula and return to the oven for a few seconds to soften. Have two or three lightly oiled wooden spoon handles to hand.

5 Taking one round cookie out of the oven at a time, turn it over and roll it around a spoon handle. Leave for a few seconds to set. Repeat to shape the remaining cookies. Put the second sheet of cookies in the oven to bake. Repeat the process of loosening, softening and rolling the cookies into shape.

6 When the cookies are set, slip them off the spoon handles on to a wire rack. Repeat with the remaining mixture and the red and green coloured chocolate until all the mixture has been used, baking only one sheet of cookies at a time. If the cookies are too hard to shape, simply return them to the oven for a few seconds to soften.

7 When the cookies are cold, tie them together with coloured ribbon and pack into boxes, glass jars or tins as gifts.

Cook's Tip

Don't be tempted to speed things up by baking more than one sheet of cookies at a time, as you won't be able to shape them all before some of them harden and set flat or scorch.

Ginger Glass Cookies

As thin, delicate and elegant as fine glass, these ginger cookies are ideal served with creamy desserts, syllabubs, sorbets and luxury ice creams.

Makes about 18

50g/2oz/¼ cup unsalted (sweet)
  butter, diced
40g/1½oz/3 tbsp liquid glucose
  (clear corn syrup)
90g/3½oz/½ cup caster
  (superfine) sugar
40g/1½oz/⅓ cup plain (all-purpose) flour
5ml/1 tsp ground ginger

1 Put the butter and liquid glucose in a heatproof bowl set over a pan of gently simmering water. Stir together until melted. Set aside.

Cook's Tip

Use unlipped baking sheets so you can roll the cookies thinly.

2 Put the sugar in a bowl and sift over the flour and ginger. Stir into the butter mixture, then beat well until combined. Cover with clear film (plastic wrap) and chill for about 25 minutes, until firm. Meanwhile, preheat the oven to 180°C/350°F/ Gas 4 and line two or three baking sheets with baking parchment.

3 Roll teaspoonfuls of the cookie mixture into balls between your hands and place them, spaced well apart to allow room for spreading, on the prepared baking sheets.

4 Place a second piece of baking parchment on top and roll the cookies as thinly as possible. Peel off the top sheet. Then stamp each cookie with a 7.5 or 9cm/3 or 3½in plain round cutter.

5 Bake for 5–6 minutes, or until golden. Leave for a few seconds on the baking sheets to firm up slightly, then either leave flat or curl over in half. Leave to cool completely.

Butterfly Cookies

Melt-in-the-mouth puff pastry interleaved with sugar, nuts and cinnamon produces a slightly outrageous-looking cookie that teams well with ice creams and fruit salads.

Makes about 12

500g/1¼lb packet ready-made
  puff pastry
1 egg, beaten
115g/4oz/generous ½ cup
  granulated sugar
25g/1oz/¼ cup chopped mixed nuts
5ml/1 tsp ground cinnamon

1 Preheat the oven to 200°C/400°F/ Gas 6. Roll out the pastry on a lightly floured surface to a rectangle measuring 50 x 17cm/20 x 6½in. Cut widthways into four pieces. Brush each piece with beaten egg.

Cook's Tip

If using frozen puff pastry, thaw it first, but keep it chilled. Handle the dough lightly so it doesn't toughen.

2 Mix together 75g/3oz/6 tbsp of the sugar, the nuts and cinnamon in a bowl. Sprinkle this mixture evenly over three of the pieces of pastry. Place the pieces one on top of the other, ending with the uncoated piece, placing this one egg side down on the top. Press lightly together with the rolling pin.

3 Cut the stack of pastry sheets widthways into 5mm/¼in slices. Carefully place one strip on a non-stick baking sheet and place the next strip over it at an angle. Place a third strip on top at another angle so that it looks like a butterfly. Don't worry if the strips separate slightly when you are transferring them to the baking sheet.

4 Using your fingers, press the centre very flat. Sprinkle with a little of the reserved sugar. Continue in this way to make more cookies until all the pastry is used up.

5 Bake the cookies for about 10–15 minutes, or until golden brown all over. Leave to cool completely on the baking sheet before serving with your dessert.

Sablés with Caramel Glaze

These are very buttery French cookies with a dark caramel glaze. The leftover glaze can be kept in the refrigerator and used to flavour fruit salads and especially oranges, both of which are good served with sablés. Use on the day of baking for the most delicious results.

Makes about 18

200g/7oz/1¾ cups plain
  (all-purpose) flour
pinch of salt
75g/3oz/⅔ cup icing
  (confectioners') sugar
130g/4½oz/generous ½ cup unsalted
  (sweet) butter, chilled and diced
3 egg yolks
2.5ml/½ tsp vanilla essence (extract)
1 egg yolk, for glazing

For the caramel syrup

50g/2oz/¼ cup granulated sugar
20ml/4 tsp water
2.5ml/½ tsp lemon juice
50ml/2fl oz/¼ cup water

1 First make the caramel syrup. Put the sugar, 20ml/4 tsp water and lemon juice into a small pan. Place over a gentle heat and stir until no longer cloudy. Boil until bubbly and allow to become a rich golden brown. Once this colour, remove the pan immediately from the heat and plunge the base of the pan into a bowl of cold water to stop the cooking. Carefully stir in the 50ml/2fl oz/¼ cup water. Set the caramel syrup aside to cool completely.

2 Preheat the oven to 180°C/350°F/Gas 4. Put all the cookie ingredients, except the egg yolks and vanilla, into a food processor then process until the mixture resembles fine breadcrumbs. Add the egg yolks and vanilla and blend until the mixture just begins to come together as a firm dough. Form into a ball, wrap in clear film (plastic wrap) then chill in the refrigerator for 15 minutes.

3 Roll the dough out on baking parchment to a thickness of just under 5mm/¼in. Using a 7.5cm/3in fluted biscuit (cookie) cutter, stamp out rounds and place them on two non-stick baking sheets. (If you do not have non-stick baking sheets, line two ordinary sheets with baking parchment.)

4 In a small bowl, beat the egg yolk together with 15ml/1 tbsp of the caramel glaze. Use this to brush sparingly over the cookies. Leave this coating to dry then apply a second thin layer. Using a fork, prick the cookies, then mark in a neat checked pattern by dragging the tines of the fork over the glaze.

5 Bake for about 10–15 minutes, or until crisp and golden brown. Transfer to a wire rack to cool.

Cook's Tip

If the caramel does not dissolve evenly when the water is added, place the pan over a gentle heat and stir until it is completely dissolved.

Almond Fingers

Sweet and crunchy, and packed with lightly spiced nuts, these very simple Middle Eastern sweetmeats are hugely popular in their natives lands. Serve with fruit salads.

Makes 48

200g/7oz/1¾ cups ground almonds
50g/2oz/½ cup ground pistachio nuts
50g/2oz/¼ cup granulated sugar
15ml/1 tbsp rose water
2.5ml/½ tsp ground cinnamon
12 sheets of filo pastry
115g/4oz/½ cup butter, melted
icing (confectioners') sugar,
    for dusting

Variation

You could substitute orange flower water, which is also a popular Middle Eastern flavouring, for the rose water.

1 Preheat the oven to 160°C/325°F/ Gas 3. Grease a large baking sheet with a little butter. Mix together the nuts, sugar, rose water and cinnamon.

2 Cut each sheet of filo pastry into four rectangles. Work with one at a time, and cover the remaining rectangles with a damp dishtowel to prevent them from drying out.

3 Brush one rectangle of filo pastry with a little of the melted butter, place a teaspoonful of the nut filling in the centre.

4 Fold in the sides of the pastry and roll into a thick finger shape. Continue until all the filo pastry and nut filling have been used up.

5 Place the almond fingers on the baking sheet and bake for 30 minutes. Transfer to a wire rack to cool, then dust with icing sugar.

Basbousa

These delicious Middle Eastern coconut sweetmeats can be served either hot as a dessert or cold with tea. To be really authentic, serve them with a glass of sweet mint tea.

Makes 12

115g/4oz/½ cup unsalted
    (sweet) butter
175g/6oz/scant 1 cup caster
    (superfine) sugar
50g/2oz/½ cup plain
    (all-purpose) flour
150g/5oz/1¼ cups semolina
75g/3oz/1 cup grated fresh coconut
175ml/6fl oz/¾ cup milk
5ml/1 tsp baking powder
5ml/1 tsp vanilla essence (extract)
almonds, to decorate

For the syrup

115g/4oz/generous ½ cup caster
    (superfine) sugar
150ml/¼ pint/⅔ cup water
15ml/1 tbsp lemon juice

1 To make the syrup, place the sugar, water and lemon juice in a heavy pan, bring to the boil, stirring until the sugar has dissolved. Lower the heat and simmer for 6–8 minutes. Remove the pan from the heat, leave the syrup to cool, then chill in the refrigerator.

2 Preheat the oven to 180°C/350°F/ Gas 4. Melt the butter in a pan. Add the sugar, flour, semolina, coconut, milk, baking powder and vanilla and mix thoroughly.

3 Pour the mixture into a shallow cake tin (pan), flatten and smooth the top with a metal spatula and bake for 30–35 minutes.

4 Remove the basbousa from the oven and cut into diamond-shape lozenges. Pour the cold syrup evenly over the top and place an almond in the centre of each diamond shape to decorate.

Cook's Tip

Once the sugar has dissolved, do not stir the syrup while it is simmering. Keep the heat low so that the syrup thickens without changing colour. If you plan to serve the basbousa hot, make the syrup while the mixture is baking and pour it over the diamond shapes without chilling it first.

Italian Glazed Lemon Rings

These delicately flavoured, pretty cookies look almost too good to eat. The icing is flavoured with Italian liqueur, so they are strictly for adult parties.

Makes about 16

200g/7oz/1¾ cups self-raising
    (self-rising) flour
50g/2oz/¼ cup unsalted (sweet)
    butter, at room temperature, diced
25ml/1½ tbsp milk
50g/2oz/¼ cup caster (superfine) sugar
finely grated rind of ½ lemon
1 egg, beaten

For the topping

150g/5oz/1¼ cups icing (confectioners')
    sugar, sifted
30ml/2 tbsp Limoncello liqueur
15ml/1 tbsp chopped candied angelica

Variation

If you are baking for children, use lemon
syrup instead of liqueur.

1 Preheat the oven to 180°C/
350°F/Gas 4. Line two large baking
sheets with baking parchment.
Put the flour into a bowl and rub in
the butter. Put the milk, sugar and
lemon rind in a small pan and stir
over a low heat until the sugar
has dissolved. Add to the flour
mixture, together with the egg,
and mix well. Knead lightly
until smooth.

2 Roll walnut-size pieces of dough
into strands 15cm/6in long. Twist
two strands together, and join the
ends to make a circle. Place on the
prepared baking sheets and bake for
15–20 minutes, or until golden.

3 To make the topping, stir the icing
sugar and liqueur together. Dip the
top of each cookie into the topping
and sprinkle with angelica.

Mini Fudge Bites

These cute little cookies have the flavour of butterscotch and fudge and are topped with chopped pecan nuts for a delicious crunch – just the right size for a special little treat with ice cream.

Makes 30

200g/7oz/1¾ cups self-raising
  (self-rising) flour
115g/4oz/½ cup butter, at room
  temperature, diced
115g/4oz/generous ½ cup dark
  muscovado (molasses) sugar
75g/3oz vanilla cream fudge, diced
1 egg, beaten
25g/1oz/¼ cup pecan nut halves,
  sliced widthways

1 Preheat the oven to 190°C/375°F/ Gas 5. Line two or three baking sheets with baking parchment. Put the flour in a bowl and rub in the butter until the mixture resembles fine breadcrumbs.

2 Add the muscovado sugar and diced vanilla cream fudge to the flour mixture and stir well until combined. Add the beaten egg and mix in well. Bring the dough together with your hands, then knead gently on a lightly floured surface. It will be soft yet firm.

3 Roll the dough into two cylinders, 23cm/9in long. Cut into 1cm/½in slices and place on the baking sheets. Sprinkle over the pecan nuts and press in lightly. Bake for about 12 minutes until browned at the edges. Transfer to a wire rack to cool.

Semolina and Nut Halva

Semolina is a popular ingredient in many desserts and pastries in the Eastern Mediterranean. Here it provides a spongy base for soaking up a deliciously fragrant spicy syrup.

Makes 20–24
115g/4oz/½ cup unsalted (sweet) butter
   at room temperature, diced
115g/4oz/generous ½ cup caster
   (superfine) sugar
finely grated rind of 1 orange
30ml/2 tbsp orange juice
3 eggs
175g/6oz/1 cup semolina
10ml/2 tsp baking powder
115g/4oz/1 cup ground hazelnuts
50g/2oz/½ cup unblanched
   hazelnuts, toasted and chopped
50g/2oz/½ cup blanched almonds,
   toasted and chopped
shredded rind of 1 orange
whipped cream, to serve (optional)

For the syrup
350g/12oz/1¾ cups caster
   (superfine) sugar
550ml/18fl oz/2¼ cups water
2 cinnamon sticks, halved
juice of 1 lemon
60ml/4 tbsp orange flower water

1 Preheat the oven to 220°C/425°F/ Gas 7. Grease and line the base of a deep 23cm/9in square heavy cake tin (pan).

2 Lightly cream the butter in a large bowl. Add the sugar, orange rind and juice, the eggs, semolina, baking powder and ground hazelnuts and beat the ingredients together until combined and smooth.

3 Tip the mixture into the prepared tin and level the surface with a spatula or palette knife. Bake for 20–25 minutes, or until just firm and golden on top. Remove from the oven and place the tin on a wire rack. Leave to cool.

4 To make the syrup, put the sugar in a heavy pan with the water and cinnamon sticks. Heat gently, stirring until the sugar has dissolved.

5 Bring the syrup to the boil and continue to boil hard for 5 minutes without stirring. The syrup should thicken, but not colour.

6 Measure half the syrup in a jug (cup) and add the lemon juice and orange flower water to it. Pour this mixture over the halva. Reserve the remainder of the syrup in the pan.

7 Leave the halva in the tin until the syrup has been absorbed, then turn it out on to a plate and cut diagonally into diamond-shape portions. Sprinkle with the chopped hazelnuts and almonds.

8 Boil the remaining syrup until slightly thickened, then pour it over the halva. Sprinkle the shredded orange rind over the top and serve the halva with lightly whipped cream, if you like.

Cook's Tip
You can make the halva up to two days in advance. At the end of step 5, leave the halva to cool in the tin, then cover with clear film (plastic wrap) and store in the refrigerator. Pour the remaining syrup into a jug (pitcher), cover and chill. Bring to room temperature to serve. Cut into diamond shapes, sprinkle with the chopped nuts, pour over the reserved syrup and decorate with the shredded orange rind.

Lace Cookies

Very pretty, delicate and crisp, these lacy cookies are ideal for serving with elegant creamy or iced desserts at the end of a dinner party. Don't be tempted to bake more than four on a sheet.

Makes about 14

75g/3oz/6 tbsp butter, diced
75g/3oz/¾ cup rolled oats
115g/4oz/generous ½ cup golden caster (superfine) sugar
1 egg, beaten
10ml/2 tsp plain (all-purpose) flour
5ml/1 tsp baking powder
2.5ml/½ tsp mixed (apple pie) spice

1 Preheat the oven to 180°C/350°F/Gas 4. Line three or four baking sheets with baking parchment. Put the butter in a pan and set over a low heat until just melted. Remove the pan from the heat.

2 Stir the rolled oats into the melted butter. Add the remaining ingredients and mix well.

3 Place only three or four heaped teaspoonfuls of the mixture, spaced well apart, on each of the lined baking sheets.

4 Bake for about 5–7 minutes, or until a deepish golden brown all over. Leave the cookies on the baking sheets for a few minutes. Carefully cut the parchment so you can lift each cookie singly. Invert on to a wire rack and carefully remove the parchment. Leave to cool.

Dark Chocolate Fingers

With their understated elegance and distinctly grown-up flavour, these deliciously decadent chocolate fingers are ideal for serving with a special dinner part dessert.

Makes about 26

115g/4oz/1 cup plain (all-purpose) flour
2.5ml/½ tsp baking powder
30ml/2 tbsp (unsweetened)
   cocoa powder
50g/2oz/¼ cup unsalted (sweet)
   butter, softened
50g/2oz/¼ cup caster (superfine) sugar
20ml/4 tsp golden (light corn) syrup
150g/5oz dark (bittersweet) chocolate
chocolate-flavour mini flakes,
   for sprinkling

1 Preheat the oven to 160°C/325°F/ Gas 3. Line two baking sheets with baking parchment. Put the flour, baking powder, cocoa powder, butter, sugar and syrup in a large mixing bowl.

2 Work the ingredients together with your hands to combine and form into a dough.

3 Roll the dough out between sheets of baking parchment to an 18 x 24cm/7 x 9½in rectangle. Remove the top sheet. Cut in half lengthways, then into bars 2cm/¾in wide. Place on the baking sheets.

4 Bake for about 15 minutes, taking care not to allow the bars to brown or they will taste bitter. Transfer to a wire rack to cool.

5 Melt the chocolate in a heatproof bowl set over a pan of hot water. Half-dip the cookies, place on baking parchment, sprinkle with chocolate flakes, then leave to set.

Strawberry Shortcakes

More of a dessert than a cookie, shortcake is as American as apple pie – only slightly more popular. It's a favourite summer dessert that is served here with sweet, fresh strawberries.

Makes 6
250g/8oz/2 cups plain (all-purpose) flour
75g/3oz/⅓ cup caster (superfine) sugar
15ml/1 tbsp baking powder
pinch of salt
225ml/8fl oz/1 cup whipping cream
fresh mint leaves, to decorate

For the filling
450g/1lb strawberries, hulled and halved
   or quartered, depending on size
45ml/3 tbsp icing (confectioners') sugar
250ml/8fl oz/1 cup whipping cream

1 Preheat the oven to 200°C/400°F/Gas 6. Grease a baking sheet.

2 To make the shortcakes, sift the flour into a mixing bowl. Add 50g/2oz/¼ cup of the caster sugar, the baking powder and salt. Stir well.

3 Gradually add the cream, tossing with a fork until clumps form.

4 Gather the clumps together, but do not knead the dough. Shape the dough into a 15cm/6in log. Cut into six slices and place the slices on the prepared baking sheet.

5 Sprinkle with the remaining caster sugar, then bake for about 15 minutes until light golden brown. Leave to cool on a wire rack.

6 Meanwhile, mash a quarter of the strawberries with the icing sugar. Stir in the remaining strawberries.

7 Just before serving, whip the cream until soft peaks form.

8 Slice each shortcake in half horizontally. Put the lower halves on individual serving plates and top with some of the cream. Divide the strawberries among the six shortcake halves. Replace the tops and decorate with mint leaves. Serve with the remaining cream.

Cook's Tip
Mix the strawberries with the icing (confectioners') sugar and leave to stand in a cool place for an hour before serving. To achieve the best results when whipping cream, chill both the bowl and beaters until thoroughly cold. If using an electric mixer, increase the speed gradually, and turn the bowl while beating to incorporate as much air as possible.

Raspberry and Rose Petal Shortcakes

Rose-water-scented cream and fresh raspberries form the filling for this delectable dessert. Although they look impressive, these shortcakes are easy to make.

Makes 6

115g/4oz/½ cup unsalted (sweet)
   butter, softened
50g/2oz/¼ cup caster (superfine) sugar
½ vanilla pod (bean), split and
   seeds reserved
115g/4oz/1 cup plain (all-purpose) flour,
   plus extra for dusting
50g/2oz/⅓ cup semolina
icing (confectioners') sugar, for dusting

For the filling

300ml/½ pint/1¼ cups double
   (heavy) cream
15ml/1 tbsp icing (confectioners') sugar
2.5ml/½ tsp rose water
450g/1lb/4 cups raspberries

For the decoration

12 miniature roses, unsprayed
6 mint sprigs
1 egg white, beaten
caster (superfine) sugar, for dusting

2 Gently knead the dough on a lightly floured surface until smooth. Roll out quite thinly and prick all over with a fork. Using a 7.5cm/3in fluted cutter, stamp out 12 rounds. Place these on a baking sheet and chill for 30 minutes.

3 Meanwhile, make the filling. Whisk the cream with the icing sugar until soft peaks form. Gently fold in the rose water with a metal spoon, cover with clear film (plastic wrap) and chill until required.

4 Preheat the oven to 180°C/350°F/Gas 4. To make the decoration, paint the roses and leaves with the egg white. Dust with sugar, then dry on a wire rack.

5 Bake the shortcakes for about 15 minutes or until lightly golden. Lift them off the baking sheet with a metal fish slice or spatula and cool on a wire rack.

6 To assemble the shortcakes, spoon the rose water cream on to half the cookies. Add a layer of raspberries, then top with a second shortcake. Dust with icing sugar. Decorate with the frosted roses and mint sprigs.

Cook's Tip

For best results, serve the shortcakes as soon as possible after assembling them. Otherwise, they are likely to turn soggy from the berries' liquid. However, unfilled shortcakes can be stored.

1 Cream the butter, caster sugar and vanilla seeds in a bowl until pale and fluffy. Sift the flour and semolina together, then gradually work the dry ingredients into the creamed mixture to make a dough.

Florentine Bites

Very sweet and rich, these little mouthfuls are great with iced desserts and you can continue serving them with after-dinner coffee and liqueurs.

Makes 36

200g/7oz good quality plain (semisweet) chocolate (minimum 70 per cent cocoa solids)

50g/2oz/2½ cups cornflakes

50g/2oz/scant ⅓ cup sultanas (golden raisins)

115g/4oz/1 cup toasted flaked (sliced) almonds

115g/4oz/½ cup glacé (candied) cherries, halved

50g/2oz/⅓ cup cut mixed (candied) peel

200ml/7fl oz/scant 1 cup can sweetened condensed milk

1 Preheat the oven to 180°C/350°F/Gas 4. Line the base of a shallow 20cm/8in cake tin (pan) with baking parchment. Lightly grease the sides. Melt the chocolate in a heatproof bowl set over a pan of hot water. Spread evenly over the base of the tin. Put in the refrigerator to set.

2 Meanwhile, put the cornflakes, sultanas, almonds, cherries and mixed peel in a large bowl. Pour over the condensed milk and toss the mixture gently, using a fork.

3 Spread the mixture evenly over the chocolate base and bake for 12–15 minutes until golden brown. Cool in the tin, then chill for 20 minutes. Cut into tiny squares.

Chocolate and Pistachio Wedges

These cookies are rich and grainy textured, with a bitter chocolate flavour. They go extremely well with vanilla ice cream and are especially delicious with bananas and custard.

Makes 16

200g/7oz/scant 1 cup unsalted (sweet)
   butter, at room temperature, diced
90g/3½oz/½ cup golden caster
   (superfine) sugar
250g/9oz/2¼ cups plain
   (all-purpose) flour
50g/2oz/½ cup (unsweetened)
   cocoa powder
25g/1oz/¼ cup shelled pistachio nuts,
   finely chopped
(unsweetened) cocoa powder, for dusting

1 Preheat the oven to 180°C/350°F/
Gas 4 and line a shallow 23cm/9in
round sandwich tin (pan) with
baking parchment.

2 Beat the butter and sugar until light and creamy. Sift the flour and cocoa powder, then add the flour mixture to the butter and work in with your hands until the mixture is smooth. Knead until soft and pliable then press into the prepared tin.

3 Using the back of a tablespoon, spread the mixture evenly in the tin. Sprinkle the pistachio nuts over the top and press in gently. Prick with a fork, then mark into 16 segments using a round-bladed knife.

4 Bake for about 15–20 minutes. Do not allow to brown at all or the cookies will taste bitter.

5 Remove the tin from the oven and dust the cookies with cocoa powder. Cut through the marked sections with a round-bladed knife and leave to cool completely before removing from the tin.

Almond and Vanilla Cookies with Praline Coating

These short-textured almond cookies, filled with vanilla cream and coated in praline, are just the thing to have with a light dessert, such as fresh fruit salad or compote.

Makes 17–18

150g/5oz/1¼ cups plain
(all-purpose) flour
75g/3oz/¾ cup ground almonds
75g/3oz/6 tbsp unsalted (sweet) butter,
at room temperature, diced
1 egg yolk
5ml/1 tsp vanilla essence (extract)
icing (confectioners') sugar, sifted,
for dusting

For the praline
25g/1oz/¼ cup whole blanched almonds
50g/2oz/¼ cup caster (superfine) sugar

For the filling
150g/5oz/1¼ cups icing (confectioners')
sugar, sifted
75g/3oz/6 tbsp unsalted (sweet) butter,
at room temperature, diced
5ml/1 tsp vanilla essence (extract)

1 First make the praline. Lightly oil a baking sheet and place the almonds on it, fairly close together. Melt the sugar in a small pan over a very low heat. Heat until it turns dark golden brown and pour immediately over the almonds. Cool then crush finely in a food processor.

2 Preheat the oven to 160°C/325°F/ Gas 3. Line three baking sheets with baking parchment.

3 Put the flour, ground almonds and butter in a bowl. Rub together until the mixture starts to cling together. Add the egg and vanilla and work together using your hands to make a soft dough. Roll out to a thickness of about 5mm/¼in on baking parchment. Stamp out rounds using a 5cm/2in cookie cutter and place on the prepared baking sheets.

4 Bake the cookies for about 15 minutes, or until light golden brown. Leave on the baking sheets for 5 minutes to firm up slightly, then transfer to a wire rack to cool.

5 To make the filling, beat together the icing sugar, butter and vanilla until creamy. Use this mixture to sandwich the cookies in pairs. Be generous with the filling, spreading right to the edges. Press the cookies gently so the filling oozes out of the sides and, using your finger, smooth around the sides of the cookie.

6 Put the praline on a plate and roll the edges of each cookie in the praline until thickly coated. Dust the tops of the cookies with icing sugar.

Cook's Tip
These cookies should be made on the day of serving or the filling will cause them to become soggy and unpleasant.

Louisiana Pralines

These classic cookies are a sweet combination of sugar, cream and milk. They resemble puddles of nut fudge and are deliciously indulgent with ice cream.

Makes 30

225g/8oz/2 cups pecan nut halves
450g/1lb/2 well-packed cups soft light
  brown sugar
200g/7oz/scant 1 cup granulated sugar
300ml/½ pint/1¼ cups double
  (heavy) cream
175ml/6fl oz/¾ cup milk
5ml/1 tsp vanilla essence (extract)

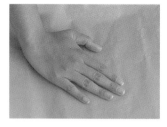

I Line two or three large baking sheets with baking parchment. Coarsely chop half the pecan nuts and set both the whole and chopped nuts aside.

2 Place both the sugars, the cream and milk together in a heavy pan and stir over a medium heat until the sugar has dissolved. Stir until the mixture reaches 119°C/238°F (soft ball stage).

Cook's Tip

Praline is traditionally made with almonds and has a characteristically granulated appearance. Named after the French aristocrat whose chef invented the recipe, Comte du Plessis-Praslin, they quickly became popular and were widely sold in fairgrounds. Peanuts were sometimes substituted for the almonds and when the recipe crossed the Atlantic, indigenous American pecans got their turn.

3 Remove the pan from the heat immediately and beat with an electric mixer or balloon whisk until the mixture loses its sheen and becomes creamy in texture and grainy looking. This could take as long as 15 minutes whisking by hand or about 5 minutes if you are using an electric mixer.

4 Stir in the vanilla essence and nuts. Drop tablespoonfuls of the mixture on to the prepared baking sheets, allowing it to spread of its own accord. Leave to cool and set at room temperature. Store stacked between layers of greaseproof (waxed) paper in an airtight container until required.

Mexican Almond Cookies

Light and crisp, these sugar-dusted cookies make a lively accompaniment to plain ice cream at the end of a family supper and also make a good accompaniment to fruit salads.

Makes 24

115g/4oz/1 cup plain (all-purpose) flour
175g/6oz/1½ cups icing (confectioners')
  sugar, plus extra for dusting
pinch of salt
50g/2oz/½ cup almonds,
  finely chopped
2.5ml/½ tsp vanilla essence (extract)
115g/4oz/½ cup unsalted (sweet) butter
  at room temperature, diced

1 Preheat the oven to 180°C/350°F/
Gas 4. Sift the flour, icing sugar
and salt into a bowl. Add the
almonds and mix well. Stir in the
vanilla essence.

2 Using your fingertips, work the
butter into the mixture to make a
dough. Form it into a ball.

Variation

*Try using other nuts such as walnuts,
peanuts or pecan nuts.*

3 Roll out the dough on a lightly
floured surface until it is 3mm/⅛in
thick. Using a round, fluted cutter,
stamp out 24 rounds, re-rolling the
trimmings as necessary.

4 Carefully transfer the cookies to
non-stick baking sheets and bake for
30 minutes until browned. Transfer
to wire racks to cool, then dust
thickly with icing sugar.

Peppermint and Coconut Chocolate Sticks

Coconut gives these chocolate mint sticks a unique flavour and texture. The mixture makes lots, so is perfect party fare when you are throwing a big dinner or buffet party.

Makes 80
115g/4oz/½ cup granulated sugar
150ml/¼ pint/⅔ cup water
2.5ml/½ tsp peppermint essence (extract)
200g/7oz dark (bittersweet)
  chocolate, chopped
60ml/4 tbsp toasted desiccated (dry
  unsweetened shredded) coconut

I Lightly oil a large baking sheet. Place the sugar and water in a small, heavy pan and heat gently, stirring occasionally, until the sugar has dissolved completely.

2 Bring to the boil and boil rapidly, without stirring, until the syrup registers 138°C/280°F on a sugar thermometer (hard ball stage).

3 Remove the pan from the heat and add the peppermint essence, then carefully pour on to the prepared baking sheet and leave until set and completely cold.

4 Break the peppermint mixture into a bowl with your hands and then use the end of a rolling pin to crush it into pieces.

5 Melt the dark chocolate in a medium-size heatproof bowl set over a pan of simmering water. Remove the bowl from the heat, add the crushed peppermint pieces and desiccated coconut and stir well until thoroughly combined.

6 Place a 30 x 25cm/12 x 10in sheet of baking parchment on the work surface. Spread the mixture over the paper, leaving a narrow border all around. Leave to set. When firm, use a sharp knife to cut into thin sticks.

Plain Chocolate and Peppermint Crisps

Crunchy peppermint caramel is crushed then stirred into chocolate to make these pretty swirls – choose good quality chocolate for the best result.

Makes 30

50g/2oz/¼ cup granulated sugar
50ml/2fl oz/¼ cup water
5ml/1 tsp peppermint essence (extract)
225g/8oz plain (semisweet)
  chocolate, chopped

I Lightly brush a large baking sheet with unflavoured oil. In a pan over a medium heat, heat the sugar and water, swirling the pan gently until the sugar dissolves. Boil rapidly until the temperature registers 138°C/280°F on a sugar thermometer (hard ball stage).

2 Remove from the heat and add the peppermint essence; swirl gently to mix. Pour on to the baking sheet and leave to set and cool.

3 When cold, break into pieces. Place in a food processor fitted with a metal blade until fine crumbs form.

Cook's Tip
You can test cooked sugar for "hard ball stage" by spooning a few drops into a bowl of cold water; it should form a hard ball when rolled between your fingers.

4 Line two baking sheets with non-stick baking parchment. Place the chocolate in a heatproof bowl over a small pan of hot water. Place over a very low heat until the chocolate has melted, stirring frequently until smooth. Remove from the heat and stir in the peppermint mixture.

5 Using a teaspoon, drop small mounds on to the prepared baking sheets. Using the back of the spoon, spread to 4cm/1½in rounds. Cool, then chill for about 1 hour, until set. Peel off the parchment and store in airtight containers with baking parchment between the layers.

Vanilla Crescents

These attractively shaped cookies are sweet and delicate, ideal to serve with creamy ice cream or a light and fluffy fruit fool for dessert. Kids love them with chocolate ice cream.

Makes 36

175g/6oz/1¼ cups unblanched almonds
115g/4oz/1 cup plain (all-purpose) flour
pinch of salt
225g/8oz/1 cup unsalted (sweet) butter
    at room temperature, diced
115g/4oz/½ cup granulated sugar
5ml/1 tsp vanilla essence (extract)
icing (confectioners') sugar, for dusting

1 Grind the almonds with a few tablespoons of the flour in a food processor, blender or nut grinder and process in short pulses until finely ground.

2 Sift the remaining flour with the salt into a bowl. Set aside.

3 With an electric mixer, cream together the butter and sugar until light and fluffy.

4 Add the almonds, vanilla essence and the flour mixture. Stir to mix well. Gather the dough into a ball, wrap in greaseproof (waxed) paper, and chill for at least 30 minutes. Preheat the oven to 160°C/325°F/Gas 3. Lightly grease two baking sheets.

5 Break off walnut-size pieces of dough and roll them into small cylinders about 1cm/½in in diameter. Bend them into crescent shapes and place on the baking sheets, spaced well apart.

6 Bake for about 20 minutes until dry but not brown. Transfer to a wire rack to cool only slightly. Set the rack over a baking sheet and dust with an even layer of icing sugar. Leave to cool completely.

Black Russian Cookies

The ingredients of the famous cocktail – coffee and vodka – flavour these fabulous cookies. These are strictly for the adults in the family, so why not go the extra mile and serve with vodka jelly?

Makes 16
30ml/2 tbsp ground espresso coffee
60ml/4 tbsp near-boiling milk
115g/4oz/½ cup butter
115g/4oz/½ cup soft light brown sugar
1 egg
225g/8oz/2 cups plain (all-purpose) flour
5ml/1 tsp baking powder
pinch of salt

For the icing
115g/4oz/1 cup icing
   (confectioners') sugar
about 25ml/1½ tbsp vodka

1 Preheat the oven to 180°C/350°F/Gas 4. Put the coffee in a small bowl and pour the hot milk over it. Leave to infuse (steep) for 4 minutes, then strain through a fine sieve and leave to cool.

2 Cream the butter and sugar until light and fluffy. Gradually beat in the egg. Sift the flour, baking powder and salt together and fold in with the coffee-flavoured milk to make a fairly stiff mixture.

3 Place dessertspoonfuls of the mixture on greased baking sheets, spacing them slightly apart. Bake the cookies for about 15 minutes until lightly browned. Cool on a wire rack.

4 To make the icing, mix the icing sugar and enough vodka together to make a thick icing. Spoon into a small greaseproof (waxed) paper piping (pastry) bag.

5 Snip off the end of the piping bag and lightly drizzle the icing over the top of each cookie. Leave the icing to set before serving.

Variations
You could adapt this recipe to re-create other classic and contemporary cocktails. For Black Magic Cookies, add a dash of lemon juice to the vodka when making the icing. For Blackout Cookies, substitute white rum for the vodka in the icing. For Brave Bull Cookies, substitute silver tequila for the vodka in the icing. For Moon Landing Cookies, substitute 15ml/ 1 tbsp amaretto liqueur for the same quantity of milk. Don't heat it, simply stir it in after straining the coffee.

Nut Lace Cookies

These cookies look so pretty, it almost seems a shame to eat them, but if you didn't, you would certainly be missing out on a treat. Serve them with smooth and creamy desserts.

Makes 18
50g/2oz/½ cup blanched almonds
50g/2oz/¼ cup butter
45ml/3 tbsp plain (all-purpose) flour
115g/4oz/½ cup granulated sugar
30ml/2 tbsp double (heavy) cream
2.5ml/½ tsp vanilla essence (extract)

Variation
Add 40g/1½oz/¼ cup finely chopped candied orange peel to the mixture with the almonds in step 3.

1 Preheat the oven to 190°C/375°F/ Gas 5. Thoroughly grease one or two baking sheets.

2 With a sharp knife, chop the almonds as finely as possible. Alternatively, use a food processor to chop the nuts very finely.

3 Melt the butter in a small pan over a low heat. Remove from the heat and stir in the remaining ingredients, including the almonds.

4 Drop teaspoonfuls of the mixture 6cm/2½in apart on the prepared baking sheets. Bake for about 5 minutes, or until golden. Cool on the sheets briefly, until the cookies are just firm enough to lift off.

5 With a metal spatula, transfer the cookies to a wire rack to cool.

Oat Lace Cookies

These thin, crisp cookies have quite a different texture from other oat cookie recipes, but they are just as tasty. Use unsalted butter for the best flavour.

Makes 36
165g/5½oz/¾ cup unsalted (sweet) butter
    or margarine
175g/6oz/1½ cups rolled oats
175g/6oz/¾ cup soft dark brown sugar
175g/6oz/¾ cup granulated sugar
45ml/3 tbsp plain (all-purpose) flour
pinch of salt
1 egg, lightly beaten
5ml/1 tsp vanilla essence (extract)
50g/2oz/½ cup pecan nuts or walnuts,
    finely chopped

1 Preheat the oven to 180°C/350°F/ Gas 4. Thoroughly grease two large baking sheets.

2 Melt the butter or margarine in a small pan over a low heat. Set aside.

3 Mix the oats, sugars, flour and salt. Add the butter or margarine, the egg and vanilla. Mix until blended, then stir in the nuts.

4 Drop rounded teaspoonfuls of the batter about 5cm/2in apart on the prepared baking sheets. Bake for 5–8 minutes, until lightly browned on the edges and bubbling. Leave to cool slightly on the baking sheets for about 2 minutes, then, using a metal spatula, transfer to a wire rack to cool completely.

Cook's Tip
Walnuts and pecan nuts are quite closely related and, when fresh, have a similar sweetness. Pecans tend to have a slightly softer texture than walnuts. Chop them with a large sharp knife.

Brownies and Bars

Cookies with attitude, brownies and bars make filling snacks, lunchtime treats, perfect picnic fare and a marvellous morale and energy boost at any time of day. There are probably more variations on the basic brownie than on any other cookie in the world and when you try some of the recipes here, you will understand why. As for bars and slices, the sky's the limit — crisp and nutty, chewy and succulent, sweet and fruity. You choose.

Fruity Lemon Drizzle Bars

These tangy iced, spongy bars are great for kids to snack on after school. This fruit and lemon mixture is lovely but you can easily experiment with other flavours such as orange or lime.

Makes 16

250g/9oz ready-made sweet
   shortcrust pastry
90g/3¼oz/¾ cup self-raising
   (self-rising) flour
75g/3oz/¾ cup fine or
   medium oatmeal
5ml/1 tsp baking powder
130g/4½oz/generous ½ cup light
   muscovado (brown) sugar
2 eggs
150g/5oz/10 tbsp unsalted
   (sweet) butter, at room
   temperature, diced
finely grated rind of 1 lemon
90g/3½oz/¾ cup sultanas
   (golden raisins)
150g/5oz/1¼ cups icing
   (confectioners') sugar
15–30ml/3–4 tsp lemon juice

1 Preheat the oven to 190°C/375°F/ Gas 5 and place a baking sheet in the oven to heat through. Generously grease a 28 x 18cm/ 11 x 7in shallow baking tin (pan).

2 Roll out the pastry thinly on a lightly floured, clean surface. Use to line the base of the baking tin, pressing the pastry up the sides. (Don't worry about rough edges.)

3 Put the flour, oatmeal, baking powder, sugar, eggs, butter and lemon rind in a mixing bowl. Beat with a hand-held electric whisk for about 2 minutes until pale and creamy. Stir in the sultanas.

4 Tip the filling into the pastry case and spread evenly into the corners using the back of a spoon.

5 Place the tin on the heated baking sheet in the oven and bake for about 30 minutes until pale golden and the surface feels firm to the touch.

6 Put the icing sugar in a small bowl with enough lemon juice to mix to a thin paste, about the consistency of pouring (half-and-half) cream.

7 Using a teaspoon, drizzle the icing diagonally across the warm cake in thin lines. Leave to cool in the tin.

8 When the icing has set, use a sharp knife to cut the cake in half lengthways. Cut each half across into eight even-size bars.

Luscious Lemon Bars

A crisp cookie base is covered with a tangy lemon topping. The bars make a delightful addition to the tea table on a warm summer's day in the garden.

Makes 12

150g/5oz/1¼ cups plain
  (all-purpose) flour
90g/3½oz/7 tbsp unsalted (sweet) butter,
  chilled and diced
50g/2oz/½ cup icing (confectioners')
  sugar, sifted

For the topping

2 eggs
175g/6oz/scant 1 cup caster
  (superfine) sugar
finely grated rind and juice of
  1 large lemon
15ml/1 tbsp plain (all-purpose) flour
2.5ml/½ tsp bicarbonate of soda
  (baking soda)
icing (confectioners') sugar, for dusting

3 To make the topping, whisk the eggs in a bowl until frothy. Add the caster sugar, a little at a time, whisking well between each addition. Whisk in the lemon rind and juice, flour and soda. Pour over the cookie base. Bake for 20–25 minutes, until set and golden.

4 Leave to cool slightly. Cut into twelve bars and dust lightly with icing sugar. Leave to cool completely.

1 Preheat the oven to 180°C/350°F/Gas 4. Line the base of a 20cm/8in square shallow cake tin (pan) with baking parchment and lightly grease the sides of the tin.

2 Process the flour, butter and icing sugar in a food processor until the mixture comes together as a firm dough. Press evenly into the base of the tin and spread smoothly using the back of a tablespoon. Bake for 12–15 minutes until lightly golden. Cool in the tin.

Lemon Cheese Bars

Using a really creamy cheese for the topping makes these bars suitable for any celebration.

Makes 24

115g/4oz/1 cup plain (all-purpose) flour
50g/2oz/½ cup chopped walnuts
75g/3oz/⅓ cup soft light brown sugar
75g/3oz/⅓ cup unsalted (sweet)
   butter, softened
grated rind and juice of 1 small lemon
225g/8oz/1 cup full-fat cream cheese
50g/2oz/¼ cup granulated sugar
15ml/1 tbsp milk
2.5ml/½ tsp vanilla essence (extract)
1 large (US extra large) egg

1 Preheat the oven to 180°C/350°F/ Gas 4. Grease a 23cm/9in square cake tin (pan).

2 Beat together the flour, walnuts, brown sugar and butter. Divide the mixture in half. Press half of the mixture into the prepared cake tin. Bake for 12–15 minutes until lightly browned. Remove from the oven.

3 Beat together the lemon rind and juice, the cheese and sugar, then beat in the milk, vanilla essence and egg. Spoon over the partly cooked pastry and crumble the remaining mixture evenly over the top. Bake for a further 25 minutes, until the top is golden. Transfer to a wire rack to cool, then chill. Cut into bars.

Citrus Spice Bars

These iced bars have a delicious rum-flavoured fruit mixture at the base, so they're strictly adults only.

Makes 50

115g/4oz/¾ cup candied orange
   peel, chopped
50g/2oz/⅓ cup seedless raisins
75ml/5 tbsp rum
50g/2oz/¼ cup clear honey
45ml/3 tbsp black treacle (molasses)
1 egg
115g/4oz/1 cup ground almonds
175g/6oz/1½ cups wholemeal
   (whole-wheat) flour
2.5ml/½ tsp baking powder
large pinch of bicarbonate of soda
   (baking soda)
5ml/1 tsp ground cinnamon
2.5ml/½ tsp ground ginger
115g/4oz/1 cup almonds, chopped
50g/2oz/½ cup sifted icing
   (confectioners') sugar
about 45ml/3 tbsp orange juice

1 Preheat the oven to 200°C/400°F/ Gas 6. Lightly grease a 33 × 23cm/ 13 × 9in cake tin (pan). Place the orange peel, raisins and rum in a bowl, cover and set aside for 1 hour.

2 Bring the honey and treacle to the boil in a pan. Cool, then beat in the egg. Combine the ground almonds, flour, baking powder, bicarbonate of soda and spices and stir into the mixture. Stir in the chopped almonds and the rum mixture and form into a dough.

3 Bake for 20 minutes. Transfer to a wire rack to cool. Sift the icing sugar into a bowl and stir in just enough orange juice to make a spreading consistency. Set aside for 1 hour.

4 Spread with the icing. Decorate if you like and cut into generous bars.

Lemon Squares

Perfect for when you crave something sweet, but don't want the richness of chocolate.

Makes 12
225g/8oz/2 cups plain (all-purpose) flour
50g/2oz/½ cup icing
   (confectioners') sugar
pinch of salt
175g/6oz/¾ cup butter or
   margarine, diced

For the lemon layer
4 eggs
450g/1lb/2¼ cups caster
   (superfine) sugar
25g/1oz/¼ cup plain (all-purpose) flour
2.5ml/½ tsp baking powder
5ml/1 tsp grated lemon rind
50ml/2fl oz/¼ cup fresh lemon juice
icing (confectioners') sugar, for sprinkling

1 Preheat the oven to 180°C/350°F/ Gas 4. Sift the flour, icing sugar and salt into a mixing bowl.

2 Rub in the butter or margarine until the mixture resembles coarse breadcrumbs. Stir in 5ml/1 tsp water with a fork until the mixture forms a ball.

3 Press the mixture evenly into an ungreased 33 × 23cm/13 × 9in ovenproof dish. Bake for 15–20 minutes, until light golden brown. Remove from the oven and leave to cool slightly.

4 Meanwhile, to make the lemon layer, beat together the eggs, caster sugar, flour, baking powder and lemon rind and juice in a bowl until smooth and combined.

5 Pour the lemon mixture over the cooked base. Return to the oven and bake for 25 minutes.

6 Leave to cool in the ovenproof dish, placed on a wire rack. Before serving, sprinkle the top with icing sugar. Cut into squares with a knife.

Variation
To make Orange Squares, substitute grated orange rind and orange juice for the lemon rind and juice.

Apricot and Almond Bars

What an utterly perfect combination. If they aren't eaten immediately, these fruity bars will stay moist for several days if stored in an airtight container.

Makes 18

225g/8oz/2 cups self-raising
   (self-rising) flour
115g/4oz/½ cup light muscovado
   (brown) sugar
50g/2oz/⅓ cup semolina
175g/6oz/¾ cup ready-to-eat dried
   apricots, chopped
2 eggs
30ml/2 tbsp malt extract
30ml/2 tbsp clear honey
60ml/4 tbsp skimmed milk
60ml/4 tbsp sunflower oil
a few drops of almond essence (extract)
30ml/2 tbsp flaked (sliced) almonds

1 Lightly grease and line a 28 x 18cm/ 11 x 7in shallow cake tin (pan) and line with greaseproof (waxed) paper.

2 Preheat the oven to 160°C/ 325°F/Gas 3. Sift the flour into a bowl and add the muscovado sugar, semolina, dried apricots and eggs. Add the malt extract, clear honey, milk, sunflower oil and almond essence. Mix well until smooth.

3 Turn the mixture into the prepared cake tin and spread to the edges and corner with a metal spatula or palette knife. Smooth the top. Sprinkle the flaked almonds all over the surface in as even a layer as possible.

4 Bake for 30–35 minutes, until the centre of the cake springs back when lightly pressed. Transfer to a wire rack to cool. Remove and discard the lining paper, place the cake on a board and cut it into 18 slices with a sharp knife.

Variation
You can substitute dried peaches or nectarines for the apricots; they all have an affinity with almonds.

Apricot and Walnut Bars

These traditional bars remain firm favourites and are still irresistible. For a truly fabulous flavour, use Hunza apricots and soak them first before poaching.

Makes 12

75g/3oz/⅓ cup soft light
 brown sugar
75g/3oz/⅔ cup plain
 (all-purpose) flour
75g/3oz/⅓ cup cold unsalted (sweet)
 butter, diced

For the topping

175g/6oz/¾ cup dried apricots
250ml/8fl oz/1 cup water
grated rind of 1 lemon
75g/3oz/⅓ cup granulated sugar
10ml/2 tsp cornflour (cornstarch)
50g/2oz/½ cup walnuts,
 coarsely chopped

1 Preheat the oven to 180°C/350°F/ Gas 4. Grease a 20cm/8in square cake tin (pan).

2 In a bowl, combine the sugar and flour. Add the butter, cut it in, then rub it in with your fingers until the mixture resembles coarse breadcrumbs.

3 Press into the prepared cake tin. Bake for 15 minutes. Remove from the oven, but leave the oven on.

4 To make the topping, combine the apricots and water in a pan and simmer for about 10 minutes until soft. Strain the liquid and reserve. Chop the apricots.

5 Return the apricots to the pan and add the lemon rind, granulated sugar, cornflour, and 60ml/4 tbsp of the reserved cooking liquid. Cook for 1 minute.

6 Remove the pan from the heat and cool slightly before spreading the topping over the base. Sprinkle over the walnuts and bake for a further 20 minutes. Leave to cool in the tin before cutting into bars.

Spiced Fig Bars

The dried fruit gives these bars a deliciously chewy texture and natural sweetness, while the spices add aroma and warmth to the flavour. Sprinkle with icing sugar just before serving.

Makes 48

350g/12oz/2 cups dried figs
3 eggs
175g/6oz/¾ cup granulated sugar
75g/3oz/⅔ cup plain (all-purpose) flour
5ml/1 tsp baking powder
2.5ml/½ tsp ground cinnamon
1.5ml/¼ tsp ground cloves
1.5ml/¼ tsp grated nutmeg
pinch of salt
75g/3oz/¾ cup walnuts, finely chopped
30ml/2 tbsp brandy or cognac
icing (confectioners') sugar, for dusting

1 Preheat the oven to 160°C/325°F/ Gas 3. Grease and line a 30 × 20 × 4cm/12 × 8 × 1½in cake tin (pan) with greaseproof (waxed) paper.

2 With a sharp knife, chop the figs coarsely. Set aside.

3 Whisk the eggs and sugar in a bowl until well blended. Sift together the flour, baking powder, spices and salt into another bowl, then gently fold into the egg mixture in several batches.

4 Stir the figs, walnuts and brandy or cognac into the mixture until evenly combined.

5 Scrape the mixture into the prepared cake tin and spread out evenly. Bake for 35–40 minutes, until the top is firm and brown. It should still be soft underneath.

6 Leave to cool in the tin for about 5 minutes, then unmould and transfer to a sheet of greaseproof paper lightly sprinkled with icing sugar. Cut into bars and leave to cool completely.

Creamy Lemon Bars

These delicious bars topped with a rich, creamy custard flavoured with lemon are a real treat, ideal for accompanying a cup of coffee.

Makes 36

50g/2oz/½ cup icing
  (confectioners') sugar
175g/6oz/1½ cups plain
  (all-purpose) flour
pinch of salt
175g/6oz/¾ cup butter, diced

For the topping

4 eggs
350g/12oz/1½ cups granulated sugar
grated rind of 1 lemon
120ml/4fl oz/½ cup fresh lemon juice
175ml/6fl oz/¾ cup whipping cream
icing (confectioners') sugar,
  for dusting

1 Preheat the oven to 160°C/325°F/ Gas 3. Grease a 33 × 23cm/ 13 × 9in cake tin (pan). Sift the sugar, flour and salt into a bowl. Rub in the butter.

2 Press the mixture into the tin.

3 Bake for about 20 minutes, until golden brown.

4 Meanwhile, to make the topping, whisk together the eggs and sugar in a bowl until blended. Add the lemon rind and juice and mix well.

5 Lightly whip the cream in another bowl and fold into the egg mixture. Pour the topping over the warm crust, return to the oven, and bake for about 40 minutes, until set. Cool completely in the tin, set on a wire rack, before cutting into bars. Dust with icing sugar.

Blueberry Streusel Slices

A pastry base, a crumbly topping and, sandwiched in between, a fruity filling that is both sweet and sharp at the same time makes these moist slices very good indeed.

Makes 30

50g/2oz/½ cup plain (all-purpose) flour
1.5ml/¼ tsp baking powder
25g/1oz/½ cup fresh white breadcrumbs
50g/2oz/¼ cup soft light brown sugar
pinch of salt
40g/1½oz/3 tbsp butter or
* margarine, diced*
50g/2oz/4 tbsp flaked (sliced) or
* chopped almonds*
225g/8oz ready-made shortcrust pastry,
* thawed if frozen*
60ml/4 tbsp blackberry or
* bramble jelly*
115g/4oz/scant 1 cup blueberries, fresh
* or frozen*

1 Preheat the oven to 180°C/350°F/
Gas 4. Grease an 18 × 28cm/
7 × 11in Swiss roll tin (jelly roll pan).

2 Sift the flour into a large bowl
and then add the baking powder,
bread, sugar and salt. Rub in the
butter or margarine, until the
mixture resembles breadcrumbs,
then mix in the almonds.

3 Roll out the shortcrust pastry
and use to line the base and sides
of the prepared tin, trimming off
any excess.

4 Spread the pastry evenly with the
blackberry or bramble jelly, sprinkle
with the blueberries, spreading them
out well, then cover evenly with the
streusel topping, pressing down
lightly with the back of the spoon.

5 Bake for 20 minutes, then lower
the oven temperature to 160°C/
325°F/Gas 3. Bake for a further
10–20 minutes, until firm.

6 Remove from the oven. Using a
sharp knife, cut into slices while still
hot, then transfer the slices to a
wire rack to cool completely. Store
in an airtight container.

Sticky Date and Apple Squares

Sometimes the simplest things are the nicest – and these squares, with their combination of fresh and dried fruit, couldn't be easier to make or more delicious to eat.

Makes 16

115g/4oz/½ cup margarine
50g/2oz/¼ cup soft dark brown sugar
50g/2oz/4 tbsp golden (light
* corn) syrup*
115g/4oz/⅔ cup chopped dates
115g/4oz/generous 1 cup rolled oats
115g/4oz/1 cup wholemeal (whole-
* wheat) self-raising (self-rising) flour*
2 eating apples, peeled, cored
* and grated*
5–10ml/1–2 tsp lemon juice
walnut halves, to decorate

1 Preheat the oven to 190°C/375°F/
Gas 5. Line an 18–20cm/7–8in
square or rectangular loose-based
cake tin (pan).

2 Gently heat the margarine, sugar
and syrup together in a large pan,
stirring occasionally, until the
margarine has melted completely.

3 Add the dates and cook until
softened. Gradually work in the
oats, flour, apples and lemon juice
until well mixed.

4 Spoon the mixture into the
prepared tin and spread out evenly.
Top with the walnut halves. Bake
for 30 minutes, then reduce the
oven temperature to 160°C/325°F/
Gas 3 and bake for a further
10–12 minutes, until firm to the
touch and golden.

5 Cut into squares or bars while
still warm if you are going to eat
them straight away, or wrap in foil
when nearly cold and keep for
1–2 days before eating.

Mincemeat Wedges

The flour used in these wedge-shaped cookies gives a nutty flavour that combines well with the mincemeat. These are great for winter tea parties around a blazing fire.

Makes 12

225g/8oz/2 cups self-raising (self-rising)
   wholemeal (whole-wheat) flour
75g/3oz/6 tbsp unsalted (sweet)
   butter, diced
75g/3oz/⅓ cup demerara (raw) sugar
1 egg, beaten
115g/4oz/½ cup good-quality mincemeat
about 60ml/4 tbsp milk
crushed brown or white café (sugar)
   cubes or a mixture, for sprinkling

Cook's Tip

If you can't find self-raising (self-rising)
flour, add 10ml/2 tsp baking powder to
the plain wholemeal (whole-wheat) flour.

1 Preheat the oven to 200°C/400°F/ Gas 6. Line the base of a 20cm/8in round sandwich tin (layer pan) and lightly grease the sides. Put the flour in a bowl, add the diced butter and rub in with your fingertips just until the mixture resembles coarse breadcrumbs.

2 Stir in the demerara sugar, egg and mincemeat. Add enough milk to mix to a soft dough. Spread evenly in the prepared tin and sprinkle generously with the crushed sugar. Bake for about 20 minutes until firm and golden. Cool in the tin, then cut into wedges to serve.

Sour Cream Streusel Bars

The German word **Streuselkuchen** simply means a cake with a crumbly topping. These tasty bars have a cinnamon-flavoured filling and topping and make a deliciously different tea-time treat.

Makes 12–14
115g/4oz/½ cup butter, diced
150g/5oz/⅔ cup granulated sugar
3 eggs, at room temperature
175g/6oz/1½ cups plain
   (all-purpose) flour
5ml/1 tsp bicarbonate of soda
   (baking soda)
5ml/1 tsp baking powder
250ml/8fl oz/1 cup sour cream

For the topping
175g/6oz/¾ cup cup dark brown sugar
10ml/2 tsp ground cinnamon
115g/4oz/1 cup walnuts, finely chopped
50g/2oz/¼ cup butter, chopped

1 Preheat the oven to 180°C/350°F/ Gas 4. Line the base of a 23cm/ 9in square cake tin (pan) with greaseproof (waxed) paper and then grease the paper.

2 To make the topping, place the brown sugar, cinnamon and walnuts in a bowl. Mix with your fingertips, then add the butter and continue working until the mixture resembles coarse breadcrumbs.

3 Cream the butter with an electric mixer until soft. Add the sugar and beat until light and fluffy.

4 Add the eggs, one at a time, beating well after each addition.

5 In another bowl, sift together the flour, bicarbonate of soda and baking powder three times.

6 Gently fold the dry ingredients into the butter mixture in three batches, alternating with the sour cream. Fold, using a rubber spatula, until all the ingredients are blended after each addition.

7 Pour half of the batter into the prepared tin and sprinkle over half of the topping.

8 Pour the remaining batter on top and then sprinkle over the remaining topping. Bake for 60–70 minutes, until browned. Leave to stand for about 5 minutes, then unmould. Transfer to a wire rack to cool, then cut into squares.

Almond-topped Squares

Sweet and crunchy with a slightly chewy nut topping, these are just the cookies you want when you need to put your feet up and have a cup of tea or coffee and a well-earned break.

Makes 18

75g/3oz/⅓ cup butter
50g/2oz/¼ cup granulated sugar
1 egg yolk
grated rind and juice of ½ lemon
2.5ml/½ tsp vanilla essence (extract)
30ml/2 tbsp whipping cream
115g/4oz/1 cup plain (all-purpose) flour

For the topping

225g/8oz/1 cup granulated sugar
75g/3oz/¾ cup flaked (sliced) almonds
4 egg whites
2.5ml/½ tsp ground ginger
2.5ml/½ tsp ground cinnamon

1 Preheat the oven to 190°C/375°F/ Gas 5. Line a 33 × 23cm/13 × 9in Swiss roll tin (jelly roll pan) with greaseproof (waxed) paper and grease the paper.

2 With an electric mixer, cream the butter and sugar until light and fluffy. Beat in the egg yolk, lemon rind and juice, the vanilla essence and cream.

3 Gradually stir in the flour. Gather the dough into a ball. With lightly floured fingers, press the dough into the prepared tin. Bake for 15 minutes. Remove from the oven but leave the oven switched on.

4 To make the topping, combine all the ingredients in a heavy pan. Cook, stirring constantly, until the mixture comes to the boil. Boil for 1 minute. Pour the topping over the base, spreading it evenly.

5 Return to the oven and bake for about 45 minutes. Remove and score into squares or bars with a sharp knife and leave to cool and set completely before serving.

Hazelnut and Raspberry Bars

The hazelnuts are ground and used to make a superb sweet pastry which is then baked with a layer of raspberry jam in the middle and sprinkled with flaked almonds.

Makes 30

250g/9oz/2¼ cups hazelnuts
300g/10oz/2½ cups plain
  (all-purpose) flour
5ml/1 tsp mixed (apple pie) spice
2.5ml/½ tsp ground cinnamon
150g/5oz/1¼ cups golden icing
  (confectioners') sugar
15ml/1 tbsp grated lemon rind
300g/10oz/1¼ cups unsalted (sweet)
  butter, softened
3 egg yolks
350g/12oz/1¼ cups seedless
  raspberry jam

For the topping
1 egg, beaten
15ml/1 tbsp clear honey
50g/2oz/½ cup flaked (sliced) almonds

1 Grind the hazelnuts in a food processor and then put in a bowl. Sift in the flour, spices and icing sugar. Add the lemon rind and mix well, then add the butter and the egg yolks and, using your hands, knead until a smooth dough is formed. Wrap in clear film (plastic wrap) and chill for 30 minutes. Meanwhile, preheat the oven to 200°C/400°F/Gas 6 and lightly grease a 33 x 23cm/13 x 9in Swiss roll tin (jelly roll pan).

2 Roll out half the dough to fit the base of the prepared tin and place in the tin. Spread the jam all over the dough base. Roll out the remaining dough and place on top of the jam.

3 To make the topping, beat the egg and honey together and brush over the dough. Sprinkle the almonds evenly over the top.

4 Bake for 10 minutes, then lower the oven temperature to 180°C/350°F/Gas 4 and bake for another 20–30 minutes until golden brown. Cool then cut into bars.

Cook's Tip
Don't use ready-ground hazelnuts for these bars as they lose their flavour very quickly.

Walnut and Honey Bars

A sweet, custard-like filling brimming with nuts sits on a crisp pastry base. These scrumptious bars are pure heaven to bite into at any time of day.

Makes 12–14

*175g/6oz/1½ cups plain
  (all-purpose) flour*
*30ml/2 tbsp icing (confectioners')
  sugar, sifted*
*115g/4oz/½ cup unsalted (sweet)
  butter, diced*

For the filling

300g/11oz/scant 3 cups walnut halves
2 eggs, beaten
*50g/2oz/¼ cup unsalted (sweet)
  butter, melted*
*50g/2oz/¼ cup light muscovado
  (brown) sugar*
90ml/6 tbsp dark clear honey
30ml/2 tbsp single (light) cream

1 Preheat the oven to 190°C/375°F/
Gas 5. Lightly grease a 28 x 18cm/
11 x 7in shallow tin (pan).

2 Put the flour, icing sugar and butter in a food processor and process until the mixture forms crumbs. Using the pulse button, add 15–30ml/1–2 tbsp water – enough to make a firm dough.

3 Roll the dough out on baking parchment and line the base and sides of the tin. Trim and fold the top edge inwards.

4 Prick the base, line with foil and baking beans and bake blind for 10 minutes. Remove the foil and beans. Return the base to the oven for about 5 minutes, until cooked but not browned. Reduce the temperature to 180°C/350°F/Gas 4.

5 For the filling, sprinkle the walnuts over the base. Whisk the remaining ingredients together. Pour over the walnuts and bake for 25 minutes.

Pecan Nut Squares

A rich, buttery, pastry-like base is topped with a fabulous nutty, toffee-like mixture to make cookies with a tempting crunch and crispness. These cookies are equally good made with walnuts.

Makes 36

225g/8oz/2 cups plain (all-purpose) flour
pinch of salt
115g/4oz/½ cup granulated sugar
225g/8oz/1 cup cold butter or
   margarine, diced
1 egg
finely grated rind of 1 lemon

For the topping

175g/6oz/¾ cup butter
75g/3oz/⅓ cup clear honey
50g/2oz/¼ cup granulated sugar
115g/4oz/½ cup soft dark
   brown sugar
75ml/5 tbsp whipping cream
450g/1lb/4 cups pecan nut halves

1 Preheat the oven to 190°C/ 375°F/Gas 5. Lightly grease a 37 x 27 x 2.5cm/15½ x 10½ x 1in Swiss roll tin (jelly roll pan).

2 Sift together the flour and salt into a large mixing bowl. Stir in the sugar. Add the butter or margarine, cut in and then rub in with your fingertips until the mixture resembles coarse breadcrumbs.

3 Add the egg and lemon rind and blend with a fork until the mixture just holds together.

4 Spoon the mixture into the prepared tin. With floured fingertips, press the mixture into an even layer. Prick the pastry all over with a fork and chill for 10 minutes.

5 Bake the pastry for 15 minutes. Remove the tin from the oven and leave to cool. Leave the oven switched on.

6 To make the topping, melt the butter, honey and both sugars in a small saucepan. Bring to the boil. Boil, without stirring, for 2 minutes. Remove from the heat and stir in the cream and pecan nuts.

7 Pour the topping over the crust, return the tin to the oven and bake for 25 minutes. Leave to cool and set completely.

8 When cool, run a knife around the edge of the tin. Invert on to a baking sheet, place another sheet on top and invert again. Dip a sharp knife into very hot water and cut into squares.

Rainbow Gingerbread Squares

These gingerbread squares have a more spongy texture than traditional gingerbread cookies and look stunning decorated with vibrantly coloured sprinkles. Ground and preserved stem ginger gives a really spicy flavour, but can easily be left out for younger children.

Makes 16

225g/8oz/2 cups plain
   (all-purpose) flour
5ml/1 tsp baking powder
10ml/2 tsp ground ginger
2 pieces preserved stem ginger from
   a jar, finely chopped
90g/3½oz/¾ cup raisins
50g/2oz/¼ cup glacé (candied)
   cherries, chopped
115g/4oz/½ cup unsalted (sweet)
   butter, diced
115g/4oz/⅓ cup golden (light
   corn) syrup
30ml/2 tbsp black treacle (molasses)
75g/3oz/⅓ cup dark muscovado
   (molasses) sugar
2 eggs, beaten

For the decoration

200g/7oz/1¾ cups icing
   (confectioners') sugar
50g/2oz/¼ cup unsalted (sweet) butter,
   at room temperature, diced
multi-coloured sprinkles

1 Preheat the oven to 160°C/325°F/ Gas 3. Grease a 20cm/8in square shallow baking or cake tin (pan) and line with baking parchment.

2 Sift the flour, baking powder and ground ginger into a bowl. Add the stem ginger, raisins and cherries and stir together well.

3 Put the butter, syrup, treacle and muscovado sugar in a small pan and heat gently until the butter melts. Pour the mixture into the dry ingredients. Add the eggs and stir well until evenly combined.

4 Tip the mixture into the baking tin and spread in an even layer, using the back of a wooden spoon. Bake for about 55 minutes, or until risen and firm in the centre. Leave to cool in the tin.

5 To make the topping, put the icing sugar and butter in a bowl with 20ml/4 tsp hot water and beat together until smooth and creamy.

6 Turn the gingerbread out of the baking tin on to a board. Using a large, sharp knife, carefully cut the gingerbread into 16 squares.

7 Using a teaspoon, drizzle a thick line of icing around the top edge of each gingerbread square. Don't worry if it falls down the sides. (If the icing is too stiff and doesn't come off the spoon easily, stir a little more hot water into the icing: about 5ml/1 tsp.)

8 Scatter the coloured sprinkles over the icing to finish and leave to set before serving.

Hermits

How these cookies gained their intriguing name is a matter of guesswork, although it is interesting that both convents and monasteries are thought to have created many original cookie recipes.

Makes 30
75g/3oz/⅔ cup plain (all-purpose) flour
7.5ml/1½ tsp baking powder
5ml/1 tsp ground cinnamon
2.5ml/½ tsp grated nutmeg
1.5ml/¼ tsp ground cloves
1.5ml/¼ tsp ground allspice
250g/9oz/1½ cups raisins
115g/4oz/½ cup butter or margarine
    at room temperature, diced
115g/4oz/generous ½ cup caster
    (superfine) sugar
2 eggs
175g/6oz/scant ½ cup black
    treacle (molasses)
50g/2oz/½ cup walnuts, chopped

1 Preheat the oven to 180°C/350°F/
Gas 4. Grease and line a 33 × 23cm/
13 × 9in tin (pan) with greaseproof
(waxed) paper.

2 Sift together the flour, baking powder and spices into a bowl.

3 Place the raisins in another bowl and toss with a few tablespoons of the flour mixture.

Cook's Tip
Don't confuse allspice and mixed (apple pie) spice. Allspice tastes like a mixture of spices, but comes from a single berry.

4 Cream the butter or margarine and sugar until light and fluffy. Beat in the eggs, one at a time, then the black treacle. Stir in the flour mixture, raisins and walnuts.

5 Spread the mixture evenly in the prepared cake tin. Bake for about 15 minutes, or until just set. Leave to cool in the tin before cutting into squares or bars.

Butterscotch Meringue Bars

Walnuts add a nutty crunch to the sweet meringue topping on these sumptuous bars.

Makes 12
50g/2oz/¼ cup butter
175g/6oz/¾ cup cup dark brown sugar
1 egg
2.5ml/½ tsp vanilla essence (extract)
50g/2oz/½ cup plain (all-purpose) flour
pinch of salt
1.5ml/¼ tsp grated nutmeg

For the topping
1 egg white
pinch of salt
15ml/1 tbsp golden (light corn) syrup
115g/4oz/½ cup granulated sugar
50g/2oz/½ cup walnuts, chopped

1 Place the butter and brown sugar in a pan and heat until melted and bubbling. Set aside to cool.

2 Preheat the oven to 180°C/350°F/
Gas 4. Grease and line a 20cm/8in square cake tin (pan) with greaseproof (waxed) paper.

3 Beat the egg and vanilla essence into the cooled sugar mixture. Sift over the flour, salt and nutmeg and fold in. Spread over the base of the prepared cake tin.

4 Beat the egg white with the salt to soft peaks. Beat in the syrup, then the sugar and beat until stiff. Fold in the nuts and spread on top of the base. Bake for 30 minutes. Cut into bars when cool.

Parkin Squares

The flavour of these richly flavoured squares will improve if they are stored in an airtight container for several days or up to a week before serving.

Makes 16–20

300ml/½ pint/1¼ cups milk
225g/8oz/1 cup cup golden (light corn) syrup
225g/8oz/⅔ cup black treacle (molasses)
115g/4oz/½ cup butter or margarine, diced
50g/2oz/¼ cup soft dark brown sugar
450g/1lb/4 cups plain (all-purpose) flour
2.5ml/½ tsp bicarbonate of soda (baking soda)
6.25ml/1¼ tsp ground ginger
350g/12oz/scant 3½ cups medium rolled oats
1 egg, beaten
icing (confectioners') sugar, for dusting

1 Preheat the oven to 180°C/350°F/Gas 4. Grease and line the base of a 20cm/8in square cake tin (pan). Gently heat together the milk, syrup, treacle, butter or margarine and sugar, stirring until smooth.

2 Stir the flour, bicarbonate of soda, ginger and rolled oats together in a bowl. Make a well in the centre, pour in the egg, then gradually pour in the warmed milk mixture, stirring to make a smooth batter.

3 Pour the batter into the tin and bake for about 45 minutes, or until firm to the touch. Cool slightly in the tin, then turn out on to a wire rack and cool completely. Cut into squares and dust with icing sugar.

Cook's Tip

These are nutritious, energy-giving squares that are a really good choice for school lunches and picnics as they don't break up too easily.

Banana Ginger Parkin

Parkin is a moist, spicy cake that keeps well and actually improves with keeping. Store in a covered container for up to two months – that is, if you can bear to wait that long.

Makes 26

200g/7oz/1⅔ cups plain
  (all-purpose) flour
10ml/2 tsp bicarbonate of soda
  (baking soda)
10ml/2 tsp ground ginger
150g/5oz/scant 1½ cups medium
  rolled oats
60ml/4 tbsp dark muscovado
  (molasses) sugar
75g/3oz/⅓ cup butter or
  margarine, diced
150g/5oz/⅔ cup golden (light
  corn) syrup
1 egg, beaten
3 ripe bananas, mashed
75g/3oz/¾ cup icing
  (confectioners') sugar
preserved stem ginger, to decorate

1 Preheat the oven to 160°C/ 325°F/Gas 3. Grease and line an 18 x 28cm/7 x 11in cake tin (pan).

2 Sift together the plain flour, bicarbonate of soda and ground ginger into a mixing bowl, then stir in the rolled oats.

3 Melt the sugar, margarine and syrup in a pan over a low heat, then stir into the flour mixture. Beat in the egg and mashed bananas.

4 Spoon the mixture into the prepared tin and bake for about 1 hour, until firm to the touch. Leave to cool in the tin, then turn out and cut into squares.

5 Sift the icing sugar into a bowl and stir in just enough water to make a smooth, runny icing. Drizzle the icing over each square and top with a piece of stem ginger.

Sticky Treacle Slices

This three-layered treat of buttery cookie base, covered with a sticky dried fruit filling, followed by an oaty flapjack-style topping, is utterly delicious and unbelievably easy to make.

Makes 14

175g/6oz/1½ cups plain
  (all-purpose) flour
90g/3½oz/7 tbsp unsalted (sweet)
  butter, diced
50g/2oz/¼ cup caster (superfine) sugar
250g/9oz/generous 1 cup mixed dried
  fruit, such as prunes, apricots, peaches,
  pears and apples
300ml/½ pint/1¼ cups apple or
  orange juice
225g/8oz/⅔ cup golden (light
  corn) syrup
finely grated rind of 1 small orange,
  plus 45ml/3 tbsp juice
90g/3½oz/1 cup rolled oats

1 Preheat the oven to 180°C/350°F/ Gas 4. Grease a 28 × 18cm/11 × 7in shallow baking tin (pan).

2 Put the flour and butter in a food processor and process until the mixture begins to resemble fine breadcrumbs. Add the sugar and mix until the dough starts to cling together in a ball.

3 Tip the mixture into the baking tin and press down in an even layer with the back of a fork. Bake for about 15 minutes until the surface is just beginning to colour.

4 Meanwhile, prepare the filling. Remove the stones (pits) from any of the dried fruits, if not already done. Chop the fruit fairly finely and put in a pan with the fruit juice. Bring to the boil, reduce the heat and cover with a lid. Simmer gently for about 15 minutes, or until all the juice has been absorbed.

5 Leaving the base in the tin, tip the dried fruit filling on top and spread out in an even layer with the back of a spoon.

6 Put the golden syrup in a bowl with the orange rind and juice and oats and mix together. Spoon the mixture over the fruits, spreading it out evenly. Return to the oven for 25 minutes. Leave to cool in the tin for several hours before cutting into squares or bars.

Butterscotch Brownies

These gorgeous treats are made with brown sugar, white chocolate chips and walnuts. Who could possibly have the will power to resist? You might want to make two batches at a time.

Makes 12

450g/1lb white chocolate chips
75g/3oz/6 tbsp unsalted (sweet) butter
3 eggs
175g/6oz/¾ cup light muscovado (brown) sugar
175g/6oz/1½ cups self-raising (self-rising) flour
175g/6oz/1½ cups walnuts, chopped
5ml/1 tsp vanilla essence (extract)

1 Preheat the oven to 190°C/ 375°F/Gas 5. Line the base of a 28 x 18cm/11 x 7in shallow tin (pan) with baking parchment. Lightly grease the sides. Melt 90g/3½oz of the chocolate chips with the butter in a bowl set over a pan of hot water. Leave to cool slightly.

2 Put the eggs and light muscovado sugar into a large bowl and whisk well, then whisk in the melted chocolate mixture.

3 Sift in the flour into the bowl and gently fold in along with the chopped walnuts, vanilla essence and the remaining chocolate chips. Be careful not to overmix.

4 Spread the mixture out in the prepared tin and bake for about 30 minutes, or until risen and golden brown. The centre should be firm to the touch but will be slightly soft until it cools down.

5 Leave to cool in the tin, then cut into twelve bars when the brownie is completely cool.

Toffee Bars

It takes no time at all to whip up a batch of these ever-popular cookies, but, equally, it takes no time at all for the family to demolish them.

Makes 32

350g/12oz/1½ cups soft light
   brown sugar
450g/1lb/2 cups butter
2 egg yolks
7.5ml/1½ tsp vanilla essence (extract)
450g/1lb/4 cups plain (all-purpose) or
   wholemeal (whole-wheat) flour
pinch of salt
225g/8oz milk chocolate, chopped
115g/4oz/1 cup walnuts or pecan nuts or
   a mixture of both, chopped

I Preheat the oven to 180°C/
350°F/Gas 4. Lightly grease a
33 x 23 x 5cm/13 x 9 x 2in cake
rectangular tin (pan).

2 Beat together the sugar and butter until light and fluffy. Beat in the egg yolks and vanilla. Stir in the flour and salt.

3 Spread the dough in the prepared cake tin. Bake for about 25–30 minutes, until lightly browned. The texture will be soft.

4 Remove from the oven and immediately place the chocolate pieces on the hot cookie base. Leave to stand until the chocolate softens, then spread evenly over the top with a spatula or palette knife. Sprinkle with the chopped nuts. While still warm, cut into 5 x 4cm/ 2 x 1½in bars. Leave to cool.

Sticky Marmalade Squares

These baked treats have a plain lower layer supporting a scrumptious nutty upper layer flavoured with orange and chunky marmalade. Cut into squares or bars – whichever you prefer.

Makes 24

350g/12oz/3 cups plain
(all-purpose) flour
200g/7oz/scant 1 cup unsalted (sweet)
butter, diced
150g/5oz/⅔ cup light muscovado
(brown) sugar
2.5ml/½ tsp bicarbonate of soda
(baking soda)
1 egg, beaten
120ml/4fl oz/½ cup single
(light) cream
50g/2oz/½ cup pecan nuts, chopped
50g/2oz/⅓ cup mixed (candied) peel
90ml/6 tbsp chunky marmalade
15–30ml/1–2 tbsp orange juice

1 Preheat the oven to 190°C/ 375°F/Gas 5. Line the base of a 28 × 18cm/11 × 7in tin (pan) with baking parchment.

2 Put the flour in a bowl and rub in the butter. Stir in the sugar and then spread half the mixture over the base of the prepared tin. Press down firmly. Bake for 10–15 minutes until lightly browned. Leave to cool.

3 To make the filling, put the remaining flour mixture into a bowl. Stir in the soda. Mix in the egg and cream, pecan nuts, peel and half the marmalade.

4 Pour the mixture over the cooled base, return to the oven and bake for 20–25 minutes, or until the filling is just firm and golden brown.

5 Put the remaining marmalade into a small pan and heat gently. Add just enough orange juice to make a spreadable glaze. Brush the glaze over the baked cookie mixture while it is still warm. Leave to cool before cutting into bars or squares.

Variation
These bars would be just as delicious made with lemon, lime, grapefruit or mixed fruit marmalade instead of orange. However, do not substitute a sharper juice, such as lemon, for the orange juice as this would spoil the flavour.

Jewelled Shortbread Fingers

These shortbread fingers are made using a classic, buttery shortbread base, drizzled with icing and decorated with sparkling, crushed sweets and glistening gold or silver balls.

Makes 14

90g/3½oz/7 tbsp unsalted (sweet)
   butter, diced
175g/6oz/1½ cups plain
   (all-purpose) flour
50g/2oz/¼ cup caster (superfine) sugar

To decorate

150g/5oz/1¼ cups icing
   (confectioners') sugar
10–15ml/2–3 tsp lemon juice
coloured boiled sweets (hard candies)
gold or silver balls

1 Preheat the oven to 160°C/325°F/ Gas 3. Grease an 18cm/7in square shallow baking tin (pan).

2 Put the butter and flour in a food processor and process until the mixture resembles breadcrumbs. Add the sugar and process until the ingredients cling together.

3 Put the dough in the baking tin and press down in an even layer using the back of a spoon. Bake for 35 minutes, or until just beginning to colour. Leave to cool in the tin.

4 To make the topping, put the icing sugar in a bowl and add enough lemon juice to make a thick paste that only just holds its shape.

5 Tap the boiled sweets (in their wrappers) gently with a rolling pin to break them into small pieces. Unwrap the sweets and mix them together in a bowl.

Cook's Tip

Use a serrated knife and a sawing action to cut the shortbread into neat fingers.

6 Turn out the shortbread base on to a board. Cut in half, then across into fingers. Drizzle with the icing, then sprinkle with the sweets and gold or silver balls. Leave to set.

Creamed Coconut Macaroons

These soft-centred cookies are very rich and gooey. Cook them on baking parchment so that they can be easily removed from the baking sheet.

Makes 16–18

50g/2oz/1 cup creamed coconut, chilled
2 large (US extra large) egg whites
90g/3½oz/½ cup caster
*   (superfine) sugar*
75g/3oz/1 cup desiccated (dry
*   unsweetened shredded) coconut*

1 Preheat the oven to 180°C/350°F/ Gas 4. Line one or two large baking sheets with baking parchment. Finely grate the creamed coconut.

2 Use an electric beater to whisk the egg whites in a large, grease-free bowl until they are holding stiff peaks. Whisk in the caster sugar, a spoonful at a time, to make a stiff and glossy meringue.

3 Gently fold the grated creamed and desiccated coconut into the whisked egg whites, using a rubber spatula or a large metal spoon until evenly combined.

4 Place dessertspoonfuls of the mixture, spaced well apart, on the baking sheet. Bake for about 15 minutes, or until slightly risen and golden brown.

5 Leave the macaroons to cool on the baking parchment, then transfer to an airtight container.

Chocolate Pecan Nut Squares

These moist and flavoursome cookies look as good as they taste. Serve to adults with tea or coffee and to children with a glass of milk or a creamy milkshake.

Makes 16

2 eggs
10ml/2 tsp vanilla essence (extract)
pinch of salt
175g/6oz/1½ cups pecan nuts,
  coarsely chopped
50g/2oz/½ cup plain (all-purpose) flour
50g/2oz/¼ cup granulated sugar
175g/6oz/scant ½ cup treacle (molasses)
75g/3oz plain (semisweet) chocolate,
  finely chopped
45g/1½oz/3 tbsp butter
16 pecan nut halves, to decorate

I Preheat the oven to 160°C/325°F/ Gas 3. Line the base and sides of a 20cm/8in square baking tin (pan) with greaseproof (waxed) paper and grease the paper lightly.

2 Whisk together the eggs, vanilla essence and salt in a bowl, using a balloon whisk. In another bowl, mix together the pecan nuts and flour. Set both bowls aside.

3 Place the sugar and treacle in a heavy pan and bring to the boil, stirring constantly.

4 Remove the pan from the heat, stir in the chopped chocolate and butter and blend thoroughly with a wooden spoon.

5 Mix in the beaten eggs, then fold in the pecan nut and flour mixture with a metal spoon. Pour the mixture into the prepared tin and bake for about 35 minutes until set.

6 Cool in the tin for 10 minutes turning out on to a board. Cut into 5cm/2in squares and press pecan nut halves into the top of each square while still warm. Transfer to a wire rack to cool completely.

Raisin Brownies

Adding dried fruit makes brownies a little more substantial, although no less moist and delicious. Try to find Californian or Spanish raisins for the best flavour and texture.

Makes 16

115g/4oz/½ cup butter or
  margarine, diced
50g/2oz/½ cup (unsweetened)
  cocoa powder
2 eggs
225g/8oz/generous 1 cup caster
  (superfine) sugar
5ml/1 tsp vanilla essence (extract)
40g/1½oz/⅓ cup plain
  (all-purpose) flour
75g/3oz/¾ cup walnuts, chopped
65g/2½oz/½ cup raisins
icing (confectioners') sugar,
  for dusting

I Preheat the oven to 180°C/350°F/ Gas 4. Line a 20cm/8in square baking tin (pan) with greaseproof (waxed) paper and grease the paper lightly.

2 Melt the butter or margarine in a small pan over a low heat. Remove from the heat and stir in the cocoa.

3 In a bowl, beat together the eggs, sugar and vanilla essence with an electric mixer until light and fluffy. Add the cocoa mixture and stir to blend.

4 Sift the flour over the cocoa mixture and fold in gently with a metal spoon. Add the walnuts and raisins, mixing them in gently, then scrape the mixture into the prepared tin. Bake for about 30 minutes until firm to the touch, being careful not to overbake.

5 Leave in the tin on a rack to cool completely before cutting into 5cm/2in squares and removing from the tin. The brownies should be soft and moist. Dust with sifted icing sugar before serving.

White Nut Brownies

Two kinds of chocolate and a topping of sweet melted chocolate and chopped macadamia nuts make these fabulous brownies irresistible to adults and children alike.

Makes 16

150g/5oz/1¼ cups plain
  (all-purpose) flour
2.5ml/½ tsp baking powder
pinch of salt
175g/6oz fine-quality white
  chocolate, chopped
90g/3½oz/½ cup caster
  (superfine) sugar
115g/4oz/½ cup unsalted (sweet)
  butter, chopped
2 eggs, lightly beaten
5ml/1 tsp vanilla essence (extract)
175g/6oz plain (semisweet) chocolate,
  chopped, or plain (semisweet)
  chocolate chips

For the topping

200g/7oz milk chocolate, chopped
215g/7½oz/scant 2 cups unsalted
  macadamia nuts, chopped

1 Preheat the oven to 180°C/350°F/ Gas 4. Thoroughly grease a 23cm/ 9in springform cake tin (pan). Sift together the flour, baking powder and salt into a small bowl and set aside.

2 Place the white chocolate, sugar and butter in a heavy pan and melt over a medium heat, stirring constantly until smooth.

3 Cool slightly, then beat in the eggs and vanilla essence. Stir in the flour mixture until well blended, then stir in the chopped chocolate or chocolate chips. Spread evenly in the prepared tin, smoothing the top.

4 Bake for 20–25 minutes, until a skewer inserted 5cm/2in from the side comes out clean. Remove from the oven. Sprinkle the milk chocolate over the surface. Return to the oven for 1 minute.

5 Remove from the oven. Spread the softened chocolate evenly over the top with the back of a spoon. Sprinkle with the nuts and gently press into the chocolate. Cool on a wire rack for 30 minutes, then chill until set. Run a knife around the side of the tin to loosen, unclip the side and remove. Cut into thin wedges.

Chocolate Brownies

Traditional American brownies are usually rich in butter. This version uses sunflower oil in place of butter. It still tastes rich and gooey, but is best eaten on the day it is made.

Makes 20

120ml/4fl oz/½ cup sunflower oil
150g/5oz plain (semisweet) chocolate, chopped
2 eggs
115g/4oz/1 cup self-raising (self-rising) flour
115g/4oz/generous ½ cup caster (superfine) sugar
5ml/1 tsp vanilla essence (extract)
75g/3oz/¾ cup halved pecan nuts

1 Preheat the oven to 200°C/400°F/ Gas 6. Use a little of the oil to grease a 23cm/9in square shallow cake tin (pan) and then line it with lightly oiled greaseproof (waxed) paper.

2 Melt the chocolate with the remaining oil in a heatproof bowl over a pan of simmering water, stirring until smooth.

Cook's Tip

Ingredients can be melted easily in a microwave oven. To soften chocolate, butter, sugar or syrup, microwave on High for a few seconds, until soft. Remember that chocolate and butter may not look melted, so check them carefully by stirring before returning them to the microwave for a few seconds more.

3 Beat the eggs lightly and add them to the melted chocolate, stirring vigorously. Beat in the flour, caster sugar and vanilla essence and pour the mixture into the prepared tin. Arrange the pecan nut halves over the top.

4 Bake for 10–15 minutes. If you like chewy brownies, take them out of the oven now. If you want a more cake-like finish, leave for a further 5 minutes. Cut into squares and leave to cool before removing from the tin.

Hazelnut Squares

Adding a topping of hazelnuts part of the way through the baking time gives the cookies a lovely toasted flavour and makes them very moreish. Cut them into chunky squares for serving.

Makes 9

50g/2oz plain (semisweet)
   chocolate, chopped
65g/2½oz/5 tbsp butter or margarine
225g/8oz/generous 1 cup caster
   (superfine) sugar
50g/2oz/½ cup plain (all-purpose) flour
2.5ml/½ tsp baking powder
2 eggs, beaten
2.5ml/½ tsp vanilla essence (extract)
115g/4oz/1 cup skinned hazelnuts,
   coarsely chopped

1 Preheat the oven to 180°C/350°F/ Gas 4. Grease a 20cm/8in square cake tin (pan).

2 Melt the chocolate and butter or margarine in a heatproof bowl set over a pan of hot water, stirring.

3 Stir the sugar, flour, baking powder, eggs, vanilla essence and half of the hazelnuts into the mixture.

4 Pour the mixture into the prepared cake tin, smoothing the top. Bake for 10 minutes, then sprinkle the remaining hazelnuts over the top. Bake for a further 25 minutes, until firm.

5 Leave to cool in the tin, set on a wire rack, for about 10 minutes, then remove from the tin, transfer to the rack and leave to cool completely. Using a sharp knife, cut into squares to serve.

Chocolate Walnut Bars

Although cookies like these are widely available in supermarkets, once you have tasted this delicious home-made version, you will never want to eat the ready-made bars again.

Makes 24

50g/2oz/½ cup walnuts
75g/3oz/⅓ cup granulated sugar
75g/3oz/⅔ cup plain (all-purpose)
  flour, sifted
75g/3oz/6 tbsp cold unsalted (sweet)
  butter, diced
icing (confectioners') sugar, for dusting

For the topping

25g/1oz/2 tbsp unsalted (sweet) butter
75ml/5 tbsp water
40g/1½oz/⅓ cup (unsweetened)
  cocoa powder
115g/4oz/½ cup granulated sugar
5ml/1 tsp vanilla essence (extract)
pinch of salt
2 eggs

1 Preheat the oven to 180°C/350°F/ Gas 4. Grease a 20cm/8in square cake tin (pan).

2 Grind the walnuts with a few tablespoons of the sugar in a food processor, blender or nut grinder.

3 Mix the ground walnuts, the remaining sugar and the flour in a bowl. Rub in the butter until the mixture resembles breadcrumbs. Alternatively, process all the ingredients in a food processor.

4 Pat the walnut mixture into the base of the prepared tin in an even layer. Bake for 25 minutes.

5 Meanwhile, to make the topping, melt the butter with the water in a small pan over a low heat. Whisk in the cocoa and sugar.

6 Remove the pan from the heat, stir in the vanilla essence and salt and leave to cool for 5 minutes.

7 Whisk in the eggs, one at a time, until thoroughly blended. Remove the cake tin from the oven and pour the topping evenly over the cooked walnut mixture.

8 Return the tin to the oven and bake for about 20 minutes, until set. Set the tin on a wire rack to cool. Once cooled, cut into 7 x 2.5cm/ 2¾ x 1in bars and dust with sifted icing sugar. Store the bars in the refrigerator.

Chocolate Cheesecake Brownies

A very dense chocolate brownie mixture is swirled with creamy cheese to give a marbled effect. Cut into tiny squares for little mouthfuls of absolute heaven.

Makes 16

For the cheesecake mixture

1 egg

225g/8oz/1 cup full-fat
*   cream cheese*

50g/2oz/¼ cup caster
*   (superfine) sugar*

5ml/1 tsp vanilla essence (extract)

For the brownie mixture

115g/4oz dark (bittersweet)
*   chocolate (minimum 70 per cent*
*   cocoa solids)*

115g/4oz/½ cup unsalted
*   (sweet) butter*

150g/5oz/¾ cup light muscovado
*   (brown) sugar*

2 eggs, beaten

50g/2oz/½ cup plain
*   (all-purpose) flour*

1 Preheat the oven to 160°C/ 325°F/Gas 3. Line the base and sides of a 20cm/8in cake tin (pan) with baking parchment.

2 To make the cheesecake mixture, beat the egg in a mixing bowl, then add the cream cheese, caster sugar and vanilla essence. Beat together until smooth and creamy.

3 To make the brownie mixture, melt the chocolate and butter together in the microwave or in a heatproof bowl set over a pan of gently simmering water. When the mixture is melted, remove from the heat, stir well, then add the sugar. Add the eggs, a little at a time, and beat well. Gently stir in the flour.

4 Spread two-thirds of the brownie mixture over the base of the tin. Spread the cheesecake mixture on top, then spoon on the remaining brownie mixture in heaps. Using a skewer, swirl the mixtures together.

5 Bake for 30–35 minutes, or until just set in the centre. Leave to cool in the tin, then cut into squares.

Fudge-nut Bars

Although your kids will be desperate to tuck into these fudgy treats, it's well worth chilling them for a few hours before slicing so that they can be cut into neat pieces.

Makes 16

150g/5oz/10 tbsp unsalted (sweet) butter, chilled and diced
250g/9oz/2¼ cups plain (all-purpose) flour
75g/3oz/scant ½ cup caster (superfine) sugar

For the topping

150g/5oz milk chocolate, broken into pieces
40g/1½oz/3 tbsp unsalted (sweet) butter
405g/14¼oz can sweetened condensed milk
50g/2oz/½ cup chopped nuts

1 Preheat the oven to 160°C/ 325°F/ Gas 3. Grease a 28 × 18cm/ 11 × 7in shallow baking tin (pan).

2 Put the butter and flour in a food processor and process until the mixture resembles breadcrumbs. Add the sugar and blend again until the mixture starts to cling together.

3 Tip the mixture into the baking tin and spread out with the back of a wooden spoon to fill the base in an even layer. Bake for 35–40 minutes until the surface is very lightly coloured.

4 To make the topping, put the chocolate in a heavy pan with the butter and condensed milk. Heat gently until the chocolate and butter have melted, then increase the heat and cook, stirring, for 3–5 minutes until the mixture starts to thicken.

5 Add the chopped nuts to the pan and pour the mixture over the cookie base, spreading it in an even layer. Leave to cool, then chill for at least 2 hours until firm. Serve cut into bars.

Fudgy Glazed Chocolate Slices

These wonderfully flavoured treats will delight the hearts of those with a really sweet tooth – they are very rich, so cut them into relatively small bars or squares.

Makes 8–10

300g/11oz plain (semisweet)
  chocolate, chopped
115g/4oz/½ cup unsalted (sweet)
  butter, diced
90g/3½oz/scant ½ cup soft light
  brown sugar
50g/2oz/¼ cup granulated sugar
2 eggs
15ml/1 tbsp vanilla essence (extract)
65g/2½oz/generous ½ cup plain
  (all-purpose) flour
115g/4oz/1 cup pecan nuts or walnuts,
  toasted and chopped
150g/5oz fine-quality white
  chocolate, chopped

For the fudgy chocolate glaze

175g/6oz plain (semisweet)
  chocolate, chopped
50g/2oz/¼ cup unsalted (sweet)
  butter, chopped
30ml/2 tbsp golden (light corn) syrup
10ml/2 tsp vanilla essence (extract)
5ml/1 tsp instant coffee powder
pecan nut halves, to decorate (optional)

1 Preheat the oven to 180°C/350°F/ Gas 4. Invert a 20cm/8in square baking tin (pan) and mould a piece of foil over the base. Turn the tin over and line with moulded foil. Lightly grease the foil.

2 Place the plain chocolate and butter in a heavy pan and melt over a very low heat, stirring until combined and smooth.

3 Stir in the brown and granulated sugars and continue stirring for about 2 minutes, until the sugar has completely dissolved.

4 Remove the pan from the heat and beat in the eggs and vanilla essence. Stir in the flour, nuts and white chocolate. Pour the batter into the prepared tin.

5 Bake for about 20–25 minutes, until a skewer inserted 5cm/2in from the centre comes out clean. Transfer the tin to a wire rack to cool for about 30 minutes. Using the foil to help, lift from the tin, place on the wire rack and leave for 2 hours to cool completely.

6 To make the glaze, melt the chocolate, butter, syrup, vanilla essence and coffee powder in a pan over a medium heat, stirring frequently, until smooth. Remove from the heat. Chill for 1 hour, until thickened and spreadable.

7 Invert the cake on to the wire rack, and remove the foil from the base. Turn the cake top side up. Using a metal palette knife or spatula, spread a thick layer of fudgy glaze over the top of the cake just to the edges. Chill for 1 hour until set. Cut into bars or squares. If you like, top each slice with a pecan nut half.

Nut and Chocolate Chip Brownies

These chunky chocolate brownies are moist, dark and deeply satisfying. They are delicious with a morning cup of coffee and will definitely boost morale on a dreary day.

Makes 16

150g/5oz plain (semisweet) chocolate, chopped
120ml/4fl oz/½ cup sunflower oil
215g/7½oz/scant 1 cup light muscovado (brown) sugar
2 eggs
5ml/1 tsp vanilla essence (extract)
65g/2½oz/scant ⅔ cup self-raising (self-rising) flour
60ml/4 tbsp (unsweetened) cocoa powder
75g/3oz/¾ cup chopped walnuts
60ml/4 tbsp milk chocolate chips

Variation

Substitute chopped pecan nuts for the walnuts, if you like.

1 Preheat the oven to 180°C/350°F/ Gas 4. Lightly grease a shallow 19cm/7½in square cake tin (pan). Melt the plain chocolate in a heatproof bowl over a pan of simmering water.

2 Beat together the oil, sugar, eggs and vanilla essence.

3 Stir in the melted chocolate, then beat well until evenly mixed.

4 Sift the flour and cocoa powder into the bowl and fold in thoroughly. Stir in the chopped nuts and milk chocolate chips, then tip the mixture into the prepared tin and spread evenly to the edges.

5 Bake for about 30–35 minutes, until the top is firm and crusty. Cool in the tin before cutting into squares.

Cook's Tip

These brownies freeze well and can be stored in the freezer for 3 months in an airtight container.

Chocolate and Coconut Slices

Very simple to make, these slices are deliciously moist and sweet. They look very tempting, too, with their sweet coconut filling and attractive, nutty topping.

Makes 24

115g/4oz/½ cup butter or
   margarine, diced
175g/6oz/scant 2½ cups crushed
   digestive biscuits (graham
   crackers)
50g/2oz/¼ cup caster
   (superfine) sugar
pinch of salt
75g/3oz/1 cup desiccated
   (dry unsweetened
   shredded) coconut
250g/9oz/1½ cups plain (semisweet)
   chocolate chips
250ml/8fl oz/1 cup sweetened
   condensed milk
115g/4oz/1 cup chopped walnuts,
   to decorate

1 Preheat the oven to 180°C/350°F/ Gas 4. Melt the butter or margarine in a pan over a low heat.

2 Combine the crushed biscuits, sugar, salt and butter or margarine. Press the mixture evenly over the base of an ungreased 33 x 23cm/ 13 x 9in ovenproof dish.

3 Sprinkle the coconut, then the chocolate chips over the base. Pour the condensed milk evenly over the chocolate. Sprinkle the walnuts on top. Bake for 30 minutes. Transfer to a wire rack and leave to cool, preferably overnight. When cooled, cut into slices.

Chocolate Raspberry Macaroon Bars

Any seedless preserve, such as strawberry or apricot, can be used instead of the raspberry in the topping for these flavour-packed, moist little bars.

Makes 16–18 bars

115g/4oz/½ cup unsalted (sweet) butter
50g/2oz/½ cup icing
   (confectioners') sugar
25g/1oz/¼ cup (unsweetened)
   cocoa powder
pinch of salt
5ml/1 tsp almond essence (extract)
150g/5oz/1¼ cups plain
   (all-purpose) flour

For the topping

150g/5oz/scant ½ cup seedless
   raspberry preserve
15ml/1 tbsp raspberry-flavour liqueur
175g/6oz/1 cup mini chocolate chips
175g/6oz/1½ cups finely ground almonds
4 egg whites
pinch of salt
200g/7oz/1 cup caster (superfine) sugar
2.5ml/½ tsp almond essence (extract)
50g/2oz/½ cup flaked (sliced) almonds

1 Preheat the oven to 160°C/325°F/Gas 3. Invert a 23 x 33cm/9 x 13in cake tin (pan). Mould a sheet of foil over the tin and evenly around the corners. Lift off the foil and turn the tin right side up; line with the moulded foil and grease.

2 In a bowl, using an electric mixer, beat together the butter, sugar, cocoa and salt until well blended. Add the almond essence and the flour and mix until the mixture forms a crumbly dough.

3 Turn the dough into the prepared tin and pat firmly over the base to make an even layer. Prick the dough with a fork.

4 Bake for 20 minutes, until just set. Remove from the oven and increase the oven temperature to 190°C/375°F/Gas 5.

5 To make the topping, combine the raspberry preserve and liqueur in a small bowl, mixing well.

6 Spread the topping evenly over the top of the chocolate crust with a palette knife or spatula, then sprinkle evenly with the chocolate chips.

7 In a food processor fitted with a metal blade, process the almonds, egg whites, salt, sugar and almond essence until well blended and foamy. Gently pour the mixture over the raspberry layer, spreading evenly to the edges of the tin. Sprinkle with the flaked almonds.

8 Bake for a further 20–25 minutes, until the top is golden and puffed. Transfer to a wire rack to cool in the tin for 20 minutes, until firm and cool enough to handle.

9 Using the edges of the foil to help, carefully remove the cake from the tin and place on the wire rack to cool completely. Peel off and discard the foil and, using a sharp knife, cut into bars.

Chocolate Butterscotch Bars

Wonderfully sticky with their sweet toffee and chocolate double topping, these rich, nutty cookie bars are very popular with children.

Makes 24

225g/8oz/2 cups plain (all-purpose) flour
2.5ml/½ tsp baking powder
115g/4oz/½ cup unsalted (sweet)
  butter, diced
50g/2oz/¼ cup light muscovado
  (brown) sugar
150g/5oz plain (semisweet)
  chocolate, melted
30ml/2 tbsp ground almonds

For the topping

175g/6oz/¾ cup unsalted (sweet) butter
115g/4oz/generous ½ cup caster
  (superfine) sugar
30ml/2 tbsp golden (light corn) syrup
175ml/6fl oz/¾ cup condensed milk
150g/5oz/1¼ cups toasted hazelnuts
225g/8oz plain (semisweet)
  chocolate, chopped

1 Preheat the oven to 160°C/325°F/ Gas 3. Grease a shallow 30 x 20cm/ 12 x 8in cake tin (pan).

2 Sift together the flour and baking powder into a large bowl. Add the butter and rub it in with your fingertips until the mixture resembles fine breadcrumbs.

3 Stir in the muscovado sugar. Gradually, work in the melted chocolate and ground almonds until thoroughly combined.

4 Press the mixture into the prepared cake tin, prick the surface all over with a fork and bake for 25–30 minutes until firm. Place the tin on a wire rack and leave to cool.

5 To make the topping, mix the butter, sugar, syrup and condensed milk in a pan. Heat gently until the butter and sugar have melted. Simmer, stirring occasionally, until golden, then stir in the hazelnuts.

6 Pour the topping over the cooked base and spread it out evenly with a spatula or palette knife. Leave in a cool place to set.

7 Melt the chocolate in a heatproof bowl set over a pan of hot water. Spread the chocolate over the butterscotch layer. Leave to set before cutting into bars.

Cook's Tip

As these bars are incredibly rich and sticky, cut them in half if serving at a children's party.

Marbled Brownies

These are the perfect brownies for those who like chocolate, but are not complete chocoholics, as they are made from a mixture of flavours swirled together before baking.

Makes 24

225g/8oz plain (semisweet)
   chocolate, chopped
75g/3oz/⅓ cup butter, diced
4 eggs
350g/12oz/1¾ cups caster
   (superfine) sugar
115g/4oz/1 cup plain (all-purpose) flour
pinch of salt
5ml/1 tsp baking powder
10ml/2 tsp vanilla essence (extract)
115g/4oz/1 cup walnuts, chopped

For the plain batter

50g/2oz/¼ cup butter
175g/6oz/⅔ cup cream cheese
115g/4oz/generous ½ cup caster
   (superfine) sugar
2 eggs
30ml/2 tbsp plain (all-purpose) flour
5ml/1 tsp vanilla essence (extract)

1 Preheat the oven to 180°C/350°F/ Gas 4. Line a 33 x 23cm/13 x 9in tin (pan) with greaseproof (waxed) paper and lightly grease the paper.

2 Melt the plain chocolate and butter in a small, heavy pan over a very low heat, stirring occasionally until smooth and combined, then remove the pan from the heat, and leave to cool slightly.

3 Meanwhile, beat the eggs with an electric mixer until they are light and fluffy. Gradually add the caster sugar and continue beating well after each addition until thoroughly blended and smooth. Sift over the flour, salt and baking powder and gently fold in with a metal spoon.

4 Stir in the cooled chocolate mixture, the vanilla essence and walnuts. Set aside 475ml/16fl oz/ 2 cups of the chocolate batter.

5 To make the plain batter, cream the butter and cream cheese with an electric mixer.

6 Add the sugar and continue beating until blended. Beat in the eggs, flour and vanilla essence.

7 Spread the chocolate batter into the tin. Pour over the plain batter. Drop spoonfuls of the reserved chocolate batter on top.

8 With a metal spatula, swirl the mixtures to marble. Do not blend completely. Bake for 35–40 minutes, until just set. Unmould when cool and cut into squares for serving.

Muffins and Scones

Marvellous muffins and scones are so quick and easy to make, you can serve them at any time of day. When you fancy a muffin, there are dozens of different flavourings to choose from, from fresh fruity blueberries, cranberries and raspberries to rich chocolate and nuts and tangy citrus. If you're looking for a wholesome healthy start to the day go for scones. Try delicious sweet combinations such as yogurt and honey or orange and raisin, or opt for savoury flavours such as bacon and corn meal or cheese and chives.

Oat and Buttermilk Muffins

In this traditional recipe, the natural acid of buttermilk activates the raising agent to produce lovely light and airy muffins. Raisins add a sweet contrast.

Makes 12

115g/4oz/generous 1 cup rolled oats
250ml/8fl oz/1 cup buttermilk
115g/4oz/½ cup butter, softened
75g/3oz/scant ½ cup soft dark
   brown sugar
1 egg
115g/4oz/1 cup plain (all-purpose) flour
5ml/1 tsp baking powder
2.5ml/½ tsp bicarbonate of soda
   (baking soda)
pinch of salt
25g/1oz/¼ cup raisins

1 Place the oats in a bowl, stir in the buttermilk and set aside to soak for about 1 hour.

2 Grease 12 muffin tins (pans), or use paper liners. Preheat the oven to 200°C/400°F/Gas 6.

3 Put the butter and sugar in a large bowl and, with an electric mixer or wooden spoon, beat together until light and fluffy. Beat in the egg.

4 Sift together the flour, baking powder, bicarbonate of soda and salt. Stir into the butter mixture, alternating with the oat mixture. Fold in the raisins.

5 Fill the muffin tins two-thirds full. Bake for 20–25 minutes. Transfer to a wire rack to cool.

Cook's Tip

Nowadays, buttermilk is made from pasteurized skimmed milk treated with a special culture and is much more stable than traditional buttermilk.

Pumpkin Muffins

Wonderfully moist, richly coloured and packed with flavour, these lightly spiced muffins are delicious whether served still warm from the oven or cold.

Makes 14

115g/4oz/½ cup butter or margarine
175g/6oz/¾ cup firmly packed
   brown sugar
115g/4oz/½ cup black
   treacle (molasses)
1 egg, beaten
225g/8oz/1 cup cooked or
   canned pumpkin
200g/7oz/1¾ cups plain
   (all-purpose) flour
pinch of salt
5ml/1 tsp bicarbonate of soda
   (baking soda)
7.5ml/1½ tsp ground cinnamon
5ml/1 tsp grated nutmeg
50g/2oz/¼ cup currants or raisins

1 Preheat the oven to 200°C/400°F/Gas 6. Grease 14 muffin tins (pans), or use paper liners.

2 With an electric mixer, cream the butter or margarine until soft. Add the sugar and black treacle and beat until light and fluffy.

3 Add the egg and pumpkin and stir until well blended.

4 Sift over the flour, a pinch of salt, the bicarbonate of soda, cinnamon and grated nutmeg. Fold in with a metal spoon until just blended, but do not overmix.

5 Fold the currants or raisins into the pumpkin mixture.

6 Spoon the batter into the muffin tins, filling them two-thirds full. Bake for 12–15 minutes, until the tops spring back when touched lightly.

Pan Dulce

These "sweet breads" of various shapes are made throughout Mexico, and are eaten as a snack or with jam or marmalade for breakfast – a great way to start the day.

Makes 12

120ml/4fl oz/½ cup lukewarm milk
10ml/2 tsp active dried yeast
450g/1lb/4 cups strong plain (all-purpose) flour
75g/3oz/6 tbsp caster (superfine) sugar
25g/1oz/2 tbsp butter, softened
4 large (US extra large) eggs, beaten
oil, for greasing

For the topping

75g/3oz/6 tbsp butter, softened
115g/4oz/½ cup granulated sugar
1 egg yolk
5ml/1 tsp ground cinnamon
115g/4oz/1 cup plain (all-purpose) flour

1 Pour the milk into a small bowl, stir in the dried yeast and leave in a warm place until frothy.

2 Put the flour and sugar in a mixing bowl, add the butter and eggs and mix to a soft, sticky dough.

3 Place the dough on a lightly floured surface and dredge it with a little more flour. Using floured hands, turn the dough over and over until it is completely covered in a light coating of flour. Cover it with lightly oiled clear film (plastic wrap) and leave to rest for 20 minutes.

4 Meanwhile, make the topping. Cream the butter and sugar together in a bowl, then gently mix in the egg yolk, ground cinnamon and flour. The mixture should have a slightly crumbly texture.

5 Divide the dough into 12 equal pieces and shape each of them into a round. Space well apart on greased baking sheets. Sprinkle the topping over the breads, dividing it more or less equally among them, then press it lightly into the surface.

6 Leave the rolls in a warm place to stand for about 30 minutes until they are about one and a half times their previous size. Preheat the oven to 200°C/400°F/Gas 6 and bake the breads for about 15 minutes. Leave to cool slightly before serving.

Orange and Pecan Scones

Serve these nutty orange scones with satiny orange or lemon curd or, for a simple, unsweetened snack, fresh and warm with unsalted butter.

Makes 10

225g/8oz/2 cups self-raising
  (self-rising) flour
50g/2oz/¼ cup unsalted (sweet) butter,
  chilled and diced
granted rind and juice of
  1 orange
115g/4oz/1 cup pecan nuts,
  coarsely chopped

1 Preheat the oven to 220°C/ 425°F/Gas 7. Lightly grease a large baking sheet.

2 Put the flour in a food processor with a pinch of salt and add the butter. Process the mixture until it resembles coarse breadcrumbs. Do not overprocess.

3 Add the orange rind. Reserve 30ml/2 tbsp of the orange juice and make the remainder up to 120ml/ 4fl oz/½ cup with water. Add the pecan nuts and the orange juice mixture to the food processor, and process very briefly to a firm dough, adding a little water if the dough seems to be dry.

4 Turn the dough out on to a lightly floured surface and roll out to 2cm/¾in thick. Cut out scones using a round cutter and transfer them to the baking sheet. Re-roll the trimmings and cut more scones. Brush the scones with the reserved juice and bake for 15–20 minutes until golden. Transfer to a wire rack to cool.

Banana Muffins

Make sure that you use really ripe bananas for these muffins, not just because those are the sweetest, but also because they are easy to mash to a smooth consistency.

Makes 12

225g/8oz/2 cups plain (all-purpose) flour
5ml/1 tsp baking powder
5ml/1 tsp bicarbonate of soda
   (baking soda)
pinch of salt
2.5ml/½ tsp ground cinnamon
1.5ml/¼ tsp grated nutmeg
3 large ripe bananas
1 egg
50g/2oz/¼ cup soft dark brown sugar
50ml/2fl oz/¼ cup vegetable oil
40g/1½oz/⅓ cup raisins

1 Preheat the oven to 190°C/375°F/ Gas 5. Grease 12 muffin tins (pans), or use paper liners.

2 Sift together the flour, baking powder, bicarbonate of soda, salt, cinnamon and nutmeg. Set aside.

3 With an electric mixer, mash the peeled bananas at medium speed.

4 Beat the egg, sugar and oil into the mashed bananas.

5 Add the dry ingredients and beat in gradually, on low speed. Mix until just blended. With a wooden spoon, stir in the raisins until just combined. Spoon the mixture into the muffin tins, filling them two-thirds full.

6 Bake for 20–25 minutes, until the tops spring back when touched lightly with your finger. Transfer the muffins to a wire rack to cool completely before serving.

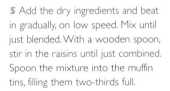

Maple Pecan Nut Muffins

The smooth, rich and distinctive flavour of maple syrup complements the nuts superbly. Make sure you buy the pure syrup, as blended varieties are disappointing.

Makes 20

150g/5oz/1¼ cups pecan nuts
300g/11oz/2⅔ cups plain
 (all purpose) flour
5ml/1 tsp baking powder
5ml/1 tsp bicarbonate of soda
 (baking soda)
pinch of salt
1.5ml/¼ tsp ground cinnamon
115g/4oz/½ cup granulated sugar
50g/2oz/¼ cup soft light
 brown sugar
45ml/3 tbsp maple syrup
150g/5oz/⅔ cup butter, softened
3 eggs
300ml/½ pint/1¼ cups buttermilk
60 pecan nut halves, to decorate

1 Preheat the oven to 180°C/350°F/ Gas 4. Grease 20 muffin tins (pans), or use paper liners.

2 Spread the pecan nuts on a baking sheet and toast in the oven for 5 minutes. Leave to cool, then chop coarsely and set aside.

3 In a bowl, sift together the flour, baking powder, bicarbonate of soda, salt and cinnamon. Set aside.

4 Combine the granulated sugar, light brown sugar, maple syrup and butter in a bowl. Beat with an electric mixer until light and fluffy. Add the eggs, one at a time, beating well to combine thoroughly after each addition.

5 Pour half of the buttermilk and half of the dry ingredients into the butter mixture, then stir until blended. Repeat with the remaining buttermilk and dry ingredients. Fold the chopped pecan nuts into the batter. Spoon the mixture into the muffin tins, filling them about two-thirds full. Top with the pecan nut halves.

6 Bake for 20–25 minutes, until puffed up and golden brown. Leave to stand in the tins for about 5 minutes before transferring the muffins to a wire rack to cool completely before serving.

Cranberry Muffins

These delicious muffins are perfect to eat at any time of day and are a real energy boost for breakfast or as a lunch box treat. Use fresh or frozen cranberries.

Makes 10–12

350g/12oz/3 cups plain
 (all-purpose) flour
15ml/1 tsp baking powder
pinch of salt
115g/4oz/generous ½ cup caster
 (superfine) sugar
2 eggs
150ml/¼ pint/⅔ cup milk
50ml/2fl oz/¼ cup corn oil
finely grated rind of 1 orange
150g/5oz/1¼ cups cranberries, thawed
 if frozen

Variation

*Replace half the cranberries with
blueberries or raspberries.*

I Preheat the oven to 190°C/375°F/
Gas 5. Line 10–12 deep muffin tins
(pans) with paper cases.

2 Mix the flour, baking powder, salt
and sugar together. Lightly beat the
eggs with the milk and oil.

3 Add the egg mixture to the dry
ingredients and blend to a smooth
batter. Fold in the orange rind and
cranberries. Divide the mixture
among the cases and bake for
25 minutes, or until risen and
golden. Serve warm or cold.

Raspberry Muffins

Low-fat buttermilk gives these muffins a light and spongy texture. Make them in the summer when fresh raspberries are at their seasonal best.

Makes 10–12

300g/11oz/2⅔ cups plain
 (all-purpose) flour
15ml/1 tbsp baking powder
115g/4oz/generous ½ cup caster
 (superfine) sugar
1 egg
250ml/8fl oz/1 cup buttermilk
60ml/4 tbsp sunflower oil
150g/5oz/1 cup raspberries

I Preheat the oven to 200°C/400°F/
Gas 6. Arrange 10–12 paper cases
in deep muffin tins (pans). Sift the
flour and baking powder into a
mixing bowl.

2 Stir in the sugar, then make a well
in the centre.

3 Mix the egg, buttermilk and
sunflower oil together in a bowl,
pour into the flour mixture and mix
quickly until just combined.

4 Add the raspberries and lightly
fold them into the mixture with a
metal spoon until just combined.
Spoon the mixture into the
prepared paper cases, filling them
about two-thirds full.

5 Bake for 20–25 minutes, until
golden brown and firm in the
centre. Transfer to a wire rack and
serve warm or cold.

Cook's Tip

*Raspberry muffins make a delicious
tea-time treat when served warm with
cream, preferably clotted.*

Double Chocolate Chip Muffins

These marvellous muffins are flavoured with cocoa and packed with chunky chips of plain and white chocolate so they are sure to be a success with children. Serve them on their own or with cherry or raspberry jam for a terrific after-school snack or teatime treat.

Makes 16

400g/14oz/3½ cups plain
  (all-purpose) flour
15ml/1 tbsp baking powder
30ml/2 tbsp (unsweetened) cocoa
  powder, plus extra for dusting
115g/4oz/½ cup dark muscovado
  (molasses) sugar
2 eggs
150ml/¼ pint/⅔ cup sour cream
150ml/¼ pint/⅔ cup milk
60ml/4 tbsp sunflower oil
175g/6oz white chocolate
175g/6oz plain (semisweet) chocolate

1 Preheat the oven to 190°C/375°F/ Gas 5. Place 16 paper muffin cases in muffin tins (pans) or lightly grease the muffin tins.

2 Sift the flour, baking powder and cocoa into a bowl and stir in the sugar. Make a well in the centre.

3 Beat the eggs with the sour cream, milk and sunflower oil in a separate bowl.

4 Add the egg mixture to the well in the dry ingredients. Beat thoroughly with a wooden spoon, gradually incorporating the flour mixture to make a thick and creamy batter. Do not overmix the batter – it's best if it's still slightly lumpy.

5 Finely chop both the white and plain chocolate using a large sharp knife and stir into the batter mixture until just mixed.

6 Spoon the mixture into the muffin cases, filling them almost to the top. Bake for 25–30 minutes, until well risen and firm to the touch. Transfer to a wire rack to cool, then dust lightly with cocoa powder before serving.

Variations

• Make sure you use good quality plain chocolate with a high cocoa content. Vary the proportions of plain and white chocolate, or add milk chocolate, if you prefer.

• To make Chocolate Chip and Apple Muffins, sift 2.5ml/½ tsp ground cinnamon, a pinch of grated nutmeg and 1.5ml/¼ tsp mixed (apple pie) spice with the dry ingredients in step 1. Halve the quantity of chocolate. Peel, core and grate two eating apples and stir into the batter with the chopped chocolate in step 3. Bake as given in the recipe, but check that the muffins are cooked by inserting a skewer into the centre of one of them. If it comes out clean, then they are ready. Cool in the tins for 4–5 minutes, then serve warm or transfer to a wire rack to cool completely.

Cook's Tip

If sour cream is not available, sour 150ml/¼ pint/⅔ cup single (light) cream by stirring in 5ml/1 tsp lemon juice and letting the mixture stand until thickened.

Chocolate Chip Muffins

Nothing could be easier – or nicer – than these classic muffins. The muffin mixture is plain, with a surprise layer of chocolate chips in the middle.

Makes 10

115g/4oz/½ cup butter or
   margarine, softened
75g/3oz/⅓ cup granulated sugar
30ml/2 tbsp soft dark
   brown sugar
2 eggs
175g/6oz/1½ cups plain
   (all-purpose) flour
5ml/1 tsp baking powder
120ml/4fl oz/½ cup milk
175g/6oz/1 cup plain (semisweet)
   chocolate chips

1 Preheat the oven to 190°C/375°F/ Gas 5. Grease ten muffin tins (pans), or use paper liners.

2 With an electric mixer, cream the butter or margarine until soft. Add both sugars and beat until light and fluffy. Beat in the eggs, one at a time, beating well after each addition.

3 Sift the flour and baking powder, twice. Fold into the butter mixture, alternating with the milk.

4 Divide half of the mixture among the muffin tins. Sprinkle the chocolate chips on top, dividing them equally among the muffins, then cover with the remaining mixture.

5 Bake for about 25 minutes, until lightly coloured. Leave to stand for 5 minutes before transferring to a wire rack to cool.

Chocolate Walnut Muffins

Walnuts and chocolate are a delicious combination and provide both smoothness and crunch while vanilla and almond essence provide extra flavour.

Makes 12

175g/6oz/¾ cup unsalted (sweet)
   butter, diced
150g/5oz plain (semisweet)
   chocolate, chopped
225g/8oz/1 cup granulated sugar
50g/2oz/¼ cup soft dark brown sugar
4 eggs
5ml/1 tsp vanilla essence (extract)
1.5ml/¼ tsp almond essence (extract)
75g/3oz/⅔ cup plain
   (all-purpose) flour
115g/4oz/1 cup walnuts,
   coarsely chopped

1 Preheat the oven to 180°C/ 350°F/Gas 4. Grease 12 muffin tins (pans), or use paper liners.

2 Melt the butter with the chocolate in a heatproof bowl set over a pan of hot water. Transfer to a large mixing bowl.

3 Stir both the sugars into the chocolate mixture. Mix in the eggs, one at a time, beating well after each addition, then add the vanilla and almond essences.

4 Sift the flour over the chocolate mixture and fold in until evenly combined. Stir the walnuts evenly into the mixture.

5 Fill the muffin tins almost to the top and bake for 30–35 minutes. Leave to stand for 5 minutes before transferring to a wire rack to cool.

Banana and Nut Muffins

Sweet, moist and full of flavour, these are bound to become family favourites. Use bananas that are ripe and soft, but not brown, and serve the muffins warm.

Makes 8

150g/5oz/1¼ cups plain
  (all-purpose) flour
7.5ml/1½ tsp baking powder
50g/2oz/¼ cup butter or margarine
175g/6oz/scant 1 cup caster
  (superfine) sugar
1 egg
1 tsp vanilla essence (extract)
3 bananas, mashed
50g/2oz/½ cup coarsely chopped
  pecan nuts
75ml/5 tbsp milk

1 Preheat the oven to 190°C/375°F/ Gas 5. Thoroughly grease eight muffin tins (pans), or use paper liners.

2 Sift the flour and baking powder into a small bowl. Set aside.

3 With an electric mixer, cream the butter or margarine and the sugar. Add the egg and vanilla essence and beat until fluffy. Mix in the bananas. Add the pecan nuts.

4 With the mixer on low speed, beat in the flour mixture alternately with the milk. Spoon into the tins. Bake for 20–25 minutes until golden brown.

5 Leave to cool in the tins for 10 minutes. Transfer to a wire rack.

Blueberry Muffins

Lightly spiced with ground cinnamon, these classic sweet muffins are extremely easy to make – and quite astonishingly delicious to eat.

Makes 8

115g/4oz/1 cup plain
  (all-purpose) flour
15ml/1 tbsp baking powder
pinch of salt
65g/2½oz/generous ¼ cup soft light
  brown sugar
1 egg
175ml/6fl oz/¾ cup milk
45ml/3 tbsp vegetable oil
10ml/2 tsp ground cinnamon
150g/5oz/1¼ cups fresh or thawed
  frozen blueberries or blackcurrants

1 Preheat the oven to 190°C/375°F/ Gas 5. Thoroughly grease eight muffin tins (pans).

2 With an electric mixer, beat together the flour, baking powder, salt, sugar, egg, milk, vegetable oil and cinnamon until smooth.

3 Fold the blueberries or blackcurrants into the flour mixture until just evenly combined.

4 Spoon the mixture into the prepared tins, filling them about two-thirds full. Bake for 25 minutes, or until golden brown.

5 Leave to cool in the tins for 10 minutes, then transfer the buns to a wire rack to cool completely.

Carrot Muffins

Carrots have a natural sweetness and moistness that makes them an ideal ingredient for cakes and muffins. If you haven't used them when baking before, you will be pleasantly surprised.

Makes 12

175g/6oz/¾ cup margarine at room
   temperature, diced
75g/3oz/⅓ cup soft dark brown sugar
1 egg
15ml/1 tbsp water
275g/10oz/2 cups grated carrots
150g/5oz/1¼ cups plain
   (all-purpose) flour
5ml/1 tsp baking powder
2.5ml/½ tsp bicarbonate of soda
   (baking soda)
5ml/1 tsp ground cinnamon
1.5ml/¼ tsp grated nutmeg
pinch of salt

1 Preheat the oven to 180°C/350°F/
Gas 4. Grease 12 muffin tins (pans),
or use paper liners.

2 With an electric mixer, cream the margarine and sugar until light and fluffy. Beat in the egg and water.

3 Stir the grated carrots into the creamed mixture until evenly combined. Sift over the flour, baking powder, bicarbonate of soda, cinnamon, nutmeg and salt. Stir to blend evenly.

4 Spoon the batter into the prepared muffin tins, filling them almost to the top.

5 Bake for about 35 minutes, until the tops spring back when touched lightly with your fingers. Leave to stand in the tins for 10 minutes before transferring to a wire rack to cool completely.

Dried Cherry Muffins

Both sweet and sour cherries are available dried. These muffins are traditionally made with a sour variety, which is, in any case, something of a misnomer as they are sharp rather than sour.

Makes 16

250ml/8fl oz/1 cup natural
   (plain) yogurt
225g/8oz/1 cup dried cherries
115g/4oz/½ cup butter, softened
175g/6oz/scant 1 cup caster
   (superfine) sugar
2 eggs
5ml/1 tsp vanilla essence (extract)
200g/7oz/1⅔ cups plain
   (all-purpose) flour
10ml/2 tsp baking powder
5ml/1 tsp bicarbonate of soda
   (baking soda)
pinch of salt

1 In a mixing bowl, combine the yogurt and dried cherries. Cover with clear film (plastic wrap) and leave to stand for 30 minutes.

2 Preheat the oven to 180°C/350°F/
Gas 4. Grease 16 muffin tins (pans),
or use paper liners.

3 Dice the butter and place in a bowl with the sugar. Cream together until light and fluffy. Add the eggs, one at a time, beating well after each addition.

4 Add the vanilla essence and the cherry mixture and stir to blend. Set aside.

5 In another bowl, sift together the flour, baking powder, bicarbonate of soda and salt. Gently fold into the cherry mixture in three batches.

6 Spoon the mixture into the prepared muffin tins, filling them about two-thirds full. Bake for 20 minutes, or until the tops spring back when touched lightly. Transfer to a wire rack to cool.

Blueberry and Lemon Muffins

Blueberries grow wild all over the United States, which is where this traditional recipe comes from. If you cannot obtain blueberries, use bilberries which are similar but slightly sharper.

Makes 12

175g/6oz/1¼ cups plain
   (all-purpose) flour
75g/3oz/scant ½ cup caster
   (superfine) sugar
10ml/2 tsp baking powder
pinch of salt
2 eggs
50g/2oz/¼ cup butter, melted
175ml/6fl oz/¾ cup milk
5ml/1 tsp vanilla essence (extract)
5ml/1 tsp grated lemon rind
150g/5oz/1¼ cups fresh blueberries

Cook's Tip

Rinse the blueberries in cold water, drain well and pat dry with kitchen paper before adding them to the batter.

1 Preheat the oven to 200°C/400°F/ Gas 6. Grease 12 muffin tins (pans), or use paper liners.

2 Sift the flour, sugar, baking powder and salt into a bowl and set aside.

3 In another bowl, lightly whisk the eggs until blended. Add the melted butter, milk, vanilla essence and lemon rind and stir well until thoroughly combined.

4 Make a well in the dry ingredients and pour in the egg mixture. Using a large metal spoon, stir until the flour is just moistened and incorporated, but not until the mixture is smooth.

5 Gently fold the blueberries into the mixture with a metal spoon until they are evenly distributed.

6 Spoon the mixture into the tins, leaving room for the muffins to rise. Bake for 20–25 minutes. Leave to cool for 5 minutes before transferring to a wire rack.

Date and Apple Muffins

These spiced muffins are delicious and very filling. If possible, use fresh medjool dates from Egypt, as they have sweet, dense flesh and a truly opulent flavour.

Makes 12

150g/5oz/1¼ cups self-raising wholemeal
  (self-rising whole-wheat) flour
150g/5oz/1¼ cups self-raising (self-rising)
  white flour
5ml/1 tsp ground cinnamon
5ml/1 tsp baking powder
25g/1oz/2 tbsp margarine
75g/3oz/⅓ cup light muscovado
  (brown) sugar
1 eating apple
250ml/8fl oz/1 cup apple juice
30ml/2 tbsp pear and apple spread
1 egg, lightly beaten
75g/3oz/½ cup chopped dates
15ml/1 tbsp chopped pecan nuts

1 Preheat the oven to 200°C/400°F/ Gas 6. Arrange 12 paper cases in a deep muffin tin (pan).

2 Sift both flours with the cinnamon and baking powder into a bowl. Rub in the margarine until the mixture resembles breadcrumbs.

Cook's Tip
If self-raising wholemeal (self-rising whole-wheat) flour is not available, use more self-raising (self-rising) white flour instead.

3 Stir in the muscovado sugar. Quarter and core the apple, chop the flesh finely and set aside. Stir a little of the apple juice with the pear and apple spread until smooth. Mix in the remaining apple juice, then add to the rubbed-in mixture with the beaten egg.

4 Add the chopped apple to the bowl and stir in the dates. Mix quickly until just combined. Divide the mixture among the prepared muffin cases.

5 Sprinkle the chopped pecans on top. Bake for 20–25 minutes, until golden brown and firm in the middle. Transfer to a wire rack and serve while still warm.

Blackberry Muffins

Blackberries are deliciously succulent with a slightly sharp flavour, but other similar berries, such as elderberries or blueberries, can be used instead.

Makes 12
275g/10oz/2½ cups plain
  (all-purpose) flour
50g/2oz/¼ cup soft light brown sugar
20ml/4 tsp baking powder
pinch of salt
65g/2½oz/generous ½ cup chopped
  blanched almonds
90g/3½oz/generous ¾ cup
  fresh blackberries
2 eggs
200ml/7fl oz/scant 1 cup milk
65g/2½oz/5 tbsp butter, melted
15ml/1 tbsp sloe gin
15ml/1 tbsp rose water

1 Preheat the oven to 200°C/400°F/ Gas 6. Grease 12 muffin tins (pans), or use paper liners.

2 Mix the flour, sugar, baking powder and salt in a bowl and stir in the almonds and blackberries, mixing them well to coat all over with the flour mixture.

3 In another bowl, mix the eggs with the milk, then gradually add the butter, sloe gin and rose water.

4 Make a well in the centre of the bowl of dry ingredients and add the egg and milk mixture. Stir well until the mixture is smooth.

5 Spoon the mixture into the prepared muffin tins or cases. Bake for 20–25 minutes, until browned. Transfer to a wire rack to cool slightly, if you want to serve them warm, or cool completely.

Cook's Tip
If you can't find sloe gin, make your own by packing pricked sloes into a sterile container and covering with dry gin. Leave to infuse (steep) in a cool, dark place for several weeks.

Chocolate Blueberry Muffins

Blueberries are one of the many fruits that combine deliciously with the richness of chocolate, while still retaining their own distinctive flavour. These muffins are best served warm.

Makes 12

115g/4oz/½ cup butter
75g/3oz plain (semisweet)
   chocolate, chopped
200g/7oz/1 cup granulated sugar
1 egg, lightly beaten
250ml/8fl oz/1 cup buttermilk
10ml/2 tsp vanilla essence (extract)
275g/10oz/2½ cups plain
   (all-purpose) flour
5ml/1 tsp bicarbonate of soda
   (baking soda)
175g/6oz/generous 1 cup fresh or
   thawed frozen blueberries
25g/1oz plain (semisweet) chocolate,
   melted, to decorate

1 Preheat the oven to 190°C/375°F/ Gas 5. Grease 12 deep muffin tins (pans), or use paper liners.

2 Melt the butter and chocolate in a medium pan over a medium heat, stirring frequently until smooth. Remove the pan from the heat and leave to cool slightly.

Cook's Tip
Do not keep the batter waiting once you have folded in the blueberries. Bake the muffins immediately or they won't rise very well during cooking.

3 Stir the sugar, egg, buttermilk and vanilla essence into the melted chocolate mixture. Gently fold in the flour and bicarbonate of soda until just blended. (Be careful not to overblend; the mixture is best slightly lumpy.) Gently fold in the blueberries.

4 Spoon the batter into the prepared tins or paper cases. Bake for 25–30 minutes, until a skewer inserted in the centre comes out with just a few crumbs attached. Transfer the muffins to a wire rack (if left in the tin they will go soggy). To decorate, drizzle with the melted chocolate and serve warm or at room temperature.

Prune Muffins

Muffins with prunes are nutritious as well as delicious and perfect as a weekend breakfast treat. These are made with oil rather than butter, so are marvellously quick to mix.

Makes 12

1 egg
250ml/8fl oz/1 cup milk
50ml/2fl oz/¼ cup vegetable oil
50g/2oz/¼ cup granulated sugar
30ml/2 tbsp soft dark brown sugar
225g/8oz/2 cups plain
  (all-purpose) flour
10ml/2 tsp baking powder
pinch of salt
1.5ml/¼ tsp grated nutmeg
150g/5oz/¾ cup cooked prunes, or
  ready-to-eat prunes, chopped

1 Preheat the oven to 200°C/400°F/ Gas 6. Grease 12 muffin tins (pans), or use paper liners.

2 Break the egg into a mixing bowl and beat with a fork. Beat in the milk and oil.

3 Stir the sugars into the egg mixture. Set aside. Sift the flour, baking powder, salt and nutmeg into a mixing bowl. Make a well in the centre, pour in the egg mixture and stir. The batter should be slightly lumpy.

4 Gently fold the prunes into the batter until just evenly distributed. Spoon into the prepared muffin tins, filling them two-thirds full.

5 Bake for about 20 minutes, until golden brown. Leave to stand for 10 minutes before transferring to a wire rack. Serve warm or cold.

Yogurt Honey Muffins

Yogurt and honey are known to boost energy levels, so these muffins go well in lunch boxes.

Makes 12

50g/2oz/4 tbsp butter
75ml/5 tbsp clear honey
250ml/8fl oz/1 cup natural (plain) yogurt
1 egg
grated rind of 1 lemon
50ml/2fl oz/¼ cup lemon juice
115g/4oz/1 cup plain (all-purpose) flour
115g/4oz/1 cup wholemeal
  (whole-wheat) flour
7.5ml/1½ tsp bicarbonate of soda
  (baking soda)
pinch of grated nutmeg

1 Preheat the oven to 190°C/375°F/ Gas 5. Grease 12 muffin tins (pans).

2 In a pan, melt the butter and honey. Remove from the heat and set aside to cool slightly.

3 In a bowl, whisk together the yogurt, egg, lemon rind and juice. Add the butter and honey mixture.

4 In another bowl, sift together the flours, bicarbonate of soda and nutmeg. Fold the dry ingredients into the yogurt mixture just enough to blend them.

5 Fill the prepared muffin tins two-thirds full. Bake for 20–25 minutes, then leave to cool in the tins for about 5 minutes before transferring to a wire rack.

Variation

To make Walnut Yogurt Honey Muffins, add 50g/2oz/½ cup chopped walnuts, folded in with the flour.

Raisin Bran Muffins

These traditional muffins remain hugely popular. This is hardly surprising as they are delicious,
served warm and spread with butter and honey.

Makes 15

50g/2oz/¼ cup butter
  or margarine
75g/3oz/⅔ cup plain
  (all-purpose) flour
50g/2oz/½ cup wholemeal
  (whole-wheat) flour
7.5ml/1½ tsp bicarbonate of soda
  (baking soda)
pinch of salt
5ml/1 tsp ground cinnamon
25g/1oz/¼ cup bran
75g/3oz/generous ½ cup raisins
50g/2oz/¼ cup soft dark
  brown sugar
50g/2oz/¼ cup granulated sugar
1 egg
250ml/8fl oz/1 cup buttermilk
juice of ½ lemon

1 Preheat the oven to 200°C/400°F/
Gas 6. Grease 15 muffin tins (pans),
or use paper liners.

2 Place the butter or margarine in
a pan and melt over a low heat. Set
aside to cool slightly. In a mixing
bowl, sift together the plain flour,
wholemeal flour, bicarbonate of
soda, salt and ground cinnamon.

3 Add the bran, raisins and sugars
and stir until blended. In another
bowl, mix together the egg,
buttermilk, lemon juice and melted
butter or margarine.

4 Add the buttermilk mixture to
the dry ingredients and stir lightly
and quickly until just moistened; do
not mix until smooth.

5 Spoon the batter into the
prepared muffin tins, filling them
almost to the top. Bake for about
15 minutes, or until golden. Serve
warm or at room temperature.

Cook's Tip
*Bran is the outer husk of cereal grains
removed during milling. Wheat bran is the
most widely available and popular variety,
but other cereal brans are available from
health food stores.*

Raspberry Crumble Muffins

Make these stylish muffins for a special occasion in the summer when raspberries are bursting with flavour. For total luxury, serve like scones, with raspberry jam and cream.

Makes 12

175g/6oz/1½ cups plain
  (all-purpose) flour
10ml/2 tsp baking powder
pinch of salt
5ml/1 tsp ground cinnamon
50g/2oz/¼ cup granulated sugar
50g/2oz/¼ cup soft light
  brown sugar
115g/4oz/½ cup butter, melted
1 egg
120ml/4fl oz/½ cup milk
225g/8oz/1⅓ cups fresh raspberries
grated rind of 1 lemon

For the crumble topping

50g/2oz/½ cup pecan nuts,
  finely chopped
50g/2oz/¼ cup soft dark
  brown sugar
45ml/3 tbsp plain (all-purpose) flour
5ml/1 tsp ground cinnamon
40g/1½oz/3 tbsp butter, melted

1 Preheat the oven to 180°C/350°F/ Gas 4. Grease 12 muffin tins (pans).

2 Sift the flour, baking powder, salt and cinnamon into a bowl. Stir in the sugars. Make a well in the centre, add the butter, egg and milk and mix until just combined. Stir in the raspberries and lemon rind.

3 Spoon the batter into the muffin tins, filling them almost to the top.

4 To make the topping, mix the pecans, sugar, flour and cinnamon in a bowl. Stir in the melted butter.

5 Spoon a little of the crumble topping over to top of each muffin. Bake for about 25 minutes. Transfer to a wire rack to cool slightly. Serve the muffins warm.

Nutty Muffins with Walnut Liqueur

These are slightly spicy and topped with a delicious crunchy sugar and nut mixture. If you're making them for children simply omit the walnut liqueur and add more milk.

Makes 12

225g/8oz/2 cups plain (all-purpose) flour
20ml/4 tsp baking powder
2.5ml/½ tsp mixed (apple pie) spice
pinch of salt
115g/4oz/½ cup soft light brown sugar
75g/3oz/¾ cup chopped walnuts
50g/2oz/¼ cup butter, melted
2 eggs
175ml/6fl oz/¾ cup milk
30ml/2 tbsp walnut liqueur

For the topping

30ml/2 tbsp soft dark brown sugar
25g/1oz/¼ cup chopped walnuts

1 Preheat the oven to 200°C/400°F/ Gas 6. Line a muffin tin (pan) with 12 paper cases. Sift the flour, baking powder, mixed spice and salt into a bowl. Stir in the sugar and walnuts.

2 Combine the melted butter, eggs, milk and liqueur in a jug (pitcher).

3 Pour the butter mixture into the dry mixture and stir for just long enough to combine the ingredients. The batter should be lumpy.

4 Fill the tins two-thirds full, then top with a sprinkling of sugar and walnuts. Bake for 15 minutes until the muffins are golden brown. Leave in the tins for a few minutes, then transfer to a wire rack to cool.

Cook's Tip

Probably the best-known walnut liqueur is brou de noix from France, which is made from green walnut husks and flavoured with cinnamon and nutmeg. Other versions are also produced.

Apple and Cinnamon Muffins

These fruity, spicy muffins are quick and easy to make and are perfect for serving for breakfast or tea. The appetizing aroma as they bake is out of this world.

Makes 6

1 egg, beaten
40g/1½oz/3 tbsp caster
  (superfine) sugar
120ml/4fl oz/½ cup milk
50g/2oz/¼ cup butter, melted
150g/5oz/1¼ cups plain
  (all-purpose) flour
7.5ml/1½ tsp baking powder
pinch of salt
2.5ml/½ tsp ground cinnamon
2 small eating apples, peeled, cored and
  finely chopped

For the topping

12 brown sugar cubes,
  coarsely crushed
5ml/1 tsp ground cinnamon

1 Preheat the oven to 200°C/400°F/ Gas 6. Line a large muffin tin (pan) with six paper cases.

2 Mix the egg, sugar, milk and melted butter in a large bowl. Sift in the flour, baking powder, salt and cinnamon. Add the chopped apple and mix roughly.

Variation

You can also make these muffins with pears or even quinces, both of which go well with cinnamon.

3 Spoon the mixture into the prepared muffin cases. To make the topping, mix the crushed sugar cubes with the cinnamon. Sprinkle over the uncooked muffins.

4 Bake for 30–35 minutes until well risen and golden brown on top. Transfer the muffins to a wire rack to cool. Serve them warm or at room temperature.

Cook's Tip

Do not overmix the muffin mixture – it should be slightly lumpy.

Pineapple and Cinnamon Drop Scones

Making the batter with pineapple juice instead of milk cuts down on the amount of fat and adds a delicious piquancy to the flavour of these delicious drop scones.

Makes 24

115g/4oz/1 cup self-raising wholemeal
  (self-rising whole-wheat) flour
115g/4oz/1 cup self-raising (self-rising)
  white flour
5ml/1 tsp ground cinnamon
15ml/1 tbsp caster (superfine) sugar
1 egg
300ml/½ pint/1¼ cups pineapple juice
75g/3oz/½ cup semi-dried
  pineapple, chopped

1 Put the wholemeal flour in a mixing bowl. Sift in the white flour, add the cinnamon and sugar and make a well in the centre. Add the egg with half of the pineapple juice.

3 Heat a griddle or electric frying pan, then lightly grease it. Drop tablespoons of the batter on to the surface, spacing them apart, and leave them until they bubble and the bubbles begin to burst.

Cook's Tips
• Drop scones do not keep well and are best eaten freshly cooked. In any case, they are especially delicious served hot.
• If self-raising wholemeal flour is not readily available, use white self-raising flour instead.

2 Gradually incorporate the flour, then beat in the remaining pineapple juice with the chopped pineapple.

4 Turn over the drop scones with a palette knife or metal spatula and cook until the underside is golden brown. Continue to cook in successive batches.

Chocolate Chip Banana Drop Scones

These scrumptious, moist scones are topped with whipped cream and toasted almonds. You may find it difficult to keep up with the speed the family can eat them.

Makes 16

2 ripe bananas
200ml/7fl oz/scant 1 cup milk
2 eggs
150g/5oz/1¼ cups self-raising (self-rising) flour
25g/1oz/¼ cup ground almonds
15ml/1 tbsp caster (superfine) sugar
pinch of salt
25g/1oz/2½ tbsp plain (semisweet) chocolate chips
butter, for frying

For the topping

150ml/¼ pint/⅔ cup double (heavy) cream
15ml/1 tbsp icing (confectioners') sugar
50g/2oz/½ cup toasted flaked (sliced) almonds, to decorate

1 In a bowl, mash the bananas with a fork, combine with half the milk and beat in the eggs. Sift in the flour, ground almonds, sugar and salt.

2 Make a well in the centre of the dry ingredients and pour in the remaining milk. Add the chocolate chips and stir with a wooden spoon to produce a thick batter.

3 Heat a knob (pat) of butter in a non-stick frying pan. Spoon the drop scone mixture into heaps, allowing room for them to spread. When the mixture starts to bubble, turn the drop scones over and cook briefly on the other side.

4 When all the batches of scones have been cooked, lightly whip the cream with the icing sugar to sweeten it slightly. Spoon the cream on to the drop scones and decorate with flaked almonds. Serve immediately, while still warm.

Teatime Scones

Although the great British institution of tea time is fast becoming a memory, there are occasions when reviving the tradition is worthwhile – and making these scones is one of them.

Makes 16
225g/8oz/2 cups plain (all-purpose) flour
pinch of salt
2.5ml/½ tsp bicarbonate of soda
  (baking soda)
5ml/1 tsp cream of tartar
25g/1oz/2 tbsp butter
about 150ml/¼ pint/⅔ cup milk
  or buttermilk

1 Preheat the oven to 220°C/425°F/ Gas 7. Flour a baking sheet. Sift the flour, salt, bicarbonate of soda and cream of tartar into a large mixing bowl.

2 Rub in the butter until the mixture resembles breadcrumbs. Gradually stir in just enough milk to make a light, spongy dough.

3 Turn out the dough on to a lightly floured surface and knead until smooth. Roll to 2.5cm/1in thick. Stamp out rounds with a floured 5cm/2in cutter.

4 Place the scones on the prepared baking sheet and brush the tops with milk. Bake for 7–10 minutes, until the scones are well risen and golden brown.

Lavender Scones

These scented scones are literally a taste of the summer and are delicious served warm with jam.

Makes 12
225g/8oz/2 cups plain (all-purpose) flour
15ml/1 tbsp baking powder
50g/2oz/¼ cup butter
40g/1½oz/3 tbsp caster (superfine) sugar
10ml/2 tsp fresh lavender florets, chopped
about 175ml/6fl oz/¾ cup milk

1 Preheat the oven to 220°C/425°F/ Gas 7. Grease a baking sheet.

2 Sift together the flour and baking powder into a bowl. Rub the butter into the dry ingredients until the mixture resembles breadcrumbs.

3 Stir in the sugar and lavender, reserving a pinch of lavender to sprinkle on the top of the scones.

4 Add enough milk to make a soft, sticky dough. Bind the mixture together and then turn the dough out on to a well-floured surface.

5 Roll out the dough to a round about 2.5cm/1in thick. Stamp out 12 scones with a floured cutter and place them on the baking sheet. Brush the tops with a little milk and sprinkle with the reserved lavender.

6 Bake for 10–12 minutes, until golden brown.

Sunflower Sultana Scones

Baking a batch of fruit scones takes very little time and is extremely easy, but it is both satisfying and rewarding. They make the perfect snack for both morning and afternoon breaks.

Makes 10–12

225g/8oz/2 cups self-raising
  (self-rising) flour
5ml/1 tsp baking powder
25g/1oz/2 tbsp margarine
30ml/2 tbsp golden caster
  (superfine) sugar
50g/2oz/⅓ cup sultanas (golden raisins)
30ml/2 tbsp sunflower seeds
150ml/¼ pint/⅔ cup natural
  (plain) yogurt
about 30–45ml/2–3 tbsp milk

Cook's Tip
These scones would be perfect served with sunflower honey, which has a wonderful floral fragrance.

I Preheat the oven to 230°C/450°F/ Gas 8. Grease a baking sheet. Sift the flour and baking powder into a bowl, add the margarine and rub in. Stir in the sugar, sultanas and half of the sunflower seeds, then mix in the yogurt.

2 Add just enough milk to the mixture to make a soft dough.

3 Roll out on a lightly floured surface to about 2cm/¾in thick. Stamp out 6cm/2½in rounds with a floured biscuit (cookie) cutter and lift on to the baking sheet.

4 Brush the tops of the scones with milk and sprinkle with the reserved sunflower seeds.

5 Bake for 10–12 minutes until well risen and golden brown. Transfer to a wire rack to cool slightly. Serve while still warm, spread with a little butter and jam.

Wholemeal Scones

These scones make a delicious and healthy option. As you would expect, they taste great spread with jam, but they are also surprisingly good with cheese – either soft or hard.

Makes 16
175g/6oz/¾ cup cold butter
225g/8oz/2 cups wholemeal
   (whole-wheat) flour
115g/4oz/1 cup plain (all-purpose) flour
30ml/2 tbsp caster (superfine) sugar
pinch of salt
12.5ml/2½ tsp bicarbonate of soda
   (baking soda)
2 eggs
175ml/6fl oz/¾ cup buttermilk
40g/1½oz/⅓ cup raisins

1 Preheat the oven to 200°C/400°F/
Gas 6. Grease and flour a large
baking sheet.

2 Dice the butter. Mix the dry
ingredients in a bowl, then add the
butter and rub in. Set aside. In
another bowl, whisk together the
eggs and buttermilk. Set aside 30ml/
2 tbsp for glazing.

3 Stir the remaining egg mixture
into the dry ingredients to form a
dough. Stir in the raisins.

4 Roll out the dough on a lightly
floured surface to about 2cm/¾in
thick. Stamp out rounds with a
floured cutter. Place on the
prepared baking sheet and brush
with the reserved egg mixture.

5 Bake for 12–15 minutes until
golden brown. Leave to cool slightly
before serving. Split the scones in
half while they are still warm and
spread with whatever you like.

Orange Raisin Scones

These sweet, tangy scones are really at their best served warm, in the traditional Cornish way, with thick cream and home-made jam.

Makes 16
225g/8oz/2 cups plain (all-purpose) flour
25ml/1½ tbsp baking powder
75g/3oz/scant ½ cup caster
   (superfine) sugar
pinch of salt
65g/2½oz/5 tbsp butter, chopped
grated rind of 1 large orange
50g/2oz/⅓ cup raisins
115g/4oz/½ cup buttermilk
milk, for glazing

1 Preheat the oven to 220°C/425°F/
Gas 7. Grease and flour a large
baking sheet.

2 Combine the dry ingredients in a
large bowl. Rub in the butter.

3 Add the orange rind and raisins
and mix well. Gradually stir in the
buttermilk to form a soft dough.

4 Roll out the dough on a lightly
floured surface to about 2cm/¾in
thick. Stamp out rounds with a
floured biscuit (cookie) cutter.

5 Place on the prepared baking
sheet and brush the tops with milk
to glaze. Bake for 12–15 minutes
until golden brown. Serve hot or
warm, with butter or whipped
cream and jam.

Cook's Tips
• For light, delicate scones, handle the
dough as little as possible.
• If you wish, split the scones when cool
and toast them under a preheated grill
(broiler). Butter them while they are still hot.

Ham and Tomato Scones

These savoury scones make an ideal accompaniment for soup. Choose a strong-flavoured ham and chop it fairly finely, so that a little goes a long way.

Makes 12

225g/8oz/2 cups self-raising
  (self-rising) flour
5ml/1 tsp mustard powder
5ml/1 tsp paprika, plus extra
  for sprinkling
pinch of salt
25g/1oz/2 tbsp margarine, diced
15ml/1 tbsp chopped fresh basil
50g/2oz/½ cup sun-dried tomatoes in oil,
  drained and chopped
50g/2oz Black Forest ham, chopped
90–120ml/3–4fl oz/⅓–½ cup skimmed
  milk, plus extra for brushing

1 Preheat the oven to 200°C/400°F/ Gas 6. Flour a large baking sheet. Sift the flour, mustard, paprika and salt into a bowl. Rub in the margarine with your fingertips.

2 Stir the basil, sun-dried tomatoes and ham into the bowl. Pour in enough milk to make a soft dough.

3 Turn the dough out on to a lightly floured surface, knead lightly and roll out to a 20 × 15cm/8 × 6in rectangle. Cut into 5cm/2in squares and arrange on the baking sheet.

4 Brush the tops of the scones with milk, sprinkle lightly with paprika and bake for 12–15 minutes, until risen and golden brown. Transfer to a wire rack to cool.

Bacon Corn Meal Muffins

Serve these tasty muffins fresh from the oven for an extra special breakfast. They would also be ideal as part of a weekend brunch menu, served with scrambled eggs or an omelette.

Makes 14

8 bacon rashers (strips)
50g/2oz/¼ cup butter
50g/2oz/¼ cup margarine
115g/4oz/1 cup plain
  (all-purpose) flour
15ml/1 tbsp baking powder
5ml/1 tsp caster (superfine) sugar
pinch of salt
175g/6oz/1½ cups corn meal
250ml/8fl oz/1 cup milk
2 eggs

1 Preheat the oven to 200°C/ 400°F/Gas 6. Grease 14 muffin tins (pans), or use paper liners.

4 Pour the milk and egg mixture into the centre of the well and stir in the dry ingredients until smooth and well blended.

5 Fold in the bacon. Spoon the batter into the prepared tins, filling them halfway. Bake for about 20 minutes until risen and golden.

2 Remove the bacon rind if necessary, then fry the bacon over a medium heat until crisp. Drain on kitchen paper, then chop into small pieces. Set aside. Melt the butter and margarine in a pan over a low heat and set aside.

3 Sift the flour, baking powder, sugar and salt into a large mixing bowl. Stir in the corn meal, then make a well in the centre. In another pan, heat the milk to lukewarm. In a small bowl, lightly whisk the eggs, then add to the milk. Stir in the melted butter and margarine.

Savoury Cheese Whirls

These make a tasty – and healthy – after-school snack for children and you may be surprised to discover that adults like them too. Serve them with carrot and cucumber sticks.

Makes 16

250g/9oz frozen puff pastry, thawed
about 15ml/1 tbsp vegetable extract
1 egg, beaten
50g/2oz/½ cup grated red Leicester or Cheddar cheese

1 Preheat the oven to 220°C/ 425°F/Gas 7. Lightly grease a large baking sheet. Roll out the pastry on a lightly floured surface to a large rectangle, measuring about 35 × 25cm/14 × 10in.

2 Spread the pastry with vegetable extract, leaving a 1cm/½in border. Brush the edges of the pastry with egg and sprinkle over the cheese to cover the vegetable extract.

3 Roll the pastry up quite tightly like a Swiss (jelly) roll, starting from a long edge. Brush the outside of the pastry with beaten egg.

4 Cut the pastry roll into thick slices and place on the prepared baking sheet.

5 Bake for 12–15 minutes, until the pastry is well risen and golden. Arrange on a serving plate and serve warm or cold with carrot and cucumber sticks.

Cook's Tip
If the shapes become a little squashed when sliced, re-form them into rounds by opening out the layers slightly with the tip of a knife.

Variation
Omit the vegetable extract and use peanut butter, if you like.

Cheese Muffins

These muffins would be terrific served straight from the oven at a brunch party or wonderfully restorative and warming after a brisk walk on a cold winter's afternoon.

Makes 9

50g/2oz/¼ cup butter

175g/6oz/1½ cups plain (all-purpose) flour

10ml/2 tsp baking powder

30ml/2 tbsp caster (superfine) sugar

pinch of salt

5ml/1 tsp paprika

2 eggs

120ml/4fl oz/½ cup milk

5ml/1 tsp dried thyme

50g/2oz mature (sharp) Cheddar cheese, cut into 1cm/½in dice

1 Preheat the oven to 190°C/375°F/ Gas 5. Grease nine muffin tins (pans), or use paper liners. Melt the butter in a small pan.

2 Sift the flour, baking powder, sugar, salt and paprika into a bowl.

3 Combine the eggs, milk, melted butter and thyme and whisk well.

4 Add the milk mixture to the dry ingredients and stir until just moistened, do not mix until smooth.

5 Place a mounded spoonful of batter into each of the prepared tins. Drop a few pieces of cheese over each, then top with another spoonful of batter.

6 Bake the muffins for about 25 minutes until puffed and golden brown. Leave to stand in the tins for about 5 minutes before unmoulding them on to a wire rack to cool slightly. These muffins are best served while still warm from the oven or at room temperature.

Feta Cheese and Chive Scones

Salty feta cheese makes an excellent substitute for butter in these tangy savoury scones. They not only go well with hot soup, but also make a delicious snack at any time of day.

Makes 9

115g/4oz/1 cup self-raising
  (self-rising) flour
150g/5oz/1¼ cup self-raising wholemeal
  (self-rising whole-wheat) flour
pinch of salt
75g/3oz feta cheese
15ml/1 tbsp chopped fresh chives
150ml/¼ pint/⅔ cup skimmed milk, plus
  extra for glazing
1.5ml/¼ tsp cayenne pepper

1 Preheat the oven to 200°C/400°F/ Gas 6. Sift together both the flours and the salt into a mixing bowl, adding any bran left over from the flour in the sieve.

2 Crumble the feta cheese roughly and rub it into the dry ingredients. Stir in the chives, then add the milk and mix lightly to form a soft, not sticky dough.

3 Turn out the dough on to a floured surface and knead lightly until smooth. Roll out to 2cm/¾in thick and stamp out nine scones with a floured 6cm/2½in biscuit (cookie) cutter.

4 Transfer to a non-stick baking sheet. Brush with skimmed milk, then sprinkle over the cayenne pepper. Bake for 15 minutes, until golden brown. Serve warm or cold.

Cook's Tip

Try to obtain genuine sheep's milk feta, as it has the best flavour. Much modern feta is made from cow's milk, but some Greek and, surprisingly, Bulgarian feta is still made in the traditional manner.

Variation

If self-raising wholemeal flour is not readily available, use white self-raising flour instead.

Chive and Potato Scones

These little scones should be fairly thin, soft inside and crisp on the outside. Traditionally served for what was once known as high tea, they are also excellent for breakfast.

Makes 20

450g/1lb potatoes
115g/4oz/1 cup plain (all-purpose) flour
30ml/2 tbsp olive oil, plus extra
*   for greasing*
30ml/2 tbsp chopped fresh chives
salt and ground black pepper

3 Roll out the dough on a well-floured surface to a thickness of about 5mm/¼in and stamp out rounds with a floured 5cm/2in plain biscuit (cookie) cutter. Lightly grease the griddle or frying pan with a little olive oil.

4 Cook the scones in batches for about 10 minutes, turning once halfway through cooking.

Cook's Tip
Cook over a low heat to avoid burning the outsides before the insides are cooked.

1 Cook the potatoes in a pan of lightly salted, boiling water for about 20 minutes, until tender, then drain thoroughly. Return the potatoes to the clean pan and mash them with a masher or a fork. Preheat a griddle or heavy frying pan.

2 Add the flour, olive oil and chives to the mashed potato. Season to taste with salt and pepper. Mix to a soft dough.

No-bake Cookies

The recipes in this chapter require even less time and effort to mix than travelling to the supermarket to buy a packet of cookies – and they taste a lot better too. Not just no-bake, some are even no-cook, making them great for kids to prepare as well. None of them requires anything more demanding than melting some chocolate, but you may have to be patient to allow the cookies enough time to set in the refrigerator before sampling them.

Fruit and Nut Clusters

This is a fun, no-bake recipe that children will like, although if they are making it themselves, adult supervision for melting the chocolate is recommended.

Makes 24

225g/8oz white chocolate
50g/2oz/⅓ cup sunflower seeds
50g/2oz/½ cup flaked (sliced) almonds
50g/2oz/¼ cup sesame seeds
50g/2oz/⅓ cup seedless raisins
5ml/1 tsp ground cinnamon

1 Break the white chocolate into small pieces. Put the chocolate in a microwave-proof container and cook in a microwave on medium for 2–3 minutes.

2 Alternatively, melt the chocolate by putting it into a heatproof bowl set over a pan of hot water on a low heat. Do not allow the water to touch the base of the bowl, or the chocolate may become too hot.

3 Stir the melted chocolate until it is smooth and glossy.

4 Mix the remaining ingredients together, pour on the melted chocolate and stir well.

5 Using a teaspoon, spoon the mixture into paper cases and leave in a cool place to set, but do not put the clusters in the refrigerator.

Cook's Tip
As with any recipe that contains nuts, always check those who will be eating the cookies do not have nut allergies. You could always substitute the nuts for other dried fruit such as dates.

Oat and Apricot Clusters

Here is a variation on an old favourite, which children can easily make themselves, so have plenty of the dried fruits and nuts ready for them to add.

Makes 12

50g/2oz/¼ cup butter or margarine
50g/2oz/¼ cup clear honey
50g/2oz/½ cup medium rolled oats
50g/2oz/½ cup chopped ready-to-eat
　dried apricots
15ml/1 tbsp dried banana chips
15ml/1 tbsp dried shreds of coconut or
　desiccated (dry unsweetened) coconut
50 75g/2–3oz/2–3 cups cornflakes or
　crisped rice cereal

1 Place the butter or margarine and honey in a small pan and warm over a low heat, stirring.

2 Remove the pan from the heat and add the oats, apricots, banana chips, coconut and cornflakes or crisped rice cereal and stir well with a wooden spoon until combined.

3 Spoon the mixture into 12 paper cake cases, piling it up roughly. Transfer to a baking sheet or place on a tray and chill in the refrigerator until set and firm.

Variations
• To make Oat and Cherry Clusters, use rinsed and chopped glacé (candied) cherries in place of the apricots.
• To make Chocolate Chip Clusters, substitute 75g/3oz/½ cup chocolate chips.

Cook's Tip
The ingredients can be changed according to what you have in your store cupboard (pantry) – try peanuts, pecan nuts, raisins or dried dates.

Apricot and Coconut Kisses

These tangy, fruity treats make a colourful addition to the tea table. Although they are easy to make, remember to allow plenty of time for the apricots to soak.

Makes 12

130g/4½oz/generous ½ cup ready-to-eat
  dried apricots
100ml/3½fl oz/scant ½ cup freshly
  squeezed orange juice
40g/1½oz/3 tbsp unsalted (sweet)
  butter, at room temperature, diced
75g/3oz/¾ cup icing (confectioners')
  sugar, plus extra for dusting
90g/3½oz/generous 1 cup desiccated
  (dry unsweetened shredded) coconut,
  lightly toasted
2 glacé (candied) cherries, cut
  into wedges

1 Finely chop the dried apricots, then tip them into a bowl. Pour in the orange juice and leave to soak for about 1 hour until all the juice has been absorbed.

2 In a large bowl, beat together the butter and sugar with a wooden spoon until pale and creamy.

3 Gradually add the soaked apricots to the creamed butter and sugar mixture, beating well after each addition, then stir in the toasted coconut.

4 Line a small baking tray with greaseproof (waxed) paper.

5 Place teaspoonfuls of the coconut mixture on to the paper, piling them up into little pyramid shapes. Gently press the mixture together with your fingers to form neat shapes.

6 Top each kiss with a tiny wedge of cherry, gently pressing it into the mixture. Chill the kisses for about 1 hour until firm, then serve lightly dusted with a little icing sugar.

Cook's Tip

It is essential that all the orange juice has been absorbed by the apricots before adding them to the butter mixture, otherwise the kisses will be too moist to set properly.

Date Crunch

A tasty mixture of dried fruit, syrup and chocolate is guaranteed to be a success with the younger members of the family – and they will need to keep an eye on the adults, too.

Makes 24

225g/8oz digestive biscuits
  (graham crackers)
75g/3oz/⅓ cup butter
30ml/2 tbsp golden (light corn) syrup
75g/3oz/½ cup finely chopped pitted
  dried dates
75g/3oz/⅔ cup sultanas (golden raisins)
150g/5oz milk or plain (semisweet)
  chocolate, chopped

1 Line an 18cm/7in square shallow cake tin (pan) with foil. Put the biscuits in a plastic bag and crush coarsely with a rolling pin.

2 Gently heat the butter and syrup together in a small pan until the butter has melted.

Variation
You could drizzle 75g/3oz each melted white and dark (bittersweet) chocolate.

3 Stir the crushed biscuits, dates and sultanas into the butter and syrup mixture and mix well with a wooden spoon until evenly combined. Spoon into the prepared tin, spreading it out evenly, press flat with the back of the spoon and chill for 1 hour.

4 Melt the chocolate in a heatproof bowl set over a pan of hot water, stirring until smooth. Spoon over the cookie mixture, spreading evenly with a palette knife (metal spatula). Chill until set. Lift the foil out of the cake tin and peel away. Cut the crunch into 24 pieces to serve.

Chocolate Nut Clusters

These delightful chocolate-coated cookies are packed with chunky nuts and are an ideal way to end a dinner party or the perfect a gift for a special friend.

Makes 30

550ml/18fl oz/2¼ cups double (heavy) cream

25g/1oz/2 tbsp unsalted (sweet) butter, diced

350ml/12fl oz/1½ cups golden (light corn) syrup

200g/7oz/scant 1 cup granulated sugar

90g/3½oz/scant ½ packed cup soft light brown sugar

pinch of salt

15ml/1 tbsp vanilla essence (extract)

425g/15oz/3¾ cups hazelnuts, pecan nuts, walnuts, brazil nuts or unsalted peanuts, or a combination

400g/14oz plain (semisweet) chocolate, chopped

25g/1oz/2 tbsp white vegetable fat

1 Lightly oil two baking sheets. Put the cream, butter, syrup, both kinds of sugar and the salt in a heavy pan and cook over a medium heat, stirring constantly until the sugars dissolve and the butter melts. Bring to the boil and cook, stirring frequently, for about 1 hour, until the caramel reaches 119°C/238°F (soft ball stage) on a sugar thermometer.

2 Place the base of the pan in a pan of cold water to stop further cooking or transfer the caramel to a smaller pan. Cool slightly, then stir in the vanilla essence.

3 Stir the nuts into the caramel until well-coated. Using an oiled tablespoon, drop spoonfuls of the mixture on to the baking sheets, about 2.5cm/1in apart. If the mixture hardens, return to the heat.

4 Chill the clusters for 30 minutes, until firm and cold, or leave in a cool place until hardened.

Cook's Tip

You can test cooked sugar for "soft ball stage" by spooning a small amount into a bowl of cold water: when taken out it should form a soft ball when rolled between finger and thumb.

5 Using a metal palette knife or spatula, transfer the clusters to a wire rack placed over a baking sheet to catch drips.

6 Melt the chocolate with the white vegetable fat in a pan over a low heat, stirring until smooth. Remove the pan from the heat and leave to cool slightly.

7 Spoon the melted chocolate mixture over each cluster, being sure to cover them completely. Alternatively, using a fork, dip each cluster, one at a time, into the chocolate mixture and lift out, tapping the fork on the edge of the pan to shake off the excess chocolate.

8 Place the nut clusters on the wire rack over the baking sheet. Leave to set for about 2 hours until hardened.

Nutty Marshmallow and Chocolate Squares

Unashamedly sweet, with chocolate, marshmallows, cherries, nuts and coconut, this recipe is a favourite with children of all ages, and sweet-toothed adults too.

Makes 9

200g/7oz digestive biscuits
 (graham crackers)
90g/3½oz plain (semisweet) chocolate
200g/7oz mini coloured marshmallows
150g/5oz/1¼ cups chopped walnuts
90g/3½oz/scant ½ cup glacé (candied)
 cherries, halved
50g/2oz/⅔ cup sweetened desiccated
 (dry shredded) coconut
350g/12oz milk chocolate

I Put the digestive biscuits in a plastic bag and, using a rolling pin, crush them until they are fairly small. Place them in a bowl. Melt the plain chocolate in the microwave or in a heatproof bowl set over a pan of hot water. Pour the melted plain chocolate over the broken biscuits and stir well. Spread the mixture in the base of a 20cm/8in square shallow cake tin (pan).

2 Put the marshmallows, walnuts, cherries and coconut in a large bowl. Melt the milk chocolate in the microwave or in a heatproof bowl set over a pan of hot water.

3 Pour the melted milk chocolate over the marshmallow and nut mixture and toss gently together until almost everything is coated. Spread the mixture over the chocolate base, but leave in chunky lumps – do not spread flat.

4 Chill until set, then cut into squares or bars.

Variation
Other nuts can be used instead of the walnuts – the choice is yours.

Almond-scented Chocolate Cherry Wedges

These cookies are a chocoholic's dream, and use the very best quality chocolate. Erratically shaped, they are packed with crunchy cookies, juicy raisins and munchy nuts.

Makes about 15

50g/2oz ratafia biscuits (almond
   macaroons) or small amaretti
90g/3½oz shortcake biscuits (cookies)
150g/5oz/1 cup jumbo raisins
50g/2oz/¼ cup undyed glacé (candied)
   cherries, quartered
450g/1lb dark (bittersweet) chocolate
   (minimum 70 per cent cocoa solids)
90g/3½oz/scant ½ cup unsalted (sweet)
   butter, diced
30ml/2 tbsp amaretto liqueur (optional)
25g/1oz/¼ cup toasted flaked
   (sliced) almonds

1 Line a baking sheet with baking parchment. Put the ratafia biscuits or amaretti in a large bowl. Leave half whole and break the remainder into coarse pieces. Break each of the shortcake biscuits into three or four jagged pieces and add to the bowl. Add the raisins and cherries and toss lightly together.

Cook's Tip

If you cannot find undyed glacé cherries in the supermarket, look for them in your local delicatessen instead.

2 Melt the chocolate and butter with the liqueur, if using, in the microwave or in a heatproof bowl set over a pan of hot water. When the chocolate has melted, remove from the heat and stir the mixture until combined and smooth. Set aside to cool slightly.

3 Pour the chocolate over the biscuit mixture and toss lightly together until everything is coated in chocolate. Spread out over the prepared baking sheet. Sprinkle over the almonds and push them in at angles so they stick well to the chocolate-coated biscuits.

4 When the mixture is completely cold and set, cut or break into crazy shapes, as you wish, such as long thin triangles, short stumpy squares or irregular shapes.

Chocolate Crispy Cookies

These little chocolate-coated cornflake cakes are always a hit with kids. They couldn't be easier to make – and are great for young aspiring cooks who want to get involved in the kitchen. The only problem is giving the mixture time to set before they've been gobbled up by hungry helpers.

4 Remove the bowl from the heat and tip in the cornflakes. Mix well until the cornflakes are thoroughly coated in the chocolate mixture.

5 Place a 6.5cm/2½in round cutter on the paper and put a spoonful of the chocolate mixture in the centre. Pack down firmly with the back of the spoon to make a thick cookie.

6 Gently ease away the cutter, using the spoon to help keep the mixture in place. Continue making cookies in this way until all the mixture has been used up. Chill for 1 hour.

Makes 10

90g/3½oz milk chocolate
15ml/1 tbsp golden (light corn) syrup
90g/3½oz/4½ cups cornflakes
icing (confectioners') sugar, for dusting

1 Line a large baking sheet with baking parchment.

2 Break the chocolate into a heatproof bowl and add the syrup. Rest the bowl over a pan of gently simmering water and leave until melted, stirring frequently.

3 Put the cornflakes in a plastic bag and, using a rolling pin, lightly crush the cornflakes, breaking them into fairly small pieces.

7 Put a little icing sugar in a small bowl. Lift each cookie from the paper and roll the edges in the icing sugar to finish.

Chocolate Nut Slice

Children of all ages will love this combination of broken cookies, chocolate and nuts. Although the unsliced bar looks small, it's very rich so is best sliced very thinly. If you have any other plain cookies in the cupboard, you can use them instead of the rich tea, with equally good results.

Makes 10 slices

225g/8oz milk chocolate
40g/1½oz/3 tbsp unsalted (sweet)
  butter, diced
75g/3oz rich tea biscuits (plain cookies)
50g/2oz/½ cup flaked (sliced) almonds
75g/3oz plain (semisweet) or white
  chocolate, roughly chopped
icing (confectioners') sugar, for dusting

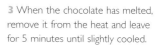

3 When the chocolate has melted, remove it from the heat and leave for 5 minutes until slightly cooled.

4 Break the biscuits into small pieces, then stir into the melted chocolate with the almonds. Add the chopped chocolate to the bowl and fold in quickly and lightly.

1 Break the milk chocolate into pieces and place in a heatproof bowl with the butter. Rest the bowl over a pan of simmering water and stir frequently until melted.

2 Meanwhile, dampen a 450g/1lb loaf tin (pan) and line the base and sides with clear film (plastic wrap). Don't worry about smoothing out the creases in the film.

5 Turn the mixture into the tin and pack down with a fork. Tap the base of the tin gently on the work surface. Chill for 2 hours until set.

6 To serve, turn the chocolate loaf on to a board and peel away the clear film. Dust lightly with icing sugar and slice thinly.

Chocolate Birds' Nests

These delightful crispy chocolate nests make a perfect Easter teatime treat and are a real favourite with kids. They're so quick and easy to make and young children can have great fun shaping the chocolate mixture inside the paper cases and tucking the pastel-coloured eggs inside.

Makes 12

200g/7oz milk chocolate

25g/1oz/2 tbsp unsalted (sweet)
   butter, diced

90g/3½oz Shredded Wheat cereal

36 small pastel-coloured, sugar-coated
   chocolate eggs

Cook's Tip

Bags of sugar-coated chocolate eggs are widely available in supermarkets at Easter time. However, if you have trouble finding them out of season, try an old-fashioned sweet store. Often they have large jars of this type of sweet (candy), which they sell all year round.

1 Line the sections of a tartlet tray (muffin pan) with 12 decorative paper cake cases.

2 Break the milk chocolate into pieces and put in a bowl with the butter. Rest the bowl over a pan of gently simmering water and stir frequently until melted. Remove the bowl from the heat and leave to cool for a few minutes.

3 Using your fingers, crumble the Shredded Wheat into the melted chocolate. Stir well until the cereal is completely coated in chocolate.

4 Divide the mixture among the paper cases, pressing it down gently with the back of a spoon and make a slight indentation in the centre. Tuck three eggs into each nest and leave to set for about 2 hours.

White Chocolate Snowballs

These little spherical cookies are particularly popular during the Christmas season. They're simple to make, yet utterly delicious and bursting with creamy, buttery flavours. If you like, make them in advance of a special tea as they will keep well in the refrigerator for a few days.

Makes 16

200g/7oz white chocolate
25g/1oz/2 tbsp butter, diced
90g/3½oz/generous 1 cup desiccated
   (dry unsweetened shredded) coconut
90g/3½oz syrup sponge or
   Madeira cake
icing (confectioners') sugar, for dusting

1 Break the chocolate into pieces and put in a heatproof bowl with the butter. Rest the bowl over a pan of gently simmering water and stir frequently until melted. Remove the bowl from the heat and set aside for a few minutes.

2 Meanwhile, put 50g/2oz/⅔ cup of the coconut on a plate and set aside. Crumble the cake and add to the melted chocolate with the remaining coconut. Mix well to form a chunky paste.

3 Take spoonfuls of the mixture and roll into balls, about 2.5cm/1in in diameter, and immediately roll them in the reserved coconut. Place the balls on greaseproof (waxed) paper and leave to set.

4 To serve, dust the snowballs with plenty of icing sugar.

Cook's Tip
You'll need to shape the mixture into balls as soon as you've mixed in the coconut and cake; the mixture sets very quickly and you won't be able to shape it once it hardens.

Ice Mountain

To create an alternative shape to rounds and squares, this refrigerator cookie is set in the corner of a cake tin, giving it a "pyramid" shape for slicing into triangles.

Makes 12

75g/3oz malted milk biscuits (cookies)
90g/3½oz milk chocolate
75g/3oz white chocolate mint sticks
250g/9oz white chocolate
60ml/4 tbsp double (heavy) cream
several clear mints (hard mint candies),
* to decorate*

I Break the biscuits into small pieces, chop the milk chocolate into small dice and break the chocolate mint sticks into short lengths. Keep these ingredients separate.

2 Reserve 50g/2oz of the white chocolate. Break up the remainder and put in a small heatproof bowl with the cream. Set the bowl over a pan of gently simmering water and leave until melted, stirring the chocolate frequently. Remove the bowl from the heat and scrape the melted chocolate into a clean bowl.

Cook's Tip

It is important to avoid overheating white chocolate when you are melting it. It is less robust than other types of chocolate as it contains no cocoa solids. Do make sure that the base of the bowl is not touching the surface of the water.

3 Cut out a 23cm/9in square piece of baking parchment. Grease one side and 5cm/2in of the base of an 18cm/7in square cake tin (pan). Fold the paper in half and fit the crease line into the greased corner of the tin so the side and part of the base and ends are lined. Make sure the ends are greased under the lining paper too.

4 Stir the biscuits into the white chocolate mixture followed by the chocolate mint sticks. Add the milk chocolate, stir quickly to combine then turn the mixture into the lined section of the tin. Hold the tin at an angle, then smooth the surface of the chocolate level. Place in the refrigerator, propping the tin up with another container to maintain the angle to form the pyramid shape. Leave for about 2 hours, until set.

5 Remove the cake from the tin, place on a flat plate and peel off the paper. In their wrappers, crush the mints with a rolling pin. Melt the reserved white chocolate in a heatproof bowl set over a pan of hot water.

6 Spread the white chocolate over the top sloping side of the pyramid, sprinkle with the crushed mints and press in lightly.

Pink Piggies

These are what you could call rainy day cookies. They are fun to make and thoroughly absorbing when the family is stuck indoors. You might want to make up icings in other colours and experiment with your own animal variations. Children's books are a great source of inspiration.

Makes 10

90g/3½oz/scant 1 cup icing
    (confectioners') sugar, plus extra
    for dusting
50g/2oz/¼ cup unsalted
    (sweet) butter, at room
    temperature, diced
10 rich tea (plain cookies) or digestive
    biscuits (graham crackers)
200g/7oz white ready-to-roll icing
pink food colouring
small, pink soft sweets (candies)
tube of black writer icing

1 To make the buttercream, put the icing sugar and butter in a bowl and beat with a hand-held electric whisk until smooth, pale and creamy.

2 Using a small palette knife (metal spatula) spread the rich tea or digestive biscuits almost to the edges with the buttercream.

3 Reserve 25g/1oz of the ready-to-roll icing and add a few drops of the pink food colouring to the remainder. Knead on a clean work surface that has been lightly dusted with icing sugar until the pink colouring is evenly distributed.

4 Reserve about 25g/1oz of the pink icing. If necessary, lightly dust your work surface with more icing sugar and roll out the remaining pink icing very thinly.

5 Using a cookie cutter that is just slightly smaller than the rich tea or digestive biscuits, cut out rounds of pink icing. Lay a round over each biscuit and press it down gently on to the buttercream.

6 Halve five of the pink sweets and press into an oval shape. Make two small holes in each one with a wooden skewer or cocktail stick (toothpick) to make a nose.

7 Using a little of the buttercream, attach a halved sweet to the centre of each cookie.

8 Using the black writer icing, pipe two small dots of icing above the nose to resemble eyes, then pipe a small, curved mouth.

9 Thinly roll out the reserved pink icing and the reserved white icing. Dampen the white icing with a little water and press the pink icing gently on top. Using a small sharp knife, cut out triangles for ears.

10 Dampen one edge of the ears with a little water and secure, pink side up, to the cookies. Gently curl the ears out at the ends.

Cook's Tip
If you cannot get black writer icing, use any dark food colouring such as black, blue or brown and paint on the features with a fine brush.

Savoury Crackers

Cheese and biscuits is a classic combination, but there are many other occasions when a savoury crunch is just what is needed. Crackers go well with home-made soup and salads for a light lunch and make delicious snacks when you want something with a little bite to it. This superb collection of tasty recipes offers something for all occasions, from sophisticated Wheat Thins to rustic Herby Seeded Oatcakes.

Polenta Chip Dippers

These tasty Parmesan-flavoured batons are best served warm from the oven with a spicy, tangy dip. A bowl of Thai chilli dipping sauce or a creamy, chilli-spiked guacamole are perfect.

2 Remove the pan from the heat and add the cheese, butter, pepper and salt to taste. Stir well until the butter has completely melted and the mixture is smooth.

3 Pour on to a smooth surface, such as a marble slab or a baking sheet. Spread the polenta out using a palette knife (metal spatula) to a thickness of 2cm/¾in and shape into a rectangle. Leave for at least 30 minutes to become quite cold. Meanwhile preheat the oven to 200°C/400°F/Gas 6 and lightly oil two or three baking sheets with some olive oil.

4 Cut the polenta slab in half, then carefully cut into even-size strips using a sharp knife.

5 Bake the polenta chips for about 40–50 minutes until they are dark golden brown and crunchy. Turn them over from time to time during cooking. Serve warm.

Makes about 80

1.5 litres/2½ pints/6¼ cups water
10ml/2 tsp salt
375g/13oz/3¼ cups instant polenta
150g/5oz/1½ cups freshly grated
   Parmesan cheese
90g/3½oz/scant ½ cup butter
10ml/2 tsp cracked black pepper
olive oil, for brushing
salt

I Put the water in a large heavy pan and bring to the boil over a high heat. Reduce the heat, add the salt and pour in the polenta in a steady stream, stirring constantly with a wooden spoon. Cook over a low heat, stirring constantly, until the mixture thickens and starts to come away from the sides of the pan – this will take about 5 minutes.

Cook's Tip
The unbaked dough can be made a day ahead, then wrapped in clear film (plastic wrap) and kept in the refrigerator until ready to bake.

Corn Meal Biscuits

These are delicious served hot, straight from the oven and spread with butter. They are great for breakfast and also go well with soup for a light lunch.

Makes 12

50g/2oz/½ cup corn meal, plus extra
    for sprinkling
175g/6oz/1¼ cups plain
    (all-purpose) flour
12.5ml/2½ tsp baking powder
pinch of salt
175g/6oz/¾ cup lard, white cooking fat or
    butter, diced
175ml/6fl oz/¾ cup milk

1 Preheat the oven to 230°C/ 450°F/Gas 8. Sprinkle a large ungreased baking sheet lightly with a little corn meal.

2 Sift together the flour, baking powder and salt into a bowl. Stir in the corn meal. Add the lard, white cooking fat or butter and rub into the dry ingredients with your fingertips until the mixture resembles coarse breadcrumbs.

3 Make a well in the centre and pour in the milk. Stir in quickly with a wooden spoon until the dough begins to pull away from the sides of the bowl.

4 Turn the dough out on to a lightly floured surface and knead lightly 8–10 times only. Roll it out to a thickness of 1cm/½in. Stamp out into rounds with a floured 5cm/2in biscuit (cookie) cutter.

5 Arrange the dough rounds on the prepared baking sheet, spacing them about 2.5cm/1in apart. Sprinkle with a little corn meal, then bake for about 10–12 minutes, until golden brown.

Cocktail Shapes

Tiny savoury crackers are always a welcome treat and make lovely party nibbles. Try making a range of shapes and flavouring them with different cheeses and spices.

Makes 80
350g/12oz/3 cups plain
  (all-purpose) flour
pinch of salt
2.5ml/½ tsp ground black pepper
5ml/1 tsp wholegrain mustard
175g/6oz/¾ cup unsalted (sweet)
  butter, chopped
115g/4oz Cheddar cheese
1 egg, beaten
5ml/1 tsp chopped nuts
10ml/2 tsp dill seeds
10ml/2 tsp curry paste
10ml/2 tsp chilli sauce

1 Line several large baking sheets with non-stick baking parchment and set aside.

2 Sift the flour into a large mixing bowl and add the salt, pepper and wholegrain mustard. Mix well.

3 Add the butter and rub it into the flour mixture with your fingertips until it resembles fine breadcrumbs. Grate the cheese then, with a fork, stir it into the butter and flour mixture until thoroughly incorporated. Add the beaten egg and mix together to form a soft dough.

4 Turn out the dough on to a floured surface, knead lightly until smooth, then divide it into four equal pieces.

5 Knead chopped nuts into one piece, dill seeds into another, and curry paste and chilli sauce into the remaining pieces. Wrap each piece in clear film (plastic wrap) and chill for at least 1 hour.

6 Preheat the oven to 200°C/400°F/Gas 6. Roll out each piece of dough in turn. Use a floured heart-shaped cutter to stamp out about 20 shapes from the curry-flavoured dough. Use a club-shaped cutter to cut out the chilli-flavoured dough. Arrange the shapes well spaced apart on the baking sheets and bake for 6–8 minutes, until slightly puffed and pale gold. Cool on wire racks.

7 Repeat with the remaining dough using spade- and diamond-shaped cutters. Knead any trimmings together, and make more shapes.

Spiced Cocktail Biscuits

These prettily specked savoury biscuits are ideal for serving with pre-dinner drinks. Each of the spice seeds contributes to the flavour and makes them very moreish indeed.

Makes 20–30

150g/5oz/1¼ cups plain
  (all-purpose) flour
10ml/2 tsp curry powder
115g/4oz/½ cup butter, chopped
75g/3oz/¾ cup grated Cheddar cheese
10ml/2 tsp poppy seeds
5ml/1 tsp black onion seeds
1 egg yolk
15ml/1 tbsp cumin seeds

1 Grease two baking sheets. Sift the flour and curry powder into a large bowl. Add the butter and rub it in with your fingertips until the mixture resembles breadcrumbs.

2 Stir in the grated cheese, poppy seeds and black onion seeds until thoroughly combined. Stir in the egg yolk and mix to a firm dough. Wrap the dough in clear film (plastic wrap) and chill for 30 minutes.

Cook's Tip
You can make these well in advance and freeze them until almost ready to serve. Spread out on baking sheets and reheat in a moderate oven.

Variation
Use caraway or sesame seeds instead of the poppy seeds, if you like.

3 Roll out the dough on a floured surface to a thickness of about 3mm/⅛in. Stamp out rounds with a floured biscuit (cookie) cutter.

4 Arrange the dough rounds on the prepared baking sheets, spaced well apart, and sprinkle with the cumin seeds. Allow to chill for 15 minutes.

5 Meanwhile, preheat the oven to 190°C/375°F/Gas 5. Bake the biscuits for about 20 minutes until crisp and golden. Serve warm, or transfer to wire racks and leave to cool and serve cold.

Cheese Scones

These delicious, old-fashioned scones make a good teatime treat. They are best served fresh and still slightly warm from the oven and are delicious served with soup.

Makes 12

225g/8oz/2 cups plain (all-purpose) flour
12.5ml/2½ tsp baking powder
2.5ml/½ tsp mustard powder
2.5ml/½ tsp salt
50g/2oz/¼ cup cold butter, chopped
75g/3oz/¾ cup grated mature (sharp)
   Cheddar cheese
150ml/¼ pint/⅔ cup milk
1 egg, beaten

I Preheat the oven to 230°C/450°F/ Gas 8. Sift the flour, baking powder, mustard powder and salt into a mixing bowl. Add the butter and rub it in until the mixture resembles coarse breadcrumbs.

2 Stir 50g/2oz/½ cup of the grated Cheddar cheese into the butter and flour mixture. Make a well in the centre and pour in the milk and beaten egg. Stir gently using a wooden spoon until the mixture forms a soft, only slightly sticky dough.

3 Turn the dough out on to a lightly floured surface.

4 Roll out the dough and cut into triangles or squares. Place them on a baking sheet, brush lightly with milk and sprinkle with the remaining grated cheese. Leave to rest for about 15 minutes, then bake for 15 minutes, until well risen.

Cook's Tip
Don't overwork the dough, or roll it out too thinly, or the scones will be hard and not rise well.

Oatcakes

These are very simple to make and are an excellent addition to any cheese board. They also make a delicious snack spread with pâté and topped with slices of hard-boiled egg.

Makes 24

225g/8oz/2¼ cups medium rolled oats,
   plus extra for sprinkling
75g/3oz/⅔ cup plain
   (all-purpose) flour
1.5ml/¼ tsp bicarbonate of soda
   (baking soda)
5ml/1 tsp salt
25g/1oz/2 tbsp lard or white cooking fat
25g/1oz/2 tbsp butter

Cook's Tip
You can store the oatcakes in an airtight container in a cool place for up to 1 week, but they are best eaten when freshly baked.

I Preheat the oven to 220°C/425°F/ Gas 7. Place the rolled oats, flour, bicarbonate of soda and salt in a large bowl and mix well. Melt the lard or white cooking fat and the butter together in a small pan over a low heat.

2 Add the melted fat and enough boiling water to the dry ingredients to make a dough. Turn out on to a surface sprinkled with rolled oats. Roll out thinly and stamp out 24 rounds. Bake on ungreased baking sheets for 15 minutes.

Curry Crackers

Crisp curry-flavoured crackers are very good with creamy cheese or yogurt dips and make an unusual nibble with pre-dinner drinks. Add a pinch of cayenne pepper for an extra kick.

Makes about 30

175g/6oz/1½ cups self-raising (self-rising) flour
pinch of salt
10ml/2 tsp garam masala
75g/3oz/6 tbsp butter, diced
5ml/1 tsp finely chopped fresh coriander (cilantro)
1 egg, beaten

For the topping

beaten egg
black onion seeds
garam masala

1 Preheat the oven to 200°C/400°F/ Gas 6. Put the flour, salt and garam masala into a bowl. Rub in the butter until the mixture resembles fine breadcrumbs. Stir in the coriander, add the egg and mix to a soft dough.

Cook's Tip

Garam masala is a mixture of Indian spices, that usually contains a blend of cinnamon, cloves, peppercorns, cardamom seeds and cumin seeds. You can buy it ready-made or make your own.

2 Turn out on to a lightly floured surface and knead gently until smooth. Roll out to a thickness of about 3mm/⅛in.

3 Using a fluted biscuit (cookie) wheel, knife or pizza wheel, cut the dough into neat rectangles measuring about 7.5 x 2.5cm/3 x 1in. Brush with a little beaten egg and sprinkle each cracker with a few black onion seeds. Place on non-stick baking sheets and bake in the oven for about 12 minutes until the crackers are light golden brown all over.

4 Remove from the oven and transfer to a wire rack using a palette knife (metal spatula). Put a little garam masala in a saucer and, using a dry pastry brush, dust each cracker with a little of the spice mixture. Leave to cool before serving.

Chilli and Herb Crackers

These spicy, crisp little crackers are ideal for serving as a nibble with drinks and would also be an interesting alternative to bread or rolls served with a seafood appetizer.

Makes 12

50g/2oz/½ cup plain
  (all-purpose) flour
pinch of salt
5ml/1 tsp curry powder
1.5ml/¼ tsp chilli powder
15ml/1 tbsp chopped fresh
  coriander (cilantro)
30ml/2 tbsp water

1 Preheat the oven to 180°C/ 350°F/Gas 4. Sift the flour and salt into a mixing bowl, then add the curry powder and chilli powder and mix well. Make a well in the centre and add the chopped fresh coriander and water. Gradually incorporate the flour and mix to a firm dough.

2 Turn the dough out on to a lightly floured surface, knead until smooth, then cover and leave to rest for about 5 minutes.

3 Cut the dough into 12 even-size pieces and knead into small balls. Roll each ball out very thinly to a 10cm/4in round, sprinkling more flour over the dough if necessary to prevent it from sticking to the rolling pin.

4 Arrange the rounds on two ungreased baking sheets, spaced apart, then bake for 15 minutes, turning the crackers over once during cooking. Using a palette knife or metal spatula, transfer the rounds to a wire rack to cool.

Dill and Potato Cakes

Serve these light savoury cakes topped with thinly sliced smoked salmon and a spoonful of sour cream for a superb light lunch or dinner party appetizer.

Makes 10

225g/8oz/2 cups self-raising
*   (self-rising) flour*
40g/1½oz/3 tbsp butter
pinch of salt
15ml/1 tbsp finely chopped fresh dill
175g/6oz/2 cups mashed potato,
*   freshly made*
30–45ml/2–3 tbsp milk

Variation

For extra flavour, sift 2.5ml/½ tsp mustard powder with flour and add ½ finely chopped onion or 2 finely chopped spring onions (scallions) with the potato.

1 Preheat the oven to 230°C/ 450°F/Gas 8. Grease a baking sheet. Sift the flour into a bowl and add the butter, salt and dill. Stir in the potato and add enough milk to mix to a soft dough.

2 Roll out the dough until fairly thin. Cut into neat rounds with a floured 7.5cm/3in biscuit (cookie) cutter. Place the cakes on the prepared baking sheet and bake for 20–25 minutes.

Wholemeal Herb Triangles

These make a good lunchtime snack when filled with chicken and salad, and are also an ideal accompaniment to a bowl of steaming soup.

Makes 8

225g/8oz/2 cups wholemeal
   (whole-wheat) flour
115g/4oz/1 cup strong white bread flour
pinch of salt
2.5ml/½ tsp bicarbonate of soda
   (baking soda)
5ml/1 tsp cream of tartar
2.5ml/½ tsp chilli powder
50g/2oz/¼ cup margarine, diced
60ml/4 tbsp chopped mixed fresh herbs
250ml/8fl oz/1 cup skimmed milk
15ml/1 tbsp sesame seeds

1 Preheat the oven to 220°C/ 425°F/Gas 7. Lightly flour a baking sheet. Put the flours into a mixing bowl. Sift together the salt, bicarbonate of soda, cream of tartar and chilli powder into the bowl, then rub in the margarine with your fingertips until the mixture resembles coarse breadcrumbs.

Variation

To make Sun-dried Tomato Triangles, replace the fresh mixed herbs with 30ml/2 tbsp drained chopped sun-dried tomatoes in oil and add 15ml/1 tbsp each mild paprika, chopped fresh parsley and chopped fresh marjoram. Add to the mixture in step 2.

2 Add the mixed fresh herbs and milk and mix quickly but thoroughly to a soft dough. Turn out on to a lightly floured surface. Knead only very briefly or the dough will become tough.

3 Roll the dough out to a 23cm/9in round and place on the prepared baking sheet. Brush lightly with water and sprinkle the top evenly with the sesame seeds.

4 Carefully cut the dough round into eight wedges, separate them slightly and bake for 15–20 minutes, until golden brown. Using a metal spatula, transfer to a wire rack to cool. Serve warm or cold.

Herb and Garlic Twists

These twists are very short and crumbly, made with garlic-flavoured dough sandwiching with fresh herbs and some chilli flakes for an extra kick. A very popular party nibble.

Makes about 20

90g/3½oz/scant ½ cup butter, at room
   temperature, diced
2 large garlic cloves, crushed
1 egg
1 egg yolk
175g/6oz/1½ cups self-raising
   (self-rising) flour
large pinch of salt
30ml/2 tbsp chopped fresh mixed
   herbs, such as basil, thyme,
   marjoram and flat
   leaf parsley
2.5–5ml/½–1 tsp dried chilli flakes
paprika or cayenne pepper,
   for sprinkling

1 Preheat the oven to 200°C/400°F/ Gas 6. Put the butter and garlic into a bowl and beat well. Add the egg and yolk and beat in thoroughly. Stir in the flour and salt and mix to a soft but not sticky dough.

2 Roll the dough out on a sheet of baking parchment to a 28cm/11in square. Using a sharp knife, cut it in half to make two rectangles.

3 Sprinkle the herbs and chilli flakes over one of the rectangles, then place the other rectangle on top. Gently roll the rolling pin over the herbs and chilli flakes to press them into the dough.

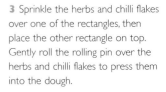

4 Using a sharp knife, cut the dough into 1cm/⅓in sticks. Make two twists in the centre of each one and place on a non-stick baking sheet.

5 Bake the twists for 15 minutes, or until crisp and golden brown. Leave on the baking sheet to cool slightly, then carefully transfer to a wire rack to cool completely. To serve, sprinkle with a little paprika or cayenne pepper, according to taste.

Cook's Tip

If the dough seems a little too soft to handle, wrap it in clear film (plastic wrap) and chill in the refrigerator for about 15 minutes to firm up. It will be much easier to roll it out.

Fennel and Chilli Rings

Based on an Italian recipe, these savoury bakes are made with yeast and are dry and crumbly. Try them with drinks, dips or with antipasti.

Makes about 30

500g/1lb 2oz/4½ cups type 00 flour
115g/4oz/½ cup white vegetable fat
5ml/1 tsp easy-blend (rapid-rise) yeast
15ml/1 tbsp fennel seeds
10ml/2 tsp crushed chilli flakes
15ml/1 tbsp olive oil
400–550ml/14–18fl oz/1⅔–2½ cups
    lukewarm water
olive oil, for brushing

1 Put the flour in a bowl and rub in the fat until the mixture resembles fine breadcrumbs. Add the yeast, fennel and chilli and mix well. Add the oil and enough water to make a soft but not sticky dough. Turn out on to a floured surface and knead lightly.

2 Take small pieces of dough and shape into sausages about 15cm/6in long. Shape into rings and pinch the ends together.

3 Place the rings on a non-stick baking sheet and brush lightly with olive oil. Cover with a dishtowel and set aside at room temperature for 1 hour to rise slightly.

4 Meanwhile, preheat the oven to 150°C/300°F/Gas 2. Bake the cookies for 1 hour until they are dry and only slightly browned. Leave on the baking sheet to cool completely.

Cook's Tip
Type 00 is an Italian grade of flour used for pasta. It is milled from the centre part of the endosperm so that the resulting flour is much whiter than plain (all-purpose) flour. It contains 70 per cent of the wheat grain. It is available from Italian delicatessens and some large supermarkets. If you cannot find it, try using strong white bread flour instead.

Bacon Twists

Making bread is always good fun, so try this simple savoury version and add that extra twist to breakfast or brunch. Choose good quality bacon, or try Italian pancetta or prosciutto for a change. Serve hot or warm with soft cheese with herbs for dipping or spreading.

Makes 12

450g/1lb/4 cups strong white
   bread flour
15ml/1 tbsp easy-blend (rapid-rise)
   dried yeast
pinch of salt
400ml/14fl oz/1¾ cups cups
   lukewarm water
12 streaky (fatty) bacon
   rashers (strips)
1 egg, beaten

1 Place the flour, yeast and salt in a large bowl and stir them together until well combined.

2 Add a little of the lukewarm water to the flour mixture and mix with a round-bladed knife. Add the remaining water and use the knife and then one of your hands to pull the mixture together, to make a soft, slightly sticky dough.

3 Turn the dough out on to a lightly floured surface and knead for about 5 minutes, or until the dough is smooth and stretchy.

4 Divide the dough into 12 even-sized pieces and roll each one into a fat sausage shape. Lightly brush a baking sheet with oil.

5 Place each bacon rasher on a chopping board and run the back of the knife along its length to stretch it slightly. Wind a rasher of bacon round each dough "sausage".

6 Brush the "sausages" with beaten egg and arrange them on the prepared baking sheet. Leave in a warm place for 30 minutes, or until doubled in size.

7 Preheat the oven to 200°C/400°F/Gas 6. Bake for 20–25 minutes until cooked and browned. Serve hot or warm with soft cheese.

Cook's Tips

The same basic dough mix can be used to make plain rolls or a loaf of bread. At the end of the cooking time, tap the base of the loaf with your knuckles – if it sounds hollow, it's cooked.

Variations

Make some meat-free versions of these twists for vegetarians by twisting the dough by hand and sprinkling with poppy or sesame seeds before baking.

Walnut Biscotti

These light crunchy cookies with toasted walnuts are flavoured with orange and coriander seeds.

Makes about 40

115g/4oz/½ cup unsalted (sweet)
   butter, diced
200g/7oz/1 cup granulated sugar
2 eggs
15ml/1 tbsp walnut or olive oil
finely grated rind of 1 large orange
350g/12oz/3 cups plain
   (all-purpose) flour
7.5ml/1½ tsp baking powder
75g/3oz/¾ cup cornmeal
115g/4oz/1 cup toasted walnuts, chopped
10ml/2 tsp coriander seeds, crushed

Cook's Tip

To toast the nuts, spread them on a baking sheet and place in the oven at 160°C/325°F/Gas 3 for 5–7 minutes until just beginning to brown.

1 Preheat the oven to 160°C/325°F/Gas 3. Put the butter and sugar into a bowl and beat together well. Add the eggs, walnut or olive oil and orange rind and mix well. Sift the flour and baking powder over the mixture and add the cornmeal, walnuts and coriander seeds. Mix thoroughly and bring together to form a soft but not sticky dough.

2 Shape the dough into four logs, about 18cm/7in long and 5cm/2in in diameter. Place slightly apart on non-stick baking sheets. Bake for 35 minutes until lightly golden.

3 Leave the logs for 10 minutes on wire racks, then slice diagonally into 1cm/½in slices. Place on the baking sheets and bake for 10 minutes.

Sun-dried Tomato Butter Cookies

These buttery cookies have all the flavours of classic pizza – cheese, tomato, oregano and olives.

Makes about 25
175g/6oz/1½ cups plain
  (all-purpose) flour
150g/5oz/10 tbsp unsalted (sweet)
  butter, chilled and diced
150g/5oz/1¼ cups grated mature (sharp)
  Cheddar cheese
15ml/1 tbsp sun-dried tomato paste
25g/1oz semi-dried sun-dried tomatoes,
  coarsely chopped
15ml/1 tbsp oregano
15g/½oz/2 tbsp pitted black olives, drained
15–30ml/1–2 tbsp cold water
50g/2oz sesame seeds

1 Put all the ingredients, except the water and sesame seeds, into a food processor. Process until the mixture forms fine crumbs.

2 Add enough water to mix to a soft dough, then shape it into a neat log about 25cm/10in long. Spread out the sesame seeds over a sheet of baking parchment or on a large plate. Roll the dough log in the seeds until the sides are thoroughly coated. Wrap in clear film (plastic wrap) and chill for about 2 hours.

3 Preheat the oven to 180°C/350°F/ Gas 4. Remove the clear film from the dough log. Using a long, sharp knife, slice the log into 5mm/¼in slices and place on non-stick baking sheets, spaced slightly apart. Bake for 15–20 minutes, or until golden brown. Transfer the cookies to a wire rack to cool.

Malted Wheat and Mixed Seed Crackers

These large crackers have plenty of crunch and flavour provided by the selection of different seeds that are used. They taste fabulous with robust farmhouse cheeses.

Makes 12–14

250g/9oz/2¼ cups Granary
   (whole-wheat) or malted wheat flour
2.5ml/½ tsp salt
2.5ml/½ tsp baking powder
115g/4oz/½ cup butter, chilled and diced
1 egg, beaten
30ml/2 tbsp milk, plus extra for brushing
15ml/1 tbsp pumpkin seeds
15ml/1 tbsp sunflower seeds
15ml/1 tbsp sesame seeds
2.5ml/½ tsp celery salt

1 Preheat the oven to 180°C/350°F/ Gas 4. Put the flour, salt, baking powder and butter in a bowl. Rub together until well combined.

2 Add the egg and milk and mix to a stiff dough. Roll out on a floured surface to about 5mm/¼in thick.

3 Using a pastry brush, brush a little milk over the rolled dough. Sprinkle all the pumpkin, sunflower and sesame seeds over the top in an even layer, then sprinkle the celery salt over the top.

4 Very gently, roll the rolling pin back and forth over the seeds to press them into the dough.

5 Stamp out rounds using a 10cm/4in plain cookie cutter, and place on a non-stick baking sheet, spacing them slightly apart. Alternatively, use a sharp knife to trim off the rough edges of the rolled out dough, then cut the dough into equal-size squares, rectangles or triangles.

6 Bake the crackers for about 15 minutes, or until just beginning to brown. Carefully transfer the crackers to a wire rack to cool completely.

Cook's Tips

• *To make your own celery salt, grind five parts lightly toasted celery seeds with one part sea salt. Transfer to an airtight container and store in a cool, dark place.*
• *You can also use other seeds if you prefer. Try using poppy seeds in place of the sesame seeds.*

Poppy Seed and Sea Salt Crackers

These attractive little crackers are ideal to use as the base of drinks party canapés, or they can be served plain as tasty nibbles in their own right.

Makes 20
115g/4oz/1 cup plain (all-purpose) flour
1.5ml/¼ tsp salt
5ml/1 tsp caster (superfine) sugar
15g/½oz/1 tbsp butter
15ml/1 tbsp poppy seeds
about 90ml/6 tbsp single (light) cream

For the topping
a little milk
sea salt flakes

Variation
You can use black or white poppy seeds – or a mixture of the two – for these crackers, or substitute sesame, caraway or celery seeds, if you like.

1 Preheat the oven to 150°C/ 300°F/Gas 2. Put the flour, salt and sugar in a bowl and rub in the butter. Stir in the poppy seeds. Add enough cream to mix to a stiff dough. Roll out on a lightly floured surface to a 20 x 25cm/8 x 10in rectangle. Cut into 20 squares.

2 Place the dough squares on an ungreased baking sheet and brush sparingly with milk. Sprinkle a few sea salt flakes over each cracker.

3 Bake in the oven for 30 minutes until crisp but still pale. Transfer to a wire rack to cool.

Rye and Caraway Seed Sticks

Wonderful with cocktails or pre-dinner drinks and a great addition to the cheese board, these long sticks are made with rye flour and have crunchy caraway seeds inside and out.

Makes 18–20

90g/3½oz/¾ cup plain (all-purpose) flour
75g/3oz/⅔ cup rye flour
2.5ml/½ tsp salt
2.5ml/½ tsp baking powder
90g/3½oz/7 tbsp unsalted (sweet)
    butter, diced
10ml/2 tsp caraway seeds
60ml/4 tbsp boiling water

1 Preheat the oven to 180°C/350°F/ Gas 4. Put the flours, salt and baking powder in a bowl and mix together. Add the butter and rub in until the mixture resembles fine breadcrumbs. Stir in 5ml/1 tsp of the caraway seeds. Add the water and mix well to form a soft dough.

2 Divide the dough into about 18 even-size pieces and, using your fingers, gently roll each one out to a long thin stick about 25cm/10in long. Do not use any flour when rolling out the sticks unless the mixture is a little too moist and try to make the sticks as uniform as possible.

3 Place the sticks on a non-stick baking sheet. Sprinkle over the remaining caraway seeds, rolling the sticks in any spilled seeds.

4 Bake the sticks in the oven for about 20 minutes until crisp. Remove from the oven and transfer carefully to a wire rack to cool.

Thyme and Mustard Biscuits

These aromatic biscuits are delicious served with herbed cheese as a light, savoury last course. Wrap them in cellophane and tie with string for a pretty gift.

Makes 40

175g/6oz/1½ cups wholemeal
   (whole-wheat) flour
50g/2oz/⅔ cup rolled oats
25g/1oz/2 tbsp caster (superfine) sugar
10ml/2 tsp baking powder
30ml/2 tbsp fresh thyme leaves
50g/2oz/¼ cup butter, diced
25g/1oz/2 tbsp white vegetable
   fat, diced
45ml/3 tbsp milk
10ml/2 tsp Dijon mustard
30ml/2 tbsp sesame seeds
salt and ground black pepper

1 Preheat the oven to 200°C/400°F/Gas 6. Grease two baking sheets. Put the flour, oats, sugar, baking powder, thyme leaves and seasoning into a bowl and mix together. Rub in the fats.

2 Mix the milk and mustard together and stir into the flour mixture until you have a soft dough.

3 Knead lightly on a floured surface then roll out to a thickness of 5mm/¼in. Stamp out 5cm/2in rounds with a floured fluted biscuit (cookie) cutter and arrange them, spaced slightly apart to allow room for spreading, on the baking sheets.

4 Re-roll the trimmings and continue stamping out rounds until all the dough is used. Prick the biscuits with a fork and sprinkle them with sesame seeds. Cook for 10–12 minutes until golden.

5 Leave to cool completely on the baking sheets, then pack the biscuits into a small airtight container. Store in a cool place for up to 5 days.

Wheat Thins

These classic wheat biscuits are especially delicious with rich-tasting creamy cheeses, and also make a quick snack simply spread with butter when you are in a hurry.

Makes 18

175g/6oz/1½ cups fine stoneground
   wholemeal (whole-wheat) flour
pinch of salt
5ml/1 tsp baking powder
50g/2oz/½ cup coarse oatmeal
40g/1½oz/3 tbsp granulated sugar
115g/4oz/½ cup unsalted (sweet) butter,
   chilled and diced

Cook's Tip

These cookies are perfect for serving with a cheeseboard and look very pretty cut into different shapes. You could make star-shaped cookies for Christmas, or heart-shaped ones for Valentine's Day.

1 Preheat the oven to 190°C/375°F/ Gas 5. Put all the ingredients into a food processor and process until the mixture starts to clump. Tip out on to a floured surface, gather the dough together with your hands and roll out.

2 Stamp out 18 rounds with a 7.5cm/3in round biscuit (cookie) cutter. Place on an ungreased baking sheet. Bake for 12 minutes until just beginning to colour at the edges. Leave to cool slightly, then transfer to a wire rack to cool completely.

Herby Seeded Oatcakes

The addition of thyme and sunflower seeds to this traditional recipe makes these oatcakes an especially good accompaniment to cheese – try them spread with goat's cheese or ripe Brie.

Makes 32

175g/6oz/1½ cups plain wholemeal (whole-wheat) flour
175g/6oz/1½ cups fine oatmeal
5ml/1 tsp salt
1.5ml/¼ tsp bicarbonate of soda (baking soda)
75g/3oz/6 tbsp white vegetable fat
15ml/1 tbsp fresh thyme leaves, chopped
30ml/2 tbsp sunflower seeds
rolled oats, for sprinkling

1 Preheat the oven to 150°C/300°F/Gas 2. Sprinkle two ungreased, non-stick baking sheets with rolled oats and set aside.

2 Put the flour, oats, salt and soda in a bowl and rub in the fat until the mixture resembles fine breadcrumbs. Stir in the thyme.

3 Add just enough cold water (about 90–105ml/6–7 tbsp) to the dry ingredients to mix to a stiff but not sticky dough.

4 Gently knead the dough on a lightly floured surface until smooth, then cut roughly in half and roll out one piece on a lightly floured surface to make a 23–25cm/9–10in round.

4 Sprinkle sunflower seeds over the dough and press them in with the rolling pin. Cut into triangles and arrange on one of the baking sheets. Repeat with the remaining dough. Bake for 45–60 minutes until crisp but not brown. Cool on wire racks.

Cream Cheese Spirals

Not totally savoury, yet not a sweet snack either, these attractive little spirals make delightfully adult canapés and are much easier to prepare than they look.

Makes 32

225g/8oz/1 cup butter
225g/8oz/1 cup cream cheese
10ml/2 tsp granulated sugar
225g/8oz/2 cups plain (all-purpose) flour
1 egg white beaten with 15ml/1 tbsp
    water, for glazing
granulated sugar, for sprinkling

For the filling

115g/4oz/1 cup walnuts or pecan nuts,
    finely chopped
75g/3oz/⅓ cup soft light brown sugar
5ml/1 tsp ground cinnamon

1 With an electric mixer, cream the butter, cream cheese and sugar until soft. Sift over the flour and mix to form a dough. Gather into a ball and divide in half. Flatten each piece, wrap in greaseproof (waxed) paper and chill for at least 30 minutes.

2 To make the filling, mix together the chopped walnuts or pecan nuts, brown sugar and cinnamon. Preheat the oven to 190°C/375°F/Gas 5. Grease two baking sheets.

3 Roll out each half of dough thinly into a round about 28cm/11in in diameter. Trim the edges with a knife, using a dinner plate as a guide.

4 Brush the surface with the egg white glaze and sprinkle each dough round evenly with half the filling.

5 With a sharp knife, cut each dough round into quarters and then cut each quarter into four sections, to form 32 triangles.

6 Starting from the base of the triangles, roll up to form spirals.

7 Place on the prepared baking sheets and brush with the remaining glaze. Sprinkle with granulated sugar. Bake for 15–20 minutes until golden. Cool on a wire rack.

Herb Popovers

These tasty puffs are really easy to prepare and cook. Serve as an imaginative alternative to garlic bread to accompany salads, soups and stews.

Makes 12

25g/1oz/2 tbsp butter
3 eggs
250ml/8fl oz/1 cup milk
175g/6oz/1½ cups plain
(all-purpose) flour
pinch of salt
1 small sprig each fresh herbs,
such as chives, tarragon, dill
and parsley

1 Preheat the oven to 220°C/425°F/ Gas 7. Grease 12 small ramekins or popover tins (pans). Melt the butter in a small pan over a low heat.

2 Beat the eggs in a bowl until well blended. Beat in the milk, then beat in the melted butter.

3 Sift together the flour and salt into another bowl, then gradually beat the flour and salt into the egg mixture.

4 Strip the herb leaves from the stems and chop finely. Stir 30ml/ 2 tbsp of the herbs into the batter.

5 Pour the batter into the prepared dishes or tins so they are half-full. Bake for 25–30 minutes, until golden. Do not open the oven door during baking time or the popovers may fall. For slightly drier popovers, pierce each one with a knife after 30 minutes baking time and bake for a further 5 minutes. Serve hot.

Cheese Popovers

Light-as-air and full of flavour, these moreish puffs are guaranteed to become a family favourite. Serve them as they are – fresh from the oven.

Makes 12

25ml/1½ tbsp butter
3 eggs
250ml/8fl oz/1 cup milk
75g/3oz/⅔ cup plain (all-purpose) flour
pinch of salt
1.5ml/¼ tsp paprika
75g/3oz/1 cup freshly grated
Parmesan cheese

1 Preheat the oven to 220°C/ 425°F/Gas 7. Grease 12 small ramekins or popover tins (pans). Melt the butter in a small pan over a low heat.

2 Beat the eggs until blended, then beat in the milk and melted butter.

3 Sift together the flour, salt, and paprika, then beat into the egg mixture. Stir in the cheese.

4 Fill the prepared ramekins or popover tins so they are half-full. Bake for 25–30 minutes until golden. Do not open the oven door during baking or the popovers will fall. For drier popovers, pierce each one with a knife after 30 minutes baking time and bake for a further 5 minutes. Serve hot.

Cook's Tip
Use an electric mixer to beat the batter to make sure that it is thoroughly blended and incorporates plenty of air.

Salted Peanut Biscuits

The combination of salt and sweet flavours in these little biscuits is delicious. The texture is delightfully crunchy and will appeal particularly to adult tastes.

Makes 70

250g/9oz/generous 1 cup soft light
  brown sugar, plus extra for dipping
350g/12oz/3 cups plain (all-purpose) flour
2.5ml/½ tsp bicarbonate of soda
  (baking soda)
115g/4oz/½ cup butter at room
  temperature, diced
115g/4oz/½ cup margarine
2 eggs
10ml/2 tsp vanilla essence (extract)
225g/8oz/2 cups salted peanuts

1 Preheat the oven to 190°C/
375°F/Gas 5. Lightly grease two
baking sheets. Grease the base of a
glass and dip in sugar.

2 Sift together the flour and
bicarbonate of soda and set aside.

3 With an electric mixer, cream the
butter, margarine and sugar until
light and fluffy. Beat in the eggs, one
at a time, and then the vanilla
essence. Gently fold in the flour
mixture with a metal spoon.

4 Add the peanuts and gently stir
them into the butter mixture until
evenly combined.

5 Drop teaspoonfuls of the
mixture, spaced 5cm/2in apart on
to the prepared baking sheets.
Flatten with the prepared glass.

6 Bake for about 10 minutes, until
lightly coloured. With a metal
spatula, carefully transfer to a wire
rack to cool.

Cheddar Pennies

Serve these tasty snacks with pre-dinner drinks. Choose a strong-flavoured Cheddar, or substitute Parmesan, Pecorino or a farmhouse Lancashire cheese.

Makes 20

50g/2oz/4 tbsp butter at room
  temperature, diced
115g/4oz/1 cup freshly grated
  Cheddar cheese
40g/1½oz/⅓ cup plain
  (all-purpose) flour
pinch of salt
pinch of chilli powder

1 With an electric mixer, cream the
butter until soft. Stir in the cheese,
flour, salt and chilli powder. Gather to
form a dough.

2 Transfer the dough to a lightly
floured work surface. Shape into a
long cylinder about 3cm/1¼in in
diameter. Wrap in greaseproof
(waxed) paper and chill for
1–2 hours.

3 Preheat the oven to 180°C/350°F/
Gas 4. Grease one large or two
medium-size baking sheets.

4 Cut the dough into 5mm/¼in
thick slices and place on the
prepared baking sheets. Bake for
about 15 minutes.

Parmesan Tuiles

These lacy tuiles look very impressive, but they couldn't be easier to make. Believe or not, they use only a single ingredient – Parmesan cheese.

Makes 8–10

115g/4oz Parmesan cheese

1 Preheat the oven to 200°C/400°F/ Gas 6. Line two baking sheets with baking parchment. Grate the cheese using a fine grater, pulling it down slowly to make long strands.

Cook's Tip

Tuiles can be made into little cup shapes by draping over an upturned egg cup. These little cups can be filled to make tasty treats to serve with drinks. Try a little cream cheese flavoured with herbs.

2 Spread the grated cheese out in 7.5–9cm/3–3½in rounds. Do not spread the cheese too thickly; it should just cover the parchment. Bake for 5–7 minutes until bubbling and golden brown.

3 Leave on the baking sheet for about 30 seconds and then carefully transfer, using a palette knife (metal spatula) to a wire rack. Alternatively, drape over a rolling pin to make a curved shape.

Savoury Parmesan Puffs

Serve these tasty popovers with home-made soup or salad for a sustaining lunch or to accompany an appetizer for an impressive start to a dinner party menu.

Makes 6

115g/4oz/1¼ cups freshly grated
    Parmesan cheese
115g/4oz/1 cup plain (all-purpose) flour
pinch of salt
15ml/1 tbsp butter or margarine
2 eggs
250ml/8fl oz/1 cup milk

1 Preheat the oven to 230°C/450°F/Gas 8. Grease six individual baking tins (pans). Sprinkle each tin with 15ml/1 tbsp of the grated Parmesan. Alternatively, you can use ramekins, in which case, heat them on a baking sheet in the oven then grease and sprinkle with Parmesan just before filling.

2 Sift the flour and salt into a small bowl. Set aside. Melt the butter or margarine in a small pan.

3 Beat together the eggs, milk and melted butter or margarine in a mixing bowl. Add the flour mixture and stir until smoothly blended.

Variation

You could also use another hard or semi-hard cheese, such as Pecorino, Gruyère or Emmenthal.

4 Divide the batter evenly among the containers, filling each one about half-full. Bake for 15 minutes, then sprinkle the tops of the puffs with the remaining Parmesan.

5 Reduce the oven temperature to 180°C/350°F/Gas 4 and continue baking for 20–25 minutes, or until the puffs are firm and golden brown.

6 Remove the puffs from the oven. To unmould, run a thin knife around the inside of each container to loosen them. Gently ease out, then transfer to a wire rack to cool.

Tiny Cheese Puffs

These bitesize portions of choux pastry are the ideal accompaniment to a glass of chilled white wine or to cocktails before dinner. They are delicious on their own, but are also good split and filled with garlic-flavoured soft white cheese, or mascarpone flavoured with fresh parsley.

Makes 45

115g/4oz/1 cup plain (all-purpose) flour
pinch of salt
5ml/1 tsp mustard powder
pinch of cayenne pepper
250ml/8fl oz/1 cup water
115g/4oz/½ cup butter, diced
4 eggs
75g/3oz Gruyère cheese, finely diced
15ml/1 tbsp finely chopped fresh chives

1 Preheat the oven to 200°C/400°F/ Gas 6. Lightly grease two large baking sheets.

2 Sift together the flour, salt, mustard powder and cayenne pepper.

Variations

To make Ham and Cheese Puffs, add 50g/2oz/⅓ cup finely diced ham or prosciutto with the cheese. For Cheese Herb Puffs, stir in 30ml/2 tbsp chopped fresh herbs or spring onions (scallions) with the cheese.

Cook's Tip

The puffs can be prepared ahead and are suitable for freezing. Thaw at room temperature for an hour or so, then reheat them in a hot oven for about 5 minutes, until crisp, before serving.

3 In a pan, bring the water and butter to the boil over a medium-high heat. Remove the pan from the heat and add the flour mixture all at once, beating with a wooden spoon until the dough forms a ball.

4 Return the pan to the heat and beat constantly for 1–2 minutes to dry out. Remove the pan from the heat and cool for 3–5 minutes.

5 Beat three of the eggs into the dough, one at a time, beating well after each addition.

6 Beat the fourth egg in a separate small bowl and add to the dough a teaspoon at a time, beating until the dough is smooth and shiny and falls slowly when dropped from a spoon. (You may not need all of the fourth egg; reserve any remaining egg for glazing.)

7 Stir the diced cheese and chives into the dough.

8 Using two teaspoons, drop small mounds of dough, spaced about 5cm/2in apart, on to the prepared baking sheets.

9 Beat any remaining egg with 15ml/1 tbsp water and brush the tops of the choux puffs with the glaze.

10 Bake for 8 minutes, then reduce the oven temperature to 180°C/350°F/Gas 4 and bake the puffs for a further 7–8 minutes until puffed and golden. Transfer to a wire rack to cool. Serve warm.

Three-cheese Crumble Cookies

A delicious combination of mozzarella, Red Leicester and Parmesan cheese and the fresh taste of pesto make these cookies totally irresistible. Make mini ones to serve with drinks.

Makes 10

225g/8oz/2 cups self-raising
  (self-rising) flour
50g/2oz/¼ cup butter, diced
50g/2oz mozzarella cheese, diced
50g/2oz Red Leicester cheese, diced
15ml/1 tbsp fresh pesto
1 egg
60ml/4 tbsp milk
15g/½oz/2 tbsp grated Parmesan cheese
15ml/1 tbsp mixed chopped nuts

1 Preheat the oven to 200°C/400°F/ Gas 6. Put the flour in a bowl and rub in the butter until the mixture resembles fine breadcrumbs.

2 Add the diced mozzarella and Red Leicester cheeses to the bowl and stir to mix well. In a separate bowl, beat together the pesto, egg and milk, then pour into the flour and cheese mixture. Stir together quickly until well combined.

3 Using a tablespoon, place in rocky piles on non-stick baking sheets. Sprinkle over the Parmesan cheese and chopped nuts. Bake for 12–15 minutes until well risen and golden brown. Transfer to a wire rack to cool.

Blue Cheese and Chive Crisps

A classic combination and one that never fails to please – serve these tasty crackers with a selection of dips and spreads as part of a party buffet.

Makes 48

225g/8oz/2 cups crumbled blue cheese
115g/4oz/½ cup unsalted (sweet) butter
   at room temperature, diced
1 egg
1 egg yolk
30ml/2 tsp chopped fresh chives
225g/8oz/2 cups plain (all-purpose)
   flour, sifted
ground black pepper

1 The day before serving, beat together the cheese and butter until well blended. Add the egg, egg yolk, chives and a little pepper and beat until just blended.

2 Add the flour in three batches, folding in between each addition.

Cook's Tip

The cheese crisps will keep for up to 10 days in an airtight container.

3 Divide the dough in half and then shape each half into a log about 5cm/2in in diameter. Wrap in greaseproof (waxed) paper and chill overnight. Preheat the oven to 190°C/375°F/Gas 5. Lightly grease two baking sheets.

4 Using a sharp knife, cut the dough logs across into slices about 3mm/⅛in thick. Place on the prepared baking sheets. Bake for about 10 minutes, until just golden around the edges. With a metal spatula, transfer to a wire rack to cool.

Wisconsin Cheddar and Chive Biscuits

These soft-textured biscuits are almost like scones. They are delicious warm, split and spread with butter. Serve with soup or to accompany a rich-flavoured stew.

Makes 20

200g/7oz/1¾ cups plain
* (all-purpose) flour*
10ml/2 tsp baking powder
2.5ml/½ tsp bicarbonate of soda
* (baking soda)*
pinch of salt
1.5ml/¼ tsp ground black pepper
65g/2½oz/5 tbsp unsalted (sweet)
* butter, diced*
50g/2oz/½ cup grated mature (sharp)
* Cheddar cheese*
30ml/2 tbsp chopped
* fresh chives*
175ml/6fl oz/¾ cup buttermilk

1 Preheat the oven to 200°C/400°F/ Gas 6. Grease a baking sheet.

2 Sift the flour, baking powder, bicarbonate of soda, salt and pepper into a large bowl. Add the butter and rub it into the dry ingredients with your fingertips until the mixture resembles coarse breadcrumbs. Add the cheese and chives and stir to mix.

3 Make a well in the centre of the mixture. Add the buttermilk and stir vigorously until the mixture comes away from the sides of the bowl.

4 Drop in 30ml/2 tbsp mounds spaced 5–7.5cm/2–3in apart on the prepared baking sheet. Bake for 12–15 minutes until golden brown.

Corn Oysters

Fried rather than baked, these savoury snacks are best served hot by themselves or as an accompaniment to meat or chicken dishes.

Makes about 8

150g/5oz/1 cup grated fresh
* corn kernels*
1 egg, separated
30ml/2 tbsp plain
* (all-purpose) flour*
pinch of salt
1.5ml/¼ tsp ground black pepper
25–50g/1–2oz/2–4 tbsp butter
* or margarine*
30–60ml/2–4 tbsp vegetable oil

1 Combine the grated corn kernels, egg yolk and flour in a bowl. Mix well. Add the salt and black pepper.

2 In a separate, grease-free bowl, whisk the egg white until it forms stiff peaks. Carefully fold it into the corn mixture with a metal spoon.

3 Heat 25g/2 tbsp butter or margarine with 30ml/2 tbsp of the oil in a heavy frying pan.

4 When the fats are very hot and almost smoking, drop tablespoonfuls of the corn mixture into the pan. Cook over a medium heat until crisp and brown on the undersides.

5 Turn the "oysters" over with a spatula and cook for 1–2 minutes on the other side. Drain well on kitchen paper and keep hot. Continue frying the remaining "oysters", adding more fat as necessary.

Cheese Straws

Everyone loves these crisp, cheesy sticks, so it is fortunate that they are so quick and easy to make. They are perfect for serving with pre-dinner drinks or as party snacks.

Makes 50 straws and 8 rings
115g/4oz/1 cup plain (all-purpose) flour, plus extra for dusting
5ml/1 tsp mustard powder
pinch of salt
115g/4oz/½ cup butter
75g/3oz/¾ cup grated Cheddar cheese
pinch of cayenne pepper
30ml/2 tbsp water
1 egg, beaten

1 Preheat the oven to 200°C/400°F/Gas 6. Grease two baking sheets. Sift the flour, mustard powder and salt into a bowl and rub in the butter until the mixture resembles fine breadcrumbs.

2 Stir in the grated cheese and cayenne pepper and sprinkle on the water. Add half the beaten egg, mix to a firm dough and knead lightly until smooth.

3 Roll out the dough pastry on a lightly floured surface and cut into strips about 10cm/4in long and 5mm/¼in wide.

4 Gather up the trimmings, roll them out and stamp out rounds using two biscuit (cookie) cutters of different sizes, a 6cm/2½in one to cut out the round and a 5cm/2in diameter one to stamp out the centre to make rings.

5 Arrange the straws and rings on the baking sheets, brush with egg and bake for 8–10 minutes.

6 Leave on the baking sheets to cool slightly for about 2 minutes, then transfer to wire racks to cool completely. To serve, push six or seven straws through each ring.

Variation
You can use other types of cheese for making the pastry. Try Parmesan, Pecorino, Emmenthal, Mahon or, for extra colour, red Leicester. For a less spicy flavour, substitute sweet paprika for the cayenne pepper.

Cook's Tip
Some or all of the cheese straws can be sprinkled with poppy, sunflower and/or sesame seeds before baking. A mixture of plain and coated straws looks attractive.

Festive Nibbles

Shape these spicy cheese snacks in any way you wish – stars, crescent moons, triangles, squares, hearts, bars or rounds. Serve them with drinks, from ice-cold cocktails to hot and spicy mulls.

Makes 60
115g/4oz/1 cup plain (all-purpose) flour, plus extra for dusting
5ml/1 tsp mustard powder
pinch of salt
115g/4oz/½ cup butter
75g/3oz/¾ cup grated Cheddar cheese
pinch of cayenne pepper
30ml/2 tbsp water
1 egg, beaten
poppy seeds, sunflower seeds or sesame seeds, to decorate

1 Preheat the oven to 200°C/400°F/Gas 6. Grease two baking sheets. Sift the flour, mustard powder and salt into a bowl and rub in the butter until the mixture resembles fine breadcrumbs.

2 Stir in the grated cheese and cayenne pepper and sprinkle on the water. Add half the beaten egg, mix to a firm dough and knead lightly until smooth.

3 Roll out the dough on a lightly floured surface and cut out a variety of shapes with cutters or freehand with a sharp knife. Re-roll the trimmings and cut out more shapes.

4 Place on the prepared baking sheets and brush with the remaining egg. Sprinkle on the seeds. Bake for 8–10 minutes until golden. Transfer to wire racks to cool completely before serving.

Wholesome Bites

When anyone is trying to lose weight or eat a
healthier diet, the first items to be scrapped
are almost always cookies, but this doesn't
have to be the case. The recipes in this chapter
are nutritious and delicious, packed with fruit,
fibre and flavour. Many are low in fat and use
natural sweeteners rather than refined sugars.
You don't even have to sacrifice "chocolate"
cookies. They are the perfect pick-me-up for
adults and ideal for after-school snacks.

Coconut Oat Cookies

Toasting the oats and coconut before mixing them with the other ingredients is the secret of both the delicious flavour and the lovely crunchy texture of these cookies. You'll need to keep an eye on the oats and coconut, as they will burn if cooked too long.

Makes 18

115g/4oz/½ cup granulated sugar

175g/6oz/2 cups quick-cooking oats

75g/3oz/1 cup shredded coconut

225g/8oz/1 cup butter or margarine
   at room temperature, diced

40g/1½oz/¼ cup firmly packed dark
   brown soft sugar

2 eggs

60ml/4 tbsp milk

7.5ml/1½ tsp vanilla
   essence (extract)

115g/4oz/1 cup plain
   (all-purpose) flour

2.5ml/½ tsp bicarbonate of soda
   (baking soda)

pinch of salt

5ml/1 tsp ground cinnamon

1 Preheat the oven to 200°C/400°F/ Gas 6. Lightly grease two baking sheets. Grease the base of a glass and dip in some granulated sugar.

2 Spread the oats and coconut on an ungreased baking sheet. Bake for 8–10 minutes until golden brown, stirring occasionally.

3 Cream the fat and both sugars. Beat in the eggs, then add the milk and vanilla. Sift the dry ingredients and fold in. Stir in the oat mixture.

4 Drop spoonfuls of the dough on to the baking sheets and flatten with the sugared glass. Bake for 8–10 minutes. Cool on a wire rack.

Crunchy Jumbles

Making up your mind about whether you prefer milk or plain chocolate chips is the perfect excuse for baking another batch of these tasty cookies.

Makes 36

115g/4oz/½ cup butter or margarine
   at room temperature, diced

225g/8oz/1 cup granulated sugar

1 egg

5ml/1 tsp vanilla essence (extract)

175g/6oz/1¼ cups plain
   (all-purpose) flour

2.5ml/½ tsp bicarbonate of soda
   (baking soda)

pinch of salt

115g/4oz/2 cups crisped
   rice cereal

175g/6oz/1 cup chocolate chips

1 Preheat the oven to 180°C/350°F/ Gas 4. Lightly grease two or three large baking sheets.

2 With an electric mixer, cream the butter or margarine and sugar until light and fluffy. Beat in the egg and vanilla essence. Sift over the flour, bicarbonate of soda and salt and fold in until just mixed.

Variation
To make Crunchy Walnut Jumbles, add 50g/2oz/½ cup walnuts, coarsely chopped, with the cereal and chocolate.

3 Add the cereal and chocolate chips and stir thoroughly to mix. Drop spoonfuls of the dough on to the baking sheets. Bake for 10–12 minutes until golden and cooked. Transfer to a wire rack to cool.

Crunchy Oatmeal Cookies

Any-time-of-day cookies, these are delicious with morning coffee or as a great after-school treat for hungry children. The combination of crunchy cereal and oats is highly nutritious, providing protein, carbohydrate, vitamins and minerals – and the cookies taste wonderful.

Makes 14

175g/6oz/¾ cup butter or margarine
   at room temperature, diced
125g/4½oz/¾ cup caster
   (superfine) sugar
1 egg yolk
175g/6oz/1½ cups plain (all-purpose)
   flour, plus extra for dusting
5ml/1 tsp bicarbonate of soda
   (baking soda)
pinch of salt
40g/1½oz/½ cup rolled oats
40g/1½oz/½ cup crunchy nugget cereal

1 Cream the butter or margarine and sugar together until light and fluffy. Mix in the egg yolk.

2 Sift over the flour, bicarbonate of soda and salt, then stir into the butter mixture. Add the oats and cereal and stir to blend. Chill for at least 20 minutes.

3 Preheat the oven to 190°C/375°F/ Gas 5. Grease a baking sheet. Flour the base of a wide, heavy glass.

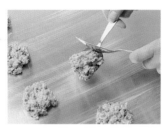

4 Using two spoons, drop teaspoons of the dough on to the prepared baking sheet, spaced well apart. Gently flatten them with the floured base of the glass, dusting it with more flour if necessary.

5 Bake for 10–12 minutes until golden. With a metal spatula, transfer the cookies to a wire rack. Allow to cool completely before serving or storing.

Variation

To make nutty oatmeal cookies, substitute an equal quantity of chopped walnuts or pecan nuts for the cereal, and prepare as described in the recipe.

Cook's Tip

These cookies will store for a week in an airtight container.

Granola Cookies

These are popular American cookies, so they also have an American name. If they were British, they would be called muesli biscuits. Whatever the name, they are packed with flavour. Use almonds, peanuts or pistachios in place of the walnuts, if you prefer.

Makes 18

115g/4oz/½ cup butter or margarine
  at room temperature, diced
75g/3oz/½ cup soft light brown sugar
75g/3oz/⅓ cup crunchy peanut butter
1 egg
50g/2oz/½ cup plain (all-purpose) flour
2.5ml/½ tsp baking powder
2.5ml/½ tsp ground cinnamon
pinch of salt
225g/8oz/2 cups muesli (granola)
50g/2oz/⅓ cup raisins
50g/2oz/½ cup walnuts, chopped

1 Preheat the oven to 180°C/350°F/ Gas 4. Lightly grease two baking sheets. Put the butter or margarine in a large bowl.

2 With an electric mixer, cream the butter or margarine and sugar until light and fluffy. Beat in the peanut butter, then beat in the egg.

3 Sift together the flour, baking powder, cinnamon and salt over the peanut butter mixture and stir with a wooden spoon to blend well.

4 Add the muesli, raisins and chopped walnuts and stir well.

5 Drop rounded tablespoonfuls of the dough on to the prepared baking sheets, spacing them about 2.5cm/1in apart. Press gently with the back of a spoon to spread each mound into a round.

6 Bake the cookies for about 15 minutes until lightly coloured. Remove the baking sheets from the oven and, with a metal spatula, transfer the cookies to a wire rack. Leave to cool completely.

Low-fat Orange Oaties

These are so delicious that it is difficult to believe that they are healthy too. As they are packed with flavour and wonderfully crunchy, the whole family will love them.

Makes about 16

175g/6oz/¾ cup clear honey
120ml/4fl oz/½ cup orange juice
90g/3½oz/1 cup rolled oats,
   lightly toasted
115g/4oz/1 cup plain (all-purpose) flour
115g/4oz/generous ½ cup golden caster
   (superfine) sugar
finely grated rind of 1 orange
5ml/1 tsp bicarbonate of soda
   (baking soda)

1 Preheat the oven to 180°C/350°F/ Gas 4. Line two baking sheets with baking parchment

2 Put the honey and orange juice in a small pan and simmer over a low heat for 8–10 minutes, stirring occasionally, until the mixture is thick and syrupy.

3 Put the oats, flour, sugar and orange rind into a bowl. Mix the bicarbonate of soda with 15ml/ 1 tbsp boiling water and add to the flour mixture, together with the honey and orange syrup. Mix well with a wooden spoon.

4 Place spoonfuls of the mixture on to the prepared baking sheets, spaced slightly apart, and bake for 10–12 minutes, or until golden brown. Leave to cool on the sheets for 5 minutes before transferring to a wire rack to cool completely.

Apricot Yogurt Cookies

These soft cookies are very quick to make and are perfect for children's school lunches, as they taste great and are low in fat, not too sweet and full of natural goodness.

Makes about 16

175g/6oz/1½ cups plain
   (all-purpose) flour
5ml/1 tsp baking powder
5ml/1 tsp ground cinnamon
75g/3oz/scant 1 cup rolled oats
75g/3oz/⅓ cup light muscovado
   (brown) sugar
115g/4oz/¾ cup chopped ready-to-eat
   dried apricots
15ml/1 tbsp flaked (sliced) hazelnuts
   or almonds
150g/5oz/⅔ cup natural
   (plain) yogurt
45ml/3 tbsp sunflower oil
demerara (raw) sugar,
   for sprinkling

1 Preheat the oven to 190°C/375°F/ Gas 5. Lightly grease a large baking sheet.

2 Sift together the flour, baking powder and cinnamon. Stir in the oats, sugar, apricots and nuts.

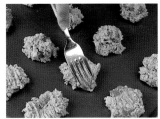

3 Beat together the yogurt and sunflower oil, then stir evenly into the flour mixture to make a firm dough. If necessary, add a little more yogurt. Use the palms of your hands to roll the mixture into about 16 small balls.

4 Place the balls on the prepared baking sheet and flatten gently with a fork. Sprinkle with demerara sugar. Bake for 15–20 minutes until firm and golden brown. With a spatula, transfer to a wire rack and leave to cool completely.

Cook's Tip
These moist cookies do not keep well, so it is best to eat them within 2 days, or to freeze them. Pack the cookies into plastic bags and freeze for up to 4 months.

Chewy Flapjacks

Flapjacks are about the easiest cookies to make and, with a little guidance, can be knocked up in minutes by even the youngest cooks. This chunky, chewy version is flavoured with orange rind.

Makes 18
250g/9oz/generous 1 cup unsalted
  (sweet) butter
finely grated rind of 1 large orange
225g/8oz/⅔ cup golden (light corn) syrup
75g/3oz/⅓ cup light muscovado
  (brown) sugar
375g/13oz/3¾ cups rolled oats

1 Preheat the oven to 180°C/350°F/Gas 4. Line the base and sides of a 28 x 20cm/11 x 8in shallow baking tin (pan) with baking parchment.

2 Put the butter, orange rind, syrup and sugar in a large pan and heat gently until the butter has melted.

3 Add the oats to the pan and stir to mix thoroughly. Tip the mixture into the tin and spread into the corners in an even layer.

4 Bake for 15–20 minutes until just beginning to colour around the edges. (The mixture will still be very soft but will harden as it cools.) Leave to cool in the tin.

5 Lift the flapjack out of the tin in one piece and cut into fingers.

Cook's Tip
Don't be tempted to overcook flapjacks; they'll turn crisp and dry and lose their lovely chewy texture.

Apricot and Pecan Flapjack

A tried-and-tested favourite made even more delicious by the addition of maple syrup, fruit and nuts. This is a real energy booster at any time of day – great for kids and adults alike.

Makes 10

150g/5oz/⅔ cup unsalted (sweet) butter, diced

150g/5oz/⅔ cup light muscovado (brown) sugar

30ml/2 tbsp maple syrup

200g/7oz/2 cups rolled oats

50g/2oz/½ cup pecan nuts, chopped

50g/2oz/¼ cup ready-to-eat dried apricots, chopped

Variations

• You can substitute walnuts for the pecan nuts if you like, although the nutty flavour won't be so intense.

• Use different dried fruits instead of the apricots if you like. Let children choose their own.

I Preheat the oven to 160°C/325°F/ Gas 3. Lightly grease an 18cm/7in square shallow baking tin (pan). Put the butter, sugar and maple syrup in a large heavy pan and heat gently until the butter has melted. Remove from the heat and stir in the oats, nuts and apricots until well combined.

2 Spread evenly in the prepared tin and, using a knife, score the mixture into ten bars. Bake for about 25–30 minutes, or until golden.

3 Remove from the oven and cut through the scored lines. Leave until completely cold before removing from the tin.

Ker-runch Cookies

An unusual coating of bran flakes covers these small cookies – a painless way of making sure that you have plenty of fibre in your diet. They are fun to make too.

Makes about 18
175g/6oz/¾ cup vegetable margarine
175g/6oz/¾ cup light muscovado
  (brown) sugar
1 egg
175g/6oz/1½ cups self-raising
  (self-rising) wholemeal
  (whole-wheat) flour
115g/4oz/generous 1 cup rolled oats
115g/4oz/⅔ cup mixed dried fruit
50g/2oz/2 cups bran flakes
  breakfast cereal

1 Preheat the oven to 160°C/325°F/ Gas 3. Line two baking sheets with baking parchment. Put the margarine and sugar in a bowl and beat until pale and creamy.

2 Add the egg to the margarine mixture and beat in until thoroughly combined. Stir in the flour, oats and fruit. Roll into walnut-size balls between the palms of your hands. Spread out the bran flakes on a shallow plate and roll the balls in them to coat.

3 Place on the prepared baking sheets and flatten each one gently with your hand.

4 Bake for about 20 minutes until firm and golden brown. Remove from the baking sheets while still hot as these cookies firm up very quickly. Place on a wire rack to cool.

Fruity Breakfast Bars

Instead of buying fruit and cereal bars from the supermarket, try making this quick and easy version – they are tastier and more nutritious than most of the commercially-made ones.

Makes 12

270g/10oz jar apple sauce
115g/4oz/½ cup ready-to-eat dried
    apricots, chopped
115g/4oz/¾ cup raisins
50g/2oz/¼ cup demerara (raw) sugar
50g/2oz/⅓ cup sunflower seeds
25g/1oz/2 tbsp sesame seeds
25g/1oz/¼ cup pumpkin seeds
75g/3oz/scant 1 cup rolled oats
75g/3oz/⅔ cup self-raising (self-rising)
    wholemeal (whole-wheat) flour
50g/2oz/⅔ cup desiccated (dry
    unsweetened shredded) coconut
2 eggs

Cook's Tip

Allow the baking parchment to hang over the edges of the tin; this makes baked bars easier to remove.

1 Preheat the oven to 200°C/400°F/ Gas 6. Grease a 20cm/8in square shallow baking tin (pan) and line with baking parchment.

2 Put the apple sauce in a large bowl with the apricots, raisins, sugar and the sunflower, sesame and pumpkin seeds and stir together with a wooden spoon until thoroughly mixed.

3 Add the oats, flour, coconut and eggs to the fruit mixture and gently stir together until evenly combined.

4 Turn the mixture into the tin and spread to the edges in an even layer. Bake for about 25 minutes or until golden and just firm to the touch.

5 Leave to cool in the tin, then lift out on to a board and cut into bars.

Chewy Fruit Muesli Slice

An easy recipe that needs just measuring out, mixing together, pressing into a cake tin and baking. The only other instruction is to eat it – and you will find that it tastes delicious.

Makes 8

75g/3oz/¾ cup ready-to-eat dried
   apricots, chopped
I eating apple, cored and grated
150g/5oz/1¼ cups Swiss-style
   muesli (granola)
150ml/¼ pint/⅔ cup apple juice
15g/½oz/1 tbsp soft
   sunflower margarine

I Preheat the oven to 190°C/375°F/ Gas 5. Place all five of the ingredients in a large bowl and mix well with a wooden spoon.

2 Press the mixture into a 20cm/ 8in non-stick sandwich tin (layer pan) and bake for 35–40 minutes, or until lightly browned and firm.

3 Mark the muesli slice into eight equal wedges with the blade of a knife and leave to cool completely in the tin.

Malted Oaty Crisps

These sweet cookies are made with rolled oats and flavoured with malt. They are very crisp and crunchy and so are ideal to serve with morning coffee or a cup of tea in the afternoon.

Makes 18

175g/6oz/1½ cups rolled oats
75g/3oz/⅓ cup light muscovado
  (brown) sugar
1 egg
60ml/4 tbsp sunflower oil
30ml/2 tbsp malt extract

Variation

To give these crisp cookies a coarser texture, substitute jumbo oats for some or all of the rolled oats.

1 Preheat the oven to 190°C/375°F/ Gas 5. Lightly grease two baking sheets. Mix the rolled oats and muscovado sugar in a bowl, breaking up any lumps in the sugar. Add the egg, sunflower oil and malt extract, mix well, then leave to soak for about 15 minutes.

2 Using a teaspoon, place small heaps of the mixture well apart on the baking sheets. Press the heaps into 7.5cm/3in rounds with the back of a dampened fork.

3 Bake for 10–15 minutes until golden brown. Leave to cool for 1 minute, then remove to cool on a wire rack.

Almond, Orange and Carrot Bars

An out-of-this-world cookie version of the ever-popular carrot cake, these flavoursome, moist bars are best eaten fresh or stored in the refrigerator after making.

Makes 16

75g/3oz/6 tbsp unsalted (sweet)
 butter, softened
50g/2oz/¼ cup caster (superfine) sugar
150g/5oz/1¼ cups plain
 (all-purpose) flour
finely grated rind of 1 orange

For the filling

90g/3½oz/7 tbsp unsalted (sweet)
 butter, diced
75g/3oz/scant ½ cup caster
 (superfine) sugar
2 eggs
2.5ml/½ tsp almond essence (extract)
175g/6oz/1½ cups ground almonds
1 cooked carrot, coarsely grated

For the topping

175g/6oz/¾ cup cream cheese
30–45ml/2–3 tbsp chopped walnuts

1 Preheat the oven to 190°C/375°F/ Gas 5. Lightly grease a 28 x 18cm/ 11 x 7in shallow baking tin (pan). Put the butter, caster sugar, flour and orange rind into a bowl and rub together until the mixture resembles coarse breadcrumbs. Add water, a teaspoon at a time, to mix to a firm but not sticky dough. Roll out on a lightly floured surface and use to line the base of the tin.

2 To make the filling, cream the butter and sugar together. Beat in the eggs and almond essence. Stir in the ground almonds and the grated carrot. Spread the mixture over the dough base and bake for about 25 minutes until firm in the centre and golden brown. Leave to cool in the tin.

3 To make the topping, beat the cream cheese until smooth and spread it over the cooled, cooked filling. Swirl with a small palette knife (metal spatula) and sprinkle with the chopped walnuts. Cut into bars with a sharp knife.

Tropical Fruit Slice

Densely packed dried exotic fruits make the filling for these deliciously moist bars. They make a popular after-school snack for hungry kids, or pop one into their lunch box as a surprise.

Makes 12–16

175g/6oz/1½ cups plain
   (all-purpose) flour
90g/3½oz/generous ½ cup white
   vegetable fat (shortening)
60ml/4 tbsp apricot jam, sieved, or
   ready-made apricot glaze

For the filling

115g/4oz/½ cup unsalted (sweet)
   butter, softened
115g/4oz/generous ½ cup caster
   (superfine) sugar
1 egg, beaten
25g/1oz/¼ cup ground almonds
25g/1oz/2½ tbsp ground rice
300g/11oz/scant 2 cups ready-to-eat
   mixed dried tropical fruits, chopped

1 Preheat the oven to 180°C/350°F/ Gas 4. Lightly grease a 28 x 18cm/ 11 x 7in tin (pan). Put the flour and vegetable fat in a bowl and rub in with your fingers until the mixture resembles fine breadcrumbs. Add enough water to mix to a firm dough.

2 Roll out on a lightly floured surface and use to line the base of the prepared tin. Spread 30ml/ 2 tbsp of the jam or glaze over the dough.

3 To make the filling, cream together the butter and sugar until light and creamy. Beat in the egg, then stir in the almonds, rice and mixed fruits. Spread the mixture evenly in the tin.

4 Bake for about 35 minutes. Remove from the oven and brush with the remaining jam or glaze. Leave to cool completely in the tin before cutting into bars.

Cook's Tip

If you cannot find a ready-mixed packet of dried tropical fruits, make your own fruit mixture, choosing from the following: mangoes, apricots, guavas, dates, apples, pears, nectarines, peaches, figs and whatever else takes your fancy.

Spicy Fruit Slice

A double-layered sweet cookie in which the topping combines dried fruit, with grated carrot to keep it moist. An indulgent teatime treat.

Makes 12–16

90g/3½oz/7 tbsp vegetable margarine
75g/3oz/scant ½ cup caster
   (superfine) sugar
1 egg yolk
115g/4oz/1 cup plain (all-purpose) flour
30ml/2 tbsp self-raising (self-rising) flour
30ml/2 tbsp desiccated (dry unsweetened
   shredded) coconut
icing (confectioners') sugar, for dusting

For the topping

30ml/2 tbsp ready-to-eat
   prunes, chopped
30ml/2 tbsp sultanas (golden raisins)
50g/2oz/½ cup ready-to-eat dried
   pears, chopped
25g/1oz/¼ cup walnuts, chopped
75g/3oz/⅔ cup self-raising
   (self-rising) flour
5ml/1 tsp ground cinnamon
2.5ml/½ tsp ground ginger
175g/6oz/generous 1 cup grated carrots
1 egg, beaten
75ml/5 tbsp vegetable oil
2.5ml/½ tsp bicarbonate of soda
   (baking soda)
90g/3½oz/scant ½ cup dark muscovado
   (molasses) sugar

1 Preheat the oven to 180°C/350°F/
Gas 4. Line a 28 x 18cm/11 x 7in
shallow baking tin (pan) with
baking parchment. In a large mixing
bowl beat together the margarine,
sugar and egg yolk until smooth
and creamy.

Cook's Tip

*There is no need to peel the carrots
before grating them. Just give them a
good scrub to remove any dirt.*

2 Stir in the plain flour, self-raising
flour and coconut and mix together
well. Press into the base of the
prepared tin, using your fingers to
spread the dough evenly. Bake for
about 15 minutes, or until firm and
light brown.

3 To make the topping, mix
together all the ingredients and
spread over the cooked base.
Bake for about 35 minutes, or until
firm. Cool completely in the tin
before cutting into bars or squares.
Dust with icing sugar.

Granola Bar Cookies

A gloriously dense fruity, nutty and oaty mixture, packed with goodness and delicious too, these bars are an ideal snack and perfect to pack for a school lunch.

Makes 12

175g/6oz/¾ cup unsalted (sweet) butter, diced
150g/5oz/⅔ cup clear honey
250g/9oz/generous 1 cup demerara (raw) sugar
350g/12oz/3 cups jumbo oats
5ml/1 tsp ground cinnamon
75g/3oz/¾ cup pecan nut halves
75g/3oz/generous ½ cup raisins
75g/3oz/¾ cup ready-to-eat dried papaya, chopped
75g/3oz/¾ cup ready-to-eat dried apricots, chopped
50g/2oz/scant ½ cup pumpkin seeds
50g/2oz/scant ½ cup sunflower seeds
50g/2oz/2 tbsp sesame seeds
50g/2oz/½ cup ground almonds

1 Preheat the oven to 190°C/375°F/ Gas 5. Line a 23cm/9in square cake tin (pan) with baking parchment. Put the butter and honey in a large heavy pan and heat gently until the butter has melted and the mixture is completely smooth.

2 Add the demerara sugar to the pan and heat very gently, stirring constantly, until the sugar has completely dissolved. Bring the butter mixture to the boil and continue to boil for 1–2 minutes, stirring the mixture constantly until it has formed a smooth caramel sauce.

3 Add the remaining ingredients and mix together. Transfer the mixture to the tin and press down with a spoon. Bake for 15 minutes until the edges turn brown.

4 Place in the refrigerator and chill well. Turn out of the tin, peel off the parchment and cut into bars.

Luxury Muesli Cookies

It is best to use a "luxury" muesli for this recipe, preferably one with 50 per cent mixed cereal and 50 per cent fruit, nuts and seeds. These buttery, crunchy cookies are ideal for a snack at any time.

Makes about 20

115g/4oz/½ cup unsalted (sweet) butter
45ml/3 tbsp golden (light corn) syrup
115g/4oz/generous ½ cup demerara
　(raw) sugar
175g/6oz/1½ cups "luxury" muesli (granola)
90g/3½oz/¾ cup self-raising (self-rising) flour
5ml/1 tsp ground cinnamon

1 Preheat the oven to 160°C/325°F/ Gas 3. Line two or three baking sheets with baking parchment.

Variation
Tropical muesli containing coconut and dried tropical fruits makes an interesting alternative to regular luxury muesli.

2 Put the butter, syrup and sugar in a large pan and heat gently. Stir constantly until the butter has completely melted. Remove the pan from the heat then stir in the muesli, flour and cinnamon and mix together well. Set aside to cool slightly.

3 Place spoonfuls of the mixture, slightly apart, on the baking sheets. Bake for 15 minutes until the cookies are just beginning to brown around the edges. Leave to cool for a few minutes on the baking sheets, then carefully transfer to a wire rack to cool completely.

Date Slice

Lemon-flavoured icing tops these scrumptious, low-fat bars, which are full of succulent fruit and crunchy seeds – the perfect mid-morning pick-me-up with a cup of decaf.

Makes 12–16

175g/6oz/¾ cup light muscovado
   (brown) sugar
175g/6oz/1 cup ready-to-eat dried
   dates, chopped
115g/4oz/1 cup self-raising
   (self-rising) flour
50g/2oz/½ cup muesli (granola)
30ml/2 tbsp sunflower seeds
15ml/1 tbsp poppy seeds
30ml/2 tbsp sultanas
   (golden raisins)
150ml/¼ pint/⅔ cup plain (natural)
   low-fat yogurt
1 egg, beaten
200g/7oz/1¾ cups icing (confectioners')
   sugar, sifted
lemon juice
15–30ml/1–2 tbsp pumpkin seeds

I Preheat the oven to 180°C/350°F/ Gas 4. Line a 28 × 18cm/11 × 7in shallow baking tin (pan) with baking parchment. Mix together all the ingredients, except the icing sugar, lemon juice and pumpkin seeds.

2 Spread in the tin and bake for about 25 minutes until golden brown. Cool.

3 To make the topping, put the icing sugar in a bowl and stir in just enough lemon juice to make a spreading consistency.

4 Spread over the baked date mixture and sprinkle generously with pumpkin seeds. Leave to set before cutting into squares or bars.

Iced Carob Cookies

If you are unable to eat chocolate but still crave it, these heavenly cookies, with their creamy topping, provide the answer to your prayers.

Makes 12–16

115g/4oz/½ cup butter
10ml/2 tsp carob powder
115g/4oz/1 cup wholemeal
    (whole-wheat) flour
5ml/1 tsp baking powder
75g/3oz/⅓ cup muscovado
    (molasses) sugar
50g/2oz/generous ½ cup rolled oats

For the topping

50g/2oz carob bar, coarsely chopped
45ml/3 tbsp double (heavy) cream
15ml/1 tbsp chopped ready-to-eat
    dried apricots

Cook's Tip

Carob is derived from the carob bean, which has a nutritious, flavoursome pulp.

1 Preheat the oven to 190°C/375°F/ Gas 5. Line the base and sides of an 18cm/7in square shallow cake tin (pan) with baking parchment. Put the butter in a large pan and add the carob powder. Stir over a low heat until the mixture is smooth and combined. Stir in the remaining ingredients and mix well.

2 Press the mixture into the prepared tin and bake for about 20–25 minutes until just set. Mark into squares or bars while still hot. Leave to cool in the tin.

3 To make the topping, stir the carob and cream in a small pan over a low heat. Spread over the cookies and sprinkle the apricots on top.

Carob and Cherry Cookies

Simplicity itself to make, these little cookies are given a chocolate-like flavour by the addition of carob and are deliciously crisp and crunchy.

Makes about 20

90g/3½oz/7 tbsp unsalted (sweet) butter, at room temperature, diced
75g/3oz/scant ½ cup caster (superfine) sugar
75g/3oz/⅓ cup light muscovado (brown) sugar
1 egg
150g/5oz/1¼ cups self-raising (self-rising) flour
25g/1oz/2 tbsp carob powder
50g/2oz/¼ cup glacé (candied) cherries, quartered
50g/2oz carob bar, chopped

1 Preheat the oven to 180°C/350°F/ Gas 4. Line two large baking sheets with baking parchment. Put the unsalted butter, caster sugar, muscovado sugar and the egg in a large mixing bowl and beat well together until the mixture is smooth and creamy.

2 Add the flour, carob powder, cherries and chopped carob bar to the mixture and mix well with a wooden spoon until thoroughly combined, making sure the carob powder is completely blended in.

3 Shape the mixture into walnut-size balls and place, spaced slightly apart to allow for spreading, on the prepared baking sheets.

4 Bake for about 15 minutes. Leave on the baking sheets for 5 minutes before transferring to a wire rack to cool completely.

Variations
• If you aren't on a diet, use unsweetened cocoa powder and a bar of chocolate instead of the carob.
• Use raisins instead of cherries if you like.

Cookies for Special Diets

Food intolerances, allergies and health problems need not deprive you of the pleasures of baking and eating home-made cookies. You will be amazed by the range of low-fat, dairy-free, reduced-sugar or gluten-free sweet treats you can make – and what's more, they're so scrumptious, the whole family will be clamouring for them. Whether layered slices or fabulous brownies, the cookies in this chapter are special in every way.

Very Low-fat Brownies

If you ever need proof that you can still enjoy sweet treats even when you are on a low-fat diet, here it is. These brownies are not just tasty, but also very quick and easy to make.

Makes 16

100g/3½oz/scant 1 cup plain
(all-purpose) flour
2.5ml/½ tsp baking powder
45ml/3 tbsp (unsweetened) cocoa
powder
200g/7oz/1 cup caster (superfine) sugar
100ml/3½fl oz/scant ½ cup natural
(plain) low-fat yogurt
2 eggs, beaten
5ml/1 tsp vanilla essence (extract)
25ml/1½ tbsp vegetable oil

1 Preheat the oven to 180°C/350°F/ Gas 4. Line a 20cm/8in square cake tin (pan) with baking parchment.

2 Sift the flour, baking powder and cocoa powder into a bowl. Stir in the caster sugar, then beat in the yogurt, eggs, vanilla and vegetable oil until thoroughly combined. Put the mixture into the prepared tin.

3 Bake for about 25 minutes until just firm to the touch. Leave in the tin until cooled completely.

4 Using a sharp knife, cut into 16 squares, then remove from the tin using a spatula.

Carob Chip Shorties

Perfect for anyone on a gluten-free or cow's-milk-free diet, these lovely cookies are best eaten freshly made, preferably while still slightly warm from the oven.

Makes 12

175g/6oz/1½ cups gluten-free flour
25g/1oz/2 tbsp soft light brown sugar
75g/3oz/6 tbsp vegetable margarine
50g/2oz/⅓ cup carob chips
15–25ml/1–1½ tbsp clear honey, warmed
demerara (raw) or caster (superfine) sugar, for sprinkling

I Preheat the oven to 160°C/325°F/ Gas 3. Line two baking sheets with baking parchment.

Cook's Tip
Gluten-free flour can be bought at most health-food stores.

2 Put the flour and brown sugar in a mixing bowl and rub in the margarine. Add the carob chips, then stir in just enough honey to bring the mixture together but not make it sticky. Roll the dough out between two sheets of baking parchment to about 8mm/⅜in.

3 Stamp out rounds using a plain 5cm/2in round biscuit (cookie) cutter. Place on the baking sheets. Prick each cookie once with a fork and sprinkle with sugar.

4 Bake for about 15–20 minutes, or until firm. Cool on a wire rack.

Rocky Road Wedges

Free from gluten and wheat, these crumbly chocolate wedges contain home-made popcorn in place of broken cookies, which are the classic ingredient in no-bake cookies such as this. This recipe uses an orange-flavoured chocolate bar, but any gluten-free chocolate can be used.

Makes 8

15ml/1 tbsp vegetable oil
25g/1oz/2½ tbsp popping corn
150g/5oz orange-flavoured plain (semisweet) chocolate
25g/1oz/2 tbsp unsalted (sweet) butter, diced
75g/3oz soft vanilla fudge, diced
icing (confectioners') sugar, for dusting

Cook's Tip

When buying products such as chocolate or fudge, always check the label to make sure they are gluten-free.

1 Heat the oil in a heavy pan. Add the popping corn, cover with a lid and heat, shaking the pan once or twice, until the popping noises die down. (It is important not to lift the lid until the popping stops.)

2 Remove the pan from the heat and leave for about 30 seconds before removing the lid. Be careful, as there may be quite a lot of steam trapped inside. Transfer the popcorn to a bowl and leave to cool for about 5 minutes.

3 Meanwhile, line the base of an 18cm/7in sandwich tin (pan).

4 Once cooled, tip the corn into a plastic bag and tap with a rolling pin to break up into small pieces.

5 Break the chocolate into a heatproof bowl. Add the butter and rest the bowl over a pan of gently simmering water. Stir frequently until melted. Remove the bowl from the heat and leave to cool for 2 minutes.

6 Stir the popcorn and fudge into the chocolate until well coated, then turn the mixture into the tin and press down firmly in an even layer. Leave to set for about 30 minutes.

7 Turn the cookie out on to a board and cut into eight wedges. Serve lightly dusted with sugar.

Meringue Squiggles

Free from gluten, wheat and cow's milk, these wiggly wands are great for children's parties. They are fun to shape and eat, and kids of all ages love making and decorating them. Be sure to check that the multi-coloured sprinkles are free from gluten and cow's milk.

Makes 14–16

2 egg whites
90g/3½oz/½ cup caster
  (superfine) sugar
45ml/3 tbsp icing (confectioners') sugar
multi-coloured sugar sprinkles,
  to decorate

1 Preheat the oven to 150°C/300°F/ Gas 2. Line a large baking sheet with baking parchment.

2 Put the egg whites in a large, clean bowl and whisk with a hand-held electric whisk until they form firm peaks.

3 Add a spoonful of caster sugar to the whisked egg whites and whisk for about 15 seconds to combine. Add another spoonful and whisk again. Continue in this way until all the sugar has been added.

4 Spoon the meringue mixture into a large piping (pastry) bag fitted with a large plain nozzle. Alternatively, spoon the mixture into a plastic bag, gently push it into one corner and snip off the tip so that the meringue can be pushed out in a 2cm/¾in-thick line.

5 Pipe wavy lines of meringue, about 13cm/5in long, on to the baking sheet and bake for about 1 hour until dry and crisp.

6 Carefully peel the meringues off the baking parchment and transfer to a wire rack to cool.

7 Put the icing sugar in a small bowl and mix in a few drops of water to make a smooth paste.

8 Using a fine pastry brush, brush the tops of the meringues with a little of the sugar paste, then scatter over the multi-coloured sugar sprinkles to decorate.

Cashew Nut Button Cookies

These light little cookies, flavoured with ground cashew nuts, are coated in toasted hazelnuts. They are suitable for people on gluten-free and cow's-milk-free diets.

Makes about 20

1 egg white

25g/1oz/2 tbsp caster (superfine) sugar

150g/5oz/1¼ cups unroasted cashew nuts, ground

50g/2oz/⅓ cup dates, finely chopped

5ml/1 tsp finely grated orange rind

30ml/2 tbsp pure maple or maple-flavoured syrup

90g/3½oz/scant 1 cup toasted hazelnuts, chopped

1 Preheat the oven to 190°C/375°F/ Gas 5. Line two baking sheets with baking parchment.

2 In a bowl, whisk the egg white until stiff. Whisk in the sugar. Stir in the cashews, dates, orange rind and syrup. Mix well. Put the chopped hazelnuts in a small bowl.

3 Drop small spoonfuls of the cookie mixture into the hazelnuts and toss until well coated.

4 Place on the prepared baking sheets and bake for about 10 minutes until lightly browned. Leave to cool on the baking sheets.

Fruit and Millet Treacle Cookies

These little cookies are quick to make, and will no doubt disappear just as quickly when they come out of the oven. They are gluten- and cow's milk-free.

Makes about 25–30

90g/3½oz/7 tbsp vegetable
  margarine
150g/5oz/⅔ cup light muscovado
  (brown) sugar
30ml/2 tbsp black treacle (molasses)
1 egg
150g/5oz/1¼ cups gluten-free flour
50g/2oz/½ cup millet flakes
50g/2oz/½ cup almonds, chopped
200g/7oz/generous 1 cup luxury
  mixed dried fruit

Cook's Tip

Make sure that you use millet flakes for these cookies rather than millet grains. The grains will swell too much during cooking and spoil the cookies.

1 Preheat the oven to 190°C/375°F/ Gas 5. Line two large baking sheets with baking parchment.

2 Put the margarine, muscovado sugar, treacle and egg in a large bowl and beat together until well combined. (The mixture should be light and fluffy.)

3 Stir in the flour and millet flakes, the almonds and dried fruit. Put tablespoonfuls of the mixture on to the prepared baking sheets.

4 Bake for about 15 minutes until brown. Leave on the baking sheets for a few minutes, then transfer to a wire rack to cool completely.

Big Macaroons

These giant macaroons are crisp on the outside, chewy in the middle and naturally free from gluten and cow's milk. Ground almonds can be a great alternative to the wheat flour used in most cookies, and macaroons don't need butter for their deliciously moist, rich taste.

Makes 9

2 egg whites

5ml/1 tsp almond essence (extract)

115g/4oz/1 cup ground almonds

130g/4½oz/generous 1 cup light
  muscovado (brown) sugar

Cook's Tips

• *These macaroons will store well in an airtight container; do not store in the refrigerator because they'll turn soft and lose their lovely crisp and chewy texture.*

• *To make a macaroon with a milder flavour, use caster (superfine) sugar in place of the light muscovado sugar.*

1 Preheat the oven to 180°C/350°F/ Gas 4. Line a large baking sheet with baking parchment. Put the egg whites in a large, clean bowl and whisk until they form stiff peaks.

2 Add the almond essence to the egg whites and whisk to combine. Sprinkle over the ground almonds and sugar and gently fold in using a large metal spoon.

3 Place nine spoonfuls of the mixture, spacing them well apart, on to the baking sheet and flatten slightly. Bake for 15 minutes until risen, deep golden and beginning to turn crisp.

4 Leave the macaroons on the baking sheets for 5 minutes, then transfer to a wire rack to cool.

Shortbread Ring Cookies

Decorated with colourful chopped sweets, these little gluten- and dairy-free cookies are great for younger kids. They make delicious lunchbox fillers or snacks during the day. Don't forget to check the ingredients on the jellied fruit sweets as some varieties could contain gluten.

Makes 8–10

150g/5oz/1¼ cups gluten-free flour
90g/3½oz/½ cup rice flour
finely grated rind of 1 lemon
75g/3oz/6 tbsp dairy-free margarine
50g/2oz/¼ cup caster (superfine) sugar
1 egg yolk
10ml/2 tsp water

For the topping

90g/3½oz/scant 1 cup icing
   (confectioners') sugar
50g/2oz/½ cup dairy-free margarine
small jellied fruit sweets (candies)

1 Put the gluten-free flour, rice flour, lemon rind and margarine in a food processor and process briefly to combine. Add the sugar, egg yolk and water and mix to a dough.

2 Turn the dough on to a lightly floured surface and knead. Wrap in clear film (plastic wrap) and chill for about 30 minutes.

3 Preheat the oven to 180°C/350°F/Gas 4. Grease a baking sheet.

4 Roll out the dough on a lightly floured surface to a thickness of about 5mm/¼in.

5 Using a 6.5cm/2½in plain or fluted cutter, cut out rounds and place on the baking sheet. Using a 4cm/1½in round cutter, cut out and remove the centre of each round.

6 Bake for about 20 minutes until beginning to turn pale golden. Leave on the baking sheet for 2 minutes, then transfer to a wire rack to cool.

7 To make the topping, put the icing sugar and margarine in a bowl and beat together until creamy.

8 Pipe or spoon the topping on to the ring cookies. Chop the jellied sweets into small pieces with a pair of scissors and gently press them into the cream to decorate.

Cornflake Caramel Slice

A wickedly decadent caramel layer nestles between the gluten-free base and the crispy cornflake topping. These cookies are simply irresistible – and fun to make too.

Makes 12

175g/6oz/¾ cup butter
150g/5oz/¾ cup caster (superfine) sugar
300g/10oz/2½ cups gluten-free flour
1 egg, beaten

For the topping

30ml/2 tbsp golden (light
   corn) syrup
397g/14oz can sweetened
   condensed milk
50g/2oz/¼ cup butter
90ml/6 tbsp sour cream
about 40g/1½oz/2 cups cornflakes
icing (confectioners') sugar (optional)

1 Preheat the oven to 190°C/375°F/ Gas 5. And proceed to line a 28 x 18cm/11 x 7in shallow cake tin (pan) with baking parchment.

2 Melt the butter in a pan, then remove from the heat. Put the sugar and flour in a bowl. Add the beaten egg and melted butter and mix well. Press the mixture evenly into the base of the prepared tin.

3 Bake for about 20 minutes until golden brown. Leave the base to cool completely in the tin.

4 For the topping, heat the syrup, condensed milk and butter over a low heat for 10–15 minutes, stirring occasionally, until the mixture is thick and turns a caramel colour.

5 Remove from the heat and stir in the sour cream. Spread over the base. Sprinkle over the cornflakes and leave to set. Sprinkle with icing sugar, if using, and cut into bars.

Double Chocolate Slices

These delicious gluten-free cookies have a smooth chocolate base, topped with a mint-flavoured cream and drizzles of melted chocolate. Perfect for a teatime treat – or at any time of day.

Makes 12

200g/7oz/1¾ cups gluten-free flour
25g/1oz/¼ tbsp (unsweetened)
   cocoa powder
150g/5oz/⅔ cup unsalted (sweet) butter,
   cut into small pieces
75g/3oz/¾ cup icing
   (confectioners') sugar

For the topping

75g/3oz white chocolate mint crisps
50g/2oz/¼ cup unsalted (sweet)
   butter, softened
90g/3½oz/scant 1 cup icing
   (confectioners') sugar
50g/2oz milk chocolate

1 Preheat the oven to 180°C/350°F/ Gas 4. Grease an 18cm/7in square shallow baking tin (pan) and line with a strip of baking parchment that comes up over two opposite sides. This will make it easier to remove the cookie base from the tin after baking.

4 To make topping, put the chocolate mint crisps in a plastic bag and tap firmly with a rolling pin until they are crushed. Beat the butter and sugar together until creamy, then beat in the crushed chocolate mint crisps. Spread the mixture evenly over the cookie base.

2 Put the flour and cocoa powder into a food processor and add the pieces of butter. Process briefly until the mixture resembles fine breadcrumbs. Add the icing sugar and mix briefly again to form a smooth soft dough.

3 Turn the flour mixture into the prepared tin and gently press out to the edges with your fingers to make an even layer. Bake for 25 minutes, then remove from the oven and leave the base to cool completely in the tin.

5 Melt the milk chocolate in a small heatproof bowl set over a pan of hot water. Lift the cookie base out of the tin; remove the paper. Using a teaspoon, drizzle the melted chocolate over the topping. Leave to set, then cut into squares.

Chocolate Chip Cookies

This gluten-free version of these perennially popular cookies is bound to be a big hit with all the family because of their lovely, light texture.

Makes 16

75g/3oz/6 tbsp soft margarine
50g/2oz/¼ cup light soft brown sugar
50g/2oz/¼ cup caster (superfine) sugar
1 egg, beaten
few drops of vanilla essence (extract)
75g/3oz/¾ cup rice flour
75g/3oz/¾ cup gluten-free corn meal
5ml/1 tsp gluten-free baking powder
pinch of salt
115g/4oz/⅔ cup plain (semisweet)
   chocolate chips, or a mixture of milk
   and white chocolate chips

1 Preheat the oven to 190°C/ 375°F/Gas 5. Lightly grease two baking sheets. Place the margarine and sugars in a bowl and cream together until light and fluffy.

2 Beat in the egg and vanilla essence. Fold in the rice flour, corn meal, baking powder and salt, then fold in the chocolate chips.

3 Place spoonfuls of the mixture on the prepared baking sheets, leaving space for spreading between each one. Bake for 10–15 minutes until the cookies are lightly browned.

4 Remove the cookies from the oven and leave on the baking sheets for a few minutes to cool slightly, then carefully transfer to a wire rack using a palette knife or metal spatula and leave them to cool completely before serving.

Cook's Tip
Once the cookies are cold, they can be stored in an airtight container for up to a week. Alternatively, pack them into plastic bags and freeze.

Cherry Coconut Munchies

You'll find it hard to stop at just one of these gluten-free munchies, which make a wonderful morning or afternoon treat. If you like, drizzle 25–50g/1–2oz melted chocolate over the cold munchies and leave to set before serving.

Makes 20

2 egg whites
115g/4oz/1 cup icing (confectioners')
   sugar, sifted
115g/4oz/1 cup ground almonds
115g/4oz/generous 1 cup desiccated (dry
   unsweetened shredded) coconut
few drops of almond essence (extract)
75g/3oz/⅓ cup glacé (candied) cherries,
   finely chopped

Variation
Use ground hazelnuts in place of the almonds and omit the almond essence.

1 Preheat the oven to 150°C/ 300°F/Gas 2. Line two baking sheets with non-stick baking parchment. Place the egg whites in a grease-free bowl and whisk until stiff.

2 Gently fold in the icing sugar, then fold in the ground almonds, coconut and almond essence to form a sticky dough. Finally, fold in the chopped glacé cherries.

3 Place mounds on the baking sheets. Bake for 25 minutes. Cool briefly on the baking sheets, then transfer to a wire rack.

Filo and Apricot Purses

Filo pastry is very easy to use. Keep a packet in the freezer ready for rustling up a speedy dairy-free teatime treat that looks as good as it tastes.

Makes 12

115g/4oz/½ cup ready-to-eat
   dried apricots
45ml/3 tbsp apricot compote or conserve
3 macaroons, crushed
3 filo pastry sheets
20ml/4 tsp soya margarine, melted, plus
   extra for greasing
icing (confectioners') sugar, for dusting

1 Preheat the oven to 180°C/ 350°F/Gas 4. Lightly grease two baking sheets with soya margarine.

2 Chop the apricots fairly finely, put them in a bowl and stir in the apricot compote or conserve. Add the crushed macaroons and mix together well.

3 Cut the filo pastry into 24 × 13cm/5in squares, pile the squares on top of each other and cover with a clean dishtowel to prevent the pastry from drying out and becoming hard and brittle.

4 Lay one pastry square on a flat surface, brush lightly with melted soya margarine and lay another square on top. Brush the top square with melted margarine. Spoon a small amount of apricot mixture in the centre of the pastry, bring up the edges and pinch together in a money-bag shape. Repeat with the remaining pastry squares and filling to make 12 purses in all.

5 Arrange on the baking sheets and bake for 5–8 minutes until golden. Transfer to a wire rack and dust lightly with icing sugar. Serve warm.

Tomato Breadsticks

Once you've tried this simple recipe you'll never buy manufactured breadsticks again. Serve as a gluten-free snack, or with aperitifs and a dip at the beginning of a meal.

Makes 16

225g/8oz/2 cups gluten-free plain (all-purpose) flour

2.5ml/½ tsp salt

2.5ml/½ tsp easy-blend (rapid-rise) dry yeast

5ml/1 tsp clear honey

5ml/1 tsp olive oil

150ml/¼ pint/⅔ cup warm water

6 halves sun-dried tomatoes in olive oil, drained and chopped

15ml/1 tbsp skimmed milk

10ml/2 tsp poppy seeds

1 Place the flour, salt and yeast in a food processor. Add the honey and oil and, with the machine running, gradually pour in the water – stop adding water as soon as the dough starts to cling together. Process for 1 minute more.

2 Turn out the dough on to a floured board and knead for about 3–4 minutes until it is springy, smooth and elastic.

3 Knead in the chopped sun-dried tomatoes until evenly distributed. Form the dough into a ball and place in a lightly oiled bowl. Cover with oiled clear film (plastic wrap) and leave to rise for 5 minutes.

4 Divide the dough into 16 pieces and roll each into a 28 × 1cm/ 11 × ½in long stick. Place on a lightly oiled baking sheet and leave to rise in a warm place for 15 minutes.

5 Preheat the oven to 150°C/ 300°F/Gas 2. Brush the sticks with milk and sprinkle with poppy seeds. Bake for 30 minutes. Leave to cool on a wire cooling rack.

Sunflower and Yogurt Scones

For people who have to watch their gluten intake, these delicious golden scones, with their fresh tart flavour and lovely crunchy topping, are a treat indeed.

Makes 10–12

225g/8oz/2 cups gluten-free self-raising
   (self-rising) flour
5ml/1 tsp baking powder
25g/1oz/2 tbsp soft sunflower margarine
30ml/2 tbsp soft light brown sugar
50g/2oz/⅓ cup raisins
60ml/4 tbsp sunflower seeds
150ml/¼ pint/⅔ cup natural (plain)
   yogurt
about 30ml/2 tbsp milk

1 Preheat the oven to 230°C/450°F/ Gas 8. Lightly oil a baking sheet. Sift the flour and baking powder into a large bowl and rub in the sunflower margarine evenly.

2 Stir in the caster sugar, raisins and about half the sunflower seeds, then mix in the yogurt, adding just enough milk to make a fairly soft, but not sticky dough.

3 Roll out the dough on a lightly floured surface to about 2cm/¾in thickness. Cut into 6cm/2½in flower shapes or stamp out rounds with a fluted cutter and lift them on to the prepared baking sheet.

4 Brush with milk and sprinkle with the reserved sunflower seeds, then bake for 10–12 minutes, until well risen and golden brown.

5 Cool the scones on a wire rack. Serve split and spread with jam.

Prune and Peel Rock Buns

These gluten-free buns are quick and easy to make and taste absolutely wonderful.

Makes 12

225g/8oz/2 cups gluten-free plain
   (all-purpose) flour
10ml/2 tsp baking powder
75g/3oz/⅓ cup demerara (raw) sugar
50g/2oz/½ cup chopped ready-to-eat
   dried prunes
50g/2oz/⅓ cup chopped mixed
   (candied) peel
finely grated rind of 1 lemon
60ml/4 tbsp sunflower oil
75ml/5 tbsp skimmed milk

1 Preheat the oven to 200°C/ 400°F/Gas 6. Lightly oil a large baking sheet. Sift the flour and baking powder, then stir in the sugar, prunes, peel and lemon rind.

2 Mix the oil and milk, then stir into the mixture, to make a dough which just binds together.

Variation

For a dairy-free version of these rock buns, you can substitute soya milk for the skimmed milk.

3 Spoon into rocky heaps on the baking sheet and bake for about 20 minutes, until golden. Transfer to a wire rack to cool.

Index

double chocolate cookies, 241
double chocolate slices, 495
fruity chocolate cookie-cakes, 233
fudgy glazed chocolate slices, 356
giant triple chocolate cookies, 239
late night cookies, 265
marbled brownies, 363
marbled caramel chocolate
slice, 226
mini chocolate Marylands, 212
nut and chocolate chip brownies,
slice, 358
nutty marshmallow and chocolate
squares, 412
peppermint and coconut
chocolate sticks, 312
plain chocolate and peppermint
crisps, 313
rich chocolate cookie slice, 238
rich chocolate square, 347
rocky road chocolate
bars, 264
tollhouse cookies, 70
triple chocolate sandwiches, 224
two-tone chocolate
florentines, 274
white chocolate brownies, 237
white nut brownies, 350
white chocolate macadamia nut
slices, 270
white chocolate snowballs, 417
Christmas cookies, 180

Christmas tree angels, 174
chunky chocolate drops, 219
churros, Spanish, 36, 284
cinnamon:
apple and cinnamon
muffins, 391
chocolate cinnamon tuiles, 223
cinnamon balls, 166
cinnamon and orange tuiles, 148
cinnamon pinwheels, 283
cinnamon refrigerator
cookies, 83
cinnamon and treacle cookies, 82
pineapple and cinnamon drop
scones, 392
citrus cheesecake topping, 41
citrus drops, 106
citrus spice bars, 322
citrus tuiles, rosemary-scented, 287
classic shortbread, 25
cocktail shapes, 426
coconut:
apricot and coconut kisses, 408
basbousa, 294
cherry coconut munchies, 496
chocolate and coconut slices, 359
coconut and lime macaroons, 111
coconut macaroons, 96
coconut oat cookies, 464
coconut pyramids, 158
coconut topping, 41
neuris, 169
peppermint and coconut
chocolate sticks, 312
white chocolate snowballs, 417
coffee:
black Russian cookies, 315
cappuccino swirls, 93
coffee biscotti, 102
coffee sponge drops with cheese
and ginger filling, 276
mocha Viennese swirls, 260
pecan toffee shortbread, 259
tiramisu cookies, 252
Cointreau chocolate colettes, 273

cornflakes:
banana cream cookies, 249
chocolate crispy cookies, 414
cornflake caramel slice, 494
corn meal:
bacon corn meal muffins, 399
corn meal biscuits, 425
fruity corn meal cookies, 104
corn oysters, 458
crackers
chilli and herb crackers, 431
curry crackers, 430
crackle-tops, chocolate, 225
cranberries:
cranberry and chocolate
squares, 256
cranberry muffins, 372
cream cheese spirals, 447
creaming method, 24
creamy fig and peach
squares, 269
creamy lemon bars, 326
crème au beurre filling, 58
crumble cookies, candied
peel, 247
crumble topping, 41
crunchy jumbles, 464
crunchy oatmeal cookies, 466
curry crackers, 430
custard: apple crumble and custard
slice, 268